Resisting Persecution

Studies in Contemporary European History

Editors:

Konrad Jarausch, Lurcy Professor of European Civilization, University of North Carolina, Chapel Hill

Henry Rousso, Senior Research Fellow at the Institut d'histoire du temps présent (Centre national de la recherche scientifique, Paris)

Recent volumes:

Volume 24
Resisting Persecution: Jews and Their Petitions during the Holocaust
  Edited by Thomas Pegelow Kaplan and Wolf Gruner

Volume 23
Peace at All Costs: Catholic Intellectuals, Journalists, and Media in Postwar Polish–German Reconciliation
  Annika Elisabet Frieberg

Volume 22
From Eastern Bloc to European Union: Comparative Processes of Transformation since 1990
  Edited by Günther Heydemann and Karel Vodička

Volume 21
Migration, Memory, and Diversity: Germany from 1945 to the Present
  Edited by Cornelia Wilhelm

Volume 20
Ambassadors of Realpolitik: Sweden, the CSCE and the Cold War
  Aryo Makko

Volume 19
Wartime Captivity in the 20th Century: Archives, Stories, Memories
  Edited by Anne-Marie Pathé and Fabien Théofilakis

Volume 18
Whose Memory? Which Future? Remembering Ethnic Cleansing and Lost Cultural Diversity in East, Central and Southeastern Europe
  Edited by Barbara Törnquist-Plewa

Volume 17
The Long Aftermath: Cultural Legacies of Europe at War, 1936–2016
  Edited by Manuel Bragança and Peter Tame

Volume 16
Memory and Change in Europe: Eastern Perspectives
  Edited by Małgorzata Pakier and Joanna Wawrzyniak

Volume 15
Tailoring Truth: Politicizing the Past and Negotiating Memory in East Germany, 1945–1990
  Jon Berndt Olsen

For a full volume listing, please see the series page on our website:
http://berghahnbooks.com/series/contemporary-european-history

RESISTING PERSECUTION

Jews and Their Petitions during the Holocaust

Edited by
Thomas Pegelow Kaplan and Wolf Gruner

berghahn
NEW YORK • OXFORD
www.berghahnbooks.com

First published in 2020 by
Berghahn Books
www.berghahnbooks.com

© 2020, 2024 Thomas Pegelow Kaplan and Wolf Gruner
First paperback edition published in 2024

All rights reserved. Except for the quotation of short passages for the purposes of criticism and review, no part of this book may be reproduced in any form or by any means, electronic or mechanical, including photocopying, recording, or any information storage and retrieval system now known or to be invented, without written permission of the publisher.

Library of Congress Cataloging-in-Publication Data

A C.I.P. cataloging record is available
from the Library of Congress
Library of Congress Cataloging in
Publication Control Number:
2020937020

British Library Cataloguing in Publication Data

A catalogue record for this book is available from the British Library.

ISBN 978-1-78920-720-0 hardback
ISBN 978-1-80539-123-4 paperback
ISBN 978-1-80539-381-8 epub
ISBN 978-1-78920-721-7 web pdf

https://doi.org/10.3167/9781789207200

Contents

List of Illustrations	vii
Acknowledgments	viii
Introduction *Thomas Pegelow Kaplan and Wolf Gruner*	1
Chapter 1 To Not "Live as a Pariah": Jewish Petitions as Individual and Collective Protest in the Greater German Reich *Wolf Gruner*	28
Chapter 2 "Did We Not Shed Our Blood for France?" Identity and Resistance in Entreaties for the Jewish Internees of Occupied France, 1940–44 *Stacy Renee Veeder*	51
Chapter 3 Honorary Czechs and Germans: Petitions for Aryan Status in the Nazi Protectorate of Bohemia and Moravia *Benjamin Frommer*	72
Chapter 4 Legal Resistance through Petitions during the Holocaust: The Strategies of Romanian Jewish Leader Wilhelm Filderman, 1940–44 *Ștefan Cristian Ionescu*	92

Chapter 5
Attempts to Take Action in a Coerced Community: Petitions
to the Jewish Council in the Łódź Ghetto during World War II
   Svenja Bethke   114

Chapter 6
Petitioning Matters: Jews and Non-Jews
Negotiating Ghettoization in Budapest, 1944
   Tim Cole   138

Chapter 7
Global Jewish Petitioning and the Reconsideration of Spatial Analysis
in Holocaust Historiography: The Case of Rescue in the Philippines
   Thomas Pegelow Kaplan   157

Chapter 8
Petitioning for "Equal Treatment": The Struggles of
Intermarried Holocaust Survivors in Postwar Germany
   Maximilian Strnad   182

Conclusion
   Thomas Pegelow Kaplan and Wolf Gruner   204

Appendix
European-Jewish Petitions during the Holocaust   221

Index   239

Illustrations

Figure 2.1. Raymond-Raoul Lambert, head of the Union Général des Israélites de France (UGIF)-South and frequent author of petitions, ca. 1941. Yad Vashem Archives.   63

Figure 3.1. Record of petitioner Karel Nowak-Reismann's (1892–194?) visit to an office of the Czech Protectorate Government, June 1940. Národní archiv České republiky, Prague.   77

Figure 4.1. Wilhelm Filderman (in the uniform of the Romanian army) together with his family, ca. 1916. Photographic Library, The Wilhelm Filderman Center for the Study of Jewish History in Romania.   99

Figure 5.1. A teenage boy hands a petition to Mordechai Chaim Rumkowski, Łódź ghetto, 17 August 1941. Photo Archives of the United States Holocaust Memorial Museum, Washington, DC, courtesy of Jehuda Widawski.   116

Figure 7.1. President Manuel L. Quezon and US High Commissioner Paul McNutt, Manila, ca. 1938. National Library of the Philippines.   163

Acknowledgments

The idea for this book came out of a conversation between the co-editors in 2014. At the time, we both agreed on the importance of exploring petitions as tools of contestation and enlisting a range of scholars with expertise in different European countries and languages. As one of many next steps, we organized a panel at the 2015 annual meeting of the Association for Jewish Studies in Boston to test this volume's approach. Marion A. Kaplan expertly chaired this panel and offered valuable advice. With the title "Rethinking Jewish Petitions during the Holocaust: Toward Integrated Histories of Collective and Individual Acts of Contestation," our panel prompted a lively discussion and raised new questions. We were pleased and grateful to the scholars—some long-time colleagues and friends, others new collaborators—who responded to our subsequent call for essays for this volume.

Over the years, one or both of the editors discussed the topic of Jewish petitioning with many colleagues in North America, Europe, and Israel, who offered advice and constructive criticism. We are particularly grateful to Jacob Borut, Christopher R. Browning, Richard Cohen, Dan Diner, Havi Dreifuss, Luca Fenoglio, Shmuel Feiner, Gaby Finder, Amos Goldberg, Philipp Graf, Atina Grossmann, Konrad Kwiet, Jürgen Matthäus, Beate Meyer, Dan Michman, Guy Miron, Dalia Ofer, Eliot Nidam-Orvieto, Iael Nidam-Orvieto, Renée Poznanski, the late Reinhard Rürup, Alan Steinweis, Stefanie Schüler-Springorum, Bill Van Norman, Michael Wildt, and Moshe Zimmermann.

Thomas Pegelow Kaplan is indebted to the International Institute for Holocaust Research, Yad Vashem; the Memorial Foundation for Jewish Culture, New York City; and the Alexander von Humboldt Foundation, Bonn, for granting him research fellowships for his work on Jewish petitioning practices. He also wishes to thank the organizers and participants of the research colloquium on the History of National Socialism at the Humboldt University of Berlin, the research colloquium at the Center for Research on Anti-Semitism at the Technical University of Berlin, the lunch talk at the Leibniz Institute for Jewish History and Culture—Simon-Dubnow, Leipzig, and the annual lecture of The John Najmann Chair of Holocaust Studies at the International Institute for Holocaust Research,

Yad Vashem, for excellent opportunities to discuss approaches and arguments used in this volume.

Wolf Gruner is grateful for the invitation by Sybille Steinbacher to present at the 2010 conference on comparative genocide at the University Vienna. He used this opportunity to work at the Vienna archives where he found the bulk of the Jewish petitions for his chapter.

We are most thankful to all the volume's contributors for diligently crafting thoughtful chapters and responding to our catalog of questions. Our gratitude also goes to Konrad H. Jarausch and Henry Rousso, the general editors of Berghahn's Contemporary European History series, for their conceptual feedback and readiness to accept this volume into their series.

Furthermore, we are indebted to the Archives Nationales, Paris; the Archives of the Center for the Study of Jewish History in Romania "Wilhelm Filderman," Bucharest; the United States Holocaust Memorial Museum Photo Archives, Washington, DC; the Archiwum Państwowe, Łódź; the Arhivele Nationale Ale României, Bucharest; the Národní Archiv České republiky, Prague; the National Library of the Philippines, especially Anne Rosette Crelencia, Edgardo Quiros, and the Library's Director Cesar Gilbert Adriano; the Wiener Stadt- und Landesarchiv, Austria; and the Yad Vashem Archives for their cooperation and permission to print petitions and photographs on entreaty processes from their respective collections. Moreover, we would like to thank the authors and Witold Kosmala for their help in translating the petitions that appear as facsimiles in the appendix of this volume.

Finally, we would like to express our appreciation to the outside readers for their nuanced comments and suggestions and the copy editor of this volume for helping us to improve the manuscript further. Our greatest gratitude is reserved for Mykelin Higham, Soyolmaa Lkhagvadorj, Elizabeth Martinez, and Chris Chappell at Berghahn Books. They have patiently walked us through the publication process, practicing the highest standards of professionalism, thoughtfulness, and guidance.

Introduction

Thomas Pegelow Kaplan and Wolf Gruner

In the conclusions of his pathbreaking 1961 study of the Holocaust, Raul Hilberg commented that "in various forms, some more eloquent than others, the Jews appealed and petitioned wherever and whenever the threat of concentration and deportation struck them: in the Reich, in Poland, in Russia, in France, in the Balkan countries, and in Hungary."[1] Indeed, throughout the 1930s and early 1940s, officials and ordinary members of Jewish Communities as well as men and women whom the Nazi state defined as racially Jewish or partially Jewish wrote tens of thousands of petitions all across German-occupied Europe and in countries allied to the Nazi regime. Any given local, regional, or state archive on the continent and beyond encompasses collections with a myriad of such entreaties. These petitions ranged from rushed appeals for exemptions from pending deportations, such as the case of Jewish war veterans, widows, and orphans who approached the Sorting Committee in the Romanian city of Dorohoi in late 1941, to very elaborate entreaties, such as Rabbi Jacob Kaplan's July 1941 appeal against Vichy France's second *Statut des Juifs* addressed to Xavier Vallat, the Commissioner-General for Jewish Affairs.[2]

In light of this magnitude, it is striking—and even problematic for the broader understanding of Jewish responses during the Holocaust—that petitions have received so little attention in the scholarship on this genocide. This volume addresses this shortcoming and places petitioning practices at the center of its analysis, understanding these entreaties as evidence for the agency and often even resistance of Jews during the Holocaust. Specialists of Jewish history in various European countries during the 1930s and 1940s discuss the origin and outcome of Jewish petitions and place them in their specific historical context.

The neglect of Jewish petitions in the scholarly literature on the Holocaust is not so much grounded in a lack of awareness—almost every researcher searching for evidence of Jewish reactions to the persecution by the Nazis or other authoritarian regimes has been struck by these en-

---

Notes for this chapter begin on page 20.

treaties and their abundance. Rather, it is based on a common disregard, resulting from an underestimation of the function, impact, and goals of petitioning practices in some of the most influential works in the field. In his aforementioned magnum opus, Raul Hilberg even used the enormous number of entreaties to make his case for the alleged absence of "actual" Jewish resistance. "Everywhere, the Jews pitted words against rifles, dialectics against force and everywhere," he argued, "they lost."[3] Over the decades, these scholarly evaluations of petitions have changed very little. In her important study on the challenges of so-called *Mischlinge* in Hamburg during the Nazi period, historian Beate Meyer, for example, has pointed to the low success rate of petitions for exemptions from the Nuremberg Racial Laws. Moreover, Nazi state officials succeeded, in her view, in misleading petitioners to believe in "sham possibilities," falsely suggesting that an "'exit' from 'racial' persecution was possible."[4]

This volume challenges the widespread notion that Jews wrote their petitions in vain. It takes them seriously, discussing petitionary letters authored by Jewish individuals and representatives of Jewish organizations as a form of communication that was frequently able to surpass the asymmetrical power relations between the oppressed and the oppressor. In most previous studies, historians have reduced petitions to futile individual or collective quests for exemptions from of all kinds of anti-Jewish measures, ranging from early dismissals from jobs to being excluded from the mass deportations that began in 1941–42. Asking for exemptions, however, already expressed a form of agency and even opposition to the Nazi or another authoritarian state. Moreover, in the 1930s and 1940s, quite a number of petitioners openly protested anti-Jewish measures and legislation in general, be it in Germany, Romania, or France, and demanded their abandonment. This volume establishes that petitions repeatedly served as a critical but overlooked political tool for the persecuted in an authoritarian environment.

In addition to requesting exemptions from or even the abolition of national or local anti-Jewish measures, victims of persecution wrote petitions as an important means to reposition and redefine the social and political status assigned to them by the perpetrators. This is especially evident in petitionary letters—be it from regular Jewish individuals or prominent Jewish representatives—addressed to authoritarian leaders such as Adolf Hitler, Rudolf Hess, or Josef Bürckel in Germany or Ion Antonescu in Romania, as Wolf Gruner and Ştefan C. Ionescu's chapters in this volume show.[5] Thus, the analyses of this collection serve the purpose of reevaluating petitions as a means of contestation that could also amount to a form of resistance. Eschewing simplifying binaries of resistance versus collaboration, the contributions in this volume offer a more nuanced understanding of these complex and often convoluted practices.

By necessity, entreaties authored by Jewish women and men combined multiple voices and languages, including, at a minimum, those of the petitioners and the petitioned. Often, they referred to traditional, scientific, or religious authorities or employed—in line with Emancipation discourses and gains—legal arguments. In other cases, entreaties revolved around personal appeals, often subservient, and outright flattery that used to be the defining characteristics of pre- and early modern supplications. All in all, they present public or semi-public documents composed by the petitioners with a more or less clear objective, received and, in their vast majority, read by the petitioned agencies or individuals of real or imagined power. Hence, these petitions constituted the kind of hybrid source that should be at the center of the much-needed "integrated histories" of the Holocaust that prominent scholars such as Saul Friedländer and Dan Michman have called for and that relate the practices of the perpetrators, victims, and—as Tim Cole's chapter on petitioners in Budapest demonstrates—neighbors alike.[6]

Why are petitions so important? In non-authoritarian societies, it is hard to imagine that writing letters to a government might be an effective way to communicate or have any noticeable impact in light of the myriad means to assert influence.[7] In a dictatorship, conversely, interactions between perpetrators and the persecuted work very differently. The persecuted are excluded from any political participation and representation. They cannot resort to a free press or rely on free speech, since any public or private critique would be in danger of being punished by law or extrajuridical means. Therefore, entreaties often constitute the petitioners' only or most prominent permissible expression of individual or collective opinion, while simultaneously some also carry considerable risk, as scholars of Soviet history have shown.[8]

At the same time, personal relationships and direct access to individuals in positions of power amount to much greater significance in an authoritarian environment than in a pluralistic society, where different branches of power exist. As a consequence, establishing a channel of communication with authoritarian leaders or their regional and local counterparts via entreaties can be a more effective way to challenge discrimination and persecution than open protest or armed resistance. As James Scott pointed out, autocratic leaders prefer to be in control of requests, which affirms their personal political power.[9] As a result, a large number of petitions in the 1930s and 1940s—despite popular belief—did not get shelved, but were discussed by the authorities and received answers.

Moreover, responses of the perpetrators to petitioners necessitated the allocation of human and other resources of the oppressors. After all, petitions functioned as a place of negotiation of two or more groups in an asymmetric field of power.[10] As the following chapters prove with striking examples, perpetrators took entreaties seriously as indicated not only by processing them, but also by, time and again, involving agencies other than the addressed to formulate an adequate response or come to a decision. These dynamics often provided the oppressed with much-needed time and even opened opportunities to manipulate perpetrator agencies. As Ștefan Ionescu's analysis of Romanian Jewish leader Wilhelm Filderman's entreaties to Ion Antonescu reveals, petitioners occasionally sought to pit one office against another by appealing to their specific institutional and personal interests. In a dictatorship, in which Jews had no political currency and often lacked the legal means, petition writing, surprisingly, served many men and women as one of the last remaining ways to defend themselves individually or as a community from anti-Jewish laws, local restrictions, and violent attacks. Astonishingly, such efforts frequently bore success.

Methodological Questions

The study of petitions poses a number of methodological and conceptual challenges. In addition to scholars of communist rule in Europe, early modernists outside the field of Jewish studies have extensively grappled with entreaties. Their pathbreaking works inform this volume's approaches, which build on these previous studies and develop their methodologies further.[11]

Our collection explores what constitutes a "petition" composed by a member or members of a Jewish Community in mid-twentieth-century Europe. The volume raises a number of interrelated questions: How or to what extent do petitions differ from other kinds of writing, such as the crafting of personal letters or completing of bureaucratic forms? Furthermore, how do petitioning practices fit in with the broad continuum of responses by European Jews to violence and oppression that evolved on a continuum from compliance and evasion to individual protest and armed uprisings? In what ways can and should petitioning practices be understood as part of the broader spectrum of Jewish resistance during the Holocaust? And, finally, how were Holocaust-era Jewish entreaties embedded in the often long histories of petition practices, particularly in centralistic or autocratic regimes, and to what extent were these processes shaped by local, regional, national, or even transnational networks and spaces?

The term "petition" derives its meaning from the Latin verb *petere*—to claim, to desire, or to demand. As scholars such as Geoffrey Koziol have shown, it was a commonly used expression of supplication rituals in the early medieval church and kingship that had its origin in Ancient Greek supplication practices and Roman imperial rescripts. In its origins in antiquity, a supplication had moral and religious, but only quasi-legal components and was marked by repetition, distinct verbiage and rules, and oftentimes calls for mercy. The act of *supplicatio* addressed a more powerful person, generally a ruler or ruling body, not a god.[12]

Over the centuries, the very concept and act of petitioning has shifted considerably. There was a range of both different and similar terms with diverse meanings in various European languages that denoted petitioning practices by Jewish and gentile petitioners alike. In German-speaking parts of Europe, for example, *Petitionen* only arose as the dominant term by the beginning of the nineteenth century and was then strongly tied to the language of constitutionalism. Most of the earlier sources contain other terms like *Suppliken, Supplikationen,* or *Gravamina*, a Latin noun meaning "burdens." Later, terms like *Bittschriften* and *Gesuche* came into use. The word *Gravamina*, less often its singular *Gravamen*, was in wide circulation across the continent in the early modern period, referencing the voicing of grievances connected to administrative and legal proceedings or outright rebellions.[13] In English, "petition" assumed the role of an overarching term much earlier. The *American Heritage Dictionary of the English Language* captures these various components by defining a petition as "a solemn supplication or request, especially to a superior authority; an entreaty. A formal written document requesting a right or benefit from a person or group in authority."[14]

For the purpose of this study, the co-editors and contributors have agreed on a deliberately broad and far-reaching concept, using "petition" as a generic term to capture the extensive range of entreaties by Jewish populations victimized or about to be victimized in authoritarian and genocidal societies. Despite this broad range, the book's petition concept encompasses several distinct characteristics in ways that differentiate these Holocaust and early post-Holocaust era practices from other forms of public acts and protests.

First, the vast majority of Jewish petitions of this period had clearly identifiable authors. In addition to individual entreaties, collective petitions emerged from the midst of Jewish religious Communities, political and cultural organizations, but also groups of individuals in distress.[15] On occasion, especially in cases of illiteracy or limited language skills, a third person, often a lawyer, would pen an entreaty with input from the aggrieved party. Anonymous submissions were very rare and, in most cases, could be more adequately classified as a written protest than an entreaty. Especially during the 1930s, these collective petitions also repeatedly assumed the form of petitionary memoranda that were printed and intended for a wider distribution among Jewish and non-Jewish audiences, as shown in this volume's chapter on petitioning in Nazi Germany.

Second, these documents addressed a variety of specific public institutions or individuals. During the Holocaust, authors approached state offices, such as ministerial bureaucracies in the European capitals, regional administrative agencies, national parliaments, courts of law, and heads of state. They also directed their petitions to officials and leaders of ruling fascist parties, mayors, church leaders, and individuals with real or imagined high standing in the regime. Furthermore, petitioners addressed the Jewish leadership, including Jewish Councils formed at the order of German authorities in ghettos and towns, especially in Eastern Europe, as intermediators as demonstrated in Svenja Bethke's chapter on the Łódź ghetto, as well as rescue organizations and governments around the globe, as examined in Thomas Pegelow Kaplan's analysis of entreaties by Central European Jews trying to escape to the Philippines.

Third, these authors' entreaties evolved around a *petitum*, that is, a specific request or demand.[16] This request could assume the form of a favor or seeking redress for a perceived injustice by the repressive or dictatorial regimes of mid-twentieth-century Europe. They did not merely convey information and were not limited to acts of denunciations. While petitions also did not exclusively focus on criticism, they, time and again, also expressed an implicit or even open form of critique or protest.

Fourth, petitions were written documents, even if authors sometimes introduced them verbally to the addressee. During the 1930s and 1940s, Jews under different European regimes employed, as the chapters in this volume demonstrate, petitions in a great variety of formats, from letters to formal memoranda, from handwritten postcards to printed interventions, and from individual to collective entreaties. Entreaties triggered by exemption clauses in racial laws often required longer written texts and an annex with a range of supporting documents.[17]

Fifth, these pleas always remained "embedded in a functional context" that meant their authors were expected and generally sought to follow specific rules of communication and adhere to regulations stated by the addressed agency, while drawing on broader cultural and national traditions of entreaty compositions.[18] These traditions encompassed various notions of deference and civility and, especially during the early years, expressed a belief in civil and constitutional rights.

Finally, petitioners, composing their pleas during the Holocaust and other periods of twentieth-century mass violence, often expressed a sense of urgency that only increased as a result of radical persecution, looming mass deportation, sudden imprisonment, and systematic murder.

All in all, petitions during the Holocaust differed from other kinds of writing such as diary keeping, family correspondence, and many other forms of letter composition. Scholars of everyday history in authoritarian regimes, such as Sheila Fitzpatrick, have subsumed petitions under public letters.[19] Still, Holocaust-era petitions remain quite distinct in their focus on a *petitum* and request and, especially at the height of the killings, often rushed form that could consist of just a few lines scribbled on a piece of crumpled paper. Furthermore, some historians of petitioning practices have begun to frame them as ego-documents. However, this understanding, we would argue, is more confusing than illuminating since it downplays the hybrid nature of entreaties and the regulations and language of the petitioned that pervade them.[20]

Entreaties belonged to the broad range of possible responses by victims of oppression and mass violence. While they might look inconsequential in comparison to armed resistance, almost all of these entreaties constituted acts of contestation, since the individual or group of petitioners would challenge—even if only for the authors and their relatives—the effects, but also often the foundations and legality, of discrimination, persecution, and violence.

Jewish petitions across the continent unfolded on a striking continuum. They ranged from expressing partial conformity with and even support for the racist discourses of petitioned regimes, while still requesting exclusion from persecution for the petitioner, as captured in Benjamin Frommer's assessment of entreaties for "Honorary Aryan" status by members of Czech families, all the way to defiance and even resistance as explicated in Wolf Gruner's examination of Jewish petitions in the Greater German Reich.

To fully grasp the defiance end of the continuum, a brief examination of the main conceptualizations of Jewish resistance is in order. The aforementioned decrying of an alleged lack of Jewish resistance during the Holocaust by Raul Hilberg was echoed by scholars like Hannah Arendt and Bruno Bettelheim.[21] Some scholars, especially in Israel, rejected Hilberg's controversial position. Yehuda Bauer has forcefully argued that armed—and unarmed—resistance by European Jews "took place wherever there was the slightest chance that it could."[22] During the next decades, the academic discussion, nonetheless, settled on narrow readings of resistance as armed, organized group activities.[23]

As a consequence, a thorough discussion of individual Jewish resistance is missing in almost all prominent Holocaust narratives, surprisingly even in those focusing on the integration of Jewish voices, such as books authored by Saul Friedländer or Moshe Zimmermann.[24] Besides the conceptual neglect, this situation can be explained by the fact that historians relied on a very limited set of sources to evaluate Jewish behavior, mostly serial political reports originated by Nazi institutions, written testimonies of survivors, and, more recently, diaries. In all of these materials, individual acts of opposition barely left traces.

Yet, already shortly after the war, the Israeli scholar Meir Dworzecki, himself a ghetto survivor, developed the concept of "standing up"—*amidah* in Hebrew—as a comprehensive term for all expressions of Jewish non-conformism and for all acts aimed at thwarting the plans of the Nazis, especially moral and spiritual acts of resistance.[25] During the 1970s, the Australian historian Konrad Kwiet and the East German scholar Helmut Eschwege also tried to open up the definition of Jewish resistance toward individual activities and included petitions in their deliberations.[26]

Picking up these ideas, some scholars recently challenged the traditional picture of Jewish passivity in Nazi Europe introducing analyses of a range of new materials. In earlier studies, the co-editors of this volume proposed novel concepts of contestation and a broader definition of resistance by Jews and other Europeans of Jewish ancestry.[27] In his study of linguistic violence and genocide, Pegelow Kaplan developed the concept of "discursive contestation" to capture and analyze the wide range of practices converts and so-called *Mischlinge* employed in the changing languages of Germanness and Jewishness to defy official racial categories and escape persecution.[28] In a pioneering article in *Yad Vashem Studies*, Gruner defined Jewish "resistance as any individual or group action in opposition to known laws, actions, or intentions of the Nazis and their collaborators, whether successful or unsuccessful, which comprises a wide range of acts of opposition and defiance, including flight, ignoring anti-Jewish restrictions, and verbal protest."[29] Both of these conceptualizations return agency to the persecuted minorities and challenge the myth of these men and women's alleged passivity. At the same time, petitions could emerge as important acts of resistance and self-determination.

In an insightful study traversing several continents and time periods, social scientist James Scott has provided a general conceptualization of petitions as a form of "public declared resistance" that resembled boycotts, demonstrations, and strikes.[30] Albeit not analyzing the persecution of the Jews and the Holocaust, Scott emphasized that in both Tokugawa Japan and Imperial Russia petitions were "commonly seen as an implicit threat to domination."[31] The "implicit" is explained by the fact that "most acts of power from below," as Scott points out, "even when they are protests . . . will largely observe the 'rules' even if their objective is to undermine them." "A petition of desperation is therefore likely," as Scott concluded, "to amalgamate two contradictory elements: an implicit threat of violence and a deferential tone of address."[32]

As this volume demonstrates, petitions sent by the persecuted to governments, state administrations, and party agencies of genocidal or authoritarian regimes have been crucial in the struggle of Jewish individuals and groups for self-determination, self-preservation, and ultimately survival. From Jewish interwar reassessments of belonging and claims for protection to Jewish populations' requests and protests in German-controlled Europe during the Holocaust and postwar struggles for care and compensation, individuals and groups used the means of writing entreaties to reclaim agency, redefine their place in society, get access to resources, and manipulate their oppressors.

As noted earlier, many historians have opted to ignore Jewish petitions, assuming they were hapless texts written in vain. Yet, a closer look, as demonstrated in this volume's chapters, reveals that a surprising number actually produced results. Upon closer scrutiny, the very question of what constitutes "success" proves to be a relative and complex phenomenon. For more than six years, Walter Jellinek, one of the Weimar Republic's most prominent scholars in administrative law and the former *rector designatus* of Heidelberg University, for example, petitioned for exemptions from the 1935 Nuremberg Laws and his racial classification as a "full Jew." Although the Reich Interior Ministry finally rejected his claims in early 1941, he was allowed to produce more evidence, which he did until US troops liberated Heidelberg in the spring of 1945.[33] Hence, long-lasting investigations of petitions for exemption repeatedly offered the petitioners invaluable time to explore alternative strategies, including securing more support from regime officials, escape, or going into hiding. In this sense, even Holocaust-era petitions that were never approved could be successful to a degree and played an important part in the petitioners' survival.

Other entreaties by persecuted Jews did not claim exemptions, but protested persecution or humiliation, reclaimed their rights as citizens, or emphasized their contributions to the fatherland; the latter is aptly demonstrated by Stacy Renee Veeder in her chapter on Jewish petitioners who sought their own or their family members' release from transit camps in France. This quest for self-determination recuperated agency and took away the power of definition from the oppressors. Others protested against specific local policies and were able to significantly influence and even reshape perpetrator policies, as Tim Cole unearths in his chapter on the flurry of entreaties prompted by the 1944 ghettoization in Budapest.

Petitions, thus, need to be re-evaluated—and beyond the purpose of this volume—as important political means for groups or individuals, not only, but especially in times of dictatorships across the European continent and globally. A closer reading reveals that petitions provided a resource for those men and women who were subjected to a lower civil status, had no political representation, and no chance to participate in a public discussion. With this volume, we argue that petitions constitute an asymmetric response to persecution often aiming to abolish discriminatory laws and local restrictions. They provide a powerful opportunity to redefine the status of the discriminated groups and individuals in front of perpetrators.

Historiographical and Historical Overview

To date, no volume exists that is exclusively devoted to analyzing petitions during the Nazi genocide of European Jewry or, more broadly, pleas composed by Jewish victim populations targeted by state sponsored violence in the mid-twentieth century. Until the 1970s and 1980s, the field of Holocaust studies in Europe and North America relied extensively on documents produced by the perpetrators of this mass crime.[34] Since the 1990s, an intensified focus on the Holocaust's victims has led to a large-scale interdisciplinary examination of diaries, memoirs, and video interviews of persecuted Jews.[35] Albeit already a well-established practice among Israeli scholars, these novel works on the persecuted have shed new light on the unfolding of the Holocaust.[36] Recently published extensive collections of primary sources on the Holocaust rightfully include many personal survivor and ego-documents. They have, nonetheless, largely ignored sources on petitioning practices. Even an, in many ways, insightful multivolume series of primary documents on Jewish responses published by the United States Holocaust Memorial Museum is representative of this phenomenon.[37]

Since the turn of the century, a number of influential Holocaust scholars have called on their colleagues to write "integrated histories" of the Holocaust with multiple combined perspectives of various groups of actors from perpetrators to victims.[38] As uniquely and inherently hybrid sources, Holocaust-era entreaties penned by Jewish men and women reflect not only the voices and demands of Jewish petitioners but also the expectations of the petitioned government and party officials and often members of other bodies such as scientists, church representatives, and lawyers. While acknowledging the very real power differentials, these entreaties emerge as far more complex and consequential as much of the previous scholarship has realized.

The small number of works that examine Jewish petitioning practices and petitioned agencies and officials during the 1930s and 1940s have largely reduced their focus to a distinct petition or specific national and regional dynamics and have thus remained limited in scope. Philipp Graf's study of the Bernheim petition uses the history of one particular entreaty submitted to the League of Nations as a vehicle to discuss Jewish politics in the interwar period. Renée Poznanski's analysis of entreaties against Vichy France's racial legislation centers on appeals against being racially categorized as Jewish. Thomas Pegelow Kaplan has analyzed petitions by Germans of Jewish ancestry, who contested their racial classification by a range of state and party agencies, as part of a broader study on the use of language in Hitler's Germany.[39]

Throughout the twentieth century, as this literature has started to demonstrate, European-Jewish petitioning processes were anything but static and unchanging. Holocaust-era entreaties assumed distinct characteristics, despite regional and national specificities. They unfolded in close interactions with persecutory practices of regional and national governments and fascist party apparatuses and often responded to quickly changing circumstances such as the enactment of new laws and violent attacks.

At the same time, Jewish petitioning processes in 1930s and 1940s Europe were thoroughly rooted in the long-term historical development of composing and employing petitions. Any study of these Holocaust-era practices has, first, to be situated in the *longue durée* of Jewish petitions. Second, Jewish entreaties have to be related to mainstream petitioning practices by non-Jewish populations since antiquity paying specific attention to dynamics in emerging autocratic and dictatorial regimes of the modern period.

Practices of Judaism in Jewish religious Communities in the Diaspora across Europe included forms of supplicatory prayers and petitions to God that, by the High Middle Ages, had largely become universally normative in the liturgy. The *Amidah* at the center of Jewish worship services, for example, contained a series of petitions asking God to hear and respond to the prayers of the congregation and individual Jewish worshippers.[40]

In more secular terms, petitions by Jewish Communities in the European Diaspora originated in antiquity in close interactions with the non-Jewish world. Many Jewish Communities and most individual Jewish *cives Romani* and *peregrini* petitioned provincial governors and directed supplications (*supplicatio*) to the emperor in Rome to secure privileges, avoid expulsion, and gain freedom to practice their religion.[41] In medieval Christian Europe, Jewish Diaspora Communities increasingly submitted pleas to popes and emperors for protection, settlement, and other rights. There was no legal framework, let alone a constitution, guaranteeing this practice. Still, a religious or secular ruler could not arbitrarily dismiss supplications.[42]

Time and again, Jewish petitions in Christendom proved successful. In 1219, for example, the Jews residing in the Kingdom of Castile submitted a petition to the Archbishop of Toledo requesting permission not to wear a distinguishing mark on their clothing decreed in the Fourth Lateran Council of 1215. Supporting the petition, the archbishop approached Pope Honorius III who granted an exemption. Jewish petitions of this period were mainly collective in form, penned by the communal leadership, and written in a highly formulized language that—like Christian entreaties—was based on the petitioners' humility and recipients' graciousness.[43] In so doing, Jewish Communities, as Kenneth R. Stow has argued, often became "adept petitioners," even finding ways to keep the Inquisition somewhat in check.[44]

With the rise of territorial rulers and imperial cities, Jewish petitioners adjusted their entreaties' language and direction. In Central European territorial states prior to Emancipation, the rapid increase of bureaucracies prompted the integration of petitioning in even the most mundane administrative procedures such as marriage licenses or local public positions.[45] As a result, entreaties already had an astounding scope. A considerable number still related to requests for residency and protection, which in the Holy Roman Empire had assumed the form of protected Jew (*Schutzjude*) status that often necessitated initial formal petitions and included a tax or other type of payment.[46] At the same time, Jewish petitioning practices also came to include a range of other objectives from trade and employment requests to complaints about slander and outright participation in supra-local politics. In fact, petitioning constitutes a key practice in those scholarly interpretations that construe the boundaries between Christian and Jewish life and politics in parts of the Holy Roman Empire as far more permeable and anything but isolated from one another.[47]

Throughout the early modern period, for example in Poland-Lithuania, Jewish petitioners often benefited from what historian Moshe Rosman has characterized as an economically oriented "marriage of convenience" between Jewish businessmen and gentile nobles. As a result, the Jewish Community in Vilna received considerable support that also included gentile petitions submitted on its behalf.[48] During the second half of the eighteenth century, Jewish Community leaders, informed by Haskalah movements, developed new forms of entreaties for legal emancipation and the end of civic restrictions. Alongside Communities' entreaties, more and more individual Jews crafted and submitted petitions. The early 1760s entreaties by a young Moses Mendelssohn to the Prussian King Frederick II to be granted the status of a protected Jew are but one, albeit prominent, example of petitioning practices that soon became more expansive in their goals and scope.[49] Regional studies, for example, of eighteenth-century Jewish petitions for the right to reside in the territory of the margravate of Baden-Durlach indicate considerable agency for members of the often-persecuted minority. Despite the rather androcentric leadership of Jewish Communities, petitioning was also much more common for Jewish women even in rural areas.[50]

When late eighteenth- and nineteenth-century liberal lawmakers gradually removed the vestiges of the early modern estates' collective privilege to state grievances and most European constitutions began to enshrine petitioning to parliament and government agencies as an individual basic right, more and more individual members of Jewish Communities joined their representatives and the much larger and rapidly growing numbers of gentile petitioners. The drafting and submission of entreaties increasingly ceased to address single rulers, appeal to their mercy, and use religious verbiage. While petitioners had fewer and fewer reasons to fear negative repercussions from their practices, the right to petition, however, was still largely a "negative" right that did not dictate when and if the petitioned bodies had to respond.

With increasing success, Jewish petitioners relied on entreaties to parliamentary bodies as a core vehicle to articulate their demands for legal equality and bring about change, most noticeable the late eighteenth-century French National Assembly in Paris and the 1848–49 Parliament in Frankfurt that resulted from revolutionary upheaval. Petitions, often supported by the first elected Jewish parliamentarians, to the Frankfurt assembly, as scholars such as Rüdiger Moldenhauer have shown, were debated and decided in committees following further reports. In addition to Jewish Community leaders, individual Jews, including a number of widowed Jewish women who challenged a ban on remarrying or sought to secure access to government bonds, came to play increasingly prominent roles.[51]

The long histories of Jewish petitioning practices were by no means limited to Diaspora Communities on the European continent. The Ottoman Empire, which at its height reached far into Southwestern and Southeastern Europe, had rich cultures of petitioning directed at shari'a courts, or regional and central authorities in the imperial capital of Istanbul. Jews generally relied on professional Muslim petition writers (*arzuhalsi*), who assumed the position of interlocutors between the aggrieved parties and the petitioned institutions, and elaborate writer's guides (*münseat*).[52] Early twentieth-century Sephardic Jewish immigrants to Ottoman Palestine, aided by their supporters on the continent, even participated in the Ottoman system directly, composing and submitting petitions to Istanbul.[53] Many were still alive in the 1930s and able to share their experiences.

The extensive scholarship on Ottoman entreaties has started to inform the study of Jewish petitioning in general. Suraiya Faroqhi has conceptualized every act of petitioning agencies of the authoritarian Ottoman system as inherently political in nature, affecting the very question of the Sultanic legitimation. Recent literature on female petitioners, whose numbers grew in the waning days of the Empire, has shed light on their practices as forms of "double-voiced" writings. They did not simply compose their entreaties as part of a male-dominated practice, but also developed a muted discourse to articulate profound challenges without being dismissed.[54]

These practices extended far beyond the shifting borders of the Ottoman Empire. In response to the ritual murder charges in Damascus in 1840, Jewish Communities under Ottoman rule resorted to petitioning as did their counterparts and other Jewish organizations based in North America and Europe, forming extensive transnational networks. An entreaty by the "Israelites of the City of New York" to US President Martin Van Buren forcefully expressed support of the arrested Jewish Community leaders in Damascus and resulted, as Jonathan Frankel has argued, in one of the first American diplomatic initiatives on behalf of Jewish Communities abroad.[55]

The tradition of petitioning practices had arrived in the Americas from the United Kingdom. Indeed, one origin of modern petitioning practices, as scholars of social and British history have demonstrated, can be traced to English law, dating back to the Magna Carta of 1215. Petitioning constituted the right of the people to lay complaints "at the foot of the throne." More importantly, this also included the right to a formal response. In the late thirteenth century, Jews were among the earliest petitioners.[56] During the following century, petitioning had become common in England. Nevertheless, petitioners could and routinely would be punished for their petitions.[57] As petitioning became more democratized and popular, the British Parliament found it increasingly difficult to ignore—let alone punish—petitioners. Scholars such as Ronald J. Krotoszynski have argued that an increase in the volume of both petitions and petitioners reflected political awareness and a new possibility of "parliamentary agitation." Essentially, petitioning secured a right of government access and served as a means of political participation that was open to anyone, including women and Jews, long before they were granted the right to vote.[58]

Even in autocratic Tsarist Russia, home to the largest Jewish populations in Europe, Jewish petitioning practices became increasingly widespread, bolstered by the reforms under Alexander II and the belated arrival of the Haskalah movement. The Maskilim—supporters of the movement—focused not only on the removal of legal restrictions, but also the opening of secular schools in the Pale of Settlement and Congress Poland. In the late nineteenth century, thousands of Jewish graduates of secondary schools petitioned the Russian Ministry of Enlightenment each year to circumvent the stifling quota system and be permitted to university.⁵⁹ In the Pale of Settlement, entreaty compositions ranged from petitions to be granted the freedom to reside anywhere in Tsarist Russia to pleas to Russian Orthodox bishops, priests, and military officers to convert or stop the conversion of Jewish children, serving for example, in the Russian army.⁶⁰

Compared to nineteenth-century Jewish petitions in England or revolutionary France, many Russian Jews continued to pen entreaties in the form of supplications, appealing to a benevolent authority figure and often without evoking the language of "rights."⁶¹ In light of the pogroms of the early 1880s, some Jewish Communities and organizations also resorted to domestic petitioning to stop the mass violence; others sought to solicit entreaties and interventions with the Tsarist government by congregations and governments abroad. In the case of forced conversions and secular education initiatives, even Judaeophobic Tsarist officials repeatedly granted the petitioners' requests.⁶²

The 1917 revolutions radically changed Jewish life and petitioning practices. The Provisional Government abolished the Pale of Settlement and outlawed discrimination on ethnic or religious grounds, a policy that the Council of People's Commissars confirmed in its condemnation of antisemitism and pogroms the following year.⁶³ Nonetheless, the new Bolshevik government also swiftly shattered the very structural foundations of Jewish existence by closing religious institutions and nationalizing the property of Jewish Communities. All the while, Soviet authorities encouraged the writing of public letters and petitions. These practices, as a number of scholars have shown, were quite widespread and constituted one of the very few instruments for the population to address the authorities in the Soviet dictatorship—and, subsequently, other communist regimes—in cases of discrimination, deportation, and exile.⁶⁴

While the pathbreaking studies of the 1990s paid scant attention to Jewish petitioners, more recent work has revealed the significance of petitions with its new languages and *petita* for Jews under the Soviet regime, who also used these writings to practice and "becom[e] Soviet Jews." Various municipalities became sites of veritable "petitioning war[s]" involving truncated Jewish Communities.⁶⁵ While some members of the Jewish Community in Minsk, for example, successfully petitioned local Soviet authorities against the confiscation of a synagogue in the late 1920s, other Jewish workers signed entreaties that prompted the conversion of Jewish Community property into Yiddish reading rooms to support their political education.⁶⁶

Elsewhere in post-World War I Europe, the number of authoritarian and dictatorial regimes also proliferated. From Hungary and Poland to Spain and Romania, the new ruling powers sought popular acclaim and legitimacy. Petitions extolling and praising the new leaders' virtues were one means toward this end, which revived many of the older elements of supplications. At the same time, in some of the new democracies, especially in Germany, new constitutions enshrined the explicit right to petition. Listed in its basic rights section, Article 126 of the Weimar Constitution guaranteed every German citizen recourse to petition parliament or the responsible authority. This constitution required, as its commentators stressed, the petitioned bodies to accept the entreaty and provide a decision.[67]

Facing new forms of antisemitism, German Jews and their organizations, most noticeably the Central Association of German Citizens of Jewish Faith (Centralverein deutscher Staatsbürger jüdischen Glaubens, CV) made use of these constitutional changes. Despite the CV's founding generation's dismissal of petitioning and "unobtrusive groveling" as ineffective and its call for more robust and public acts, the largest Jewish organization in Germany adjusted this tool of political involvement and contestation in their local and national work in the 1920s and, as Wolf Gruner's chapter shows, even more effectively in the 1930s.[68]

While the Weimar Constitution formally remained in effect during the Nazi dictatorship, few opted for a post-1933 petition to the Reichstag, the German parliament.[69] Like other dictatorial regimes in Europe, the emerging Nazi state, however, condoned and even encouraged petitioning. Formal early anti-Jewish legislation, including the April 1933 Reich Law for the Restoration of the Professional Civil Service, already alluded to avenues of petitioning, for example for a decision on descent by the Expert in Racial Research at the Reich Minister of the Interior.[70] In November 1934, the newly established Chancellery of the Führer of the Nazi Party also began to accept and process literally hundreds of thousands of petitions, including by Germans of real or imagined Jewish descent, to the regime's leader, an influential component of the *Führerkult*.[71]

At the onset of the Holocaust, Jews across the continent had been engaging in a wide array of different petitioning practices as one of their key means of political and cultural participation and, increasingly, struggle. Jews used entreaties to navigate complex political landscapes, mobilize support, and pit gentile government agencies and political groups against one another. While some knowledge of the centuries-long traditions of Jewish entreaties writing with all their intricacies had been lost and other forms of supplication seemed antiquated, there were numerous forms, experiences and complex skills to draw from. In addition, many acculturated Western and Central European Jews were exposed to universal and petitioning letter-writing manuals that gained prominence during the second half the nineteenth century and into the early twentieth century.[72]

Jews frequently used petitions for exemptions from anti-Jewish restrictions and to oppose racist policies of all authoritarian regimes in Europe, including in Germany. Individual petitions could influence and even reshape authoritarian policies, as Tim Cole in his chapter proves for the ghettoization in Budapest in 1944. Even when the Nazi regime started the systematic deportation of Central European Jews to killing sites and ghettos in the east in the fall of 1941 and Romanian army units and their civilian collaborators engaged in mass killings of Jews in Bessarabia and North Bukovina in the summer of that year, Jewish Communities across the continent responded by drawing on the proven tool of entreaties. With rapidly shrinking options, Jewish leaders and other Community members, however, were hardly naïve or easily duped, but used petitions as one of the means to resist that was still available to them. As the chapters in this volume reveal, quite a number of petitioners failed in their immediate request, but many achieved short-term and even long-term success.

Petitioning, it is important to note, did not end in 1945. Even after the Nazis and their allied regimes across the continent had systematically murdered many authors of entreaties, Jewish survivors once more opted for and often were forced to rely on petitions to newly formed postwar bodies such as the Victims of Fascism committees and international aid organizations. Relatively few scholars have, as Maximilian Strnad does in his chapter for this collection, systematically analyzed the struggles and entreaty writing practices of German-Jewish survivors in occupied Germany, most of whom had survived due their marriage to a non-Jewish German. These survivors' petitions sought to secure food, other forms of aid, and even their very recognition as victims. In East Germany and other parts of Cold War Eastern Europe, petitioning, including complaints, remained key components of everyday life, revealed the social praxis of authoritarian rule, and a plurality of voices initially drowned out in the socialist regimes' ritualized language. By the mid-1950s, fewer and fewer entreaties in these countries came from the truncated Jewish Communities. Most that did were requests for emigration to Israel or the West.[73]

Battling the Diversity of Persecution: Jewish Petitions of the 1930s and 1940s

This volume offers the first extensive analysis of entreaties from persecuted Jews in authoritarian circumstances in mid-twentieth century Europe. While scholars have hitherto overlooked petitions as largely worthless, this book demonstrates the opposite. Tens of thousands of entreaties sent by the persecuted to authoritarian governments and party agencies have been crucial in the struggle of Jews for self-determination, self-preservation, and ultimately, survival.

Our collection provides a reassessment of petitions for two reasons. First, entreaties demonstrate Jewish agency. Second, petitions represent a political means by which Jews countered their racial discriminatory redefinition as groups and individuals as well as other discriminatory actions by an authoritarian regime. This approach is the result of a discussion between the co-editors who agreed on the common misperception of entreaties and their overlooked importance as well as the need for a renewed methodological discussion of Jewish contestation and resistance, which included a range of practices of petition writing. The co-editors solicited chapters from specialists in Jewish and Holocaust history in different countries and different regions. None of the other contributors had worked specifically on petitions before, but all had used them in their research. They all responded positively to our call to revisit the importance of these texts. Based on more in-depth studies employing nuanced methodological approaches, the contributions of this volume provide scholarly reassessments that will change the previous underestimation and misperception of Jewish entreaties in Holocaust studies and contemporary European Jewish history.

The chapters offer analyses of petitions and their historical context authored by Jews in Germany, Austria, and annexed Bohemia-Moravia, occupied France and Poland, as well as the independent Hungary and Romania as distinct loci of contestation and victim-perpetrator interaction. The collection brings together original research from accomplished senior and junior scholars, who collectively offer a broad array of different approaches, language skills, and insights from archives around the world. While advancing far-reaching analyses of Jewish petitioning practices in Europe during the Holocaust, the volume also examines transnational networks on a global scale, reaching all the way to the Philippines. Central European Jews used and reworked these networks and means of communication in ways, as Thomas Pegelow Kaplan's chapter argues, that require a much-needed rethinking of the spatial terms of analysis of Holocaust and European-Jewish histories.

To allow for a thorough analysis and as a basis for comparison, the contributors to this volume address a series of key questions developed by the co-editors. These questions included basic inquiries such as: Who were the petitioners? Why did they resort to the instrument of entreaties in their genocidal and/or authoritarian societies? Whom did the authors of petitions approach and why? What were the aims of the analyzed petition? Did individual or collective entreaties revolve around a protest against state discrimination or claims of property, requests for exemption from racial classification, a fight for specific rights, or the insistence of self-determination?

Other, more complex questions asked authors to identify ways or patterns of self-determination in various petitions by members of a group. What difference did gender dynamics and hierarchies make in the petitioning processes? Did these petitions result in discernible changes for the authors or the communities? Did they have any direct positive outcomes or negative consequences? To what extent did petitions in genocidal and/or authoritarian societies serve to negotiate, protect or enhance the authors' agency? How were these practices of crafting entreaties embedded in the often-long histories of petitions? What impact, if any, did transnational networks and exchanges have on the composition of petitions? Finally, to what extent does the close examination of petitioning processes demand a rethinking of practices of contestation or even (unarmed) individual and group resistance?

In sum, this volume examines the form and scope of a broad array of Holocaust-era petitions, identifies their aims and merits, evaluates the complex strategies of their authors and the broader political and cultural contexts, emphasizes the agency of the persecuted, and probes into the reactions of the addressed agencies to establish its merits as overlooked tools of Jewish self-determination, contestation and, repeatedly, resistance.

Thomas Pegelow Kaplan is the Louis P. Singer Endowed Chair in Jewish History, Professor of History, and Interim Director of the Program in Jewish Studies at the University of Colorado Boulder. He is the author of *The Language of Nazi Genocide* (2009) and *The German-Jewish Press and Journalism Beyond Borders, 1933-1943* (2023, in Hebrew) as well as the co-editor of *Beyond "Ordinary Men": Christopher R. Browning and Holocaust Historiography* (2019) and *Police and Holocaust* (2023, in German). He is currently completing a manuscript entitled *Naming Genocide: Protesters, Imageries of Mass Murder, and the Remaking of Memory in West Germany and the United States.*

Wolf Gruner is the Shapell-Guerin Chair in Jewish Studies, Professor of History and Founding Director of the USC Dornsife Center for Advanced Genocide Research at the University of Southern California, Los Angeles. He is the author of eleven books, ten of them on the Holocaust, including *Jewish Forced Labor under the Nazis* (2006), *The Holocaust in Bohemia and Moravia* (2019) and *Resisters: How Ordinary Jews fought Persecution in Hitler's Germany* (2023).

Notes

1. Raul Hilberg, *The Destruction of the European Jews* (Chicago, 1961), 663–64.
2. Jean Ancel, *The History of the Holocaust in Romania* (Lincoln, NE, 2011), 300–1; Jacob Kaplan, "French Jewry under the Occupation," *The American Jewish Year Book* 47 (1945–46): 89.
3. Hilberg, *Destruction*, 664. Although Hilberg revised and updated *The Destruction of the European Jews* for every new edition, he never substantially changed this harsh judgment.
4. Beate Meyer, *"Jüdische Mischlinge": Rassenpolitik und Verfolgungserfahrung 1933–1945* (Hamburg, 1999), 158.
5. See, among others, pp. 28–50, 91–113, this volume.
6. Dan Michman, "The Jewish Dimension of the Holocaust in Dire Straits? Current Challenges of Interpretation and Scope," in *Jewish Histories of the Holocaust: New Transnational Approaches*, ed. Norman J. W. Goda (New York, 2014), 17–38; Saul Friedländer, *Nazi Germany and the Jews*, vol. 1: *The Years of Persecution 1933–1939* (New York, 1997).
7. Richard W. Taylor, "When Germans Complain: The Right to Petition and Grievance Redress by Parliamentary Committee," *The Ombudsman Journal* 1 (1981): 70.
8. See, for example, Sheila Fitzpatrick, "Supplicants and Citizens: Public Letter-Writing in Soviet Russia in the 1930s," *Slavic Review* 55 (1996): 103–4.
9. James C. Scott, *Domination and the Arts of Resistance: Hidden Transcripts* (New Haven, CT, 1990), 94.
10. Andreas Würgler, "Asymmetrie und Reziprozität: Herrschaft und Protektion in Suppliken der Frühen Neuzeit," in *Protegierte und Protektoren: Asymmetrische politische Beziehungen zwischen Partnerschaft und Dominanz* (16. bis frühes 20. Jahrhundert), ed. Tilmann Haug, et al. (Cologne, 2016), 279–94.
11. See, for example, ibid.; Peter Blickle, ed., *Gemeinde und Staat im Alten Europa* (Munich 1998); Lex Heerma van Voss, ed., *Petitions in Social History* (Cambridge, 2002). For works on petitions in the Soviet Union and Communist Eastern Europe, see Alf Lüdtke and Peter Becker, eds., *Akten. Eingaben. Schaufenster: Die DDR und ihre Texte: Erkundungen zu Herrschaft und Alltag* (Berlin, 1997); and Fitzpatrick, "Supplicants and Citizens."
12. Geoffrey Koziol, *Begging Pardon and Favor: Ritual and Political Order in Early Medieval France* (Ithaca, NY, 2011), 26; Fred S. Naiden, *Ancient Supplication* (Oxford, 2006), 6–8, 289.
13. Andreas Würgler, "Voices from Among the 'Silent Masses': Humble Petitions and Social Conflict in Early Modern Central Europe," *International Review of Social History* 46, Supplement 9 (2001): 14
14. *American Heritage Dictionary of the English Language*, s.v. "Petition."
15. In her theoretical reflections, Anita Hodgkiss stresses the importance of collective petitions and empowerment. See her "Petitioning and the Empowerment Theory of Practice," *Yale Law Journal* 96, no. 3 (1987): 572.
16. *Staatslexikon*, comp. Görres-Gesellschaft, 7th ed. (Freiburg, 1985), s.v. "Petitionsrecht."
17. For some petitioning provisions in Nazi racial legislation, see Decree of the Reich Minister of the Interior, 4 December 1935, *Ministerialblatt für die Preußische Innere Verwaltung* 50 (1935): 1455–56.
18. Würgler, "Voices," 32. On the importance of rhetorical convention in other contexts preceding the Holocaust, see also David Zaret, "Petitions and the 'Invention' of Public Opinion in the English Revolution," *American Journal of Sociology* 101, no. 6 (1996): 1514–17.
19. Fitzpatrick, "Supplicants and Citizens," 80.

20. Claudia Ulbrich, "Zeuginnen und Bittstellerinnen: Überlegungen zur Bedeutung von Ego-Dokumenten für die Erforschung weiblicher Selbstwahrnehmungen in der ländlichen Gesellschaft des 18. Jahrhunderts," in *Ego-Dokumente. Annäherung an den Menschen in der Geschichte*, ed. Winfried Schulze (Berlin, 1996), 223. On ego-documents, see the defining work by Rudolf Dekker, including his edited collection *Egodocuments and History: Autobiographical Writing in Its Social Context since the Middle Ages* (Hilversum, 2002).
21. For key discussions of Jewish resistance, see Michael Marrus, "Jewish Resistance to the Holocaust," *Journal of Contemporary History* 30, no. 1 (1995): 86; Konrad Kwiet, "Problems of Jewish Resistance Historiography," *Leo Baeck Institute Yearbook* 24 (1979): 37; Robert Rozett, "Jewish Resistance," in *The Historiography of the Holocaust*, ed. Dan Stone (Houndmills, 2004), 343.
22. Yehuda Bauer, *Rethinking the Holocaust* (New Haven, CT, 2000), 141–42, 165–66; Richard Middleton-Kaplan, "The Myth of Jewish Passivity," in *Jewish Resistance against the Nazis*, ed. Patrick Gerard Henry (Washington, DC, 2014), 11–12.
23. For an account of the historiography of Jewish resistance, see Wolf Gruner, "'The Germans Should Expel the Foreigner Hitler': Open Protest and Other Forms of Jewish Defiance in Nazi Germany," *Yad Vashem Studies* 39, no. 2 (2011): 14–17.
24. Saul Friedländer, *Nazi Germany and the Jews*, vol. 1; Saul Friedländer, *Nazi Germany and the Jews, 1939–1945*, vol. 2: *The Years of Extermination, 1939–1945* (New York, 2007); Moshe Zimmermann, *Deutsche gegen Deutsche: Das Schicksal der Juden 1938–1945* (Berlin, 2008).
25. Meir Dworzecki, "The Day to Day Stand of the Jews," in *Jewish Resistance during the Holocaust: Proceedings of the Conference on Manifestations of Jewish Resistance*, Jerusalem, April 7–11, 1968 (Jerusalem, 1971), 152–81.
26. Konrad Kwiet and Helmut Eschwege, *Selbstbehauptung und Widerstand: Deutsche Juden im Kampf um Existenz und Menschenwürde, 1933–1945*, 2nd ed. (Hamburg, 1986), 18–19.
27. Gruner, "Germans Should Expel"; Thomas Pegelow Kaplan, *The Language of Nazi Genocide: Linguistic Violence and the Struggle of Germans of Jewish Ancestry* (New York, 2009).
28. Ibid., 9–14.
29. Gruner, "Germans Should Expel," 18.
30. Scott, *Domination*, 198.
31. Ibid., 63.
32. Ibid., 94–95.
33. Walter Jellinek to Adolf Hitler, 22 November 1935, copy, Bundesarchiv Berlin (hereafter BAB) R1509/91, p. 38; E. Schircks to Stellvertreter des Führers, 25 February 1941, BAB R1509/91, p. 257; Pegelow Kaplan, *Language of Nazi Genocide*, 156–57, 201.
34. See, for example, Jewish Black Book Committee, *The Black Book: The Nazi Crime against the Jewish People* (New York, 1946), Hilberg, *Destruction*; Uwe Dietrich Adam, *Judenpolitik im Dritten Reich* (Düsseldorf, 1972).
35. In the 1990s, the Visual History Archive of the USC Shoah Foundation, for example, amassed some 52,000 audio-visual testimonies mostly from Holocaust survivors interviewed around the globe. See USC Shoah Foundation, n.d., "Visual History Archive."
36. See, for instance, David Bankier and Dan Michman, eds., *Holocaust Historiography in Context: Emergence, Challenges, Polemics and Achievements* (Jerusalem, 2008).
37. Jürgen Matthäus et al., eds., *Jewish Responses to Persecution*, 5 vols. (Lanham, MD, 2010–2015). A large multivolume German-language source collection on the persecution and extermination of the European Jews likewise includes only a few entreaties by Jewish authors. Götz Aly et al., eds., *Die Verfolgung und Ermordung der europäischen Juden durch*

das nationalsozialistische Deutschland 1933–1945, 16 vols. (Munich, 2008). An English translation is under way. Volumes 1–3 were published in 2019.

38. Michman, "Jewish Dimension of the Holocaust in Dire Straits?" 17–38; Friedländer, *Nazi Germany and the Jews*, vol. 1.
39. Philipp Graf, *Die Bernheim-Petition 1933: Jüdische Politik in der Zwischenkriegszeit* (Göttingen, 2008); Renée Poznanski, *Jews in France during World War II* (Waltham, MA, 2001); Pegelow Kaplan, *Language of Nazi Genocide*.
40. Leo Trepp, *A History of the Jewish Experience* (Springfield, NJ, 2001), 353.
41. Fergus Millar, *The Emperor in the Roman World* (31 BC–AD 337) (Ithaca, NY, 1977), 541–44; Naiden, *Ancient Supplication*, 224–25.
42. Würgler, "Voices," 15; Koziol, *Begging Pardon*, 26.
43. Koziol, *Begging Pardon*, 8; Rebecca Rist, *Popes and Jews, 1095–1291* (Oxford, 2016), 127.
44. Kenneth R. Stow, *Popes, Church, and Jews in the Middle Ages: Confrontation and Response* (Aldershot, 2007), 42–43.
45. Würgler, "Voices," 26.
46. J. Friedrich Battenberg, "Die Privilegierung von Juden und der Judenschaft im Bereich des Heiligen Römischen Reiches deutscher Nation," in *Das Privileg im europäischen Vergleich*, ed. by Barbara Dölemeyer et al. (Frankfurt/Main, 1997), 1:151–56.
47. On the suprapolitical aspects, see Christopher R. Friedrichs, "Jews in the Imperial Cities: A Political Perspective," in *In and Out of the Ghetto: Jewish-Gentile Relations in Late Medieval and Early Modern Germany*, ed. Ronnie Po-chia Hsia et al. (New York, 1995), 275–88.
48. M. J. Rosman, *The Lords' Jews: Magnate-Jewish Relations in the Polish-Lithuanian Commonwealth during the Eighteenth Century* (Cambridge, MA, 1991), 201.
49. Mordechai Breuer and Michael Graetz, *German-Jewish History in Modern Times*, vol. 1: *Tradition and Enlightenment, 1600–1780* (New York, 1996), 267–68.
50. See André Holenstein, "Bitten um den Schutz: Staatliche Judenpolitik und Lebensführung von Juden im Lichte der Schutzsupplikationen aus der Markgrafschaft Baden (Durlach) im 18. Jahrhundert," in *Landjudentum im deutschen Südwesten während der Frühen Neuzeit*, ed. Rolf Kießling et al. (Berlin, 1999), 97–153. On female petitioners, see Ulbrich, "Zeuginnen und Bittstellerinnen," 221–26.
51. Rüdiger Moldenhauer, "Jewish Petitions to the German National Assembly in Frankfurt 1848/49," *Leo Baeck Institute Year Book* 16 (1971): 189–90, 192, 194. See also Uri R. Kaufmann, "The Jewish Fight for Emancipation in France and Germany," in *Jewish Emancipation Reconsidered: The French and German Models*, ed. Michel Brenner et al. (Tübingen, 2003), 79–92.
52. Fruma Zachs and Yuval Ben-Bassat, "Women's Visibility in Petitions from Greater Syria during the Late Ottoman Period," *International Journal of Middle East Studies* 47 (2015): 766–67.
53. Yuval Ben-Bassat, *Petitioning the Sultan: Protests and Justice in Late Ottoman Palestine, 1865–1908* (London, 2013), 171.
54. Suraiya Faroqhi, ed., *Coping with the State: Political Conflict and Crime in the Ottoman Empire, 1550–1720* (Istanbul, 1995); Zachs and Ben-Bassat, "Women's Visibility in Petitions," 766–67. The concept of "double-voiced" is borrowed from feminist literary critic Elaine Showalter's work.
55. Jonathan Frankel, *The Damascus Affair: "Ritual Murder", Politics, and the Jews in 1840* (Cambridge, 1997), 226–27.
56. Paul Brand, "Petitions and Parliament in the Reign of Edward I," *Parliamentary History* 23 (2004): 34.

57. Ronald J. Krotoszynski, Jr., *Reclaiming the Petition Clause: Seditious Libel, "Offensive" Protest, and the Right to Petition the Government for a Redress of Grievances* (New Haven, CT, 2012), 86, 81.
58. Ibid., 16, 90, 82, 94; Todd M. Endelman, *The Jews of Britain, 1656–2000* (Berkeley, CA, 2002), 101–2.
59. Benjamin Nathans, *Beyond the Pale: The Jewish Encounter with Late Imperial Russia* (Berkeley, CA, 2002), 272–73.
60. Jay Michael Harris et al., eds. *Everyday Jewish Life in Imperial Russia: Select Documents, 1772–1914* (Waltham, MA, 2013), 143–44, 507, 515–19.
61. For a representative example, see Gregory L. Freeze, *From Supplication to Revolution: A Documentary Social History of Imperial Russia* (New York, 1988), 189–90.
62. John Klier, *Russians, Jews, and the Pogrom Crisis of 1881–1882* (Cambridge, 2011), 234, 245.
63. Benjamin Pinkus, *The Jews of the Soviet Union: The History of a National Minority* (Cambridge, 1988), 84–85.
64. Sheila Fitzpatrick, *Everyday Stalinism: Ordinary Life in Extraordinary Times, Soviet Russia in the 1930s* (Oxford, 1999), 128; Fitzpatrick, "Supplicants and Citizens," 95–97.
65. Elissa Bemporad. *Becoming Soviet Jews the Bolshevik Experiment in Minsk* (Bloomington, IN, 2013), 117.
66. Ibid.
67. Karl Hüfner, "Artikel 126," in *Die Grundrechte und Grundpflichten der Reichsverfassung. Kommentar zum zweiten Teil der Reichsverfassung*, ed. Hans Carl Nipperday (Berlin, 1930), 2:176–79.
68. Avraham Barkai, *Hoffnung und Untergang: Studien zur deutsch-jüdischen Geschichte des 19. und 20. Jahrhunderts* (Hamburg, 1998), 113.
69. Rupert Schick, *Petitionen: Von der Untertanenbitte zum Bürgerrecht*, 3rd ed. (Heidelberg, 1996), 20.
70. Erste Verordnung zur Durchführung des Gesetzes zur Wiederherstellung des Berufsbeamtentums, 11 April 1933, *Reichsgesetzblatt* 1 (1933): 195.
71. Thomas Pegelow Kaplan, "Petitioning the Führer: The Construction of Germanness and Jewishness in Personal Appeals to the Nazi Leader, 1934–1941" (unpublished AHA paper, 7 January 2007). As scholars of petitioning in the Soviet Union have already discerned, petitioning, even if unintended by its authors, could also help to stabilize authoritarian regimes by providing a means to gauge the impact of regime policies, provide the illusion of an accessible leader, and diffuse tensions. See Merle Fainsod, *Smolensk under Soviet Rule* (Cambridge, MA, 1958), 407.
72. In the German-speaking lands, Otto Friedrich Rammler's *Universal Brief-Steller*, which printed its 65th edition in 1895, was one of the most successful examples. See Christa Hämmerle, "Requests, Complaints, Demands. Preliminary Thoughts on the Petitioning Letters of Lower-Class Austrian Women, 1865–1918," in *Gender and Politics in the Age of Letter-Writing, 1750–2000*, ed. Caroline Bland et al. (New York, 2004), 116–17, 130.
73. Felix Mühlberg, Bürger, *Bitten und Behörden: Geschichte der Eingabe in der DDR* (Berlin, 2004); Lüdtke and Becker, *Akten. Eingaben. Schaufenster*; Boris Morozov, *Documents on Soviet Jewish Emigration* (London, 2015).

Bibliography

Adam, Uwe Dietrich. *Judenpolitik im Dritten Reich*. Düsseldorf: Droste, 1972.
Aly, Götz et al., eds. *Die Verfolgung und Ermordung der europäischen Juden durch das nationalsozialistische Deutschland 1933–1945*, 16 vols. Munich: Oldenbourg, 2008.
Ancel, Jean. *The History of the Holocaust in Romania*. Lincoln: University of Nebraska Press, 2011.
Bankier, David, and Dan Michman, eds. *Holocaust Historiography in Context: Emergence, Challenges, Polemics and Achievements*. Jerusalem: Yad Vashem, 2008.
Barkai, Avraham. *Hoffnung und Untergang: Studien zur deutsch-jüdischen Geschichte des 19. und 20. Jahrhunderts*. Hamburg: Christians, 1998.
Battenberg, J. Friedrich. "Die Privilegierung von Juden und der Judenschaft im Bereich des Heiligen Römischen Reiches deutscher Nation." In *Das Privileg im europäischen Vergleich*, edited by Barbara Dölemeyer et al., 1:139–190. Frankfurt am Main: Vittorio Klostermann, 1997.
Bauer, Yehuda. *Rethinking the Holocaust*. New Haven, CT: Yale University Press, 2000.
Bemporad, Elissa. *Becoming Soviet Jews the Bolshevik Experiment in Minsk*. Bloomington: Indiana University Press, 2013.
Ben-Bassat, Yuval. *Petitioning the Sultan: Protests and Justice in Late Ottoman Palestine, 1865–1908*. London: I. B. Tauris, 2013.
Blickle, Peter, ed. *Gemeinde und Staat im Alten Europa*. Munich: R. Oldenbourg Verlag, 1998.
Brand, Paul. "Petitions and Parliament in the Reign of Edward I." *Parliamentary History* 23 (2004): 14–38.
Breuer, Mordechai, and Michael Graetz. *German-Jewish History in Modern Times*. Vol. 1: *Tradition and Enlightenment, 1600–1780*. New York: Columbia University Press, 1996.
Dekker, Rudolf, ed. *Egodocuments and History: Autobiographical Writing in Its Social Context since the Middle Ages*. Hilversum: Verloren, 2002.
Dworzecki, Meir. "The Day to Day Stand of the Jews." In *Jewish Resistance during the Holocaust: Proceedings of the Conference on Manifestations of Jewish Resistance, Jerusalem, April 7–11, 1968*, 152–181. Jerusalem: Yad Vashem, 1971.
Endelman, Todd M. *The Jews of Britain, 1656–2000*. Berkeley: University of California Press, 2002.
Fainsod, Merle. *Smolensk under Soviet Rule*. Cambridge, MA: Harvard University Press, 1958.
Faroqhi, Suraiya, ed. *Coping with the State: Political Conflict and Crime in the Ottoman Empire, 1550–1720*. Istanbul: Isis, 1995.
Fitzpatrick, Sheila. *Everyday Stalinism: Ordinary Life in Extraordinary Times, Soviet Russia in the 1930s*. Oxford: Oxford University Press, 1999.
———. "Supplicants and Citizens: Public Letter-Writing in Soviet Russia in the 1930s." *Slavic Review* 55, no. 1 (1996): 78–105.
Frankel, Jonathan. *The Damascus Affair: "Ritual Murder," Politics, and the Jews in 1840*. Cambridge: Cambridge University Press, 1997.

Freeze, Gregory L. *From Supplication to Revolution: A Documentary Social History of Imperial Russia*. New York: Oxford University Press, 1988.
Friedländer, Saul. *Nazi Germany and the Jews, 1933–1939*. Vol. 1: *The Years of Persecution*. New York: HarperCollins, 1997.
———. *Nazi Germany and the Jews, 1939–1945*. Vol. 2: *The Years of Extermination*. New York: HarperCollins, 2007.
Friedrichs, Christopher R. "Jews in the Imperial Cities: A Political Perspective." In *In and Out of the Ghetto: Jewish-Gentile Relations in Late Medieval and Early Modern Germany*, edited by Ronnie Po-chia Hsia et al., 275–88. New York: Cambridge University Press, 1995.
Graf, Philipp. *Die Bernheim-Petition 1933: Jüdische Politik in der Zwischenkriegszeit*. Göttingen: Vandenhoeck & Ruprecht, 2008.
Gruner, Wolf. "'The Germans Should Expel the Foreigner Hitler': Open Protest and Other Forms of Jewish Defiance in Nazi Germany." *Yad Vashem Studies* 39, no. 2 (2011): 13–53.
Hämmerle, Christa. "Requests, Complaints, Demands. Preliminary Thoughts on the Petitioning Letters of Lower-Class Austrian Women, 1865–1918." In *Gender and Politics in the Age of Letter-Writing, 1750–2000*, edited by Caroline Bland et al., 115–33. New York: Routledge, 2004.
Harris, Jay Michael, et al., eds. *Everyday Jewish Life in Imperial Russia: Select Documents, 1772–1914*. Waltham, MA: Brandeis University Press, 2013.
Heerma van Voss, Lex, ed. *Petitions in Social History*. Cambridge: Cambridge University Press, 2002.
Hilberg, Raul. *The Destruction of the European Jews*. Chicago: Quadrangle Books, 1961.
Hodgkiss, Anita. "Petitioning and the Empowerment Theory of Practice." *Yale Law Journal* 96, no. 3 (1987): 569–92.
Holenstein, André. "Bitten um den Schutz: Staatliche Judenpolitik und Lebensführung von Juden im Lichte der Schutzsupplikationen aus der Markgrafschaft Baden(-Durlach) im 18. Jahrhundert." In *Landjudentum im deutschen Südwesten während der Frühen Neuzeit*, edited by Rolf Kießling et al., 97–153. Berlin: Akademie Verlag, 1999.
Hüfner, Karl. "Artikel 126." In *Die Grundrechte und Grundpflichten der Reichsverfassung. Kommentar zum zweiten Teil der Reichsverfassung*, edited by Hans Carl Nipperday, 2:176–92. Berlin: Hobbing, 1930.
Jewish Black Book Committee. *The Black Book: The Nazi Crime against the Jewish People*. New York: Nexus Press, 1946.
Kaplan, Jacob. "French Jewry under the Occupation." *The American Jewish Year Book* 47 (1945–46): 71–118.
Kaufmann, Uri R. "The Jewish Fight for Emancipation in France and Germany." In *Jewish Emancipation Reconsidered: The French and German Models*, edited by Michel Brenner et al., 79–88. Tübingen: Mohr Siebeck, 2003.
Klier, John. *Russians, Jews, and the Pogrom Crisis of 1881–1882*. Cambridge: Cambridge University Press, 2011.
Koziol, Geoffrey. *Begging Pardon and Favor: Ritual and Political Order in Early Medieval France*. Ithaca, NY: Cornell University Press, 2011.

Krotoszynski, Jr., Ronald J. *Reclaiming the Petition Clause: Seditious Libel, "Offensive" Protest, and the Right to Petition the Government for a Redress of Grievances.* New Haven, CT: Yale University Press, 2012.

Kwiet, Konrad. "Problems of Jewish Resistance Historiography." *Leo Baeck Institute Yearbook* 24 (1979): 37–57.

Kwiet, Konrad, and Helmut Eschwege. *Selbstbehauptung und Widerstand: Deutsche Juden im Kampf um Existenz und Menschenwürde, 1933–1945*, 2nd ed. Hamburg: Christians, 1986.

Lüdtke, Alf, and Peter Becker, eds. *Akten. Eingaben. Schaufenster: Die DDR und ihre Texte: Erkundungen zu Herrschaft und Alltag.* Berlin: Akademie Verlag, 1997.

Matthäus, Jürgen, et al., eds. *Jewish Responses to Persecution*, 5 vols. Lanham, MD: AltaMira Press, 2010–2015.

Marrus, Michael. "Jewish Resistance to the Holocaust." *Journal of Contemporary History* 30, no. 1 (1995): 83–110.

Meyer, Beate. *"Jüdische Mischlinge": Rassenpolitik und Verfolgungserfahrung 1933–1945.* Hamburg: Doelling und Galitz, 1999.

Michman, Dan. "The Jewish Dimension of the Holocaust in Dire Straits? Current Challenges of Interpretation and Scope." In *Jewish Histories of the Holocaust: New Transnational Approaches*, edited by Norman J. W. Goda, 17–38. New York: Berghahn, 2014.

Middleton-Kaplan, Richard. "The Myth of Jewish Passivity." In *Jewish Resistance against the Nazis*, edited by Patrick Gerard Henry, 3–36. Washington, DC: Catholic University of America Press, 2014.

Millar, Fergus. *The Emperor in the Roman World (31BC–AD 337).* Ithaca, NY: Cornell University Press, 1977.

Moldenhauer, Rüdiger. "Jewish Petitions to the German National Assembly in Frankfurt 1848/49." *Leo Baeck Institute Year Book* 16 (1971): 185–223.

Morozov, Boris. *Documents on Soviet Jewish Emigration.* London: Frank Cass, 2015.

Mühlberg, Felix. *Bürger, Bitten und Behörden: Geschichte der Eingabe in der DDR.* Berlin; Dietz, 2004.

Nathans, Benjamin. *Beyond the Pale: The Jewish Encounter with Late Imperial Russia.* Berkeley: University of California Press, 2002.

Naiden, Fred S. *Ancient Supplication.* Oxford: Oxford University Press, 2006.

Pegelow Kaplan, Thomas. *The Language of Nazi Genocide: Linguistic Violence and the Struggle of Germans of Jewish Ancestry.* New York: Cambridge University Press, 2009.

―――. "Petitioning the *Führer*: The Construction of Germanness and Jewishness in Personal Appeals to the Nazi Leader, 1934–1941." Unpublished AHA paper, 7 January 2007.

Pinkus, Benjamin. *The Jews of the Soviet Union: The History of a National Minority.* Cambridge: Cambridge University Press, 1988.

Poznanski, Renée. *Jews in France during World War II.* Waltham, MA: Brandeis University Press, 2001.

Rist, Rebecca. *Popes and Jews, 1095–1291.* Oxford: Oxford University Press, 2016.

Rosman, M. J. *The Lords' Jews: Magnate-Jewish Relations in the Polish-Lithuanian Commonwealth during the Eighteenth Century.* Cambridge, MA: Harvard University Press, 1991.

Rozett, Robert. "Jewish Resistance." In *The Historiography of the Holocaust,* edited by Dan Stone, 341–63. Houndmills: Palgrave, 2004.

Schick, Rupert. *Petitionen: Von der Untertanenbitte zum Bürgerrecht.* 3rd ed. Heidelberg: Hüthig, 1996.

Scott, James C. *Domination and the Arts of Resistance: Hidden Transcripts.* New Haven, CT: Yale University Press, 1990.

Stow, Kenneth R. *Popes, Church, and Jews in the Middle Ages: Confrontation and Response.* Aldershot: Ashgate, 2007.

Taylor, Richard W. "When Germans Complain: The Right to Petition and Grievance Redress by Parliamentary Committee." *The Ombudsman Journal* 1 (1981): 53–76.

Trepp, Leo. *A History of the Jewish Experience.* Springfield, NJ: Behrman House, 2001.

Ulbrich, Claudia. "Zeuginnen und Bittstellerinnen: Überlegungen zur Bedeutung von Ego-Dokumenten für die Erforschung weiblicher Selbstwahrnehmungen in der ländlichen Gesellschaft des 18. Jahrhunderts." In *Ego-Dokumente. Annäherung an den Menschen in der Geschichte,* edited by Winfried Schulze, 207–226. Berlin: Akademie Verlag 1996.

van Voss, Lex Heerma, ed. *Petitions in Social History.* Cambridge: Cambridge University Press, 2002).

Würgler, Andreas. "Asymmetrie und Reziprozität: Herrschaft und Protektion in Suppliken der Frühen Neuzeit." In *Protegierte und Protektoren: Asymmetrische politische Beziehungen zwischen Partnerschaft und Dominanz (16. bis frühes 20. Jahrhundert),* edited by Tilmann Haug, et al., 279–294. Cologne: Böhlau, 2016.

———. "Voices from among the 'Silent Masses': Humble Petitions and Social Conflict in Early Modern Central Europe." *International Review of Social History* 46, Supplement 9 (2001): 11–34.

Zachs, Fruma, and Yuval Ben-Bassat. "Women's Visibility in Petitions from Greater Syria during the Late Ottoman Period." *International Journal of Middle East Studies* 47 (2015): 765–81.

Zaret, David. "Petitions and the 'Invention' of Public Opinion in the English Revolution." *American Journal of Sociology* 101, no. 6 (1996): 1497–1555.

Zimmermann, Moshe. *Deutsche gegen Deutsche: Das Schicksal der Juden 1938–1945.* Berlin: Aufbau-Verlag, 2008.

Chapter 1

TO NOT "LIVE AS A PARIAH"
Jewish Petitions as Individual and Collective Protest in the Greater German Reich

Wolf Gruner

Introduction

On 23 February 1933, a Jewish woman, Frieda F., appealed to German Reich President von Hindenburg to stop "the public incitement to pogroms and violent attacks on Jews." Hindenburg expressed his discontent with the ongoing violence to the woman and handed over the letter to the responsible Reich Chancellor Adolf Hitler.[1] While written appeals of Jews to employers, private organizations, local, regional, and central administrations as well as to the German government, Hitler and other Nazi Party leaders are mentioned in the vast literature on the persecution of the Jews, they are neither systematically researched nor perceived as valid tools of opposition.[2]

However, for German, Austrian, and Czech Jews, the use of written petitions as a non-violent action provided them with a means in a normally powerless situation. Petitions are important for people in dictatorships for three reasons. First, entreaties represent a rare political tool for the oppressed group stripped of their rights to directly address the perpetrators. Second, in order to achieve certain objectives, members of the victimized group can appeal to general interests and personal aspirations of individual or groups of perpetrators. Finally, petitioners can publicly express their opinion in these petitions and reclaim agency. Thus, for the Third Reich, research must shed light on the responses by Jewish individuals and their distinct strategies of writing petitions to protest Nazi violence, anti-Jewish laws, or local restrictions, which affected them personally or the community as a whole.

Notes for this chapter begin on page 44.

Jews in the Greater German Reich authored petitions individually or collectively in the form of letters and memoranda. In most cases, petitionary letters were written by individuals, a group of individuals, or by representatives of Jewish organizations and institutions. Many letters were handwritten and sometimes composed in very informal ways, especially when addressing private individuals such as employers. In most cases, though, Jews used a formal style to address authorities and relied on typewriters. By contrast, petitionary memoranda were either issued by Jewish organizations or local Jewish Communities. They employed an even more formal style. Occasionally, the responsible officials even printed those petitionary memoranda for wide distribution and public attention. However, such public forms of written protest were limited to the years between 1933 and 1938; after Kristallnacht, the Nazi regime tightened control over the remaining Jewish organizations.

Jewish petitioners aimed at putting violence-free pressure on the oppressor to stop violence or persecution. While many historians, including this author, have dismissed such petitions as written in vain for a long time, a closer look reveals two important achievements. For one, in these writings addressed to specific persons, the authors formulated goals and demands to abolish anti-Jewish measures (or to be exempted from them). While the quantity of protests and demands to end discriminatory policies decreased over time, the number of requests for individual exemption from anti-Jewish policies grew. However, this does not mean that general protest or the quest for abolishing anti-Jewish laws stopped entirely.

Many entreaties appealed to specific perpetrators in power, from a local party leader or a mayor to the Reich ministers or the Nazi leadership. While Hitler seldom answered any petition addressed to him,[3] numerous officials of his staff, in state institutions and local offices vetted thousands of such demands, committing considerable resources and time. The outcomes were hardly forgone conclusions and occasionally turned out to be successful for petitioners. Furthermore, Jewish men and women used their individual and collective protests or demands to redefine their status as a discriminated minority by emphasizing their previous roles as valuable citizens, important taxpayers, and innovative contributors to German culture.

Such open expression of opposition was much more widespread than hitherto assumed. In written appeals to employers and private organizations to local and regional administrations as well as to ministries and Hitler himself, countless Jewish individuals, men and women, reclaimed their own violated rights as workers, citizens, and Germans or on behalf of others. Analyzed in their historical context of an equally overlooked variety of individual and collective acts of defiance and opposition, these findings help to restore the agency of German, Austrian, and Czech Jews and alter the traditional picture of their supposed passive behavior under oppression in Nazi Germany.[4]

With a few notable exceptions, historians were almost entirely inattentive to critique and protests expressed by individual Jews in the historiography on the Holocaust and Jews in Germany. Even these few exceptions either dismissed the value of petitions or mentioned them only briefly without a more thorough analysis.[5] By contrast, Konrad Kwiet and Helmut Eschwege started their discussion of non-conformity by German Jews with the description of written interventions as forms of open protest.[6] For the most part, either because of not being spectacular or being perceived to have been drafted in vain, such individual or collective efforts slipped under the radar, quite similar to other individual and collective forms of non-violent protest, defiance, and opposition.

To reinstate the importance of such individual acts of Jewish resistance throughout the Nazi period, a different approach is necessary that allows for a meticulous investigation of the actions and reactions of German, Austrian, and Czech Jews as well as of their organizations under Nazi persecution. In my earlier research, I defined Jewish resistance as any individual or group action in opposition to known laws, actions, or intentions of the Nazis and their collaborators, whether successful or unsuccessful.[7] This understanding shares many features with the older concept of *amidah* (standing up) that has been discussed in Israeli historiography since the 1950s.[8] Such an approach almost immediately uncovers a wide variety of individual and collective Jewish actions, ranging from breaking Nazi laws and ignoring local regulations to protesting in public. Recent research on the diversity of local, regional, and central institutions that initiated, shaped, and radicalized highly complex and even contradictory anti-Jewish persecutions enabled us to understand much better what Jews actually responded to.[9] Individual acts of opposition occurred not only during the formative years of the Nazi regime, but astonishingly also during the war under fierce oppression. Jews performed sabotage at the workplace, escaped camps, broke national laws, ignored local prohibitions to access places, resisted adoption of discriminatory middle names, and even wrote leaflets with powerful protests.[10]

As part of the broader individual and communal resistance against the Nazis, which was unarmed, non-violent, and less organized, petitions played an important role. An assessment of the function and impact of such interventions demands an analysis of petitionary letters and memoranda of Jewish organizations and Communities, private groups, and networks as well as individuals. Petitions in the Greater German Reich, authored by Jews in the form of letters or memoranda, shall thus be re-evaluated as important political means of the racially oppressed during the 1930s and early 1940s.

This chapter argues that petitions constitute an asymmetric response to persecution aiming at abolishing discriminatory laws and local restrictions and redefining the individual and collective identity of the oppressed against the perpetrator. While most historians tend to neglect its actual virtue, a closer look reveals that petitions seem to promise some power indeed for people who are subjected to a lower civil status, have no political representation, and no chance to participate in a public discussion.

This chapter will thus describe how Jews as representatives of Jewish organizations or as individuals used this form of non-violent resistance to formally protest anti-Jewish restrictions at various administrative levels whether in the public or private sector. They did so to protect individual Jews, groups of Jews, or the Jewish population as a whole from specific persecution measures, ease their burden as well as free incarcerated people in the Greater German Reich, including annexed Austria and the Protectorate Bohemia and Moravia.

Protest by Jewish Organizations and Their Representatives, 1933–38

Looking more closely into the matter, one notices a variety of systematic approaches taken by Jewish organizations and their representatives to respond to and counter persecution. During the Weimar Republic, Jews developed sturdy defense systems against antisemitic attacks by legal means or public intervention.[11]

After Hitler took power in 1933, Jewish political and social organizations, local Jewish Communities, and the newly founded umbrella organization for the German Jewish organizations and Communities, the Reich Representation of German Jews (Reichsvertretung der deutschen Juden),[12] first organized immediate material, social, educational, and spiritual support for individuals and the community as a whole affected by violence and persecution.[13] At the same time, however, functionaries of the German Jewish organizations intervened directly at perpetrator agencies at all levels, ranging from the government to municipal departments. When they appealed to politicians, state officials, or party functionaries, Jewish representatives often mobilized existing personal connections, or old and even new relationships. They employed private and official petitionary letters, yet also used phone conversations and personal meetings.[14]

Together, the Jewish Community of Berlin and the Reichsvertretung drafted a petition against the planned nationwide anti-Jewish boycott announced by the Nazi Party for 1 April 1933, which they sent to the Reich Chancellery on 29 March. In this entreaty, they protested against the Nazi defamation that the Jews had harmed the German people.[15] In a similar vein, on the day before the nationwide boycott Alfred Neumeyer wrote a protest letter on behalf of the Association of Bavarian Jewish Communities to the new head of the Bavarian state, Ritter von Epp, culminating in the line: "We issue the strongest protest against the monstrous accusations raised against us German Jews." He underlined that the German Jews had always worked for Germany and that many thousands Jews had sacrificed their lives for Germany during the war. In addition, he underscored that the well-being of the fatherland had always been the highest priority for German Jews.[16] On the same day, the Zionist Federation for Germany (Zionistische Vereinigung für Deutschland) protested against the "elimination fight against the Jews [*Vernichtungskampf*]."[17]

During the following months, Jewish organizations authored entreaties against the general anti-Jewish policy as well as very specific discriminations. In June 1933, the Reich Representation protested with a petition to Hitler against the increasing legal and political discrimination against the Jews,[18] and in August, they opposed, with a petition to the Reich Ministry of Labor, the professional restrictions for Jewish physicians.[19] In January 1934, Leo Baeck, the head of the Reich Representation, printed an eighty-page memorandum for German government consumption, requesting that the defamation of the Jewish people in Germany cease. Baeck demanded the myriad of central and local anti-Jewish measures in all spheres of life be abolished and suggested negotiations.[20]

Specific acts of discrimination or humiliation would trigger responses of the Reichsvertretung in the form of entreaties. In May 1934, the Jewish representatives wrote protest letters to Hitler, Reich Minister of the Interior Wilhelm Frick, and—in a call for solidarity—to the Reich Bishop Ludwig Müller against an issue of the antisemitic journal *Der Stürmer* in which the Jews were accused of "ritual murder."[21] In January 1935, the Reichsvertretung issued a public statement against the editor of *Der Stürmer*, Julius Streicher, for his anti-Jewish remarks.[22] In March 1935, Leo Baeck directed a letter on behalf of the Reichsvertretung to the Reich Minister of Defense, protesting against the exclusion of Jews from the German army by a new law. He reminded him that twelve thousand Jews gave their lives during the last world war.[23] After an antisemitic speech by Julius Lippert, State Commissar of Berlin, Otto Hirsch, acting as a representative of the Reichsvertretung, wrote to him, to the Foreign Office, and Hjalmar Schacht, the Reich Minister of Economy. Hirsch criticized the dire situation of German Jews, using the term "elimination fight" (*Vernichtungskampf*). In this petitionary memorandum, he laid out the facts about the systematic cultural and economic exclusion of the Jews, the constant exposure to fierce antisemitic propaganda, and the lack of a future, especially for the Jewish youth. Furthermore, if the authorities cared about opinions abroad, Hirsch reasoned, they would need to abolish the causes for the deteriorating situation of the Jews.[24]

Besides the umbrella organization, the Reichsvertretung, Jewish organizations such as the Reich Association of Jewish Frontline Soldiers (Reichsbund jüdischer Frontsoldaten), the Central Association of German Citizens of Jewish Faith (Centralverein deutscher Staatsbürger jüdischen Glaubens), the League of Jewish Women (Jüdische Frauenbund), and the Reich Union of Orthodox Synagogue Communities (Reichsbund gesetzestreuer Synagogengemeinden) defended the Jewish population in Germany by petitioning the German government, regional and local administrations, or the police with letters and open memoranda, denouncing anti-Jewish policies and demanding that they should be abolished.[25]

On 6 May 1933, the Reich Association of Jewish Frontline Soldiers, for example, sent a petition to Adolf Hitler. In this entreaty and other letters, their officials expressed the opinion that the German Jews needed full equality regarding their citizenship and complete access to the German army. Jews should be able to keep their religious, cultural, and social education Jewish and the education in Jewish schools German. Although representatives of the Reich Association of Jewish Frontline Soldiers experienced a friendly reception at the Reich Chancellery, their demands were not seriously discussed.[26] In October, the organization of Orthodox Jews spoke in a petitionary memorandum to the Reich government of the "slow, but steady starvation" of the Jews and requested that Jews could live and practice their religion unhindered.[27] By contrast, the Zionist Federation for Germany offered in a June 1933 memorandum to the Reich government to contribute to the solution of the Jewish problem by relieving the Jewish position in Germany through emigration.[28]

Local Jewish Communities also intervened on a frequent basis. In May 1933, the Jewish Community in Munich complained in a letter to the Foreign Office about the frequent raids perpetrated by the Bavarian political police on the facilities of Jewish organizations under the pretext of "antinational" activities.[29] At the same time, the representatives of the Jewish Community in Berlin authorized the soon-to-be Community president Heinrich Stahl to protest formally against recent measures taken by the city government, which were not covered by any legislation. Stahl sent a petition to State Commissioner Julius Lippert, the new authority over the German capital, and demanded a list of municipal anti-Jewish measures be abolished in areas such as business, welfare, and access to swimming pools for Jewish schools. In this petitionary letter, he underlined the historical contributions of Jewish citizens to the "prosperity of the city of Berlin." The state commissioner, however, rejected the demands under the pretext of not being the responsible institution and advised the Community to address the state regulatory body instead. Hence, in mid-June, the Jewish Community approached the Prussian Minister President Hermann Göring with the same petition. At the end of June, they sent him an addendum referring to further discriminatory measures, such as the dismissal of Jewish city employees and welfare doctors. Göring transferred the petition to the Berlin municipality and asked for clarification. Some city departments reported back with elusive statements, others rejected the complaints outright with antisemitic language. The administrative back and forth lasted until 1935, when the petition was finally shelved.[30]

The Jewish representatives often went beyond writing mere protest letters. They employed more sophisticated techniques, which researchers have often overlooked. Jewish representatives would use petitions to pit Nazi institutions against each other by calling upon their individual interests, their unique responsibilities, and their respective status in the local, regional, or central power scenario. Moreover, they repeatedly did this in successful ways. In 1933, the Jewish Community of Essen submitted a petition to the Prussian Ministry of Interior, requesting the restitution of a youth home that the local Hitler Youth had occupied and the Gestapo had confiscated. It took a year and the involvement of the Reich Ministry of Interior and the head of the SS, Heinrich Himmler, to convince the local Gestapo to admit that the seized material did not justify the confiscation of the facility. They had to return the building to the Jewish Community.[31]

In June 1933, stormtroopers raided a Jewish learning center in Wolzig near Berlin. They supposedly found some weapons, communist propaganda material, and party membership booklets. The forty mostly Jewish teenagers and the five teachers were beaten, later detained, and brought to a concentration camp. The learning center facility was confiscated. The Jewish Community immediately intervened at the Prussian Ministry of Interior and requested the release of the prisoners and the restitution of the seized building. With the help of witnesses who testified that the SA planted the materials, the arrestees were able to leave the concentration camp a month later. Yet, in this case, they never got the facility back.[32] In Merzig (Saar), several times the windows of the local synagogue of the small Jewish Community had been broken. In November 1937, the representative, therefore, wrote to the education department of the Reich commissar of the Saar territory and requested that they oblige the local mayor to repair the windows.[33]

During the November pogrom in 1938, the Jewish Community of Vienna petitioned the SS to stop the violence, the mass arrests of Jewish males, the closing of Jewish institutions, schools and offices, the demolition of apartments, and the eviction of tenants.[34] After the pogrom, the German umbrella organization of the Jewish Communities intervened at the Gestapo headquarters in Berlin, because all so-called retraining camps in Germany had been closed, often after violent raids, and all teachers who prepared Jews for emigration had been arrested. Since the whole point of the violent pogrom was to push the remaining Jews out of the country by all means, the Reichsvertretung could successfully draw on the Nazis interest in emigration. The Gestapo released some teachers from concentration camps so that they could resume the preparation of Jewish teenagers for emigration.[35]

Even after 1938, a year that ended with very strict control of all forms of Jewish life by local Gestapo offices, Jewish Communities used petitions to protest against anti-Jewish measures. They were able to mobilize conflicting interests of various institutions involved in the increasingly radicalized persecution. When forced labor deployment hindered someone from emigration, for example, the local Gestapo could be appealed to and turned against labor offices. When robbery or violence got out of hand, the secret police could be involved against the local Nazi Party. Jewish petitioners also mobilized ministry officials against municipalities in questions of food provision or mayors against the Gestapo regarding welfare benefits.[36]

From 1933, Jewish organizations and their representatives protested, sometimes successfully, with numerous memoranda and letters against the anti-Jewish policies. Initially, such petitions were directed against general policy as well as specific measures and instances of humiliation. Subsequently, entreaties increasingly turned against certain laws and local restrictions. Jewish officials employed these petitionary letters and memoranda to reclaim the status of Jews as citizens and emphasize their important contributions to the German nation state. After 1938, petitions requesting the release of arrestees and seeking to play one Nazi institution against another dominated.

Collective Protest against the German and Czech Persecution in Annexed Bohemia and Moravia

On 15 March 1939, the German Reich occupied the Czech part of the former Czechoslovak Republic. In the newly established Protectorate of Bohemia and Moravia, a number of parties persecuted Jews from the outset: on the German side, the Office of the Reich Protector, the Security Police, and the chief county commissioners; on the Czech side, the Protectorate government and its ministries, the district and local authorities. The Czech government implemented the first anti-Jewish measures to eliminate Jews from the state apparatus and public professions. While the Gestapo focused on arresting prominent Jews, ethnic Germans and Czechs attacked synagogues and Jewish institutions. In June 1939, the German Reich Protector issued a decree defining the Jews and preparing the "Aryanization" of Jewish property. Driven by local and regional authorities, discrimination against Jews in the public sphere increased. From July 1939, the Prague-based Central Office for the Emigration of the Jews, run by Adolf Eichmann, streamlined the process of forced Jewish emigration and controlled the Jewish Communities.[37]

How did Jewish organizations and Communities in the Protectorate of Bohemia and Moravia react to the persecution and, compared to the Reich, even tighter control? Jewish representatives approached both the German and Czech authorities with informal interventions and formal petitions. On 24 April 1940, the Protectorate law gazette published a decree of the Czech government to revise the status of Jews in various professions. The Prague Jewish Community intervened directly at the Czech Ministry of Justice since it feared Jewish physicians and lawyers would be forced to give up their practices and firms and hundreds of families would lose their income. During this month alone, the staff of the legal department of the Prague Community intervened 112 times and wrote forty-five petitions on behalf of the Community or individuals.[38]

At the same time, the first wave of local efforts to ghettoize Jews in small towns occurred. In Jitschin (Jičin) District in particular, several local Czech administrations started to ghettoize Jews. In June, the Jewish Communities of Jungbunzlau, Turnau, Semil, and Jitschin received orders to clear all homes and concentrate the Jewish inhabitants into a single street or separate facilities. The Prague Jewish Community informed Eichmann's Central Office and urged their officials to help. The Jews were also ordered to relocate in the town Lissa. Here, Jews had to move into an abandoned factory building. During the following months, the Jewish Community in Prague protested immediately against relocations in several districts, writing several petitions to the authorities. While most of the forced relocations could not be stopped, the intervention at Eichmann's Central Office regarding plans to ghettoize Jews in the district of Königgrätz proved successful, as did the petition against the ghettoization of the Jews in the town of Wischau.[39]

On 7 August 1940, the Czech government ordered the exclusion of all Jewish students from Czech public schools. Thus, in September many children aged six to fourteen missed school because the Jewish Communities could not provide enough rooms and teachers for all of them. The

Prague Jewish Community repeatedly intervened on behalf of all Protectorate Communities at the Education Department of the German Reich Protector to provide a solution for the acute problem.[40]

In the second week of January 1941, the Jewish Community of Prague directed sixteen petitions to the Czech Ministry of Finance alone. They addressed issues regarding the forced submission of gold and jewelry. During the same week, employees of the Jewish Community gave legal and economic advice to 365 parties, drafted fifty-three letters and thirteen petitions, and started one lawsuit. In forty-four cases, they intervened at different authorities regarding questions of citizenship, taxes, and pensions. Some 250 Jews received legal help regarding evictions from their homes, for which sixty letters were drafted and submitted. During the third week of January, the employees of the Prague Jewish Community helped 331 families with advice and intervened sixty-five times with different authorities.[41]

In fact, this activism, including frequent petitioning, by Jewish officials challenges our traditional understanding of Jewish Communities under total Nazi control. At the height of the mass deportations in August 1942, the Jewish Community in Prague still sent forty-one "petitions and reports" to Eichmann's Central Office; during the first week in September, eighteen; and during the last week of September, twenty-six. While some of the reports had been requested by the Central Office, the majority contained complaints about problems that had emerged from persecution and deportations and were brought forward by the Jewish Community representatives to actively seek solutions.[42]

Hence, the Prague Jewish Community was not a willing executioner of Eichmann's Central Office plans or paralyzed under his total control. Quite the opposite, Jewish representatives and employees undertook many efforts to ease effects of the persecution for the Jewish population and even to oppose new measures. As in the Reich, Jews tried to appeal to the various institutions and to exploit the little room for maneuver originating from different responsibilities, initiatives, and conflicting interests of the German and Czech regional and local institutions.

Individual Jewish Petitionary Efforts to Protest, 1933–38

While most of the previous analysis highlighted the efforts of Jewish organizations and their staff, the following section sheds light on the responses of individual men and women. Thousands of their handwritten or typed entreaties can be found in local, regional, and federal archives as well as in holdings of private organizations of all kinds.

As early as April 1933, when the first anti-Jewish laws excluded them from the civil service and from the law profession and while private employers and organizations were swiftly following suit, Jews protested against their dismissal from jobs and memberships in private organizations. On 22 April, Berlin lawyer Fritz Beer begged Reich President Hindenburg to protect him as a person, who had paid all his dues for his country in times of peace and war, from humiliation as a professional and from being hindered violently from doing his job, which, as a result, had ruined him emotionally and economically.[43] Professor James Goldschmidt sent a letter of protest to the Prussian Ministry for Education that had revoked his university teaching license.[44] Hans Kantorowitz fought against his expulsion in a letter to the Berlin Gymnastic Federation.[45] They were hardly exceptions. Konrad Kwiet, Helmut Eschwege, and Saul Friedländer cite other examples, especially of university professors, that are all too similar.[46]

Beyond losing work and livelihood, Jews also protested against attempts to sever their ties to the German homeland. In 1934, Julius Fromm, a well-known Berlin merchant, complained in a petition to the police president of Berlin that his citizenship had been revoked. He emphasized his Germanness and his business success that made him the biggest taxpayer in his district in Berlin and reiterated that he had fulfilled more than his duty to his country and the "people's community."[47] In May 1935, Paula Tobias wrote to the German War Ministry protesting the new law that excluded her sons from German army duty and a military career. She emphasized that her family had done everything for the German fatherland without asking for any compensation.[48] Many German Jews also protested against their racial categorizations by the Nazi state, as Thomas Pegelow Kaplan has shown us, which they perceived as taking away their Germanness.[49]

In some cases, mostly regarding economic exclusion, individuals joined forces and acted together as a group. For example, textile merchants in Berlin complained in a petition to the municipal government about the exclusion of Jews from the public market in 1933.[50] In Pomerania, Jewish businessmen sent a telegram to the Reich Ministry of Economy, protesting against regional boycott measures during seasonal sales in July 1935.[51]

During the 1930s, the majority of petitioners had been Jewish men. After all, men were more present in the business world, in legal and medical professions, and in public service, and thus more affected by the discriminatory policies enacted from the time Hitler took power. However, with the violent November 1938 pogrom and the mass arrest of thirty thousand Jewish men, this situation changed drastically as many more women started to author petitions. Female family members, wives, mothers, daughters, and nieces protested in letters to the local police or Gestapo in desperate attempts to free their husbands, sons, fathers, or uncles from their internment in concentration camps. On 27 December 1938, Adele Klinger, for example, petitioned the Vienna Gestapo to arrange for the release of her husband Isidor Klinger from the Buchenwald concentration camp. She emphasized that he had no criminal record and had served as a frontline soldier during the entire duration of World War I. Interestingly, he was not one of victims of the sweeping actions during the November pogrom, but had been already incarcerated since May as part of the mass arrests following the annexation of Austria. He was only released in April 1939.[52]

Individual Wartime Petitions and Protests by German and Austrian Jews

Since the annexation in March 1938, many Austrian Jews had protested the increasingly radicalized persecution in entreaties to the Reich Commissar and Party leader Josef Bürckel in Vienna. Besides requests for exemptions from various national and local anti-Jewish restrictions, petitions protesting the eviction from Viennese homes and rental apartments turned out to be especially numerous. These evictions took place in two waves in the early summer of 1939 and in the spring/summer of 1940, each time prompting a new wave of entreaties.[53]

In March 1940, Adolf Fleischmann, born in Austria in 1873, was evicted and given forty-eight hours to remove himself from his flat, his residence since 1914. He authored a petition to the Nazi Party Gauleiter, in which he mentioned that he had fought for his homeland during World War I. He emphasized that he even fought for the Burgenland after the war had already ended, since his family originated from there. Fleischmann mentioned a list of prominent people, including the new Nazi mayor of Vienna, Hermann Neubacher, who could vouch for him. Among other details, he added that he had lived without practicing a religion for twenty years by then and had always fought for Germanness. Fleischmann ended his petition by stating that he could poison himself, but he would be too anxious. He would rather emigrate but had nowhere to go.[54]

Arnold Goldner, notified that he had to leave his apartment of twenty-seven years, wrote to Gauleiter Bürckel in February 1940. He requested an exemption from the eviction listing several reasons. He was a disabled war veteran. He had served as a senior lieutenant and had earned several medals for his honorable service during the war. He described all the war theaters he had fought in, and in many cases, he led various units in big offensives. Goldner had rented an apartment in a house owned by another

Viennese Jew. As a result of the ghettoization efforts in Vienna, he already had to share his 2.5 room apartment (living room and 1.5 bedrooms) with several other parties. A blind woman lived in one room. The other one was occupied by a woman with her daughter. The woman's husband was currently in a forced labor camp in the Harz Mountains. They had been forced to move into his apartment a year ago. Goldner and his wife occupied the remaining room. Goldner had no idea how to handle the situation after the eviction notice, especially where to move the seventy-year-old blind woman. He asked for help and signed as "Goldner, (reserve) senior lieutenant of Regiment, No. 26, in Marburg."[55]

In one case, the "Aryan" wife of a Jewish tenant tried to prevent the forcible relocation. After having received the eviction notice in February 1940, Anna Boskowitz pleaded with the German Reich Chancellor to let her and her husband stay in their apartment, criticizing the upcoming expulsion solely as a result from the fact her husband was Jewish. She made her case by emphasizing that her husband had fought as a volunteer for Germany, received war medals as an officer, and suffered from a severe form of rheumatism as a result of the war. She added by hand to the typewritten petition that her husband was born in Vienna and closed with "Heil Hitler." Amazingly, she did not make use of her status and potential advantage as a non-Jew in her petition to Adolf Hitler, but rather emphasized her Jewish husband's merits.[56]

While many of the petitions found in the archival holding of the Nazi Gau leadership of Vienna desperately protested the discriminatory eviction from their private homes because of the particular measures taken in Vienna, other entreaties focused on improving the deteriorating individual living situations. In a handwritten petition of 6 March 1940, Heinrich Kindler, for instance, requested from the Viennese Nazi Party leadership to grant him and his wife permission to visit a public park. Like the rest of the city's Jewish population, they had been prohibited from doing so for more than a year. He emphasized that he had been born in the Austrian capital in 1889 and was a state pensioner without any criminal record. He underlined that he was severely war disabled and consequently almost entirely deaf, which he hoped would justify the permission to visit a public park.[57]

In a very similar case, in Leipzig, Albert Koppenheim petitioned a municipal office, requesting an exemption from the prohibition to visit the city's public parks. He argued that he had served in World War I from 1914 to the war's last days. For his bravery, he had been awarded the Iron Cross First and Second Class. Because of serious brain injuries, he had not been released from the military hospital until 1921. Still fully paralyzed on his right side, Koppenheim emphasized that he counted as a 100 percent disabled war veteran and received a pension. For these reasons, he insisted that he get permission to visit the parks with his wife Dora and also make use of the benches, which was forbidden for Jews. Toward the end of his letter from June 1940, he requested an affirmative answer, but not just for him. He insisted that the answer of the city government should be valid also for other severely disabled Jewish war veterans in Leipzig.[58]

While such petitions contained a very specific request to improve each individual's personal situation affected by the results of the local anti-Jewish measures, Adolf Katzenstein wrote a petition to Hamburg's Gauleiter Kaufmann and complained about his generally dire economic situation originating from the persecution. In 1941, Katzenstein, a former chef, toiled as a forced laborer in construction works. In addition to protesting the results of persecution, he refused to sign the letter with "Israel." He also did not include his special identity card number for Jews, although he had already been punished once for not providing the authorities with his card on another occasion. Hence, Adolf Katzenstein rejected the idea of being branded and subdued by Nazi categorizations, even—or especially—in his protest to the Nazi Gauleiter.[59]

In a very different case, Moritz Glattauer handwrote a petition to request clemency for his wife, who had recently received a one-year prison sentence by a Special Court for insulting the "Führer." In his December 1939 entreaty to the Gauleiter in Vienna, Glattauer emphasized that he himself had worked for forty-five years in his own business as a butcher and had always paid his taxes on time and in their entirety. He added that he had no criminal record and was a disabled veteran of World War I.[60]

In May 1940, Rudolf Hess, Hitler's Party deputy and Reich Minister without portfolio, received a petition from Hans Kauders in Vienna. In addition to the forced ID number and the imposed middle name "Israel," his address on the typescript letter contained also "captain (retired)." With the latter denomination, he already signaled in his address line that he disputed the Nazi discriminatory definition. In a similar vein, he started the letter by defining himself as a "non-Aryan, severely war-disabled, veteran frontline officer of the world war." Kauders added, "I am Viennese-born, married, without children, a captain (retired), sixty years old, and have lived in Vienna all my life." Next, he mentioned the amputation of his left thigh, which resulted in a 90 percent disability rating. Having set the stage, Kauders then introduced the reason for his petition. In the course of the annexation of Austria in March 1938, he had lost his tobacco kiosk license (*Tabak Trafik*), which had provided him with a decent livelihood since 1917. As a Jew, Kauders was no longer permitted to be a contractor of the Reich. From then on, he had had no income, was forced to live with his wife on an invalid's pension, and, as he underlined, had been excluded from all cultural events. He could not even visit a public park in Vienna to get a breath of fresh air because he had four Jewish grandparents. Subsequently, he started to describe his war experiences: fighting on the Eastern Front, being wounded and captured, getting his leg amputated as a prisoner of war of the Russians, only to be transferred to a grim winter in Siberia, from where he came home as part of a prisoner exchange in 1915. Despite his retirement from active duty, Kauders volunteered in 1916 and worked for the war propaganda department until the spring of 1919. Later, he gave more than a hundred public lectures using picture slide shows about his experience in Russian captivity for the Austrian veteran welfare department. All earnings of the lecture series went to various charities, including the Austrian Red Cross. For this enormous volunteer work as a disabled veteran, he received several honors and medals. He proudly attached copies of the award letters to his petition. He also mentioned that he voluntarily reported for service again during the mobilization, resulting from the Sudeten crisis in September 1938. Finally, Kauders stressed the fact that because of his war disability and his advanced age, he would not find a place to build a new livelihood. He underlined that he was still close to his fatherland with all his heart and would love to serve in any capacity, as he had done in the past. Kauders emphasized that he had no criminal record and had never been politically active. Citing Hitler, who had said after the annexation of Austria that the "war disabled are the first citizens of the state," he requested Hess's attention and help. Kauders expressed that he deserved this, because he had fought shoulder to shoulder with his "Aryan comrades" for the fatherland and had sacrificed a lot of his own blood for his people. Without being at fault, he, as an army officer and an honest and truthful man, felt deeply hurt to be forced "to live as a pariah."[61]

Conclusion

In their search for rare organized and armed group resistance, historians have often overlooked that many Jewish men and women actively tried to stop, circumvent, or at least ease persecution by directing oral and written petitions to the perpetrators. Despite Saul Friedländer's call for an integrated Holocaust history that includes the full Jewish perspective,[62] research has yet to understand petitions as an integral part of the diverse and changing set of active Jewish responses to the Nazi regime. Introducing a wider definition of resistance that encompasses all individual Jewish activities directed against Nazi actions, ideas, and intentions, this chapter presents such written interventions as one element of a large array of defiant actions of Jews under Nazi rule, ranging from breaking Nazi laws and ignoring local restrictions to verbal public protest and physical self-defense.

Based on research on Germany, Austria, and the Protectorate of Bohemia and Moravia, this chapter reveals how numerous functionaries of German Jewish organizations and local Jewish Communities as well as Jewish individuals protested with individual letters, collective petitions, and printed memoranda against anti-Jewish measures and humiliations. From 1933, thousands of such petitions—sent to local, regional, or ministry officials, the Nazi government, Hitler and other high-ranking Nazi functionaries as well as private employers and organizations—criticized antisemitic boycotts, newspaper articles, Nazi laws, violent attacks, or local segregation.

The Reichsvertretung, Jewish organizations, and religious Communities tried to negotiate with the Nazi government, with Reich ministries, or regional or local perpetrator agencies in order to attempt to stop or ease persecution. Individuals complained to private organizations, local administrations, the police, ministries, as well as state and Nazi Party officials such as Bürckel, Hess, and even Hitler himself. This is true not only for Nazi Germany proper but also for annexed territories such as Austria and the Protectorate of Bohemia and Moravia.

The number of individual petitions claiming exemptions from anti-Jewish policies spiked following the nationwide boycott and the first anti-Jewish laws in 1933, the November pogrom in 1938, and in the wake of the mass deportations in 1941.[63] Since more men had been directly affected by the new anti-Jewish measures after 1933, they also responded more often by employing petitions as their favored tool of defense in the Nazi dictatorship. From the beginning, Jewish women, however, also protested with petitions against discrimination. After the persecution started to affect the whole Jewish Community and especially after the violent pogrom of November 1938 with its mass arrests of Jewish men, Jewish women started to address the Nazi authorities with entreaties in larger numbers.

In their appeals and interventions, Jewish petitioners repeatedly insisted on existing laws, addressed specific interests of the petitioned, emphasized their contributions to society or sought to manipulate Nazi state and party institutions by pitting them against each other. The latter reveals that Jewish petitioners actively developed multilayered strategies in their negotiations with perpetrators. Thus, these petitions were distinct loci of interaction with the perpetrators and need to be understood as sophisticated acts of opposition from the perspective of the victims rather than as a pointless waste of paper.

Indeed, not all of these efforts were in vain. And yet, even if they did not achieve their specific goal of abolishing some anti-Jewish measure or the exclusion from some form of discrimination, these petitions need to be seen as acts of contestation and resistance. Moreover, this asymmetric means of opposition allowed Jewish petitioners to get back their agency by publicly protesting against persecution. They claimed their violated rights as workers, property owners, and citizens. With these entreaties, they redefined their political and social position in the dictatorship.

Instead of accepting the second-class status as "subhuman" victims forced upon them by the Nazis, German, Austrian, and Czech Jews reclaimed agency with their petitions. They insisted on being regular members of German society with civil and political rights by underlining the undisputed fact that the Jews paid taxes, have been part of the nation-building process, and defended their country in previous wars. This can be seen clearly in Frieda F.'s petition to von Hindenburg from February 1933, cited at the beginning of the chapter. In her entreaty, she addressed the German Reich President and emphasized her request to stop anti-Jewish violence with the simple line: "We are Jews and we fulfilled our duty to the fatherland to the fullest." When Hitler saw her petition, he angrily disputed the Jewish "lies" about the occurrence of violence in Nazi Germany. Amazingly, however, he did not reject Frieda F.'s claim that Germany was the Jews' fatherland, too.[64]

Wolf Gruner is the Shapell-Guerin Chair in Jewish Studies, Professor of History and Founding Director of the USC Dornsife Center for Advanced Genocide Research at the University of Southern California, Los Angeles. He is the author of eleven books, ten of them on the Holocaust, including *Jewish Forced Labor under the Nazis* (2006), *The Holocaust in Bohemia and Moravia* (2019) and *Resisters: How Ordinary Jews fought Persecution in Hitler's Germany* (2023).

Notes

1. Konrad Kwiet and Helmut Eschwege, *Selbstbehauptung und Widerstand: Deutsche Juden im Kampf um Existenz und Menschenwürde 1933–1945*, 2nd ed. (Hamburg, 1986), 218.
2. Saul Friedländer, *Nazi Germany and the Jews*, vol. 1: *The Years of Persecution, 1933–1939* (New York, 1996); Marion A. Kaplan, *Between Dignity and Despair: Jewish Life in Nazi Germany* (New York, 1998).

3. Kwiet and Eschwege, *Selbstbehauptung*, 219.
4. On the historiography regarding Jewish resistance, see Wolf Gruner, "'The Germans Should Expel the Foreigner Hitler': Open Protest and Other Forms of Jewish Defiance in Nazi Germany," *Yad Vashem Studies* 39, no. 2 (2011): 13–17.
5. See also p. 2, this volume.
6. Kwiet and Eschwege, *Selbstbehauptung*, 217–22. More recently, Thomas Pegelow Kaplan analyzed in depth petitions against the racial definition of individuals. See Thomas Pegelow Kaplan, *The Language of Nazi Genocide: Linguistic Violence and the Struggle of Germans of Jewish Ancestry* (New York, 2009), 150–59, 177, 203–18. The author of this chapter includes them in his spectrum of broader resistance activities. See Gruner, "The Germans Should Expel the Foreigner Hitler," 18.
7. For the definition, see Gruner, "The Germans Should Expel the Foreigner Hitler," 18.
8. See pp. 7–8, this volume.
9. For example, Wolf Gruner, *Öffentliche Wohlfahrt und Judenverfolgung: Wechselwirkungen lokaler und zentraler Politik im NS-Staat (1933–1942)* (Munich, 2002); Wolf Gruner, "Local Initiatives, Central Coordination: German Municipal Administration and the Holocaust," in *Networks of Nazi Persecution: Bureaucracy, Business, and the Organization of the Holocaust*, ed. Gerald D. Feldman and Wolfgang Seibel (New York, 2005), 269–94.
10. The author is currently completing the book manuscript "'This Thug Hitler!' Forgotten Stories of Individual Jewish Protest and Defiance in Nazi Germany." See also the subchapters on resistance in Wolf Gruner, *The Holocaust in Bohemia and Moravia: Czech Initiatives, German Policies, Jewish Responses* (New York, 2019).
11. Avraham Barkai, *"Wehr dich!" Der Centralverein deutscher Staatsbürger jüdischen Glaubens (C.V.) 1893–1938* (Munich, 2002); Johann Nicolai, *"Seid mutig und aufrecht!" Das Ende des Centralvereins deutscher Staatsbürger jüdischen Glaubens 1933–1938* (Berlin, 2016).
12. Esriel Hildesheimer, *Jüdische Selbstverwaltung unter dem NS-Regime: Der Existenzkampf der Reichsvertretung und Reichsvereinigung der Juden in Deutschland* (Tübingen, 1994); Otto Dov Kulka, ed., *Deutsches Judentum unter dem Nationalsozialismus*, vol. 1: *Dokumente zur Geschichte der Reichsvertretung der deutschen Juden 1933–1939* (Tübingen, 1997).
13. Shalom Adler-Rudel, *Jüdische Selbsthilfe unter dem Naziregime 1933–1939: Im Spiegel der Berichte der Reichsvertretung der Juden in Deutschland* (Tübingen, 1974); Clemens Vollnhals, "Jüdische Selbsthilfe bis 1938," in *Die Juden in Deutschland: Leben unter nationalsozialistischer Herrschaft*, ed. Wolfgang Benz (Munich, 1988), 314–412; Volker Dahm, "Kulturelles und geistiges Leben," in Benz, *Die Juden in Deutschland*, 75–267. See Avraham Margaliot, "The Struggle for Survival of the Jewish Community in Germany in the Face of Oppression," in *Jewish Resistance during the Holocaust: Proceedings of the Conference on Manifestations of Jewish Resistance, Jerusalem, April 7–11, 1968* (Jerusalem, 1971), 101, 106; Ernst Simon, "Jewish Adult Education in Nazi Germany as Spiritual Resistance," *Leo Baeck Institute Yearbook* I (1956): 68–104; Michael Brenner, "Jewish Culture in a Modern Ghetto: Theater and Scholarship among the Jews of Nazi Germany," in *Jewish Life in Nazi Germany: Dilemmas and Responses*, ed. Francis Nicosia and David Scrase (New York, 2010), 170–84.
14. On the mobilization of old relationships, David Jünger, *Jahre der Ungewissheit: Emigrationspläne deutscher Juden 1933–1938* (Göttingen, 2016), 141–42, 166.
15. Kwiet and Eschwege, *Selbstbehauptung*, 218–19.
16. "Wir legen schärfste Verwahrung ein gegen die ungeheuerlichen Anschuldigungen, die gegen uns deutsche Juden erhoben wurden," cited by Marion Detjen, *"Zum Staatsfeind ernannt": Widerstand, Resistenz und Verweigerung gegen das NS-Regime in München* (Munich, 1998), 256.

17. Kwiet and Eschwege, *Selbstbehauptung*, 219. For a more detailed analysis of the Zionists, see Francis Nicosia, *Zionism and Anti-Semitism in Nazi Germany* (New York, 2008).
18. Document of 2 June 1933, in Kulka, *Deutsches Judentum*, 1:51–52; see also Kulka, *Deutsches Judentum*, 48.
19. Wolf Gruner, ed., *The Persecution and Murder of the European Jews by Nazi Germany 1933–1945*, vol. 1, *German Reich 1933–1937* (Munich/Jerusalem, 2019), doc. 68, 247–48: letter, 11 August 1933.
20. Bundesarchiv Berlin (hereafter BAB), R 3001/5107, Fol. 27: document of January 1934, excerpt in Gruner, *Persecution and Murder*, vol. 1, doc. 99, 317–20. Introduction in Kulka, *Deutsches Judentum*, 1:117–22. See also Kwiet and Eschwege, *Selbstbehauptung*, 225; Jünger, *Jahre der Ungewissheit*, 149.
21. Documents of 26 April and 2 May 1934 in Kulka, *Deutsches Judentum*, 1:140–41. See also Kwiet and Eschwege, *Selbstbehauptung*, 225.
22. Document of 31 January 1935, in Kwiet and Eschwege, *Selbstbehauptung*, 189–90.
23. Document of 23 March 1935, in Yitzhak Arad, Israel Gutman, and Avraham Margaliot, eds., *Documents on the Holocaust: Selected Sources on the Destruction of the Jews in Germany and Austria, Poland and the Soviet Union*, 8th ed. (Jerusalem and Lincoln, NB, 1999), 71–72.
24. Kwiet and Eschwege give April (Jünger gives March) 1935 as the date for the petition. Kwiet and Eschwege, *Selbstbehauptung*, 219; Jünger, *Jahre der Ungewissheit*, 187.
25. For examples, see Kwiet and Eschwege, *Selbstbehauptung*, 218–19; Gruner, *Persecution and Murder*, vol. 1, doc. 110 and 141, 315–16 and 381–85; Arad, Gutman, and Margaliot, *Documents on the Holocaust*, Document, no. 22; Jürgen Matthäus and Mark Roseman, eds., *Jewish Responses to Persecution*, vol. 1: *1933–1938* (Lanham, MD, 2010), 103–4, 150–51.
26. Jünger, *Jahre der Ungewissheit*, 147.
27. Kwiet and Eschwege, *Selbstbehauptung*, 219.
28. Jünger, *Jahre der Ungewissheit*, 147–48.
29. Letter to the German Foreign office, 13 May 1933, in Gruner, *Persecution and Murder*, vol. 1, doc. 42, 173–74. See also Kwiet and Eschwege, *Selbstbehauptung*, 222.
30. Landesarchiv Berlin, A Rep. 001–02, No. 214, fol. 21: letter, 29 May 1933. The document is printed in Gruner, *Persecution and Murder*, vol. 1, doc. 47, 164–66. For the other details, see Wolf Gruner, "Die Reichshauptstadt und die Verfolgung der Berliner Juden 1933–1945," in *Jüdische Geschichte in Berlin: Essays und Studien*, ed. Reinhard Rürup (Berlin, 1995), 232. For more examples, see Kwiet and Eschwege, *Selbstbehauptung*, 220–24.
31. Kwiet and Eschwege, *Selbstbehauptung*, 222.
32. Ibid., 222–23.
33. Leo Weil to Reich Commissar Saar Territory, 29 November 1937, in Gruner, *Persecution and Murder*, vol. 1, doc. 313, 783.
34. BAB, ZB 7050, A. 17, printed in Susanne Heim, ed., *Persecution and Murder of the European Jews by Nazi Germany 1933–1945*, vol. 2, *1938–1939* (Munich, 2019), doc. 135, 396–99.
35. Cable, Sicherheitshauptamt to SD-OA, 12 December 1938, Yad Vashem Archives (hereafter YVA), O.51/OSOBI, Nr. 92 (Moskau 500/1/387), Fol. 43; Note SD-Ref. II 112, 19 November 1938; YVA, O.51/OSOBI, Nr. 92 (Moskau 500/1/387), Fol. 58. See also Wolf Gruner, *Jewish Forced Labor under the Nazis: Economic Needs and Racial Aims (1938–1944)* (New York, 2006), 45.
36. For examples, see Wolf Gruner, "Poverty and Persecution: The Reichsvereinigung, the Jewish Population, and the Anti-Jewish Policy in the Nazi-State, 1939–1945," *Yad Vashem Studies* 27 (1999): 23–60; Gruner, *Öffentliche Wohlfahrt und Judenverfolgung*; and Heim, *Persecution and Murder*, vol. 2, doc. 119, 356–57. For a different view on collaboration and defiance, see Beate Meyer, "Gratwanderung zwischen Verantwortung und Verstrickung: Die Reichsvereinigung der Juden in Deutschland und die Jüdische Gemeinde zu

Berlin 1938–1945," in *Juden in Berlin 1938 bis 1945*, ed. Beate Meyer and Hermann Simon (Berlin, 2000), 291–337. For Vienna, see Doron Rabinovici, *Instanzen der Ohnmacht: Wien 1938–1945: Der Weg zum Judenrat* (Frankfurt, 2000).

37. For more details on anti-Jewish policies in the Protectorate, see Gruner, *The Holocaust in Bohemia and Moravia*.
38. Based on the weekly reports of the Jewish Community in Prague to Eichmann, in ibid., 146.
39. Based on the reports of the Jewish Community Prague to Eichmann's Central Office, in ibid., 142–43 and 187–88.
40. Based on the reports of the Jewish Community Prague to Eichmann's Central Office, in ibid., 185.
41. Based on the reports of the Jewish Community Prague to Eichmann's Central Office, in ibid., 209.
42. Based on the reports of the Jewish Community Prague to Eichmann's Central Office, in Ibid, 322–23.
43. Kwiet and Eschwege, *Selbstbehauptung*, 220.
44. James Goldschmidt to the Prussian Ministry of Education, 22 June 1933, in Gruner, *Persecution and Murder*, vol. 1, doc. 58, 219–20.
45. Hans F. Kantorowitz to Rupert Naumann, Berliner Turnerschaft, 1 July 1933, in Gruner, *Persecution and Murder*, vol. 1, doc. 61, 227–28.
46. Kwiet and Eschwege, *Selbstbehauptung*, 220–22; Friedländer, *Nazi Germany*, 50 and 55.
47. Julius Fromm to the police president, Berlin, 4 January 1934; Gruner, *Persecution and Murder*, vol. 1, doc. 95, 303–07. On Fromm, see Götz Aly and Michael Sontheimer, *Fromms: How Julius Fromm's Condom Empire Fell to the Nazis* (New York, 2009).
48. Paula Tobias to Reich Defense Ministry, 24 May 1935, in Gruner, *Persecution and Murder*, vol. 1, doc. 167, 465. For the exclusion of Jews from the German army, specifically *Mischlinge*, see Bryan Mark Rigg, *Hitler's Jewish Soldiers: The Untold Story of Nazi Racial Laws and Men of Jewish Descent in the German Military* (Lawrence, KS, 2002).
49. Pegelow Kaplan, *The Language of Genocide*.
50. Gruner, "The Germans Should Expel the Foreigner Hitler," 27. For collective as well as individual response strategies of Jewish merchants in Berlin, see part III in Christoph Kreutzmüller, *Final Sale in Berlin: The Destruction of Jewish Commercial Activity, 1930–1945* (New York, 2015).
51. Kwiet and Eschwege, *Selbstbehauptung*, 222.
52. Adele Klinger, Vienna, to Gestapo, 27 December 1938, in Heim, *Persecution and Murder*, vol. 2, doc. 214, 587–88.
53. Wiener Stadt- und Landesarchiv (hereafter WSLA), Rassenpolitisches Amt der Stadt Wien, Gauleitung, Diverses, A-Z Nr. 1, 1938–45. For details on the eviction actions, see Herbert Exenberger, *Kündigungsgrund Nichtarier: Die Vertreibung jüdischer Mieter aus den Wiener Gemeindebauten in den Jahren 1938–1939* (Vienna, 1996); Wolf Gruner, *Zwangsarbeit und Verfolgung: Österreichische Juden im NS-Staat 1938–1945* (Innsbruck, 2000), 103–23, 151–63, 189–92.
54. WSLA, Rassenpolitisches Amt der Stadt Wien, Gauleitung, Diverses, A-Z Nr. 1, 1938–45, no fols.: Letter Fleischmann, Vienna, to Bürckel (no date, ca. March 1940), 1–3.
55. WSLA, Rassenpolitisches Amt der Stadt Wien, Gauleitung, Diverses, A-Z Nr. 1, 1938–45, no fols.: Goldner, Vienna, to Bürckel, 14 February 1940.
56. WSLA, Rassenpolitisches Amt der Stadt Wien, Gauleitung, Diverses, A-Z Nr. 1, 1938–44, no fols.: Anna Boskowitz, Vienna, to Gauleiter Bürckel, 21 January 1940.
57. WSLA, Rassenpolitisches Amt der Stadt Wien, Gauleitung, Diverses, A-Z Nr. 1, 1938–45, no fols.: Heinrich Kindler to Nazi Party Vienna, 6 March 1940.

58. Letter, 24 June 1940, excerpt translated and printed in Alexandra Garbarini, ed., *Jewish Responses to Persecution*, vol. 2: *1938–1940* (Lanham, MD, 2011), 282–83.
59. State Archives Hamburg, 213–11_5659/41 Katzenstein, Adolf David.
60. WSLA, Rassenpolitisches Amt der Stadt Wien, Gauleitung, Diverses, A-Z Nr. 1, 1938–45, no fols.: Glattauer to Bürckel, 18 December 1939.
61. WSLA, Rassenpolitisches Amt der Stadt Wien, Gauleitung, Diverses, A-Z Nr. 1, 1938–45, no fols.: Kauders to Hess, 9 May 1940, 1–4 and attachments. For the original petition, see pp. 222–28, this volume. The Yad Vashem Database lists a Hans Kauders, born in 1880, as "murdered during the Shoah." "During the war he was in Vienna, Austria. Deported with Transport 40, Train Da 513 from Wien, Vienna, Austria to Theresienstadt, Ghetto, Czechoslovakia on 10/09/1942." His place and date of death are noted as: Theresienstadt, 18 September 1943, retrieved 29 December 2018 from https://yvng.yadvashem.org/nameDetails.html?language=en&itemId=4856660&ind=0.
62. Friedländer, *Nazi Germany and the Jews*, 1:2.
63. See also Pegelow Kaplan, *Language of Nazi Genocide*, 203.
64. Kwiet and Eschwege, *Selbstbehauptung*, 218.

Bibliography

Adler-Rudel, Shalom. *Jüdische Selbsthilfe unter dem Naziregime 1933–1939: Im Spiegel der Berichte der Reichsvertretung der Juden in Deutschland*. Tübingen: Mohr Siebeck, 1974.

Aly, Götz, and Michael Sontheimer. *Fromms: How Julius Fromm's Condom Empire Fell to the Nazis*. New York: Other Press, 2009.

Arad, Yitzhak, Israel Gutman, and Avraham Margaliot, eds. *Documents on the Holocaust: Selected Sources on the Destruction of the Jews in Germany and Austria, Poland and the Soviet Union*, 8th ed. Jerusalem and Lincoln: Yad Vashem and University of Nebraska Press, 1999.

Barkai, Avraham. *"Wehr dich!" Der Centralverein deutscher Staatsbürger jüdischen Glaubens (C.V.) 1893–1938*. Munich: Beck, 2002.

Brenner, Michael. "Jewish Culture in a Modern Ghetto: Theater and Scholarship among the Jews of Nazi Germany." In *Jewish Life in Nazi Germany: Dilemmas and Responses*, edited by Francis Nicosia and David Scrase, 170–84. New York: Berghahn Books, 2010.

Dahm, Volker. "Kulturelles und geistiges Leben." In *Die Juden in Deutschland: Leben unter nationalsozialistischer Herrschaft*, edited by Wolfgang Benz, 75–267. Munich: Beck, 1988.

Detjen, Marion. *"Zum Staatsfeind ernannt": Widerstand, Resistenz und Verweigerung gegen das NS-Regime in München*. Munich: Buchendorfer Verlag, 1998.

Exenberger, Herbert. *Kündigungsgrund Nichtarier: Die Vertreibung jüdischer Mieter aus den Wiener Gemeindebauten in den Jahren 1938–1939*. Vienna: Picus, 1996.

Friedländer, Saul. *Nazi Germany and the Jews*. Vol. 1: *The Years of Persecution, 1933–1939*. New York: HarperCollins, 1996.

Garbarini, Alexandra, ed. *Jewish Responses to Persecution*. Vol. 2: *1938–1940*. Lanham, MD: AltaMira, 2011.

Gruner, Wolf. *The Holocaust in Bohemia and Moravia: Czech Initiatives, German Policies, Jewish Responses*, New York: Berghahn Books 2019.

———. "Die Reichshauptstadt und die Verfolgung der Berliner Juden 1933–1945." In *Jüdische Geschichte in Berlin: Essays und Studien*, edited by Reinhard Rürup, 229–66. Berlin: Edition Hentrich, 1995.

———, ed. *Persecution and Murder of the European Jews by Nazi Germany 1933–1945*. Vol. 1: *German Reich 1933–1937*. Munich: Oldenbourg/Jerusalem: Yad Vashem, 2019. (Original German edition, 2008.)

———. "'The Germans Should Expel the Foreigner Hitler': Open Protest and Other Forms of Jewish Defiance in Nazi Germany." *Yad Vashem Studies* 39, no. 2 (2011): 13–53.

———. *Jewish Forced Labor under the Nazis: Economic Needs and Racial Aims (1938–1944)*. New York: Cambridge University Press, 2006.

———. "Local Initiatives, Central Coordination: German Municipal Administration and the Holocaust." In *Networks of Nazi Persecution: Bureaucracy, Business, and the Organization of the Holocaust*, edited by Gerald D. Feldman and Wolfgang Seibel, 269–94. New York: Berghahn Books, 2005.

———. *Öffentliche Wohlfahrt und Judenverfolgung: Wechselwirkungen lokaler und zentraler Politik im NS-Staat (1933–1942)*. Munich: Oldenbourg, 2002.

———. "Poverty and Persecution: The Reichsvereinigung, the Jewish Population, and the Anti-Jewish Policy in the Nazi-State, 1939–1945." *Yad Vashem Studies* 27 (1999): 23–60.

———. *Zwangsarbeit und Verfolgung: Österreichische Juden im NS-Staat 1938–1945*. Innsbruck: Studien Verlag, 2000.

Heim, Susanne, ed. *Persecution and Murder of the European Jews by Nazi Germany 1933–1945*. Vol. 2: *1938–1939*. Munich: Oldenbourg/Jerusalem: Yad Vashem, 2019. (Original German edition, 2009.)

Hildesheimer, Esriel. *Jüdische Selbstverwaltung unter dem NS-Regime: Der Existenzkampf der Reichsvertretung und Reichsvereinigung der Juden in Deutschland*. Tübingen: Mohr, 1994.

Jünger, David. *Jahre der Ungewissheit: Emigrationspläne deutscher Juden 1933–1938*. Göttingen: Vandenhoeck und Ruprecht 2016.

Kaplan, Marion A., *Between Dignity and Despair: Jewish Life in Nazi Germany*. New York: Oxford University Press, 1998.

Kreutzmüller, Christoph. *Final Sale in Berlin: The Destruction of Jewish Commercial Activity 1930–1945*. New York: Berghahn Books, 2015.

Kulka, Otto Dov, ed. *Deutsches Judentum unter dem Nationalsozialismus*. Vol. 1: *Dokumente zur Geschichte der Reichsvertretung der deutschen Juden 1933–1939*. Tübingen: Mohr Siebeck, 1997.

Kwiet, Konrad and Helmut Eschwege. *Selbstbehauptung und Widerstand: Deutsche Juden im Kampf um Existenz und Menschenwürde 1933–1945*. 2nd ed. Hamburg: Christians, 1986.

Margaliot, Avraham. "The Struggle for Survival of the Jewish Community in Germany in the Face of Oppression." In *Jewish Resistance during the Holocaust: Proceedings of the Conference on Manifestations of Jewish Resistance, Jerusalem, April 7–11, 1968*, 100–12. Jerusalem: Yad Vashem, 1971.

Matthäus, Jürgen, and Mark Roseman, eds. *Jewish Responses to Persecution.* Vol. 1: *1933–1938.* Lanham, MD: AltaMira, 2010.

Meyer, Beate. "Gratwanderung zwischen Verantwortung und Verstrickung: Die Reichsvereinigung der Juden in Deutschland und die Jüdische Gemeinde zu Berlin 1938–1945." In *Juden in Berlin 1938 bis 1945,* edited by Beate Meyer and Hermann Simon, 291–337. Berlin: Philo, 2000.

Nicolai, Johann. *"Seid mutig und aufrecht!" Das Ende des Centralvereins deutscher Staatsbürger jüdischen Glaubens 1933–1938.* Berlin: Bebra Wissenschaft, 2016.

Nicosia, Francis. *Zionism and Anti-Semitism in Nazi Germany.* New York: Cambridge University Press, 2008.

Pegelow Kaplan, Thomas. *The Language of Nazi Genocide: Linguistic Violence and the Struggle of Germans of Jewish Ancestry.* New York: Cambridge University Press, 2009.

Rabinovici, Doron. *Instanzen der Ohnmacht: Wien 1938–1945: Der Weg zum Judenrat.* Frankfurt: Jüdischer Verlag, 2000.

Rigg, Bryan Mark. *Hitler's Jewish Soldiers: The Untold Story of Nazi Racial Laws and Men of Jewish Descent in the German Military.* Lawrence: University Press of Kansas, 2002.

Simon, Ernst. "Jewish Adult Education in Nazi Germany as Spiritual Resistance." *Leo Baeck Institute Yearbook* I (1956): 68–104.

Vollnhals, Clemens. "Jüdische Selbsthilfe bis 1938." In *Die Juden in Deutschland: Leben unter nationalsozialistischer Herrschaft,* edited by Wolfgang Benz, 314–412. Munich: Beck 1988.

Chapter 2

"DID WE NOT SHED OUR BLOOD FOR FRANCE?"

Identity and Resistance in Entreaties for the
Jewish Internees of Occupied France, 1940–44

Stacy Renee Veeder

> I address this letter to a man and a French patriot, I know you
> will understand me. But, will you intervene? I hope so, and I
> thank you in the name of humanity.
>
> —Letter from the mother of a Drancy camp internee
> to the General Commissariat for Jewish Affairs
> Chief Xavier Vallat, March 1942[1]

Introduction

On 20 February 1942, the wives and families of Jews interned in the Drancy camp outside of Paris mounted a prodigious effort to petition the Vichy regime's General Commissariat for Jewish Affairs (Commissariat général aux question juives, CGQJ) to recognize the pain and deprivation internees were experiencing in the camp's disease-ridden squalor.[2] Resolute petitions were signed collectively by the "wives of those interned in the camp at Drancy," the "deeply sorrowful Jewish mothers and wives," or "the mother" and "wife" of an internee, and circulated widely throughout Paris in a bold display.[3] To increase awareness and sway public opinion, Jewish families and their advocates wrote extensively to Vichy authorities, police prefectures, and aid organizations. Authors appealed to Maréchal Philippe Pétain, General Commissioners for Jewish Affairs Xavier Vallat and Louis Darquier de Pellepoix, and Head of the French Government

---

Notes for this chapter begin on page 66.

Pierre Laval as men, husbands, veterans, military leaders, and French patriots. For example, Lili B., the wife of a man interned in Compiègne, beseeched the Commissioner-General of Jewish Affairs Xavier Vallat "as a just and humane man" in March 1942, demanding: "Why are we suffering? Did we not shed our blood for France? Did we not work honestly?"[4] Internees, their relatives and friends, and humanitarian and religious activists wrote fervent appeals to French officials as a method of unarmed, individual and collective resistance for those deprived of their status, rights, and resources by the German occupying forces and Vichy regime.[5] Both letters sent from the camps and entreaties from outside the camps were strategic in their aims, mobilizing familial, friendship, and professional networks in their resistance and looking to assert the specifically French character and loyalty of those interned. Within these writings, authors employed the lexicon of republicanism, universalism, and rights to give their claims weight. Authors firmly placed themselves in French national life by highlighting their fulfillment of the obligations of assimilation, namely service, integration, acceptance, naturalization, and citizenship.

Entreaties written on behalf of those interned in the camps of France, correspondence from the camps themselves, and the response of French officials reveal a multifarious and complicated discourse concerning national belonging and identity. Petitions display the powerful draw and extensive use of the terminology of assimilation and universal rights by Jews living in France and their advocates, drawing on political principles and processes extolled and contested in the Third Republic. Authors claimed the interned were entitled to respect for their rights based on republican principles and the crucial fact that internees were working and contributing to the nation. Recounting the fate of her son who volunteered in the French armed forces and was interned in the Pithiviers camp "as a reward for his services to France," a mother brutally chastises CGQJ officials: "We must act. If not, the blood of the innocent will forever stain the history of France."[6] The occupation facilitated a complex and shifting continuum of acts of collaboration, opportunism, accommodation, sympathy, dissidence, and passive and active resistance. Far more than symbolic or resigned gestures, internees and their advocates often expressed the conviction that recognition of their citizenship, service, or motivation to assimilate held an emancipatory power.

The interwar Jewish community in France was highly diverse in its origins, political beliefs, practices, and identity. Yet there was a commonly held belief that Jews in France were more accepted and deeply intertwined with the national community than in some other countries.[7] The advent of the "Jewish Statutes" of October 1940 and July 1941, the establishment of Vichy's General Commissariat for Jewish Affairs and Institute for the

Study of Jewish Questions (the Institut d'étude des questions juives, IEQJ), and the process of ostracism and disenfranchisement generated a painful feeling of betrayal and internal deliberations regarding identity and assimilation. Vichy founded these institutions and funded their racially charged studies as part of the larger antisemitic National Revolution, laying blame for France's defeat at the feet of those deemed weak and corrupting.

Appeals and petitions written to officials from Jewish and non-Jewish individuals and groups constituted acts of what historian Werner Rings refers to as "polemic" resistance against anti-Jewish measures, meaning opposition and protest to the occupying and collaborating powers in spite of considerable risk, considering these messages were sent directly to Vichy authorities.[8] Within France, Jews were extensively engaged in a wide range of unarmed and armed resistance activities. Within the intricate structure of the armed French resistance, Jews joined communist and non-communist units, making up 15 to 20 percent of the general *marquis* forces and also forming specifically Jewish units, such as the Jewish Combat Organization (OJC) or Jewish Army (AJ), which worked with the Zionist Youth Movement (MJS), the Jewish Scouts (EIF), and the Children's Aid Society (Oeuvre de Secours aux Enfants, OSE).[9] These resistance groups often pursued multilayered efforts in cooperation with organizations like the Rue Amelot Committee and OSE to provide forged papers, hiding places, routes to flee France, and prodigious assistance networks to sustain the disenfranchised Jewish Communities in both zones, including organizing relief, post, and petitions to officials on behalf of camp internees.[10] This writing was part of a greater language of gestures and "signs and symbols" of autonomy that developed in private and public response to the occupation.[11] Jews in France were confined to an increasingly limited space to negotiate based on their needs and communal and national identity.

Personal post was allowed out of certain camps at differing times, more broadly during 1941 and early 1942 and then sporadically prior to the mass deportations of later 1942 through 1944. Correspondence served the pragmatic function of securing relief provisions, but through this writing relatives and friends gleaned an intimate awareness of arrests, camp conditions, and deportations. Letters allowed internees to retrieve the documentary proof of citizenship, naturalization, marriage, military service, or good character they perceived to be necessary for their defense. These writings experienced myriad limitations, from basic material constraints to the censorship efforts of the police prefecture Censorship Bureau (Préfecture de Police-Bureau de Censure) and the looming fear of punishment. The German Military Commander in France (Militärbefehlshaber in Frankreich) General Otto von Stülpnagel and SD Advisor in Jewish Affairs

(Sicherheitsdienst der SS, Security Service of the SS, SD) Theodor Dannecker explicitly instructed the Camp Liaison Office that internees should include reassuring phrases such as "I am in good health," "send packages," and "I embrace you" within their letters presumably to assuage panic.[12] However, the writing of internees and their advocates relayed emotional strength and an enormous amount of information. Entreaties were written to assist as many Jews as possible, with the long-term goal of securing liberation and preventing the fulfillment of Nazi and Vichy plans.[13]

The Cosmos of the Camps in the Occupied Zone of Wartime France

In 1938 and 1939, the French government and "Research Commission on Concentration and Collection Camps" developed a system of forced residencies and camps to hold many thousands of refugees and foreign nationals. In the south and west, the camps of Vernet, Gurs, Saint Cyprien, Argelès-sur-Mer, Rivesaltes, and many smaller forced residences and camps were either hastily constructed or improvised from barracks for prisoners of war (POWs) or former soldiers. May 1940 marked the beginning of large-scale arrests in France. In total there were forty thousand civilians interned within the southern camps, 70 percent of whom were Jewish. Over the course of 1939 and 1940, major internment camps were developed in what would become the northern, German Occupied Zone of France to prepare for prisoners of war and those considered threats to national security. Among the core Occupied Zone camps of Drancy, Pithiviers, Beaune-la-Rolande, Compiègne, and Poitiers, Drancy's structure and location in the suburbs directly outside of Paris made it the main French internment and transit camp and the primary transit point to Auschwitz.[14] Transformed into a camp from a large-scale, interwar housing project, German and French authorities saw Drancy's large block towers as easy to control and fence in with barbed wire.[15] Drancy fell under the command of the Gestapo Office of Jewish Affairs in France and SS Captain Theodor Dannecker and was administered by French police until 3 July 1943, when German authorities established direct rule under camp commandant SS Officer Alois Brunner. Sixty-seven of the seventy-nine convoys of Jews deported from France left from Drancy, accounting for at least 67,000 of the approximately 77,000 Jewish people deported.[16]

The camp of Royallieu-Compiègne, located ninety kilometers northeast of Paris, was created on 22 June 1940 to intern French and foreign political prisoners and "threats," POWs, and hundreds of notable Jewish French people.[17] Within Compiègne, conditions for internees were brutal, with post allowed for a very brief period in early 1942 so internees could obtain their own clothing, bedding, and necessities. Non-Jewish prisoners transmitted clandestine letters and vital provisions bequeathed to Jewish internees by their families and the Detainee Assistance Committee of the Compiègne Camp.[18] The Poitiers camp in the Vienne district and the Pithiviers and Beaune-la-Rolande camps in the Loiret were first designed in 1939 to prepare for prisoners of war, refugees, "undesirable" foreign nationals, and internal "threats" to the state. The Pithiviers and Beaune-la-Rolande camps of the Loiret district became the main camps for Jewish families after the mass arrest campaigns of late 1941 and 1942, before internees were transferred to Drancy. Infamously, thousands of the children arrested during the mass arrests of summer 1942 were brutally separated from their families in the Loiret camps and then deported alone to Drancy and then Auschwitz.[19] Jacques Bronstein, born on 4 September 1925 in Paris, wrote to his aunt and uncle of this horror: "I stayed alone" in Pithiviers after the "very sad news" of his family being sent to "an unknown destination."[20] On 16 March 1942, a woman wrote the head of the Vichy bureau in charge of the implementation of discriminatory measures, the General Commissariat for Jewish Affairs, requesting "an intervention in favor of my husband interned at Pithiviers. My husband is naturalized French since his childhood."[21] This petition joined many dozens of entreaties written on behalf of those ripped from their homes and families and imprisoned, amounting to a chorus of demands to French officials.

The mass Occupied Zone arrests of July 1942 organized by SS Captain Dannecker, CQGJ Commissioner-General Darquier de Pellepoix, and French government and police officials marked a sea change in the internment and deportation process.[22] In the Paris region, 13,152 victims were arrested and forced to endure days of extreme heat, deprivation, and overcrowding in the Vélodrome d'Hiver (winter cycling stadium) before being interned.[23] Thousands of people were forced into the camps without proper resources or sanitation, the stairwells and rooms were filled with refuse and human waste, making disease and cachexia imminent.[24] The subsequent frenetic flow of internees of all ages between camps made it clear that deportees were not heading for forced labor. On 16 July 1942, Sara Schlafman was sent to Drancy with her husband Joseph. On 21 July, she wrote to her children: "Dear children . . . my morale is good. I am leaving tomorrow morning together with Papa for an unknown destination . . ." before telling them to eat well, look after the youngest son, and have courage in their absence.[25] Sara and Joseph were deported to Auschwitz on convoy no. 9 the following day with 994 other deportees.[26] Within this grave humanitarian crisis requests made to relief agencies, most notably the semi-clandestine Rue Amelot Committee, reveal an efficient network of aid. Many made requests to Rue Amelot and the UGIF (the General Union of Jews in France, the forced Jewish representational organization), stating a lack of family or friends who were capable of providing aid. These appeals included messages such as: "I am within Pithiviers since the summer months and have received nothing, having nobody in Paris, being without family," and a request from 11 February 1942 imploring for "something for the interned comrades in the Pithiviers camp," who did not have shoes on their feet despite the bitter winter.[27]

Aid and Agency in Petitions

After the mass arrests of thousands in the Occupied Zone in August and December 1941 and spring and summer of 1942, the wives and mothers of internees set up committees to collect funds, provisions, signatures, and letters. Jewish and non-Jewish advocates gathered funds to purchase food, medicine, and necessities for Drancy packages, while simultaneously requesting signatures and letters that protested the arrests. Authors referenced the first mass murders of the internees via "reprisal" executions in December 1941 and February 1942 at Fort Mont-Valérien. From 1941 to 1944, the Wehrmacht executed over a thousand people at the Fort.[28] In the spring of 1942, relatives, signing their letters "a group of wives and mothers of internees at Drancy and Compiègne," "a group of wives from Clichy," "the wife" or "the mother" of an internee, wrote collectively to the CGQJ decrying the "terrible injustice" of the arrests and internments, demanding they answer for their policies: "You are also a man, and a Frenchman, can you allow the idea that such things have happened in France without interference?"[29] Simultaneously deferent, critical, heartbroken, and pleading, authors sought to relay some of the perpetual agony their lives had become: "[E]very day I am afraid of receiving a notice of death, not of a natural death but by shooting."[30] Distraught over the unsanitary camp conditions and famine rations, the mother of one internee sought to shame officials and insisted they provide her with an explanation for the internments: "but why! Because they are Jews! Do you know what it is to live with that anguish and that anxiety, having to wait for the news?"[31] The authors of these appeals made the case that internees deserved the full attention and efforts of the French government. Correspondence and appeals may not have led to releases, but their significance in the survival strategies of internees cannot be underestimated, providing a vital channel for rations, medicine, hygiene, and bedding provisions, and psychological and spiritual morale.

Early epidemics of malnourishment and disease within the camps garnered international attention and compelled authorities to allow relief organizations limited access in 1941. The efforts of international humanitarian and Jewish aid organizations resulted in straw mats and bunks in many camps, increased hygiene and clothing provisions, limited heating in winter, and one postcard every two weeks in some Occupied Zone camps.[32] On 20 September 1941, French authorities allowed the Red Cross to establish itself within Drancy, providing food from the UGIF-affiliated Rue Amelot Committee. The UGIF and UGIF-North in the Occupied Zone, Rue Amelot Committee, and French and international relief organizations including the International Committee of the Red Cross, the American Friends Service Committee, the Children's Aid Society, the Intermovement Committee to Aid Evacuees (Comité inter-mouvements auprès des évacués, CIMADE), the Joint Distribution Committee, and the Jewish migration organization HICEM (formed from the Hebrew Immigrant Aid Society, the Jewish Colonization Association, and the Berlin-based migration organization Emigdirect) all provided relief for internees and their families via canteens, children's homes, hospitals, and efficient networks of camp aid. Rue Amelot and OSE used funds from various sources to pursue an ambitious, clandestine effort to find safe housing for thousands of Jewish children.[33] Directly after the first waves of arrests, the Red Cross relayed the import of camp correspondence to the German authorities: "The question of the correspondence of the Jews who have been interned should be clarified."[34]

The speed of the mass arrest and deportation processes and the grave lack of communal resources hindered resistance, yet groups such as OSE, CIMADE, the Joint Distribution Committee, HICEM, the Organization for Rehabilitation and Training (Organisation Reconstruction Travail, ORT), the Rue Amelot Committee, *landsmanshaftn* (social organizations formed by Jewish immigrants who originated from the same cities and regions in Central and Eastern Europe), and synagogues all mounted exhaustive efforts to organize medical dispensaries, assistance offices, pantries, and soup kitchens. As many as 150,000 Jewish refugees and immigrants had restricted access to work and residency permits as well as assistance in the late interwar period, necessitating a robust network of communal aid and assistance programs. This network created enough pressure on camp administration to permit correspondence, provision parcels from family and friends, limited cultural and social activities, and restricted visits within certain camps.[35] To limit deaths from malnourishment and disease Drancy authorities were forced to release over nine hundred infirm, elderly, and dying in October 1941.[36] As of November, they allowed family and friends to send food parcels of three kilograms a week, with the Bulletin of the UGIF providing public instructions.[37]

Concurrent with these practical efforts, the communist Solidarité group circulated informational pamphlets and calls for petition campaigns to French officials.[38] Petitions and letters joined demonstrations organized by Solidarité outside of the gates of internment camps and Vichy and Coordination Committee offices, hoping to disseminate information and raise awareness of camp conditions and rights violations.[39] The underground Jewish press echoed this work by issuing warnings and broadcasting messages of non-compliance and unity to the Jewish community.[40] Within the camps, the UGIF eventually took over for the Red Cross in the fall of 1941, organizing massive amounts of packages, clothes, blankets, and letters from families, private sources, and relief organizations.[41] A letter home from Drancy internee Gabriel Ramet, who was arrested on 20 August 1941, deported to Auschwitz on 23 June 1943 and survived, gives insight into how messages and relief from family tethered one to home and normalcy: "[A]ll your kindness helps me to get out of this sad reality, and the good things you send me alleviate my painful confinement."[42]

Identity, Self-Determination, and Assimilation in Entreaties

An analysis of the claims made in petitions and private correspondence elucidates the authors' perceptions and how they decided to maneuver within their increasingly desperate circumstances. Entreaties written on behalf of the interned contained deliberate, allegorical messages that resonated in the French national context. Internees and their relatives and advocates were hyper-focused on integration, citizenship, naturalization, employment, and service to France, convinced of their own agency in interactions with French officials. For both Jews whose families had lived in France for generations and more recently arrived Jewish immigrants and asylum-seekers, it was not merely a reassuring parlance that membership in France would be extended to anyone willing to wholly adopt the language, culture, and law. For example, on 3 November 1942, Lisa David wrote to her sister Nana Dachy in Paris: "my little sister, you must do something for us because here those that have French ties are freed . . . please mark on a card that you are a woman of French nationality with your date of birth and date of your wedding which you should legalize with the police."[43] Motifs of loyalty, service and self-determination within entreaties and letters reveal a crisis of faith for those who deeply identified with their homeland and found these events inconceivable. National belonging and service were symbolic of a more secure past, in which there was a logical exchange of duties with protection and rights.

Naturalization was hard-won against the immense challenge of securing and maintaining interwar employment, housing, and financial security. In September 1941, a group of "Christian wives married to French *israélite* workers" opened their petition to the CGQJ by stipulating that their husbands had been "naturalized for fifteen years and more, i.e., from a time when it took a minimum ten-year consecutive stay and a serious investigation of the morality of the naturalized," illustrating their exhaustive efforts.[44] A common strategy in these petitions was to highlight their devotion to the nation that had granted them respite or asylum, as in this plea to Pétain: "Allow us to continue to live honestly in . . . our motherland, which we all defended whether by blood or through our constant cooperation, continue to consider us as children."[45] Letters from camp internees were frequently oriented toward acquiring the birth certificates, naturalization cards, employment and service records, and letters of good character perceived as necessary for formal petitions to French authorities. In his forty-one recovered letters, internee Gabriel Ramet repeatedly beseeched his family for such paperwork: "I want you to give me a card with the date of my entry into France and the date of my naturalization." Later he wrote: "you must send my act of naturalization decree."[46] On 31 July 1942, Mme. Waycman desperately wrote to her son Levi from the Beaune-la-Rolande camp only one week before Convoy 16 brought her to Auschwitz, saying, "I need you to give me my naturalization card," believing it to be vital to her survival.[47] Paulette Stockfisz, who was arrested in the infamous Paris roundup of July 1942, wrote desperately from Drancy to her sister, instructing her to find their identity cards quickly. She described the harrowing events of her family's arrest:

> [T]he police came to arrest us, with all the Jews in the house, we were abducted, me and my two children. I'm writing to tell you that we will be transported to the Vélodrome d'Hiver, I ask you to go home . . . take all my belongings . . . the little boy forgot his identity card . . . [when] you find this card, bring it to the Vélodrome d'Hiver in the 15th arrondissement.[48]

The interwar Jewish community in France was far from monolithic, and categorization of identity informed patterns of arrest and deportation and how perpetrators and victims understood these measures. During the late interwar period, police, immigration, and customs officials established a pattern of registering and scrutinizing refugees and migrants, limiting professional and educational opportunities for Jews in particular.[49] One of the Vichy regime's first actions was to review and revoke recent naturalizations, stripping thousands of Jews of citizenship.[50] The arrest measures of 1941 focused on foreign-born Jews, with

French officials primed to "take the necessary measures to ensure the expulsion or internment of foreign Jews residing in occupied territory."[51] German and French authorities targeted Jews of Eastern and Central European descent who were asylum-seekers or naturalized. These men and women resided in more visible, Yiddish-speaking neighborhoods and often lacked the funds and networks of support that were necessary to flee, hide, or pay officials. French officials mollified Jewish leaders with promises of respecting and protecting certain categories of internees, namely citizens and veterans. In spite of this, Head of the Vichy Government Pierre Laval promised German officials that French authorities would seize citizens and veterans if foreign Jews (*juifs étrangers*) did not meet their arrest quotas.[52] The term *juif étranger* was frequently employed as a pejorative for immigrant and refugee Jews living in France, while *israélite* was used to denote French Jews who were considered more "assimilated." On 12 June 1942, a wife wrote to the second head of the General Commissariat for Jewish Affairs, Louis Darquier de Pellepoix, protesting her husband's arrest explicitly based on the fact that he was assimilated. She appealed, "[M]y husband was arrested as a Jew, and it is regarding this that I want to get your attention. So my husband came to the world of a Jewish mother, he had the misfortune of being small and never knowing her, since his poor mother died twenty years ago, while bringing him into the world. In his family, they have been assimilated for many generations."[53] Her entreaty conveyed the conviction, no doubt strained, that commitment to multi-generational integration proved one's merit. Since her husband "knows nothing of the Hebrew language or religion," she believed that "race was completely extinguished" for him, a fact explicitly contradicted in the Vichy regime's Second Jewish Statute, which tied belonging to the "Jewish race" to the religion of one's grandparents.[54]

In light of these measures and the propaganda efforts of Vichy's National Revolution, the Institute for the Study of Jewish Questions, and the popular Palais Berlitz *The Jew and France* exhibitions, internees and their advocates understandably fixated on their Frenchness. Veteran service, military awards, and time held captive in prisoner of war camps were signs that one had proven a deep, formidable union with France, which was sometimes taken into consideration by camp administration when creating deportation lists.[55] Within Drancy, a Commission of Jewish Veterans attempted to organize on behalf of veterans and former prisoners of war. Some internees proudly displayed their uniforms and decorations, inciting the rage of the gendarme guards who accosted them, saying, "[T]hey were only filthy Jews and nothing else."[56] Internee Josef Schlafman had his Military Service booklet card with him at the time of his arrest, listed as #3825, class of 1919, Second class. The card stated he did not have to pay rail tariffs, yet it was not enough to keep him free.[57] Petitions to Vichy authorities asserted internees were not merely *israélites* or *juifs*, but "hundreds of war veterans, including wounded veterans and amputees, hundreds of men who, during the war, had fought for France with the same passion and love as the French."[58] The reality that veteran victims were to be deported regardless of their citizenship or service was not a settled fact in 1941 or 1942.[59] Letters detailing military service were addressed intentionally to veteran Xavier Vallat and the hero of Verdun, Maréchal Pétain, revealing shock at being imprisoned despite enduring the horrors of war: "Monsieur, my case is special . . . I returned to France from Germany quite recently as a veteran of two wars, you can see my ribbons."[60] In June 1942, a woman wrote to the second Commissariat général aux questions juives Chief Louis Darquier de Pellepoix insisting on the release of her husband as her son was a French army volunteer: "I recognize very well that at the moment we must resign ourselves to the laws that we are under, but I think a case like my husband's could be examined closely and that we could do something for him. My son, a nineteen-year-old army volunteer, has waged war in the tanks and did his duty as a good Frenchman."[61]

"A Completely Unnecessary Correspondence": Petitions for Release and Official Responses

While an official response to personal letters and entreaties was rare, Jewish leaders, aid societies, and the Union Générale des Israélites de France took up their demands with French officials. As in the other occupied territories, German authorities commanded the creation of the representative organizations UGIF and UGIF-North, giving the impression of influence. While some Jewish leaders refused to cooperate, others participated in the UGIF in hopes of continuing to provide assistance and representation after all other non-religious Jewish organizations were banned in November 1941. Commissariat général aux questions juives head Xavier Vallat agreed to many meetings with Jewish leaders and compromised on some of the details of the UGIF's directives, allowing enough room for some belief that *israélite* status could mean a certain level of protection and space for contestation.[62] The larger negotiations between French officials and Jewish leaders were nebulous and designed to placate and mislead the Jewish community. CGQJ officials rarely responded directly to the entreaties of average people, outside of some letters in 1941 and early 1942, which largely assigned responsibility for the measures to the German authorities. On 2 July 1941, CGQJ Chief Vallat lamented to the General Secretary for Information:

> The CGQJ receives a number of letters from Jewish people who state that they think they can ask for a waiver of the prohibitions imposed by the law of 2 June 1941, they can dispense with being recognized in accordance with the law presiding over the census of the Jews (Official Journal of 14 June). I have the honor to request that you kindly publish the attached note in the press to avoid a completely unnecessary correspondence with the parties concerned.[63]

On 27 September 1941, Fanny Lantz of Paris wrote to her husband Robert, who was interned in Drancy: "Like you, I sincerely hope for a quick release. But it is difficult to have hope without any formal affirmation from the associations of former combatants, nor the prefecture of police, nor the prefecture of the Seine in charge of your return."[64] Dozens of relatives like Fanny Lantz along with non-Jewish neighbors, friends, coworkers, and priests, pursued a multipronged strategy, demanding internee release from a variety of French government and police bureaus, while simultaneously working to secure the resources necessary for their daily survival. The very limited early releases of veterans of the heads of families were the result of prodigious efforts of the Rue Amelot Committee and its devoted leader David Rapoport.[65] Outside of controlled releases for health reasons in the early stages of Drancy and a limited number of children, exemption and release was almost impossible.[66] Nevertheless, social workers and Jewish organization employees labored tirelessly to garner support and recommendations for release applications made to local police departments.[67] Rue Amelot and OSE organized false papers, transit, and housing for escapees and rescued hidden children. Rue Amelot organized the provision of identification cards within the camps to maintain contact and relief efforts, along with post and parcel distribution and educational, social, medical and relief activities.[68] This wide range of assistance and resistance activities became drastically limited after the mass arrest and brutal internments in the Paris region in the summer of 1942. In reality, release was only possible through the arduous process of garnering a "Certificate of Non-Belonging to the Jewish Race" issued by the CGQJ. To do so required proof of conversion, "of adherence to one of the other denominations recognized by the State" prior to 25 June 1940 or that two or more of an applicant's grandparents were not Jewish.[69]

Leaders of Jewish organizations, including the Central Consistory president Jacques Helbronner, Chief Rabbi Isaïe Schwarz, and UGIF and UGIF-North leaders Raymond-Raoul Lambert and André Baur requested the release of children, veterans, the infirm and elderly, and those in Christian-Jewish marriages from Vichy officials.[70]

FIGURE 2.1. Raymond-Raoul Lambert, head of the Union Général des Israélites de France (UGIF)-South and frequent author of petitions, ca. 1941. Yad Vashem Archives.

CGQJ Chief Vallat bolstered the illusion of release by compromising on some details in these meetings and correspondence, allowing these leaders to believe that they had a degree of influence.[71] Camp authorities fixated on their elaborate administrative memoranda, constantly changing the "hierarchy" of internees and thereby sustaining hope of release.[72] Meanwhile, in response to petitions for exemption requests, Vichy officials reiterated formulaic answers that their hands were tied by German measures. In late 1941, Xavier Vallat wrote in response to one petition: "It is impossible for me to accommodate your request, as the measures forbidding such action emanate from German occupation authorities." On another occasion, Vallat responded to the wife of an internee: "I have the honor to inform you that in this measure, arising from a decision of the occupying authorities, they alone have the power to examine applications for release."[73]

Despite the extremely low numbers of releases, the impossibility of liberation was incomprehensible. Many endeavored to obtain the necessary documentation for a Certificate of Non-Belonging to the Jewish Race from the CGQJ.[74] In 1941, some very restricted releases for health, diplomatic, and pragmatic reasons were allowed, but as of 1942, releases were only permitted if the German military authority issued a specific order.[75] Despite the near impossibility of release, advocacy and petition efforts had a profound effect on aid and communication to the camps. The fact that correspondence and personal and organized relief was permitted was in part the result of the protests and appeals of internees and their families, whose demands were brought to French and German officials via humanitarian groups. In addition to providing camp resources, the UGIF and Red Cross insisted officials recognize the necessity of correspondence within their aid networks, questioning to what extent "these internees have the right to correspond with the outside world and the number of letters which may be given to them addressed."[76]

Deprivation and fear consumed daily life in wartime France. Whether living in the German Occupied or Vichy Zone, all French people possessed awareness of the dangers inherent in advocating on behalf of Jewish internees and their families. While each author was influenced by a myriad of motivational factors, the brutal, public arrests of mid-1942 had an especially powerful impact on public opinion.[77] Hundreds of Jewish and non-Jewish persons tried to intervene vociferously in defense of those persecuted. The yellow star decree of 7 June 1942 sparked "innumerable manifestations of sympathy" on the part of non-Jewish French people for their beleaguered compatriots. Dozens were arrested and brought to Drancy as "friends of Jews."[78] The correspondence of non-Jewish French people conveys their impression that hard-working people who served France would be found valuable and liberated, with one employer pleading on behalf of an employee: "Return him home soon. Can you intervene on his behalf and obtain his release?"[79]

Letters of defense were complex and sometimes not entirely free of prejudice. On 22 December 1941, a Parisian man wrote to Vallat to defend his friend and client.[80] Even if his friend possessed, the author acknowledged, "the legacy of his parents, that is to say a Jewish name," he "has none of that category of people."[81] Along with relatives and friends, French children wrote to officials. A young boy sent a letter to Maréchal Pétain on behalf of his friends: "[T]heir mother cries all day because it seems that their father cannot do his job anymore, since he was not born in France and he is also Jewish." In another case, a young girl beseeched Vallat: "[M]y dad has been in a camp for a long time . . . If you have children, you will understand how much my father is missed at home."[82] At times, priests, cardinals, and bishops conveyed their objections to the anti-Jewish measures and arrests. The Archbishop of Paris, Cardinal Emmanuel Célestin Suhard, was tasked with contacting Maréchal Pétain privately on behalf of a group of cardinals and bishops, writing, "we cannot stifle the cry of our conscience" and advocating for "the inalienable rights of the human person."[83] On 28 October 1941, a priest demanded of Pétain that Jews have their property and rights reinstated and those "wrongfully interned for their religion" be released.[84]

Conclusion

The families and advocates of the interned Jews of France wrote extensively and passionately to the French government and police authorities, aid organizations, and their own friends and neighbors to increase awareness and sway public opinion. Their entreaties to officials demanded the release of internees, the provision of aid for the interned and their families, and explanations for anti-Jewish measures. In spite of seemingly insurmountable property requisitions, communal taxes, and exclusion from economic and public life, Jewish families and organizations, along with French and international humanitarian networks, fronted a massive effort to organize provisions for internees and their families. Appeals and correspondence were key to the Sisyphean organizational effort necessary to sustain the internees and their families, drawing from a community left disenfranchised and destitute by the brutal "Aryanization" in the form of property requisitions. This writing was integral to manifold relief efforts and to reinforcing fortitude and resistance. Letters were predominantly focused on the immediate and perilous conditions facing Jews in France. Yet, they also contained powerful motifs regarding service and individual and collective identity through which the interned and their families tried to understand impediments and opportunities within their struggle. Despite the many limitations placed on correspondence from the camps and entreaties, internees and their advocates were able to relay the complexities and lived reality of those persecuted. These strident declarations of self-determination challenged anti-Jewish measures using the same lexicon of integration and service that French officials had mobilized against them, speaking to the agony of their betrayal.

Entreaties were written to reassure, gather information, and secure relief, while simultaneously contesting the internments based on specifically French principles. It was indispensable for authors to mount a defense against the infringement of rights, which they understood as inherent via service, integration, asylum, naturalization, or citizenship. Since French and German officials targeted recently arrived and less secure refugee and immigrant Jews, proving one's commitment to France and fulfillment of duties became an integral part of their complex survival strategies. Relatives and advocates appealed to Vichy officials as men, husbands, veterans, and patriots who were compelled to recognize the value and claims of their loved ones, with the wife of an internee pleading: "I believe that if you are father of a family, you must understand me. It's been fifteen days since I have had any news from my husband, we do not know what's become of him."[85] Letters of petition from camp internees, their relatives, and advocates in France display an unflagging search for the space to negotiate, navigate, and resist despite their oppression and increasingly dire circumstances.

Stacy Renee Veeder is an instructor of law, society, and history at Columbia University. She holds a doctorate in History from the University of New York at Albany and is currently completing law school at the Benjamin N. Cardozo School of Law. Her work has been supported by the United States Holocaust Memorial Museum Lydia and David Zimmern Memorial Fellowship, the Claims Conference Saul Kagan Fellowship in Advanced Shoah Studies, the Auschwitz Jewish Center, the Northwestern University Holocaust Educational Foundation, the American Academy of Jewish Research, and the Morris Altman and Samuel Zippin Scholarships. She has held roles with the Department of Justice, the United Nations Department of Political Affairs, and the New York Office of the Attorney General.

Notes

1. Archives Nationales, Paris (hereafter AN), AJ 38/67: 22059, entreaty sent to the Commissariat général aux questions juives (CGQJ) on 15 March 1942. The AN, AJ 38/67 and AJ 38/6 collections hold letters written to the Vichy administration. Hundreds of letters of entreaty and personal correspondence between internees of the Occupied Zone camps, their families, and officials are found in the Centre de documentation Juive Contemporaine in Paris (hereafter CDJC), in the DCCCXXIV, DCCCXCI, CCXXI, and CDXXXIV collections (letters were primarily preserved by families and friends and then bequeathed to the archive), along with the Yad Vashem Archives (hereafter YVA) O.41 and O.75 collections, and the United States Holocaust Memorial Museum Archives, Washington, DC (hereafter USHMMA) CCCLXXV–CCCLXXVII and DXXXIII collections. A collection of these letters can be found in Antoine Sabbagh, ed., *Lettres de Drancy* (Paris, 2002), which includes a comprehensive introduction by Denis Peschanski.
2. Letters from internees' wives and mothers can be found in AN, AJ 38/67: 1979, 1980, 2027, 2160, 2246, 2276, 2277, 22038, 22042, 22043, 22059. Renée Poznanski, *Jews in France during World War II* (Boston, 2001), 235–37; Adam Rayski, *The Choice of the Jews Under Vichy: Between Submission and Resistance* (Notre Dame, IN, 2005), 49–53.

3. Poznanski, *Jews in France*, 235–37.
4. AN, AJ 38/67: 2160, 19 March 1942.
5. Hillel J. Kieval, "Legality and Resistance in Vichy France: The Rescue of Jewish Children," *Proceedings of the American Philosophical Society* 124, no. 5 (1980): 339–40.
6. AN, AJ 38/67: 22059, 15 March 1942.
7. Richard Cohen, "The Jewish Community of France in the Face of Vichy-German Persecution: 1940–1944," in *The Nazi Holocaust*. Part 6: *The Victims of the Holocaust*, ed. Michael R. Marrus (Berlin, 1989), 756–79.
8. Werner Rings, *Life with the Enemy: Collaboration and Resistance in Hitler's Europe 1939–1945*, trans. J. Maxwell Brownjohn (New York, 1982), 162; Michael R. Marrus, "Jewish Resistance to the Holocaust," *Journal of Contemporary History* 30, no. 1 (1995): 92–97.
9. Susan Zuccotti, *The Holocaust, the French, and the Jews* (Lincoln, NE, 1999), 260–78; David Diamant, *Les Juifs dans la Résistance Française 1940–1944* (Paris, 1971); Jacques Ravine, *La Résistance Organisée des Juifs en France 1940–1944* (Paris, 1973); Jacques Lazarus and Lucien Lazare, *Organisation juive de combat: Résistance/sauvetage. France 1940–1945* (Paris, 2008).
10. Nechama Tec, *Jewish Resistance: Facts, Omissions, and Distortions* (Washington, DC: The Miles Lerman Center for the Study of Jewish Resistance, USHMM, 1997), 2–6; Marrus, "Jewish Resistance to the Holocaust," 92–97; Yehuda Bauer, *A History of the Holocaust* (New York, 1982), 246–50; Wolf Gruner, "'The Germans Should Expel the Foreigner Hitler': Open Protest and Other Forms of Jewish Defiance in Nazi Germany," *Yad Vashem Studies* 39, no. 2 (2011): 13–20.
11. Jacques Semelin, *Unarmed against Hitler: Civilian Resistance in Europe, 1939–1943* (Santa Barbara, CA, 1993), 36.
12. CDJC, CCCLXXVI-13b; DCCCXXIV-10, doc. 2–3.
13. Kieval, "Legality and Resistance," 339–40; Robert O. Paxton, *Vichy France: Old Guard and New Order, 1940–1944* (New York, 1972), 291–92.
14. Serge Klarsfeld, *French Children of the Holocaust: A Memorial* (New York, 1996), 418–19; Renée Poznanski, Denis Peschanski, and Benot Pouvreau, *Drancy, un Camp de France* (Paris, 2015), 15–44; Annette Wieviorka and Michel Laffitte, *À l'intrieur du camp de Drancy* (Paris, 2012), 22–25. At least 77,000 Jewish individuals were deported from France to Auschwitz. USHMMA, 31062 Database.
15. Maurice Rajsfus, *Drancy: Un camp de concentration très ordinaire, 1941–1944* (Paris, 1996), 35–45.
16. Ibid., 16.
17. Denis Peschanski, *La France des camps: L'internement, 1938–1946* (Paris, 2002), 175–82, 203–7; Poznanski, *Jews in France*, 224–27; CDJC, XXVI-19, *MBF report*, April–May 1942.
18. Benjamin Schatzman, *Journal d'un interné: Compiègne, Drancy, Pithiviers, 12 décembre 1941–23 septembre 1942* (Paris, 2005), 62, 515–25; Jean-Jacques Bernard, *Le camp de la mort lente: Compiègne* (Paris, 2006), 122; AN, F 9, 5579; CDJC, CCXIII-138.
19. Éric Conan, *Sans oublier les enfants: Les camps de Pithiviers et de Beaune-la-Rolande, 19 juillet–16 septembre 1942* (Paris, 1991).
20. CDJC, DCCCXXIV-15, 5a and 5b. Letter from Pithiviers on 7 August 1942.
21. AN, AJ 38/67: 22938, from 16 March 1942.
22. Conan, *Sans oublier les enfants*, 22–23.
23. Maurice Rajsfus, *La Police de Vichy—Les forces de l'ordre au service de la Gestapo, 1940/1944* (Paris, 1995), 118.
24. Myriam Foss and Lucien Steinberg, *Vie et mort des Juifs sous l'Occupation: Récits et témoignages* (Paris, 1995), 264–74.
25. CDJC, DCCCXXIV-8.

26. Ibid.
27. YIVO Archives, New York (hereafter YIVO), Rue Amelot- 343, Series 2- Box 48.
28. AN, AJ 38/67: 2191, from 19 March 1942.
29. AN, AJ 38/67: 22059, from 15 March 1942; AN, AJ 38/67: 27042, from 9 April 1942; AN, AJ 38/67: 2191, from 19 March 1942.
30. AN, AJ 38/67: 2027, from 14 March 1942.
31. AN, AJ 38/67: 22036, from 16 March 1942.
32. Bernard, *Le camp*, 237; AN, F-9, 5579.
33. Poznanski, *Jews in France*, 65, 333; CDJC, CDXXX-39.
34. David Diamant, *Le Billet Vert: la vie et la résistance à Pithiviers et Beaune-la-Rolande* (Paris, 1977), 42–51, Letter from Dr. Ernst to the Militärbefehlshaber General Staff Chief on 18 January 1942.
35. Lucien Lazare, *Rescue as Resistance: How Jewish Organizations Fought the Holocaust in France* (New York, 1996), 87.
36. Henri Bulawko, *Les Jeux de la mort et de l'espoir: Auschwitz-Jaworzno* (Paris, 1993), 87.
37. *Bulletin de l'UGIF* from 30 January 1942. This record indicates some 5,658 *colis* were sent in an eighteen-day period. CDJC, CCXXI-18.
38. Lazare, *Rescue as Resistance*, 84–86.
39. Ibid., 86–87.
40. Rayski, *The Choice of the Jews*, 49–50, 84–87; Lazare, *Rescue as Resistance*, 84–86.
41. CDJC, CCXIII-106, testimony regarding Rue Amelot within the camp; Noël Calef, *Drancy 1941: Camp de représailles, Drancy la faim* (Paris, 1991), 94–140; CDJC, CCXIII-45, letter from November 16, 1941 to the FSJF; CDJC, CCXIII- 48, "Our Relations with the UGIF" from January 1942; Richard Cohen, *The Burden of Conscience: French Jewish Leadership during the Holocaust* (Bloomington, IN, 1987), 63–107.
42. CDJC, DCCCXCI-15, letter 5 from 31 July 1942.
43. CDJC, DCCCXXIV-15, Doc. 12a and 12b (3 November 1942).
44. AN, AJ 38/67: 2937, from September 1941.
45. AN, AJ 38/67: 18656.
46. CDJC, DCCCXCI-3, 15 (15 March 1942) and 35 (13 April 1943).
47. CDJC, DCCCXCI-5, Letter from a Mme. Waycman to Maréchal Pétain on 31 July 1942.
48. CDJC, DCCCXXIV-15, document 3, Letter from Paulette Stockfisz to her sister on 16 July 1942.
49. Vicki Caron, *Uneasy Asylum: France and the Jewish Refugee Crisis, 1933–1942* (Stanford, CA, 1999), 27–63; Vicki Caron, "Prelude to Vichy: France and the Jewish Refugees in the Era of Appeasement," *Journal of Contemporary History* 20, no. 1 (1985): 157–76; David Weinberg, *A Community on Trial: The Jews of Paris in the 1930s* (Chicago, 1977), 15.
50. AN, *Journal Officiel*, Number 29, 18 October 1940, p. 5324.
51. CDJC, CXCIV-81.
52. CDJC, CCXIII-10; Klarsfeld, *French Children*, 418–19; Paxton, *Vichy France*, 182; Rajsfus, *Drancy*, 76–77.
53. AN, AJ 38/67: 3091.
54. Ibid.
55. Diamant, *Le Billet Vert*, 33–35.
56. Rajsfus, *Drancy*, 69.
57. CDJC, DCCCXXIV-12.
58. AN, AJ 38/67: 22037, from 20 February 1942.
59. CDJC, DCCCXXIV-10, document 10; Billig, *Le Commissariat général aux questions juives*, 1:62; David Carroll, "What It Meant to Be 'A Jew' in Vichy France: Xavier Vallat, State Anti-Semitism, and the Question of Assimilation," *SubStance* 27, no. 3 (1998): 39–42.

Vallat did request the German High Command grant an exemption for veterans in 1941, albeit pragmatically based on the notion that the relatively small number of interned veteran exceptions could prevent protests.
60. Georges Wellers, *L'étoile Jaune à L'heure de Vichy: de Drancy à Auschwitz* (Paris, 1973), 72–73; AN, AJ 38/67, 3091.
61. AN, AJ 38/67, 3091.
62. Cohen, *Burden of Conscience*, 57–107; Jacques Adler, *The Jews of Paris and the Final Solution: Communal Response and Internal Conflicts, 1940–1944* (Oxford, 1987), 81–99. The creation of the UGIF was predicated on the subterfuge that leaders in the Jewish community could maintain some influence over Jewish communal assistance, sparking a wide range of opinions and reactions among Jewish organizations and leaders.
63. AN, AJ 38/67: 2039, from 2 July 1941.
64. CDJC, DCCCXCI-891, 5. Robert Lantz was interned from 20 August 1941 until 21 August 1943 in the Drancy camp, Block 2, Stair 9, Room 14.
65. YIVO, Rue Amelot Committee Collection, RG 343, file 8.
66. Susan Zuccotti, *Holocaust Odysseys: The Jews of Saint-Martin-Vésubie and Their Flight through France and Italy* (New Haven, CT, 2007), 205–6.
67. Lazare, *Rescue as Resistance*, 88–9; YIVO, RG 343, file 22–31.
68. YIVO, RG 343, Series 2- Box 55.
69. Richard H. Weisberg, *Vichy Law and the Holocaust in France* (New York, 1997), 103.
70. Adler, *The Jews of Paris*, 81–99; Poznanski, *Jews in France*, 77–80, 231; YVA, O.9, 60 and 67.
71. Cohen, *Burden of Conscience*, chapter 8; Adler, *The Jews of Paris*, 81–99; YVA, O.9, 60 and 67; Carroll, "What It Meant to Be 'A Jew,'" 39–42; Xavier Vallat, *Le Nez de Cléopâtre, souvenirs d'un homme de droite, 1919–1944* (Paris, 1957), 234, quote from 23 June 1941.
72. Diamant, *Le Billet Vert*, 33–35.
73. Ibid., 222. CDJC, DCCCXCI-2 (17 December 1941).
74. Joseph Billig, *Le Commissariat général aux questions juives* (Paris, 1955), 1:163.
75. AN, F- 9–5579; Bernard, *Le camp*, 237; Adler, *The Jews of Paris*, 118; CDJC, CCXXI-18.
76. Diamant, *Le Billet Vert*, 42–51, Letter from Dr. Ernst to the Militärbefehlshaber General Staff Chief on 18 January 1942.
77. Pierre Laborie, "1942 et le sort des Juifs: Quel tournant dans l'opinion?" *Annales. Histoire, Sciences Sociales*, 48, no. 3 (1993): 657.
78. Wellers, *L'étoile Jaune*, 42.
79. AN, AJ 38/67, from 2 February 1942.
80. Sabbagh, *Lettres*, 95–6; AN, AJ 38/6: 5580.
81. Ibid.
82. AN, AJ 38/67: 148, from April 21, 1942 and AN, AJ 38/67: 22041, from 16 March 1942.
83. Conan, *Sans oublier les enfants*, 49.
84. Sabbagh, *Lettres*, 73–4; AN, AJ 38/6: 3768.
85. AN, AJ 38/67: 22037, from 15 March 1942.

Bibliography

Adler, Jacques. *The Jews of Paris and the Final Solution: Communal Response and Internal Conflicts, 1940–1944*. Oxford: Oxford University Press, 1987.
Bauer, Yehuda. *A History of the Holocaust*. New York: Franklin Watts, 1982.
Bernard, Jean-Jacques. *Le camp de la mort lente: Compiègne*. Paris: Le Manuscrit, 2006.

Billig, Joseph. *Le Commissariat général aux questions juives*. Vol. 1. Paris: Éditions du Centre de documentation juive contemporaine, 1955.
Bulawko, Henri. *Les Jeux de la mort et de l'espoir: Auschwitz-Jaworzno*. Paris: Montorgueil, 1993.
Calef, Noël. *Drancy 1941: Camp de représailles, Drancy la faim*. Paris: FFDJF, 1991.
Caron, Vicki. "Prelude to Vichy: France and the Jewish Refugees in the Era of Appeasement." *Journal of Contemporary History* 20, no. 1 (1985): 157–76.
———. *Uneasy Asylum: France and the Jewish Refugee Crisis, 1933–1942*. Stanford, CA: Stanford University Press, 1999.
Carroll, David. "What It Meant to Be 'A Jew' in Vichy France: Xavier Vallat, State Anti-Semitism, and the Question of Assimilation." *SubStance* 27, no. 3 (1998): 36–54.
Cohen, Richard. *The Burden of Conscience: French Jewish Leadership during the Holocaust*. Bloomington: University of Indiana Press, 1987.
———. "The Jewish Community of France in the Face of Vichy-German Persecution: 1940–1944." In *The Nazi Holocaust. Part 6: The Victims of the Holocaust*, vol. 2, edited by Michael R. Marrus, 756–79. Berlin: Walter de Gruyter, 1989.
Conan, Éric. *Sans oublier les enfants: Les camps de Pithiviers et de Beaune-la-Rolande, 19 juillet–16 septembre 1942*. Paris: Grasset, 1991.
Diamant, David. *Le Billet Vert: la vie et la résistance à Pithiviers et Beaune-la-Rolande*. Paris: Éditions Renouveau, 1977.
———. *Les Juifs dans la Résistance Française 1940–1944*. Paris: Le Pavillon, 1971.
Foss, Myriam, and Lucien Steinberg. *Vie et mort des Juifs sous l'Occupation: Récits et témoignages*. Paris: Plon, 1995.
Gruner, Wolf. "'The Germans Should Expel the Foreigner Hitler': Open Protest and Other Forms of Jewish Defiance in Nazi Germany." *Yad Vashem Studies* 39, no. 2 (2011): 13–53.
Kieval, Hillel J. "Legality and Resistance in Vichy France: The Rescue of Jewish Children." *Proceedings of the American Philosophical Society* 124, no. 5 (1980): 339–66.
Klarsfeld, Serge. *French Children of the Holocaust: A Memorial*. New York: New York University Press, 1996.
Laborie, Pierre. "1942 et le sort des Juifs: Quel tournant dans l'opinion?" *Annales: Histoire, Sciences Sociales* 48, no. 3 (1993): 655–66.
Lazare, Lucien. *Rescue as Resistance: How Jewish Organizations Fought the Holocaust in France*. New York: Columbia University Press, 1996.
Lazarus, Jacques, and Lucien Lazare. *Organisation juive de combat: Résistance/sauvetage. France 1940–1945*. Paris: Éditions Autrement, 2008.
Marrus, Michael R. "Jewish Resistance to the Holocaust," *Journal of Contemporary History* 30, no. 1 (1995): 83–110.
Paxton, Robert O. *Vichy France: Old Guard and New Order, 1940–1944*. New York: Alfred A. Knopf, Inc. 1972.
Peschanski, Denis. *La France des camps: L'internement, 1938–1946*, Paris: Gallimard, 2002.
Poznanski, Renée. *Jews in France during World War II*. Boston, MA: Brandeis University Press, 2001.

Poznanski, Renée, Denis Peschanski, and Benot Pouvreau. *Drancy, un Camp de France*. Paris: Fayard, 2015.

Rajsfus, Maurice. *Drancy: Un camp de concentration très ordinaire, 1941–1944*. Paris: Le Cherche Midi Èditeur, 1996.

———. *La Police de Vichy—Les forces de l'ordre au service de la Gestapo, 1940/1944*. Paris: Le Cherche Midi, 1995.

Ravine, Jacques, *La Résistance Organisée des Juifs en France 1940–1944*. Paris: Julliard, 1973.

Rayski, Adam. *The Choice of the Jews Under Vichy: Between Submission and Resistance*. Notre Dame, Indiana: University of Notre Dame Press, 2005.

Rings, Werner. *Life with the Enemy: Collaboration and Resistance in Hitler's Europe 1939–1945*, trans. J. Maxwell Brownjohn. New York: Doubleday, 1982.

Sabbagh, Antoine ed. *Lettres de Drancy*. Paris: Editions Tallandier, 2002.

Schatzman, Benjamin. *Journal d'un interné: Compiègne, Drancy, Pithiviers, 12 décembre 1941–23 septembre 1942*. Paris: Fayard, 2005.

Semelin, Jacques. *Unarmed against Hitler: Civilian Resistance in Europe, 1939–1943*. Santa Barbara, CA: Praeger, 1993.

Tec, Nechama. *Jewish Resistance: Facts, Omissions, and Distortions*. Washington, DC: The Miles Lerman Center for the Study of Jewish Resistance, USHMM, 1997.

Vallat, Xavier. *Le Nez de Cléopâtre, souvenirs d'un homme de droite, 1919–1944*. Paris: Éditions Les Quatre fils Aymon, 1957.

Weinberg, David. *A Community on Trial: The Jews of Paris in the 1930s*. Chicago: University of Chicago Press, 1977.

Weisberg, Richard H. *Vichy Law and the Holocaust in France*. New York: New York University Press, 1997.

Wellers, Georges. *L'étoile Jaune à L'heure de Vichy: de Drancy à Auschwitz*. Paris: Fayard, 1973.

Wieviorka, Annette, and Michel Laffitte. *À l'intrieur du camp de Drancy*. Paris: Perrin, 2012.

Zuccotti, Susan. *The Holocaust, the French, and the Jews*. Lincoln: University of Nebraska Press, 1999.

———. *Holocaust Odysseys: The Jews of Saint-Martin-Vésubie and Their Flight through France and Italy*. New Haven, CT: Yale University Press, 2007.

Chapter 3

HONORARY CZECHS AND GERMANS
Petitions for Aryan Status in the
Nazi Protectorate of Bohemia and Moravia

Benjamin Frommer

Introduction

At the beginning of May 1939, six weeks after the German army occupied Prague and established the Protectorate of Bohemia and Moravia, Konstantin von Neurath, the highest ranking Nazi in the territory, remarked to his staff: "The Führer has ordered that the Czechs should regulate the Jewish question themselves."[1] Within a week the Czech Protectorate Government prepared a decree "to remove Jews from public life" through their purge from a range of professions, including government service, medicine, and education. In its final form, the Protectorate Government's decree authorized the Czech State President, Emil Hácha, to exempt specific persons from antisemitic restrictions. In response, more than a thousand Bohemians and Moravians, whom the Nuremberg Laws designated to be Jews, petitioned for recognition as "honorary Aryans." The petitioners—many of whom had converted to Christianity, had married non-Jews, or were the offspring of intermarriages—filled out extensive forms and compiled detailed family trees. They wrote plaintive autobiographies and sought affidavits from gentile friends, neighbors, and colleagues. Despite the repeated attempts of petitioners to learn the results of their pleas, their efforts were in vain. When the Protectorate Government finally proposed only forty-one candidates for exemption, von Neurath rejected them all. In October 1941, on the eve of mass transports of Jews to enclosed ghettos, his successor, SS-Obergruppenführer Reinhard Heydrich, summarily declared an end to the process altogether with a demand that "the concept of so-called honorary Aryan-ness must disappear."[2]

Notes for this chapter begin on page 88.

"And, with that," commented Miroslav Kárný, the pioneering historian of the Holocaust in Bohemia and Moravia, "the whole history of 'honorary Aryan-ness' was brought to a close."[3] Kárný's conclusion may be true for the unfortunate petitioners, many of whom subsequently perished in the Holocaust, but the exemption process left behind an invaluable source from which historians can learn much about the authors' attempts to seek redress from antisemitic persecution. In particular, this chapter examines the arguments mustered by petitioners to claim that they deserved to be "returned" to Czech or German society. The chapter further explores how authorities both shaped and responded to those arguments. The ultimate failure of the petitioners to gain exemption should not obscure their determination to oppose the Nazi program to rip them from the environment in which they had theretofore lived.[4]

The Creation and Limits of "Honorary Aryan" Status

In his gloss to the Protector's Office on the proposed decree "to remove Jews from public life," Czech Premier Alois Eliáš labeled the exclusion of Jews "a most important and urgent problem whose fastest solution and speedy announcement is in the interest of the orderly development of the Protectorate."[5] Czech leaders hardly needed encouragement to remove Jews from prominent public positions or exclude them from the economy. Following the Munich Pact, in October 1938 the associations of Czech lawyers, doctors, and notaries expelled Jews from their organizations and called for the state to remove them from government positions and revoke their professional licenses.[6] In January 1939, the government of the Second Czechoslovak Republic, the official name of the post-Munich rump state, initiated the forced retirement from the state bureaucracy of employees of "Jewish origin," defined as anyone with two parents who at any point in time had belonged to the Jewish Community or had declared Jewish nationality in a census. In one of their last autonomous acts after the German invasion of March 1939, the Czech ministers ordered the removal of Jews from a range of professions, including law and medicine.[7]

A month later, on 29 April, a special interministerial government committee met to discuss further measures to exclude Jews from public life. The first paragraph of their draft decree denied all Jews full citizenship in the Protectorate. The definition of a Jew laid out in the second paragraph was marginally more flexible than that of the Nuremberg Laws, but the provision nonetheless put a Czech imprimatur on the division of society into Jews and non-Jews. Anyone determined to be a Jew could not be a member in the National Partnership, the all-encompassing Czech national organization that replaced political parties in the Protectorate. More significantly, no Jew could serve as a teacher, prosecutor, defense attorney, doctor, veterinarian, pharmacist, or periodical editor. Furthermore, Jews were to be banned from membership in research institutions and from any significant role in theater and film.[8]

The planned purge of Jews was restricted only by Paragraph Four of the draft, which authorized: "On order of the government, the State President [Emil Hácha] can exempt individuals, who are Jews . . . from the scope of this act." From the outset, however, the value of any such exemption was clearly limited. It would only apply to measures enacted by Czech Protectorate authorities, not to any of the growing number of more serious sanctions instituted by the German occupiers. An exempted person could regain Protectorate citizenship and become a member of the National Partnership, but both were of dubious value even in 1939. The most significant benefit of an exemption concerned employment, but the directive mandated that Jews could make up at most two percent of all lawyers or doctors and could only serve other Jews. Even reinstated Jewish teachers could only teach Jewish pupils.[9]

German occupation officials responded critically to the Czech draft. In particular, they objected to the draft's more elastic understanding of who was a Jew. On 21 June 1939, von Neurath issued the First Regulation on Jewish Property in the Protectorate, which instituted the Nuremberg definition of a Jew and mandated German control of so-called Jewish property. In response, two weeks later, the Protectorate Government approved a modified draft of its original proposal, now named "the order on the legal status of Jews in public life." Although the new draft accepted the Nuremberg definition, German officials still questioned the provisions regarding the State President's authority to grant exemptions. The occupiers further objected that the Protectorate Government's proposed purge was too hasty. By impoverishing Jews in Bohemia and Moravia, it could undermine the Protectorate's economy and endanger efforts to prioritize Jewish emigration from the Reich.[10] On 5 March 1940, von Neurath approved the decree with the amendment that individual offices and sectors of the economy should remove Jews in a piecemeal process to make the impact more gradual. He further reserved for the Reich Protector's Office the power to veto any exemptions before they were even forwarded to the Czech State President for approval. Finally, on 24 April 1940, more than nine months after the Protectorate Government approved it, the "directive on the legal status of Jews in public life" was formally issued.[11]

The Protectorate Government tasked the Interior Ministry in Prague to assemble case files and then forward them to the office of the government premier, which would recommend a select number of individuals to be reviewed by the president. First, however, local authorities were to verify the claims of the petitions and investigate the petitioners. According to the official directive, they were to determine:

> The personal information of the petitioner, her or his spouse, their forbears, and the descendants of the petitioner, if they are resident here, in particular, their dates of birth, domiciliary and state affiliation (if appropriate, prior changes), nationality, religious denomination (if appropriate, prior changes), residence, profession, length of residence in the Protectorate, education and religious training in school, familial relations (family tree), property and income, moral and political standing, public activity, and especially also the petitioner's ties, respectively, that of his whole family, also of prior generations, if applicable, to the Aryan environment, [and], if appropriate, any contributions to cultural, scientific, economic or public life.

The directive stressed in its first paragraph that a person who applied for an exemption remained subject to any anti-Jewish measures until the resolution of the case. It further noted that exemption should be granted only in the rarest, "most extraordinary of cases," where the applicant demonstrated a "genuine desire to join Aryan life and thinking." Approval also had to be in "the particular interests of the Aryan environment, in which [the petitioner] lived, and, above all, the general interest." In the end, only that small minority of supposedly worthy applicants would have their files forwarded to the government, which would then send them on to the Protector and State President for a final decision. For the vast majority of petitioners, however, the directive ordered that they be kept in the dark: "In the other cases . . . the Ministry of the Interior will not end the investigation, but will let it rest in peace for the time being without informing the petitioner."[12] In that statement, we see perhaps one particularly cynical goal of the entire process: to quiet precisely those individuals who were most likely, due to their willingness to resort to legal means or thanks to their ties to non-Jews, to appeal to authorities and seek redress. The blanket of silence drawn over unresolved petitions could also have had the effect of assuaging the conscience and ensuring the inaction of those non-Jews.[13]

Arguments for Exemption

From the moment in spring 1939 that rumors first spread about the Protectorate Government's discussion of honorary Aryan status until long after Heydrich had finally rejected that possibility in the fall of 1941, more than a thousand men, women, and children sought every means possible to demonstrate they had assimilated into the Aryan environment and had significantly contributed to public life. In the words of one Czech policeman who handled such matters during the war, "In droves the Jews submitted petitions, acquired official stamps, and hunted for documents."[14] Those documents, now housed in dozens of boxes in the Czech National Archives, are what remain of the process. Most files begin with the plea, usually a typewritten document, sometimes prepared by a lawyer. The pleas introduce the petitioners and their families and detail their noteworthy contributions to public life, their strong ties to the non-Jewish community, and often their distance from other Jews, in thought and deed. To reinforce their claims, plaintiffs included letters of support from non-Jewish friends, acquaintances, and employers. With those documents, and other examples of public service, applicants approached the authorities, who instructed them to fill out an established form with twenty-nine questions about the religion and nationality of their whole families, including their spouses, children, parents and grandparents. The form asked whether the petitioner was still a member of the Jewish Community and, if not, when he or she had left it. The form further demanded information about education, employment, and any public service. For the most part applicants answered those questions formulaically, but the last query was more open-ended: "What basic benefit does the applicant seek to gain through possible exemption of his person from the government directive . . . on the legal status of Jews in public life?"[15]

Many petitioners continued to press their cases after submitting their personal data and supporting materials. In an effort to learn the outcome of the interminable process, they waited at government offices and repeatedly queried state officials. Some visited time and time again; others left their business cards behind in the hope that someone would follow up. The officials, however, simply affixed them to a standard form letter that confirmed that the petitioner had been warned that only the rarest of cases would be recommend for exemptions. Ordered in calmer times, the cards testify to their namesakes' former professions. On the one he left in the Interior Ministry, Karel Nowak-Reismann drew a single, clean line through the words, "Editor-in-chief of The Czechoslovak Revue."[16]

Nowak-Reismann not only petitioned for exemption from the anti-Jewish measures. Nine months later, when a Prague policeman arrested and fined him for entering an area of the city off-limits to Jews, he appealed to the regional authorities. Neither that appeal nor his petition for exemption received a positive hearing. Instead, despite his allegedly pending exemption petition, Karel Nowak-Reismann was summoned for deportation on one of the very first mass transports from the Protectorate to the Łódź ghetto, where all trace of him disappeared.[17]

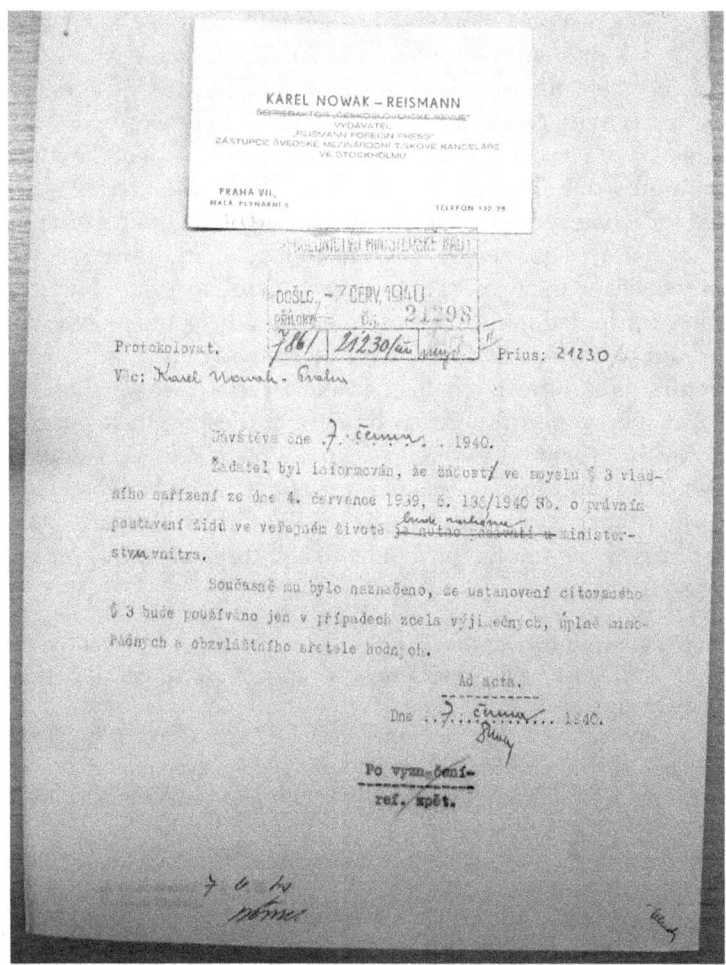

FIGURE 3.1. Record of petitioner Karel Nowak-Reismann's (1892–194?) visit to an office of the Czech Protectorate Government, June 1940. Národní archiv České republiky, Prague.

The petition files are valuable sources, but they are not a representative sample of the Jewish community of Bohemia and Moravia as a whole. Petitioners, unsurprisingly, came more frequently from wealthier and more highly educated individuals. Doctors, lawyers, and government officials had the most to lose from antisemitic purges, while factory and business owners felt most threatened by Aryanization. They could also make a stronger claim to have contributed to society in the past and had a greater chance to find prominent non-Jews willing to vouch for their character. Most of all, however, petitioners came overwhelmingly from individuals who had already broken to a lesser or greater extent with the Jewish community of Bohemia and Moravia, through intermarriage to a non-Jew or conversion to Christianity, or often both. Although on the whole the intermarried and their offspring were a significant minority of Jews (by Nazi racial criteria), they comprised a disproportionately large portion of the petitioners.[18] As a result, the sample is representative not of the entire Jewish community of Bohemia and Moravia, but of those "racial" Jews who believed for whatever reason they had a strong case for an exemption. To make that claim, petitioners resorted to a range of arguments centered on who they believed themselves to be (Czech, German, or not Jewish), what they had contributed to the lives of others and the country, and whom or what would be harmed by their exclusion from society.

Plaintiffs most directly challenged Nazi racial theory when they insisted that they were fully Czech or German despite their alleged race. In his May 1939 petition to the Protectorate State President Emil Hácha, František Kraus appealed to an older concept of nation based on language. As a former official, purged from his position in the Post and Telegraph Office, Kraus wrote (in the third person) about his life-long commitment to the Czech nation:

> From the above it is clear that the petitioner was always a loyal Czech in his conduct and beliefs and never sought his own personal benefit. He demonstrated through his marriage to a Czech woman that he entirely and without reservation assimilated [sžil] into the Czech nation in whose land he was born and whose language is his mother tongue because ... every person has only one mother tongue, which he already speaks at home, in which he thinks, in short, a language which is dearest to him. Because the petitioner has perfectly mastered only and solely the Czech language and because his only wish and goal is to raise his son as a [nationally] conscious Czech and to secure a livelihood for his Aryan wife and Aryan son, he asks that he be given the possibility of those premises through the kind recognition for him of honorary Aryanness.[19]

In his appeal to language, Kraus demonstrated the bind of those caught between traditional linguistic nationalism, which demanded that Jews identify with a "mother" tongue, and contemporary Nazi racism, for which linguistic skills had no meaning.[20] Kraus also rejected, or did not understand, that the authorities no longer considered even his son to be a full Czech, not to mention an Aryan. Instead, the child was at best a *Mischling* and at worst would have been a "designated Jew" (*Geltungsjude*), which put him in an even more precarious position than that of his intermarried father.[21] Kraus was not easily dissuaded. He first tried to gain exemption on 29 May 1939, before the government had even approved the regulations governing such applications. When the Nazis finally consented to allow the Protectorate authorities to consider such petitions, Kraus applied and then repeatedly inquired on the status of his case.[22]

Similarly to Kraus, Artur Fischl asserted, "My ancestors were mostly of Czech origin and my grandfather came from the totally Czech village of Všeň near Turnov." He claimed that his mother's uncle had been the archbishop of the diocese of New York. He wrote:

> I am of Czech nationality, and in [the] 1930 [census], I together with my family was counted among the Czech nationality and my children from my first marriage have been brought up in the Czech spirit. My first-born son Heřman [*not* Hermann] was already during the Austro-Hungarian Monarchy a pupil at the Czech grammar school. My daughters Jana and Betina attended only Czech schools.

Although his first wife had been Jewish, his (current) wife could demonstrate Catholic, Czech, and "Aryan" roots all the way back to the seventeenth century. Fischl admitted, however, that they had lived together for seven years until they married in 1937: "At that time we couldn't have known that the racial laws would come into existence and now, not only I, but also my wife indirectly, we're afflicted as a result of that law."[23]

One of the most emphatic claims to membership in the Czech nation came from Luisa Hejdová, whose non-Jewish husband had divorced her in February 1940, but who still sought to leverage his status, as a former editor of two major Czech dailies and the chief director of one of the country's most important industrial firms, to help her. Hejdová resorted to a range of arguments. She stressed that her parents had been wholly Czech and had not raised her to be religious. Her father had worked to close the separate Jewish school in his town and had been the first to send his children to a Czech-language school. She noted, "I never considered myself Jewish." Nonetheless, in a poignant hint of discomfort, she introduced a caveat: "Not that I would be ashamed of it, but I simply was not conscious of it, nor were any of the visitors to our home or our friends from eminent Czech and German circles."[24]

Rudolf Korsakov wrote directly to the Reich Protector's Office on the assumption that as a German Christian he had no reason to appeal to Czech authorities. The Germans, however, forwarded his materials to the Protectorate Interior Ministry, where they make for incongruous reading today. Born Rudolf Krausz in 1884, he argued the fact he was uncircumcised demonstrated his family's lack of commitment to Judaism. Nonetheless, they apparently were not Christians at that time because he was not baptized until more than two decades after his birth. He served with distinction in the Austrian Army during World War I, suffered severe injuries as a result, and earned the Iron Cross Second Class. He married a

Russian woman whom he met while serving as part of the occupation force in Odessa, converted for a second time (to Orthodox Christianity), and changed his name to the more Russian-sounding Korsakov. Now, he wrote in German, "almost at the end of my life I have been thrown back again into a community with which in my entire life I have had nothing to do and did not wish to have anything to do." He appealed to the authorities also on behalf of his wife, who was "from a country and a family in which the principles were no less strict on the Jewish question than those of National Socialism."[25]

Similarly, Viktor Zimmer, a converted, intermarried Jew, appealed for an exemption on the basis of his service to the German nation. In Slavonice (Zlabings), a picturesque Baroque town on the prewar border with Austria, he had actively worked to promote German culture and even helped the local leader of the fascist Sudeten German Party. His service did not spare him when the town was annexed by Germany after the Munich Pact. He had to flee to Brno and he feared that he would have to wear a Star of David together with other Jews. He wrote: "For my roots I have already been severely punished, especially as I have had to leave my wife and children, my homeland, my ancestral home, and my existence behind."[26]

Some German officials, perhaps disingenuously, objected on behalf of petitioners like Zimmer that the Protectorate Government's guidelines unfairly disadvantaged Jews who had contributed to German public life.[27] The local Nazi party in the city of České Budějovice (Budweis) supported the petition of one Jewish mother because her son, a *Mischling*, was in the German army. The top Nazis in Prague, however, saw no reason to make exceptions for Jews who had contributed to German culture or who had relatives in the Wehrmacht. The Chief of the Security Police and the Security Service of the SS in Prague, SS-Standartenführer Horst Böhme, cruelly responded to the plea from České Budějovice that a true German mother would accept the burden. Instead, he attributed the petition to nothing more than "Jewish arrogance."[28] The Protector's Office was equally unsympathetic when the Oberlandrat (Nazi governor) of Prague wrote about pleas from intermarried German men on behalf of their Jewish wives. The "Aryan" German men had complained that their own children could not play in the city's parks because their mothers had been banned from entrance. The Protector's Office rejected the plea because measures meant to ensure the separation of German blood could not be compromised for mere sentiment.[29]

Other petitioners avoided the Czech-German conflict and focused instead on their devotion and contribution to the Christian faith and its institutions. Overall, converts from Judaism comprise a large portion of the petitions, which reflects their greater opportunity to make a plausible claim to having severed ties to the Jewish community. A number of those petitioners had converted only in 1938–39, likely in the hope that they could thus avoid some measure of antisemitic persecution, but others had been Christians for decades. Alfred Fuchs, a top official in the premier's office before he was purged in 1940, had converted to Catholicism in 1921 and married a Catholic woman (who had since died). According to the very positive police background report, Fuchs had shown a deep commitment to Christianity, especially through his prodigious publications on Catholic themes and his participation in the international Catholic movement. He had received numerous Church honors and had lectured at Catholic congresses in Salzburg, Warsaw, Poznan, Budapest, and Paris. To demonstrate his bona fides, the police noted letters Fuchs had included with his petition, including one from "the current pope, former state secretary Cardinal Pacelli." For his own part, Fuchs emphasized, "My activities never spread the spirit of Judaism. To the contrary, they were always directed against it, as far as the spirit of Jewry was in conflict with Christian principles, which I can directly prove through my articles and books."[30] What the police downplayed in their report, and Fuchs ignored entirely in his own plea, was his deep pre-conversion commitment to the Czech-Jewish movement for Jewish assimilation into the Czech nation, a topic that both reasonably believed might not find favor among the leading Nazis. With the support of his former colleagues, the Protectorate Government included Fuchs among the forty-one persons it recommended for "honorary Aryan" status, but the Gestapo arrested him nonetheless and sent him to his death in Dachau in February 1941.[31]

Perhaps the most surprising claims came from a small group of petitioners who argued that they were not descended from Jews at all. To the contrary, they argued, during the seventeenth-century Counter-Reformation their ancestors had chosen to convert from the Protestant Czech Brethren to Judaism rather than return to the hated Catholic Church. Stanislav Šteindler explained that his family, "after the [1620] Battle of the White Mountain, forced to choose between emigration and Catholicism, chose a third evil: they converted to Judaism."[32] Another plaintiff, who made similar claims to Czech Brethren heritage, expressed his fears in April 1940: "Honorable, Mr. Premier [Eliáš], please do not allow that I be thrown into a ghetto and into exile ... Believe me, that for me it is a question of life or death."[33] Unfortunately, the petitioners offered nothing beyond their own family stories to support the claims to non-Jewish origins. A report in Olga Chmelařová's file simply noted that her brother's attempts to conduct genealogical research proved inconclusive, but still ventured that conversions to Judaism in the Counter-Reformation had been common in their home region around the Hussite citadel of Tábor.[34]

The largest group of applicants comprised individuals who were married to non-Jews or were the offspring of such unions. Among all those deemed to be Jews, the intermarried and their "mixed-race" children had the strongest claims to fulfill the conditions for "Aryan status." A marital union with a non-Jew could be taken as prima facie evidence for a petitioner's "genuine desire to join Aryan life and thinking," a requirement for a successful claim. Even in cases where intermarried Jews could not demonstrate that they would contribute significantly to the "Aryan environment," another key criterion for evaluation, they frequently argued that their exclusion would cause their non-Jewish spouses and children harm. Jana Kalusová, who had married a non-Jewish army officer, stressed that their son did not even know of her origins and now was threatened with not being able to continue his secondary school studies. Her husband's teaching position also was in danger.[35] Viktor Glücklich, an intermarried, former bank executive, pleaded on behalf of his daughter who had been registered with the Jewish Community in 1935 (and, therefore, counted as a Jew [*Geltungsjüdin*]), which prevented her from attending school.[36] Alice Nová, the wife of the debonair leading man of interwar Czech film, Oldřich Nový, pleaded for an exemption on the grounds that her exclusion from public life damaged his career and thereby hurt an Aryan individual and Aryan society as a whole. She further worried about the effect on their adopted, non-Jewish daughter. On his wife's behalf, Oldřich, who defied pressure to divorce her throughout the war, expressed his distress that their assets had been frozen and that Alice could no longer attend his films or plays.[37]

Although both intermarried Jewish men and women petitioned for exemptions, Czech authorities apparently viewed the Jewish wives of "Aryan" men as worthier of support. In December 1940, Eliáš sent a letter to the Protector's office, in which he made a special plea for the Jewish wives of non-Jewish Czechs, especially those who were state officials: "For those women and their families, exemption . . . would allow them once again to set their familial or social relations in order. The government here has in mind, in particular, those cases where children have resulted from the marriages with those Jewish women." If those women were not exempted, the Premier argued, their children would be lost to the "Aryan environment."[38] In the end, all fourteen of the women the Protectorate Government proposed to the Protector's Office for exemption were married to non-Jewish men. On the government's internal list of the forty-one individuals recommended for exemption, the professions of the men are noted, but next to the women's names we can find only the occupations of their husbands.[39] The government's proposal mirrored the gendered approach visible in the distinction that the Nazis drew between "privileged" and "unprivileged" intermarriages in both the core Reich and the Protectorate.[40]

Some parents took more radical steps in their efforts to protect their children. In January 1941, Kamill Resler, the most renowned Czech defense lawyer of his time, submitted a petition on behalf of a six-year-old girl, whose intermarried parents had originally registered her with the Jewish Community, but then had her baptized as a Catholic in November 1938.[41] Three months later, the Jewish father converted to Catholicism himself, but two days after the German occupation her mother petitioned for a divorce. Czech courts legalized the divorce, granted the mother sole custody, and approved a change in the girl's last name. Later judgments, however, determined her to be a Jew because her conversion had taken place after 1935. In the petition, Resler argued for a forward-looking standard of evaluation: "[T]he petitioner through her separation and divorce had ensured that the influence of the father on the future upbringing of the child is in fact completely excluded."[42]

Among those who claimed to have contributed to national life, a group of industrialists argued for their significance to the economy. Ervín Mandelík drew attention to his economic role in his local area, in particular, to the fact that his sugar factory had employed thirty-five workers and thus "contributed to the lessening of unemployment" during the Great Depression. He stressed that he had cared well for his workers and offered the absence of any strikes for more than fifty years as proof of his benevolence.[43] Emil Pick, aged seventy-four, petitioned for exemptions for himself, his wife, their children and spouses, and their grandchildren, all of whom were Catholics. The family owned enterprises that employed eight hundred workers in 1940 and by extension supported more than three thousand of their dependents. In the petition, Pick noted that he was the biggest taxpayer in his city and a major benefactor of local causes, including a pool, which he had donated on the condition that local children could go for the most nominal of sums (one crown). In 1935, he had been made an honorary citizen of the city; now he faced life as an outcast, despite the fact that "no one from our family was aware up until the present day that there was any difference between them and the Czechs around them."[44] The government placed both Pick and Mandelík on the list of forty-one persons along with several other industrialists, including Mandelík's brother and Emil Kolben, who had apprenticed with Thomas Alva Edison, worked as the chief engineer of General Edison, and founded one of the largest enterprises in the Bohemian lands.[45]

In their efforts to secure supportive letters from non-Jews, petitioners challenged the occupation regime's attempts to sever their contacts with mainstream society. In turn, the files demonstrate the willingness of a significant number of non-Jewish Czechs to support at least those Jews whom they knew well. Although such help was limited to familiar faces, the act of declaring that at least some individuals did not deserve to be afflicted by the antisemitic measures challenged the belief that so-called Aryans and Jews were two wholly separate peoples. In addition to a range of local letters of support, the number of such notes from very prominent Czechs is noteworthy, especially because the source of some is surprising. Rudolf Beran, the last prime minister of the Second Republic who presided over the initial purges of Jews from public service, law and medicine, wrote on behalf of several individuals to help them gain exemption from some of the very measures he had once approved.[46] Tomáš Krejčí, a top figure in the unambiguously named Czech Union for Collaboration with Germans, wrote on behalf of a woman, who he claimed had never lived in "a Jewish environment." In this case, the motive was familial: she was the widow of his wife's half-brother.[47] Other prominent recommenders included the leading interwar Czech historian, Josef Pekař, and the heads of two of Bohemia's most important noble families, Counts Leopold Sternberg and Karel Belcredi.[48] While we have records to document those who decided to support their Jewish (or formerly Jewish) relatives, friends, or colleagues, we cannot know how many non-Jews found reasons not to get involved. Petitioners who turned to non-Jews faced the risk of rejection and humiliation that could leave them even more isolated in the future.

Appealing to the Authorities

Although petitioners mainly focused on their own character and contributions, some nonetheless resorted to negative stereotypes about Jews in an attempt to distinguish themselves from others. A butcher from Volyně appealed to the Czech belief that Jews had failed to assimilate to the majority around them and had continued to speak German. He claimed that non-Jews repeatedly told him, "He's the only Jew in Bohemia who's really a Czech and doesn't know any other language."[49] Other petitioners parroted Nazi language about race. An "Aryan" husband wrote on behalf of his Jewish-born wife, "All of her siblings also have demonstrated for many years a deviation from Judaism, which attests to the fact that the Jewish race is foreign to them."[50] Other petitioners turned to physical signs of Jewishness. One claimed that his parents' decision not to circumcise him illustrated that they did not consider him to be a Jew.[51] Another claimed more vehemently in his own defense, "I've hated the Jewish race."[52] Similar to denunciations, however, petitions are "never written in a vacuum," to quote Sheila Fitzpatrick. She explained, "First, and most important, they are letters to authority, and authority in any given context has its own codes, conventions, preferences, and spheres of action. People write the kinds of denunciations [*and petitions*] they think are likely to be heard and acted upon by authority."[53] We cannot know whether the petitioners truly shared the antisemitic views they voiced or whether they simply believed that their audience, Czech and German officials, would respond more positively to someone who had thus verbalized his or her break with the Jewish Community.

The officials in Prague rarely left written evidence of their views on individual cases, but in their background checks of petitioners some local police and gendarmes demonstrated that they either shared the antisemitic sentiments voiced in those pleas or shared the belief that their superiors would respond more readily to such language. The background checks mainly focused on the petitioners' personal and familial data, employment, wealth, criminal record, and contributions to public life. For the most part, the reports are straightforward recitations of facts, but occasionally the officials justified their endorsement of a petition or their belief that it should not be granted. In a twist on the butcher's self-praise of his linguistic skills, one police report recommended against another petitioner because he spoke Czech poorly, which indicated that for some local authorities, at least, language was a measure of integration into the so-called Aryan environment.[54] The same report, however, went a few steps further in its antisemitism and claimed that the plaintiff, a local gas station owner, had "demonstrated nothing in the public interest that would attest to his complete unshackling from Jewish methods."[55]

Even in cases where the local authorities supported the petitioners, they sometimes resorted to antisemitic arguments to distinguish the plaintiffs from the supposedly typical Jew. The police report, which enthusiastically supported Alice Nová's petition, noted on her behalf, "From the outside, the petitioner does not demonstrate any Jewish traits. After all, she has a tall, slim figure, fair hair, and blue eyes."[56] A report on a different petition expanded the definition of Jewish-ness to include behavior: "The wife herself neither by character nor name reminds one of a Jewess. That is why most of her fellow citizens did not even know about her Jewish origin."[57] Another background report noted that the investigation of the applicant had turned up "no personality traits typical of Jews, for example, the piling up of wealth at the expense of the Aryan population and the like."[58]

The police also called for the denial of petitions from Jews who had been caught violating the very restrictions from which they now hoped to be exempt. The Gestapo had already punished Artur Fischl with imprisonment for six weeks in the Theresienstadt Small Fortress for being caught outside his home after the curfew. In response to his petition for exemption, the Prague police cited his prior arrest as reason to recommend denial.[59] Thanks to the enthusiasm of some authorities, petitioners exposed themselves to danger when they submitted their materials. When Rudolf Stein presented his identity card as part of his petition, the Czech policewoman on duty impounded it because, according to her report, "it was on first glance apparent that he added the letter 'J' with a red pencil himself." Since he should have appeared at his local police station the previous year to have his papers stamped with a "J" for "Jew" (*Jude*), the officer now fined him a thousand crowns.[60]

Even before the Germans brought a formal end to the concept of "honorary Aryan," a number of applicants withdrew their petitions. Some learned that the anti-Jewish purges and laws did not apply to them in particular because they either counted as so-called *Mischlinge* or not as Jews at all, and, thus, they had no cause to ask for exemption. Individuals who had converted to Judaism to marry a Jewish spouse discovered that they counted "racially" as Aryans.[61] Others procured visas and emigrated successfully, in one case to Shanghai.[62] Some passed away.[63] Some doctors gained permission to serve as so-called "Jewish physicians" to care only for fellow Jews and therefore no longer sought professional reinstatement.[64] Others, however, decided that their petitions had no chance according to the alleged bases of evaluation. Karl Robert Hayek originally sought "honorary Aryan" status, but after more than seven months in the SS vocational labor camp for Jews in Linden (Lípa), he concluded that he could no longer make a persuasive claim to having lived primarily among Aryans.[65] Hayek's acceptance of the official terms by which petitions were to be evaluated came in October 1941, at the same moment that Heydrich declared a complete end to the process altogether. The authorities, however, never informed the petitioners that their pleas had been and would be ignored.

Conclusion

The chimera of "honorary Aryan" status may have temporarily given hope to those who submitted petitions. Their efforts to gain supporting letters from non-Jews may have served to temporarily lessen their sense of isolation. In the end, however, the petitions seem to have had no effect on the ultimate fate of those who submitted them. Despite his allegedly pending petition, Hubert Gerold, a lawyer who had converted to Christianity and married a so-called Aryan, was deported to the Łódź ghetto on the second transport in October 1941 and died there two years later.[66] Even among the list of forty-one petitioners whom the Protectorate Government deemed most worthy of redress, several prominent individuals did not survive deportation, including renowned Prague doctor Jan Levit, who perished in Auschwitz in 1944, and the great industrialist Emil Kolben, who died in the Theresienstadt ghetto the previous year. A considerable number of those who submitted petitions did survive the war, but not thanks to their attempts to gain exemption from the antisemitic decrees. Their survival resulted largely from their marriages to non-Jews, which meant that most did not suffer deportation to Theresienstadt until the winter of 1945.[67]

Although the petitioners ultimately failed to achieve redress, their efforts represented a fundamental challenge to the application of the Nuremberg Laws in the Protectorate and to the Nazi program to divide Bohemians and Moravians into Jews and Aryans with nothing in between. In their pleas, many petitioners presented themselves as patriotic citizens who had loyally served and contributed to the Czech (or, occasionally, the German) nation and thereby implicitly contradicted Nazi rhetoric about Jewish parasites and "culture destroyers." Others, especially converts to Christianity, explicitly rejected the antisemitic belief that Jewishness was inherited and inescapable and instead argued that they were not Jews at all.

At a time when the authorities had effectively banned contact between Jews and so-called Aryans (German and Czech), the petitioners' efforts to enlist the written support of non-Jews represented an outspoken refusal to acquiesce in the process of social isolation. The threat that such interactions posed to vehement antisemites was illustrated by the hysterical reaction of the National Aryan Cultural Union, one of the more odious groups that sprouted during the occupation, to the rumor that Dr. Jan Levit had already been granted honorary Aryan status. The Union threatened the authorities: "We cannot under any circumstances agree with the declaration of anyone to be an honorary Aryan and we will mobilize all means so that similar actions do not occur, because a Jew will always remain a Jew, even if he is baptized. No declaration that he is an honorary Aryan can remove his Jewish origin, Jewish blood, and native Jewish mannerisms."[68]

In their attempts to gain personal exemption for themselves and their families, however, the petitioners did not contest the logic or implementation of antisemitic measures as a whole. Instead, they challenged only the fairness of the antisemitic regulations as they applied to them in particular. Furthermore, many denied any ties to the Jewish Community. Thus, petitions functioned as individual acts of resistance that could nonetheless be read by the authorities as endorsements of the very system the pleas challenged. As a result, within the ever-narrower constraints that bound those considered by the Nazis to be Jews, the petitions are examples both of individual attempts to resist persecution and of accommodations with the occupation regime's collectivist rhetoric.

Benjamin Frommer is Associate Professor of History at Northwestern University. He is the author of *National Cleansing: Retribution against Nazi Collaborators in Postwar Czechoslovakia* (2005), which was also published in Czech translation (2010), and the co-editor of *Intermarriage from Central Europe to Central Asia: Ethnic Mixing under Nazism, Communism and Beyond* (2020). Frommer is currently completing a book project entitled *The Ghetto Without Walls: The Holocaust in the Nazi Protectorate of Bohemia and Moravia*.

Notes

1. Jaroslava Milotová, "Die Zentralstelle für jüdische Auswanderung in Prag: Genesis und Tätigkeit bis zum Anfang des Jahres 1940," *Theresienstädter Studien und Dokumente* 4 (1997): 8.
2. Miroslav Kárný, "Vyřazení židů z veřejného života Protektorátu a historie 'čestného árijství,'" *Terezínské studie a dokumenty* 3 (1998): 28.
3. Miroslav Kárný, *"Konečné řešení": Genocida českých židů v německé protektorátní politice* (Prague, 1991), 58–60.
4. For more on the impressive efforts of the official Jewish Community to intervene on behalf of its constituents in regard to confiscated possessions, legal questions, matters of employment, pensions, housing, and citizenship, see Wolf Gruner, *The Holocaust in Bohemia and Moravia. Czech Initiatives, German Policies, Jewish Responses* (New York, 2019).
5. Miroslav Kárný, *"Konečné řešení,"* 30.
6. Livia Rothkirchen, *The Jews of Bohemia and Moravia: Facing the Holocaust* (Lincoln, NE, 2012), 89–91; Kárný, *"Konečné řešení,"* 23.
7. Národní archiv, Prague (hereafter NA), f. Úřad Říšského protektora (ÚŘP), k. 390, 398–402; Kárný, *"Konečné řešení,"* 23–24.
8. Miroslav Kárný and Jaroslava Milotová, eds., "Anatomie okupační politiky hitlerovského Německa v 'Protektorátu Čechy a Morava.' Dokumenty z období říšského protektora Konstantina von Neuratha," *Sborník k dějinám imperialismu* 21 (1987): 207–12.
9. Kárný and Milotová, "Anatomie okupační politiky hitlerovského," 207–12.
10. NA, f. Úřad Říšského protektora-Archiv Ministerstva vnitra (ÚŘP-AMV), signatura (sign.) 109–98-2-84, s. 212.
11. Kárný, "Vyřazení židů," 17–22.
12. NA, f. ÚŘP, k. 388, s. 795–96.
13. For a similar argument on petitions in Hamburg and the Altreich, see Beate Meyer, *"Jüdische Mischlinge": Rassenpolitik und Verfolgungserfahrung 1933–1945* (Hamburg, 1999).
14. Archiv bezpečnostních služeb, Prague (hereafter ABS), sign. 305–569–7, s. 17.
15. See, for example, NA, f. Ministervo vnitra—Nová registratura (MV-NR), k. 5169, s. 140–42.
16. NA, f. Presidium ministerská rada (PMR), k. 3414, s. 288.
17. Database of Holocaust Victims, retrieved 31 January 2019 from https://www.holocaust.cz/en/database-of-victims/victim/143707-karel-nowak-reismann/.
18. During the five-year period from 1928 to 1933, interfaith unions comprised 43.8 percent of all marriages involving a Jew in Bohemia. In traditionally more religious Moravia, the corresponding figure was still 30 percent. Ezra Mendelsohn gives a lower, but still significant figure of 32 percent for 1931 Bohemia. Kateřina Čapková, Michal Frankl, and Peter Brod, "Czechoslovakia," in *The YIVO Encyclopedia of Jews in Eastern Europe*, vol.

1, ed. Gershon David Hundert (New Haven, 2008), 376; Ezra Mendelsohn, *The Jews of East-Central Europe between the World Wars* (Bloomington, 1983), 145.
19. NA, f. PMR, k. 3415, s. 783.
20. For a similar appeal to language by German Jews, see Thomas Pegelow Kaplan, *The Language of Nazi Genocide: Linguistic Violence and the Struggle of Germans of Jewish Ancestry* (New York, 2009), 53, 143, 148, 154–56.
21. Children of mixed marriages who had been registered at any point in 1935 or after in the Jewish Community were "deemed to be Jews" (*Geltungsjuden*) and treated as "full" Jews. Intermarried Jews who remained wedded to their non-Jewish spouses were exempt from general deportation until the winter of 1945, but their *Geltungsjude* children were summoned earlier for transport if and when they reached the age of fourteen. *Mischlinge* were also frequently summoned for forced labor before their Jewish parent faced deportation. See Benjamin Frommer, "Privileged Victims: Intermarriage between Jews, Czechs and Germans in the Nazi Protectorate of Bohemia and Moravia," in *Intermarriage from Central Europe to Central Asia: Mixed Families in the Age of Extremes*, ed. Adrienne Edgar and Benjamin Frommer (Lincoln, NE, 2020).
22. NA, f. PMR, k. 3415, s. 780–803.
23. Fischl was baptized at the end of January 1939 after a half-year waiting period. NA, f. Ministerstvo vnitra—Stará registratura (MV-SR), k. 6583, sign. 9/51, s. 44.
24. The "eminent friends" she listed comprised a "who's who" of the Czech political and economic elite, including several current Protectorate Government ministers. NA, f. MV-SR, k. 6583, sign. 9/51, s. 495–97.
25. NA, f. ÚŘP, k. 389, s. 535–36.
26. NA, f. ÚŘP, k. 389, s. 562–63.
27. Kárný, "Vyřazení židů," 58.
28. NA, f. ÚŘP, k. 389, s. 542.
29. NA, f. ÚŘP, k. 389, s. 545.
30. NA, f. PMR, k. 3416, s. 51–52, 60.
31. Helena Krejčová, "Alfred Fuchs," in *The YIVO Encyclopedia of Jews in Eastern Europe*, retrieved 31 January 2019, http://www.yivoencyclopedia.org/article.aspx/Fuchs_Alfred.
32. NA, f. PMR, k. 3414, s. 610. For more on similar cases in Germany, see Pegelow Kaplan, *Language of Nazi Genocide*, 156–57.
33. NA, f. PMR, k. 3414, s. 613.
34. NA, f. MV-SR, k. 6583, sign. 9/51–8, s. 52.
35. NA, f. PMR, k. 3416, s. 154–56.
36. NA, f. MV-SR, k. 6583, sign. 9/51–22, s. 356.
37. NA, f. MV-SR, k. 6589, sign. 9/53–8, s. 276–87.
38. NA, f. PMR, k. 589, s. 203–4.
39. Kárný, *Konečné řešení*, 59; NA, f. PMR, k. 589, s. 10–13.
40. According to the regulations put into place after Kristallnacht, German authorities distinguished between "privileged" and "unprivileged" intermarriages. In the first category were families with minor children who had not been registered with the Jewish Community in 1935 or after. By contrast, intermarried families were unprivileged if their children were "deemed to be Jews" (*Geltungsjuden*) because they had been registered with the Jewish Community in 1935 or after. For those without children, the Nazis distinguished by sex: a childless Jewish woman with an "Aryan" husband was considered privileged, but a childless intermarried Jewish man (like Victor Klemperer) was not. As in Nazi Germany, in the Protectorate the status of property depended on the identity of the male head of household, such that intermarried gentile women lived in "Jewish homes," while intermarried Jewish women lived in "Aryan" ones. In contrast

to Nazi Germany, however, "privileged" Jews married to Czechs had to wear Stars of David in public after September 1941. See Frommer, "Privileged Victims."
41. Among other noteworthy defendants, Resler represented Karl Hermann Frank, the most powerful Nazi in the Protectorate from Heydrich's death till the end of the war, in his 1946 trial before a Czech retribution court. See Benjamin Frommer, *National Cleansing: Retribution against Nazi Collaborators in Postwar Czechoslovakia* (New York, 2005), 233–37; Jakub Drápal, *Defending Nazis in Postwar Czechoslovakia: The Life of K. Resler: Defence Counsel Ex Officio of K.H. Frank* (Prague, 2017).
42. NA, f. MV-SR, k. 6583, sign. 9/51–29, s. 432–39.
43. NA. f. PMR, k. 3414, s. 366.
44. NA, f. PMR, k. 3415, s. 717–18.
45. Kárný, "Vyřazení židů," 36–37.
46. NA, f. PMR, k. 3414, s. 740; NA, f. PMR, k. 3416, s. 172; NA, f. PMR, k. 3416, s. 309. For more on Beran, see Frommer, *National Cleansing*, 293–95; Jaroslav Rokoský, *Rudolf Beran a jeho doba: Vzestup a pád agrární strany* (Prague, 2011).
47. NA, f. PMR, k. 3414, s. 680.
48. NA, f. PMR, k. 3416, s. 11; Miroslav Kárný, "Vyřazení židů," 34; For more on Pekař, see Zdeněk Kalista, *Josef Pekař* (Prague, 1994).
49. NA, f. PMR, k. 3416, s. 310.
50. NA, f. MV-SR, k. 6583, sign. 9/51–8, s. 54–56.
51. NA, f. MV-NR, k. 5169, s. 22.
52. NA, f. MV-SR, k. 6583, sign. 9/51–42, s. 588.
53. Sheila Fitzpatrick, "Signals from Below: Soviet Letters of Denunciation of the 1930s," *The Journal of Modern History* 68, no. 4 (1996): 864.
54. NA, f. MV-SR, k. 6583, sign. 9/51–32, s. 466.
55. NA, f. MV-SR, k. 6583, sign. 9/51–32, s. 477.
56. NA, f. MV-SR, k. 6589, s. 278–79.
57. NA, f. MV-SR, k. 6583, sign. 9/51–8, s. 56.
58. NA, f. MV-SR, k. 6581, s. 179.
59. NA, f. MV-SR, k. 6583, sign. 9/51–7, s. 39–40.
60. ABS (AMV), sign. Z-6–371: s. 552–53; Database of Holocaust Victims, retrieved 16 November 2018 from https://www.holocaust.cz/databaze-dokumentu/dokument/400307-stein-rudolf-nezpracovano/.
61. NA, f. PMR, k. 3416, s. 653; NA, f. MV-SR, k. 6583, sign. 9/51–56, s. 715; NA, f. MV-SR, k. 6581, sign. 9/50–42, s. 534.
62. NA, f. PMR, k. 3416, s. 464.
63. NA, f. PMR, k. 3416, s. 621; NA, f. PMR, k. 3416, s. 770.
64. NA, f. PMR, k. 3416, s. 104.
65. NA, f. MV-SR, k. 6583, sign. 9/51–48, s. 759–62]
66. NA. f. PMR, k. 3414, s. 659–60.
67. See Frommer, "Privileged Victims."
68. NA, f. Národní arijská kulturní jednota, k. 2, korespondence.

Bibliography

Čapková, Kateřina, Michal Frankl, and Peter Brod. "Czechoslovakia." In *The YIVO Encyclopedia of Jews in Eastern Europe*. Vol. 1, edited by Gershon David Hundert, 376–81. New Haven, CT: Yale University Press, 2008.

Drápal, Jakub. *Defending Nazis in Postwar Czechoslovakia: The Life of K. Resler: Defence Counsel Ex Officio of K.H. Frank*. Prague: Karolinum Press, 2017.
Fitzpatrick, Sheila. "Signals from Below: Soviet Letters of Denunciation of the 1930s." *The Journal of Modern History* 68, no. 4 (1996): 831–66.
Frommer, Benjamin. *National Cleansing Retribution against Nazi Collaborators in Postwar Czechoslovakia*. New York: Cambridge University Press, 2005.
———. "Privileged Victims: Intermarriage between Jews, Czechs and Germans in the Nazi Protectorate of Bohemia and Moravia." In *Intermarriage from Central Europe to Central Asia: Mixed Families in the Age of Extremes*, edited by Adrienne Edgar and Benjamin Frommer. Lincoln: University of Nebraska Press, 2020.
Gruner, Wolf. *Die Judenverfolgung im Protektorat Böhmen und Mähren: Lokale Initiativen, zentrale Entscheidungen, jüdische Antworten 1939–1945*. Göttingen: Wallstein Verlag, 2016.
———. *The Holocaust in Bohemia and Moravia. Czech Initiatives, German Policies, Jewish Responses*. New York: Berghahn Books, 2019.
Kalista, Zdeněk. *Josef Pekař*. Prague: Torst, 1994.
Kárný, Miroslav. "*Konečné řešení*": *Genocida českých židů v německé protektorátní politice*. Prague: Academia, 1991.
———. "Vyřazení židů z veřejného života Protektorátu a historie 'čestného árijství.'" *Terezínské studie a dokumenty* 3 (1998): 11–41.
Kárný, Miroslav, and Jaroslava Milotová, eds., "Anatomie okupační politiky hitlerovského Německa v 'Protektorátu Čechy a Morava.' Dokumenty z období říšského protektora Konstantina von Neuratha." *Sborník k dějinám imperialismu* 21 (1987): 1–347.
Krejčová, Helena. "Alfred Fuchs." In *The YIVO Encyclopedia of Jews in Eastern Europe*. Retrieved 31 January 2019 from http://www.yivoencyclopedia.org/article.aspx/Fuchs_Alfred.
Mendelsohn, Ezra. *The Jews of East-Central Europe between the World Wars*. Bloomington: Indiana University Press, 1983.
Meyer, Beate. "*Jüdische Mischlinge*": *Rassenpolitik und Verfolgungserfahrung 1933–1945*. Hamburg: Doelling und Galitz, 1999.
Milotová, Jaroslava. "Die Zentralstelle für jüdische Auswanderung in Prag: Genesis und Tätigkeit bis zum Anfang des Jahres 1940." *Theresienstädter Studien und Dokumente* 4 (1997): 7–30.
Pegelow Kaplan, Thomas. *The Language of Nazi Genocide: Linguistic Violence and the Struggle of Germans of Jewish Ancestry*. New York: Cambridge University Press, 2009.
Rokoský, Jaroslav. *Rudolf Beran a jeho doba: Vzestup a pád agrární strany*. Prague: Vyšehrad, 2011.
Rothkirchen, Livia. *The Jews of Bohemia and Moravia: Facing the Holocaust*. Lincoln: University of Nebraska Press, 2012.

Chapter 4

LEGAL RESISTANCE THROUGH PETITIONS DURING THE HOLOCAUST
The Strategies of Romanian Jewish Leader Wilhelm Filderman, 1940–44

Ştefan Cristian Ionescu

Introduction

An outstanding lawyer from Bucharest, Wilhelm Filderman was one of the most important leaders in the history of the Romanian Jews, who advocated for their rights for over three decades. The head of the Union of Native Jews (UER) and later of the Federation of Jewish Communities (henceforth, the Federation), Filderman was the official (until December 1941) and the unofficial (until August 1944) leader of the Romanian Jewish community during World War II. Attempting to deflect the antisemitic persecution unleashed by the regime of General (Marshal from 1941) Ion Antonescu and relying on several decades of petitioning experience, Filderman complained relentlessly to the authorities, emphasizing not only the injustice of these measures, but also the negative consequences they could have on Romania's foreign policy, the national economy, and the possibility of Jews to support their country's war effort. He also emphasized that by adopting radical antisemitic measures, Romania behaved not as a sovereign state but as a German subaltern and a second-class Axis member. Filderman drafted his petitions with detailed references to domestic laws, administrative measures, international politics, and antisemitic newspaper articles, sometimes supporting them with economic statistics and comparisons with the Jewish policies of other Axis countries. While many of his petitions failed to achieve positive or even discernible results, others succeeded and managed to stop or abolish specific antisemitic measures.

Notes for this chapter begin on page 109.

Influenced by his mentor, Adolphe Stern—the first Jewish lawyer in Romania (in the 1870s) and, for several decades before and after World War I, one of the Romanian Jewish leaders—Filderman built on the Jewish community's tradition of petitioning and intervening to local and international authorities.[1] Filderman joined politics around the time local Jewish political organizations emerged and benefited from their institutional support; their resources and status facilitated his access to higher officials and increased his negotiating power. He thus built a stronger position in relation to the authorities compared to his predecessors who often had to act supported only by the Jewish Community and their devoted collaborators. Additionally, unlike his predecessors, Filderman had better connections with foreign politicians, diplomats, and international Jewish organizations. Even though he was stripped of his official leadership position in late 1941, Filderman still enjoyed the reputation as an influential man and as the unofficial leader of Romanian Jews domestically and internationally—even among many of the Antonescu regime officials—with direct access to the dictator himself.[2]

Based on official documents, diaries, and memoirs, this chapter investigates the legal resistance strategies—understood as belonging to a broader form of armed and unarmed resistance to antisemitic persecution encapsulated by the Hebrew term *amidah*[3]—employed by Filderman to negotiate the Jewish community's place in Romanian society during the Holocaust. Due to the arguments used in his petitions, addressing and channeling the fears and expectations of Antonescu and his subordinates, Filderman's persuasive efforts amount to a subtle and sophisticated manipulation of the Romanian dictator and other officials that was partially successful and, thus, disproves the myth of Jewish passivity during the Holocaust.[4] Because Filderman's numerous petitions covered all the problems of Romanian Jews, which cannot be exhaustively addressed here due to space limitations, this chapter will focus only on a selection of Filderman's most representative petitioning efforts, such as the effort to stop the antisemitic violence unleashed by the Legion of the Archangel Michael (henceforth, the Legion) between September 1940 and January 1941, the campaign for restitution and reparations following the failure of the January 1941 Rebellion, and the fight to stop the planned 1942 deportations.

Born in Bucharest in 1882 in a lower middle-class Jewish family that owned a small printing business, Filderman and his family struggled with hardships after his father died at a young age. His mother had to support her five children by running a small tailor workshop. A gifted and ambitious child, Filderman attended Matei Basarab high school in Bucharest, just like the future dictator Ion Antonescu, who remembered during a 1940 meeting that Filderman was considered the best orator of his high school. After graduation, Filderman chose to study law at the University of Bucharest, even though he lacked Romanian citizenship, which made him ineligible to join the Bar Association. The chances of obtaining citizenship were very low due to the complicated procedures aimed to discourage Jews from acquiring it.[5] Aware of local antisemitism, Filderman later explained his decision to study law—instead of medicine as some had urged him—with his desire to learn about the country's legal-administrative system in order to advocate for Jewish rights: "What can a medic do for the cause of the persecuted Jews? . . . Would I be better prepared to fight for justice if I will study medicine?"[6] After graduating from Bucharest's Law School, Filderman obtained his law doctorate from the Sorbonne in Paris in 1909. Returning to Romania from his study abroad, Filderman entered local politics by founding, together with several Jewish notables, a political party called the Union of Native Jews (UEP, later known as UER). Filderman continued his political career and advocacy for Jewish rights during the interwar years, when he became the leader of UER, and later of the Federation, and even after Antonescu dismissed him from his leadership position in 1941. After the collapse of the Antonescu regime (August 1944), Filderman reassumed the leadership of local Jewish Communities, but the new communist authorities gradually marginalized and persecuted him. In order to escape arrest, Filderman had to flee Romania illegally in 1948. He went to France, where he continued his lifetime struggle on behalf of Romanian Jews.[7]

Several historians of the Romanian chapter of the Holocaust have recognized Filderman's major role in the rescue of local Jews. According to Dennis Deletant, two factors contributed to Antonescu's decision to soften his antisemitic policy, namely the Red Army's advance on the Eastern Front and Filderman's constant petitioning of Antonescu and his officials, demanding the repatriation of all Romanian Jews from Transnistria.[8] Additionally, Jean Ancel has argued that Filderman's petitioning campaign to Antonescu and other regime officials was partially successful, because it skillfully framed the "Jewish Question" as a crucial problem on which Romania's future depended and thus contributed to the survival of hundreds of thousands of Jews.[9] Lya Benjamin has also recognized the importance of Filderman's approach for the survival of Romanian Jews.[10] Theodor Lavi was one of the survivor-scholars who acknowledged that Filderman's legalistic approach of petitioning to Antonescu and other regime officials was almost the only available option to protest antisemitic measures and of informing the dictator about specific abuses perpetrated against the Jews by bureaucrats and gentile citizens.[11] My analysis of Filderman's petitions complements these scholars' findings and provides a more nuanced assessment of their content by examining in more detail his petitions corroborated with the content of the recently published (2015) second volume of his memoirs and diaries covering World War II.

Less than two decades after they were emancipated—as a result of Jewish advocacy and the Entente's pressures at the end of World War I—Romanian Jews found themselves targeted by antisemitic governments, fascist parties, and prejudiced public opinion. Aiming to marginalize the increasingly popular Legion and to gain the sympathy of Nazi Germany, King Carol II and the right-wing National Christian Party government led by Octavian Goga, a notorious antisemite, promoted an openly anti-Jewish policy in late 1937 and early 1938 that reversed the Emancipation of many Romanian Jews. The 21 January 1938 Decree Law (no. 169) for the Revision of Citizenship had a particularly negative impact on the Jewish Communities. As a result, 225,222 Jews lost their Romanian citizenship. Moreover, the Goga government adopted other antisemitic measures such as employment restrictions, the appointment of surveillance commissars at Jewish-owned factories, the ban of Jewish newspapers, and the nationalization of certain businesses.[12]

After Filderman and his colleagues mobilized the support of international Jewish organizations, including the World Jewish Congress, the Alliance Israélite Universelle, and the American Jewish Joint Distribution Committee, as well as the League of Nations, the French and the British governments, they organized a domestic economic boycott. These activities added to the political crisis and Carol II sacked the Goga government in February 1938. Worried about negative foreign policy consequences like losing the support of Romania's French and British allies and an economic collapse, the king cancelled or postponed some of Goga's antisemitic projects such as nationalizing several Jewish companies and introducing employment restrictions and proclaimed a royal dictatorship. Unlike Goga, Carol II was not an antisemitic believer, but rather an opportunistic antisemite.[13] Following territorial losses and the political crisis that engulfed Romania in the summer of 1940, the Romanian monarch enacted the first racial and Nazi-style law, the Jewish Statute, concerning the legal status of the Jews in Romania on 8 August 1940.[14]

During the last years of Carol II's regime, Filderman and his wife left Romania for France, from where they planned to move to the United States. During a short visit to Romania, when he planned to liquidate his law practice and sell his properties, Filderman witnessed how the situation of his coreligionists had worsened. As a result, Filderman decided that it was his duty as a prominent leader with substantial legal and life experience in navigating local society to stay in Romania to defend his fellow Jewish countrymen—through legal resistance methods—against the growing number of antisemitic measures in spite of the personal risks he was to encounter. He framed this decision in his postwar memoir as follows:

> If I left Romania, would I not be betraying the life, liberty, and rights that I had won for my coreligionists, at the price of so much personal suffering? If I left, wouldn't the massacre of the Jews be my responsibility? . . . Wasn't my responsibility greater than that of those who could not fight, because they had never fought? Resistance can lead to averting injustice and illegality only if it is based on arguments of fact and law, as well as on arguments about the interest of the country and of the government itself.[15]

In addition to depicting the principles of his legal resistance strategy against antisemitic measures, which he based on petitioning to local officials, courts, and foreign diplomats and governments, this excerpt shows how Filderman perceived his devotion to his community and to the defense of its rights.

Even though King Carol II implemented an antisemitic policy between 1937 and 1940, the worst was still to come for the Jews. Following Romania's 1930s international isolation after the rise of revisionist powers, the collapse of its allies, especially France in May 1940, the loss of territory—Bessarabia, Northern Bukovina, Southern Dobrogea, and Northern Transylvania—to its neighbors in the summer of 1940, and the domestic political crisis, Carol II abdicated in favor of his son, Michael in September 1940. He also relinquished power to General Ion Antonescu. The new dictator formed the government together with the Legion, joined the Axis, and pursued a harsher antisemitic policy that aimed to disenfranchise the Jews, dispossess them, and eliminate them from the local economy—a process called Romanianization—and society.[16]

After a short time, the relation between Antonescu and the Legion became sour and ended up in a conflict known as the January 1941 Legionary Rebellion due to disagreements on power sharing and governance methods, including on how to resolve the "Jewish Question." In this respect, while the fascists favored a radical and violent antisemitic policy, Antonescu preferred a gradual and "legal" persecution of the Jews.[17] Enjoying the support of the Romanian army and Hitler, Antonescu won the short civil war against the legionaries and stayed in power until August 1944. The violence and pogroms that targeted the Jews in 1940 were surpassed by the systematic mass murder campaign implemented by Antonescu after the entrance of Romania into the war against the Soviet Union in June 1941, which led to the recuperation of Bessarabia and Northern Bukovina and the wartime occupation of Transnistria (a Soviet region located between the Dniester and Bug rivers). Transnistria became a deportation area and a graveyard for hundreds of thousands of Jews mostly from Bessarabia, Northern Bukovina, and Ukraine, who died as a result of mass executions, deportation, ghettoization, and slave labor perpetrated by the Romanian and sometimes German authorities.[18]

Advocating against the Legionary Violence between September 1940 and January 1941

After Antonescu and his fascist partners took power, the legionaries targeted the Jews in a wave of violence. As a result of these attacks, Filderman started to constantly petition Antonescu and other regime officials about the numerous cases of beatings, torture, killing, looting, and the forced Romanianization of property, invoking the legitimacy of Jewish rights in Romania based on the World War I Paris Peace Treaty, the Constitution, and the other laws. In his entreaties, he requested authorities "to respect legality."[19]

Sometimes these petitions were successful. During the audience with Alexandru Ghica, the head of the security police, Siguranța, and Alexandru Rioşanu, the Undersecretary of State at the Ministry of Interior Affairs, on 31 October 1940, for example, Filderman raised issues about several cases of illegal evictions of Jews from their homes and businesses and the illegal arrest of a Jewish man named Zentler. His entreaties were resolved favorably.[20] Another example of successful petitioning took place in August/September 1941. After submitting several petitions and an audience with Antonescu, Filderman achieved the cancellation of the government order requiring Jews to wear the yellow star.[21]

Other times, Filderman's petitions did not succeed. Especially during the Antonescu-Legionary power sharing, Filderman obtained several audiences with Antonescu to complain about the fascist violence only to receive repeated promises that were rarely fulfilled. For instance, during his 31 October 1940 audience with Ion Antonescu, Filderman brought with him numerous files of documents and petitions proving the legionary crimes against the Jews. Antonescu assured him that he had been informed about those "abuses" and that they would not be repeated.[22] Nevertheless, the antisemitic abuses continued. During this audience with Antonescu, Filderman also emphasized that the local authorities misinterpreted and abused the law for the expropriation of Jewish rural real estate. After the expropriation law was adopted, these authorities were setting arbitrary limits for urban areas in order to seize Jewish cemeteries and other properties considered to be located outside urban areas. In response to Filderman's petition, Antonescu promised that he would return the Bucharest Jewish cemetery to the Jewish Community.[23] Later, Filderman petitioned

Antonescu once again about the return of the Jewish cemetery, located on Giurgiului Street in Bucharest, which was targeted by the local officials in spite of Antonescu's assurances.[24]

In fact, protests against various confiscations of Jewish property, especially for communal properties belonging to the Jewish Communities across the country, coupled with requests for restitution and reparation, constituted one of the main points raised by Filderman in his petitions to government officials.[25] Protesting against the exclusion of Jews from employment was another aspect of his fight against the economic disenfranchisement of the Jews. In his petitions to Antonescu's officials, Filderman emphasized, for example, that a radical exclusion from employment such as the March 1941 measure canceling Jewish artisans' licenses and Jewish apprentices' contracts would not benefit ethnic Romanians. Instead, other gentile minorities would profit, Filderman pointed out, by seizing the jobs formerly held by Jews. This would happen, he argued, because only few ethnic Romanians had the necessary skills and experience to replace Jewish technicians and because local Christian minorities such as Germans, Hungarians, and Armenians preferred to hire their own co-nationals rather than ethnic Romanians.[26]

In his petitions and during audiences and private meetings, Filderman constantly emphasized the patriotism of the Jews who fought in the Romanian army and supported the creation of Great Romania.

He also underlined the injustices done to the Jews, who were decorated for their bravery on the battlefield, or were wounded or disabled during their military service.[27] For example, in his 9 April 1941 petition requesting the restitution or reparation for the property losses caused by fascists during the Legionary Rebellion, Filderman invoked the military merits of some of the Jewish victims and their loyalty to Romania:

> Dear General,
>
> Over the centuries, the Jewish population of Romania has demonstrated a deep attachment to the country and to the Romanian people. During the World War [I] the number of Jews killed, wounded, decorated, or captured, and also of deserters was proportional to the [ethnic] Romanians, who were killed, wounded, decorated, taken prisoners, or deserted. Among the 1,274 victims [of the vandalism and theft that took place during the Rebellion] there are 336 veterans of Romanian wars, of whom 89 took part in both the [Second] Balkan War and the World War; 110 of them are decorated.[28]

Even though it became clear that Antonescu distrusted the loyalty of Jewish soldiers—he banned them from military service in December 1940—Filderman hoped that these arguments would appeal to Antonescu's sense of military honor and solidarity with former Jewish comrades in arms as

FIGURE 4.1. Wilhelm Filderman (in the uniform of the Romanian army) together with his family, ca. 1916. Photographic Library, The Wilhelm Filderman Center for the Study of Jewish History in Romania.

wartime military service and blood sacrifice for the country were held in the highest esteem by the Romanian dictator.

All the while, Filderman was not pursuing the legal resistance campaign against the Antonescu regime alone. He benefited from the help of a group of close collaborators, including Arnold Schwefelberg, Matatias Carp, David Rosenkranz, and Elias Costiner—most of them lawyers—who studied the regime's antisemitic laws and administrative measures; suggested legal strategies for intervention; drafted and co-signed the petitions to be submitted to various authorities. These lawyers were devoted advocates for Jewish rights, who accepted Filderman as the main leader and defender of Romanian Jews and recognized his legalistic approach as the most suitable strategy to defend their community.[29] Lawyers Rosenkranz and Schwefelberg, for example, contributed to the process of drafting many of the petitions sent by Filderman on behalf of the Jewish Community to Antonescu officials.[30] Carp, the General Secretary of the Federation, also helped Filderman and his legal resistance activity, especially by gathering official documents and testimonies about the persecution of the Jews, which were to be used as evidence for the petitions sent to Antonescu and for the postwar restitution, reparation, and memorialization campaigns.[31] As one of the secretaries of the Jewish Community, Costiner proved particularly active in the efforts to help the deportees in Transnistria. Filderman and his collaborators also engaged in other activities that aimed at defending Jewish rights against specific antisemitic policies. They sent guidelines to Jewish Communities throughout the country that contained instructions on how to respond to the persecutions by using legal resistance strategies. These instructions advocated petitioning, especially of courts, as one of the main responses.[32]

Filderman and his collaborators did not only send entreaties to government officials, influential gentile businessmen, and opposition politicians, but also to foreign diplomats accredited in Romania. On 23 October 1940, he, for example, petitioned the British ambassador Reginald Hoare, asking him to allow some local Jews as well as Jewish refugees from Germany, Austria, and Poland based in Romania to immigrate to British-ruled Palestine.[33] Filderman thought of this emigration as a possible solution that would save some foreign and local Jews from the growing antisemitism. To that end, he hoped to persuade the British authorities, who severely restricted the Jewish immigration to Palestine from May 1939 onwards, to accept more Jews in Palestine, in other parts of their colonial empire, or to allow their transit to other countries.[34] Undeterred by the British authorities' negative response, Filderman wrote again to the British legation on 24 December 1940, requesting its help with the emigration of local Jews from Romania to British colonies.[35] Filderman continued to advocate for immigration to Palestine by emphasizing the Jews' willingness to emigrate from Romania and demanded a law to facilitate it.[36]

Many Romanian Jews trusted Filderman's strategy of petitioning and intervening with the authorities on their behalf. For instance, when the government publicized its decision to postpone all deportations of Jews to Transnistria in fall 1942, a police informer reported on 13 October 1942 that the Jewish circles of Bucharest attributed that great piece of news and the liberation of hundreds of Jews who awaited deportation in local detention centers to Filderman's petitions to Antonescu.[37] Later on when rumors about future deportations circulated among Bucharest Jews in February 1943, a Special Intelligence Service informer reported that the "Jewish circles" hoped that Filderman and the Jewish Center—established by the Antonescu authorities in December 1941 to control the Jews—would be able to cancel those nefarious plans.[38] Even antisemitic public opinion pundits such as journalist I. P. Prudeni acknowledged in their newspaper articles Filderman's crucial role in the defense of Jewish rights and the popularity and trust he enjoyed among Jews all over Romania.[39]

However, not all the Jews trusted Filderman's legal resistance strategy and some of them criticized his petitioning campaign. According to survivor and historian Theodor Lavi, local right-wing Zionists, for example, mocked Filderman's petitioning strategy as a humiliating form of begging that lacked dignity.[40]

The Post (Legionary) Rebellion Campaign for Restitution and Reparations

Even though Antonescu constantly stated that he had publicly guaranteed the property rights of all inhabitants of Romania, including the Jewish citizens, many Jews were skeptical[41] While Filderman frequently invoked Antonescu's legalistic arguments in his petitions, trying to defend the rights of his coreligionists, the Jewish leader recorded his distrust of Antonescu's legalistic statements in his memoirs. Filderman also noted the fact that local fascists frequently disregarded such "guarantees."[42]

During the National Legionary regime (September 1940–January 1941), and especially after the defeat of the January 1941 Rebellion, Filderman and his collaborators petitioned for restitution and reparations for the damages to Jewish property, businesses, jobs, and other losses caused by the fascists.[43] He argued that a revision of the antisemitic laws and a restitution of the property Romanianized through violence would help the country avoid economic collapse.[44]

In his petition of 9 April 1941, Filderman, who had experience in requesting and obtaining compensations for the losses caused to the Jewish community during the interwar period, estimated the damages to Jewish property caused by legionaries during their January 1941 Bucharest Pogrom at 382,981,800 lei. Advocating for correcting the wrongs, Filderman's petition emphasized the consistent loyalty shown by local Jews to the Romanian state, the poverty confronted by many of his coreligionists, and the urgency of restitution and reparations.[45]

To stimulate Antonescu's ego of an ambitious general and aspiring great leader and, thus, to persuade him to agree to restitution and reparations for the property seized by legionaries through violence, Filderman further commended the fairness of previous Romanian rulers who compensated the Jews for their losses caused by various pogroms since the nineteenth century:

> In 1866, the Coral Temple on Sf. Vineri Street was vandalized. His Majesty, King Carol I, at his own initiative . . . contributed 6,000 gold sovereigns from his privy purse for the reconstruction of the Temple. In 1897, the stores in the Jewish quarter were vandalized. The victims were compensated from the state budget. In 1926, after the student riots in Oradea Mare, the government paid compensation of 16 million lei . . . I myself was the one who asked for and obtained payment of this compensation . . . The Jewish population, which is peaceable and industrious, deprived of the means of existence, calls on the Head of State to follow the example of his great predecessors and succor the pain and need of those who have suffered unjustly by arranging to pay pensions to the widows and minor children of those who were murdered and to provide compensation to those who were robbed and vandalized on 21–23 January [1941] . . . In accordance with the memorandum of 8 March, we respectfully ask you to be so gracious as to speed up the restoration of the property found thus far [at Legionaries].[46]

In response to such a well-crafted petition, Antonescu accepted Filderman's request to establish pensions for the Jews, who became orphans, widows, and invalids as a result of fascist pogroms. Those Jewish survivors were awarded the same rights as the war invalids, orphans, and widows, through article 22 of the Invalid Law of 4 September 1941.[47]

Meanwhile, the courts and administrative offices only returned some of the property seized through violence by the legionaries to its Jewish owners after January 1941. Usually, these acts followed Jewish complaints.[48] Considering the violent and rapid Romanianization pursued by local legionaries during their short power-sharing as a major breach of law, contradictory to his domestic policy of gradual and "legal" dispossession of the Jews, and as a threat to Romania's economic stability, Antonescu allowed limited restitution of Jewish property. In accordance with his plan to exclude Jews from the local economy and society, he wanted to completely dispossess the Jews at a later stage.[49]

The Government Perspective on Filderman and His Petitioning Campaign

While Antonescu usually accepted, read, and responded to Filderman's petitions that informed him about the abuses against the Jews, he often criticized them as "fake complaints." The Romanian dictator also issued several press communiqués warning that whoever would send such complaints in the future would be investigated immediately. If these complaints proved baseless, their authors would be prosecuted for the crime of spreading false rumors.[50]

Although Filderman eventually lost his position as the head of the Federation in December 1941 and faced Antonescu's suspicion for allegedly using calumnies about the wrongdoings of state bureaucrats, the government frequently discussed Filderman's petitions. During the 15 April 1941 government meeting, General Dumitru Popescu, the Minister of the Interior, for instance, reported to Antonescu that he had informed Filderman about Antonescu's warning that Jews who "speculated" on the black market should stop their baneful activity. If they did not, the government would adopt extremely harsh measures against them. According to Popescu, Filderman responded that he would send circular letters to all Jewish Communities, warning them about the harsh repercussions in case of economic speculation. Yet Filderman also pointed out that the Jews represented only fifteen percent of those accused of economic sabotage. Hearing Filderman's argument, Antonescu burst out and claimed that such a low proportion was due to "Jewish cunningness" and threatened "to let the crowd loose to massacre the Jews," if they did not comply with his directives.[51]

During its 30 September 1941 meeting, the government discussed another complaint of Filderman, this time against the National Romanianization Center (NRC)'s measure of expropriating a Bucharest Jewish health-care center. The NRC, the country's main Aryanization agency, sought to transform the center into a hospital for war invalids. According to Antonescu's officials, Filderman argued that at least a part of the hospital should be left to the Jewish Community, because it was built with the money donated by several private organizations from the United States. These organizations might request the return of their donations if the funds were used for a different purpose. Eugen Zwiedeneck, who was the head of the Romanianization Center, responded that the money donated by US organizations was given to local Jews unofficially and that he believed that Romania lacked a law to allow the authorities to seize the properties of the Jewish Community. While Antonescu disagreed with Zwiedeneck and argued that the Romanianization laws stipulated that

Jewish property could be expropriated from both "individual and collective persons/entities," he advised Zwiedeneck to examine carefully the legal and factual details of the case.⁵²

In general, most of Antonescu's officials were hostile to Filderman, but some of them were cautious in their attitudes toward the Jewish leader and first inquired about Ion Antonescu's opinion before taking a specific stance toward Filderman. During its 24 November 1941 meeting, for instance, the government discussed the case of Filderman who, as a lawyer, was sent in front of the disciplinary commission of the Ilfov (Bucharest) Bar Association for his alleged breaches of ethical principles following a public letter sent by Ion Antonescu to Filderman. This correspondence responded to a private letter, in which Filderman had pleaded in favor of local Jews. The Minister of Justice, Constantin Stoicescu, was wondering what should be done about it. Antonescu adopted a legalistic attitude and argued that he did not make a formal complaint against Filderman at the Bar Association. He wanted to stay out of that controversy and let justice take its course in order to avoid appearing to help Filderman. Yet, Stoicescu seemed concerned. The public may believe that Antonescu and the government ordered the persecution of the Jewish leader.⁵³ In the end, the Bar Association excluded Filderman, who had been a member since 1912.

Another incident from November 1941 shows how Antonescu officials' challenged Filderman's petitioning strategy. Responding in the name of Ion Antonescu to one of Filderman's petitions that emphasized the Jews' loyalty to Romania and pleaded against deportations, Ovidiu Vlădescu, the head of the government Chancellery, reproached Filderman. "There is no point," Vlădescu stressed, "in using this lawyerly and specifically Jewish pettifogging with Marshal Antonescu."⁵⁴

Overall, these examples prove that Filderman's strategy of defending the rights of local Jews through petitions was well known among the Antonescu regime officials, who resented his petitioning activity, but repeatedly failed to undermine it.⁵⁵

The Campaign to Stop the 1942 Deportations to Transnistria and Poland

Perhaps Filderman's greatest achievement was the protest campaign against the 1942 German-Romanian plans to deport local Jews from Banat and Southern Transylvania and, later, from the rest of Romania to Transnistria and Poland. Once more, he based it on petitioning and mobilizing gentile support. Antonescu first postponed the planned deportations in the fall of 1942 and eventually abandoned them.⁵⁶ Hearing news and rumors about the upcoming deportations on 22 August 1942, Filderman planned to intervene with Antonescu via a memo against the deportation projects. Instead, he proposed an alternative plan—namely immigration to Palestine—if Romania would be forced by Germany to adopt a radical solution to the "Jewish Question."[57] During this most urgent campaign, Filderman spared no effort and petitioned not only the Antonescu government, but also other officials such as Dimitrie G. Lupu, the head of the Supreme Court, opposition politicians such as Iuliu Maniu, Constantin Brătianu, and Nicolae L. Lupu as well as some Church officials.

According to their reports sent to Berlin, the German diplomats in Bucharest worried about Filderman's activity against their planned deportation of Romanian Jews to Poland.[58] Following the intervention of Jewish notables from Banat, Filderman wrote a petition against the upcoming deportations and asked Maniu and Brătianu for help. The leaders of the two main opposition parties agreed with Filderman's request, made a few changes to his draft petition, signed it, and submitted it to the government. The petition argued that local Jews should not be deported to German-occupied Poland, because such a radical antisemitic measure would be damaging to Romania's claims at a potential postwar peace conference.[59] Filderman also managed to mobilize the support of other influential gentiles against the deportation plan. General Constantin Vasiliu, Minister of the Interior, opposed the plan of deporting the Jews from Banat and Southern Transylvania to Poland for several reasons, including his belief that such a measure would cause economic hardships for Romania and its national community, because Jewish companies would be taken over by local ethnic Germans. The head of Bucharest's Medical University and Antonescu's personal physician Dr. Nicolae Gh. Lupu also intervened with the Romanian dictator and received assurances that only the pro-communist and pro-Hungarian Jews from Banat and Southern Transylvania would be deported. National Peasant Party politicians—such as Ion Mihalache; Nicolae L. Lupu, and Aurel Leucutia—also discussed the antisemitic measures and projects in one of their meetings and planned to intervene in favor of the Jews.[60]

Filderman's petitions vigorously denied any Judeo-Bolshevik accusations. By invoking the book of right-wing nationalist and antisemitic politician and economist Mihail Manoilescu to support the petition, Filderman strategically emphasized the major economic losses Romania would suffer as a result of the deportation of the Jews, since even the previous milder Romanianization measures had created an economic disaster. He also argued that the Jews of Banat, Southern Transylvania, and the Old Kingdom had lived in those territories for hundreds of years and had repeatedly proven their loyalty to Romania and to earlier premodern principalities. Moreover, in contrast to Bessarabian and Bukovinian Jews, they had never been accused of communist subversion and pro-Soviet sympathy. Filderman emphasized that Romania had already adopted the most radical antisemitic policies among the Axis powers by reducing its Jewish Community to a third of what it was before World War II in just two years. Before deporting the remainder of its Jews, Romania, he stressed, was entitled to ask all other Axis countries to follow its example and deport two-thirds of their own Jews.[61]

In order to stop the 1942 deportations, Filderman also petitioned foreign diplomats believed to have influence over Antonescu and his ministers. German diplomats in Bucharest complained to Berlin that, under Filderman's influence, Transylvanian and Banat Jews submitted a petition for help against the deportation plan to the Swiss, Swedish, and Vatican diplomatic representatives in Romania.[62]

Risks and Dangers Filderman Faced as a Result of His Petitioning

As early as 1918, Filderman faced serious personal risks due to his courageous and relentless petitioning campaign on behalf of Romanian Jews. Meanwhile, threats to his life sharply increased during the interwar period and especially during the Antonescu regime.[63] On 25 November 1940, for example, a band of legionaries attacked his house under the pretext of a police search, but failed to break in, and later fled after Filderman managed to contact the police authorities who sent help.[64]

Beseeching the Romanian authorities with seemingly endless petitions and organizing help for the Jews posed an even greater danger for Filderman during the war. Enraged by Filderman's constant petitioning on behalf of local Jews and his "negative" influence among the Jews that interfered with the government's fiscal policy—specifically, the request of 4 billion lei as contribution for the war effort—and other antisemitic measures, Antonescu deported Filderman to Transnistria at the end of May 1943. Afraid that the Germans might kill Filderman in Transnistria and following the interventions of Swedish, Swiss, and Vatican diplomats, Antonescu repatriated the Jewish leader to Romania after three months.[65] According to Eugen Cristescu, the former head of the Special Intelligence Service, Filderman was "temporarily interned in Transnistria as a result of the accusations brought against him by the Jewish Center officials" who blamed Filderman for "instigating [the Jews] and sabotaging the public subscription of money collected from the Jews by the Jewish Center."[66] Filderman had petitioned the Jewish Center officials and Antonescu, arguing that the Jews were not able to pay the enormous sum requested by the authorities in spring 1943, because Romanianization and other antisemitic policies had left them impoverished.[67]

Threats to Filderman's well-being came not only from officials close to Antonescu, but also from the German personnel in Romania and Transnistria. Considering him a danger to their interests in Romania, the German legation in Bucharest kept Filderman under constant surveillance.[68] Gustav Richter, the SS expert in Aryanization and anti-Jewish legislation of the German legation in Bucharest, attacked Filderman in the local German-language press in April 1943. Richter even threatened to kill Filderman following the latter's refusal to meet with him in 1942, when Filderman campaigned against the German-initiated deportation plan.[69] Later on, when Filderman was in Transnistria, several German military officials searched the Mogilev ghetto. Since the ghetto inhabitants effectively protected Filderman, the Germans failed to locate him.[70] Many of the Jews deported to Transnistria regarded Filderman as a providential leader and a savior.[71] Overall, it seems that Filderman's public activity and international reputation protected him. The authorities worried that the assassination of Filderman might have a negative impact on Romania's stand at the end of the war. When Romanian officials found out that Richter planned to kill Filderman, they protested in Berlin, achieving the cancelation of that plan.[72]

Despite the constant threats to his life and to his community, Filderman continued to care for his country, envisioned a future in Romania, and thought about how to reconcile the Jews and ethnic Romanians after the end of the war.[73]

Conclusion

Continuing the petitioning tradition of previous Romanian Jewish leaders in fighting antisemitism and advocating for Emancipation, Filderman's interventions, discussed in this chapter, fit into the broader trend of Jewish resistance efforts against Nazi policies in Europe, as depicted by the Hebrew term *amidah*. While Filderman neither advocated for nor engaged in armed resistance against the Antonescu regime—a type of response that would have been impossible in wartime Romania, site of a dictatorship that was popular among the local inhabitants for most of this period—he organized a legal resistance movement together with other Jewish notables. It involved petitions, court litigation, and interventions with Antonescu officials and other influential gentiles and foreign diplomats, aiming to ensure the survival of the community. In combination with other reasons mostly related to the evolution of the war, this strategy was partially successful and most Romanian Jews survived the war and kept some of their property and jobs. The success of some of his petitions resulted from Filderman's deep understanding of the Romanian officials' egos, fears, and hopes, and of the international events and power shifts between influential Axis, Allied, and neutral countries. In particular, the skillful framing of his petitions—claiming that the contested antisemitic measures were detrimental to Romania's national aspirations, its independence, prosperity, security, and reputation—and the effective timing within the war context contributed to their occasional success. Sometimes, specific political and military events helped Filderman's arguments and persuaded the Romanian decision makers to postpone or abandon specific antisemitic measures in order to improve the wartime credentials of Romania at the future peace negotiations. Despite its failures, Filderman's persistent petitioning campaign reveals the agency of this Jewish leader and of his legal professional colleagues, who found the most suitable strategy in informing Antonescu and his officials about the various antisemitic "abuses" and challenging antisemitic measures. This petitioning strategy that required a lot of effort, including gathering evidence, reading the legislation, framing the petitions, enlisting gentile support, and obtaining audiences, contradicts the myth of Jewish passivity during the Holocaust and illustrates the agency of Jewish leadership.

While some of his petitions succeeded, many of his complaints remained unresolved despite the assurances from Antonescu that antisemitic abuses would be stopped or reversed. Filderman's petitions are as much about the untiring work of a responsible individual deeply concerned with the fate of the Jewish community in Romania during World War II as they are about the collective solidarity and shared work ethics of key members of the Jewish community in Romania. As indicated in this chapter, these memoranda, occasionally, had negative consequences for Filderman, such as death threats, professional interdictions, and his deportation to Transnistria. But those did not deter him from continuing to write petitions. In the end, Filderman survived the Antonescu regime and was able to contribute decisively to the survival of many Romanian Jews.

Ștefan Cristian Ionescu is the Theodore Zev and Alice R. Weiss-Holocaust Education Foundation Visiting Associate Professor in Holocaust Studies, Department of History, Northwestern University. Ionescu holds a Ph.D. in history from Clark University in Worcester, Massachusetts. He is the author of *Jewish Resistance to Romanianization: 1940-1944* (2015) and several book chapters and articles in journals such as the *Journal of Genocide Research*, *Yad Vashem Studies*, *Holocaust Studies: A Journal of Culture and History*, and *Culture & Psychology*.

Notes

Research for this chapter was supported by a grant of the Romanian National Authority for Scientific Research, UEFISCDI, for grant PN-III-P1–1.1-TE-2016–0091, no. 5/2018, Transcultural Networks in Narratives about the Holocaust in Eastern Europe.

1. On Stern's and Filderman's advocacy for Jewish rights around World War I, see Carol Iancu, ed., *Lupta Internațională pentru Emanciparea Evreilor din România: Documente și mărturii, 1913–1919*, 2 vols. (Bucharest, 2004).
2. Marcel Dumitru-Ciucă et al. eds., *Stenogramele ședințelor Consiliului de Miniștri: Guvernarea Ion Antonescu*, 11 vols. (Bucharest, 1997–2008).
3. See p. 8, this volume.
4. On the myth of Jewish passivity, see Richard Middleton-Kaplan, "The Myth of Jewish Passivity," in *Jewish Resistance against the Nazis*, ed. Patrick Henry (Washington, DC, 2014), 3–26.
5. Constantin Iordachi, *Liberalism, Constitutional Nationalism, and Minorities: The Making of Romanian Citizenship, 1750–1918* (Leiden, 2019).
6. S[imon] Schaffermann, *Dr. W. Filderman: 50 de ani din istoria judaismului român* (Tel Aviv, 1986), 17.
7. Ibid.
8. Ottmar Trașcă and Dennis Deletant, eds., *Al III-lea Reich și România, 1940–44: Documente din arhivele germane*. (Bucharest, 2007), 46–47.
9. See Jean Ancel, "Introduction," in Wilhelm Filderman, *Memoirs and Diaries*, vol. 2 (Tel Aviv, Jerusalem, 2015), iii–xxiv.
10. Lya Benjamin, *Prigoană și rezistență în istoria evreilor din România: 1940–1944* (Bucharest, 2001); Tuvia Friling, Radu Ioanid, and Mihail Ionescu, eds. *Final Report* (Iași, 2004), 205–21.
11. Quoted in S. Schafferman, *Dr. W. Filderman*, 213.
12. Carol Iancu, *Evreii din România: De la emancipare la marginalizare, 1919–1938* (Bucharest, 2000), 249–56.
13. See Jean Ancel, *The History of the Holocaust in Romania* (Lincoln, NE, and Jerusalem, 2011), 25–50; Lya Benjamin, ed., *Evreii din România între anii 1940–1944: Legislația antievreiască* (Bucharest, 1993); Iancu, *Evreii din România*, 256–260; Dennis Deletant, *Hitler's Forgotten Ally: Ion Antonescu and His Regime, Romania 1940–44* (Basingstoke, 2006); Radu Ioanid, *Evreii sub regimul Antonescu* (Bucharest, 1998); Dan Stone, "Romania and the Jews in BBC Monitoring Service Reports," *East European Politics and Societies, and Cultures* 31, no. 3 (2017): 550.
14. For the 8 August 1940 Decree Law no. 2560 for the Jewish Statute, see Ancel, *History*, 78–82; Benjamin, *Legislația*, 37–56; Deletant, *Hitler's Forgotten Ally*, 103–4; Iancu, *Evreii din România*, 260–65; Ioanid, *Evreii*, 26–29; Leon Volovici, "The Response of Jewish Leaders and Intellectuals to Antisemitism," in *The History of the Jews of Romania*, vol. 3: *Between the Two World Wars*, ed. Liviu Rotman and Raphael Vago (Tel Aviv, 2005), 171–76.
15. Filderman, *Memoirs and Diaries*, 2:9–10.
16. On the Romanianization policy, see Jean Ancel, *The Economic Destruction of Romanian Jewry* (Jerusalem, 2007); Ștefan Cristian Ionescu, *Jewish Resistance to "Romanianization," 1940–44* (Basingstoke, 2015).
17. On the legionary violence, see Ancel, *History*, 119–64; Armin Heinen, *Holocaustul și logica violenței* (Iași, 2011); Vladimir Solonari, *Purifying the Nation: Population Exchange and*

Ethnic Cleansing in Nazi-Allied Romania (Baltimore, MD, 2010), 125–36; Roland Clark, "Fascists and Soldiers: Ambivalent Loyalties and Genocidal Violence in Wartime Romania," *Holocaust and Genocide Studies* 31, no. 3 (2017): 408–32.
18. Ancel, *History*; Deletant, *Hitler's Forgotten Ally*; Diana Dumitru, *The State, Antisemitism, and Collaboration in the Holocaust: The Borderlands of Romania and the Soviet Union* (Cambridge, 2016); Heinen, *Romania*; Ioanid, *Evreii*; Ion Popa, *The Romanian Orthodox Church and the Holocaust* (Bloomington, IN, 2017); Solonari, *Purifying the Nation*.
19. Lya Benjamin, ed., *Strategii comunitare de supraviețuire în contextul statului național legionar: Documente* (Bucharest, 2013), 179–82.
20. Filderman, *Memoirs and Diaries*, 2:58.
21. Ibid., 187–202.
22. Ibid., 58–60.
23. Ibid., 60.
24. Ibid., 75–76.
25. See Filderman's petition (from 12 August 1941) against the evacuation of rural Jews to county seats and the forced Romanianization of small Jewish businesses in four villages in Vaslui County. Arhivele Naționale ale României (hereafter ANR), Ministerul Economiei Naționale-Direcția Secretariat (MEN-DS) 64/1941, p. 14. For a facsimile and translation of this petition, see pp. 231–32, this volume.
26. See, for instance, Filderman's petition to MEN from 26 March 1941. ANR, MEN-Direcția Organizării Profesionale Comerț Interior (DOPCI) 80/1941, pp. 259–61.
27. Filderman, *Memoirs and Diaries*, 2:66, 70–72, 78, 83–83, 113–15.
28. Ibid., 2:113–14.
29. Ibid.
30. Adina Rosenkranz-Herscovici, *Dadu: Viața și activitatea avocatului David Rosenkranz* (Sydney, 2018), 19; Arnold Schwefelberg, *Amintirile unui intelectual evreu din România* (Bucharest, 2000); Filderman, *Memoirs and Diaries*, 2:346.
31. Carp published many of those documents as a book—*The Black Book of Romanian Jewry*—during the first postwar years. Matatias Carp, ed., *Cartea Neagră: Suferințele evreilor din România, 1940–1944*, 3 vols. (Bucharest, 1946–1948).
32. See Filderman's circular letter (23 September 1940) in Benjamin, *Strategii comunitare*, 164–69; Jean Ancel, ed., *Documents Concerning the Fate of Romanian Jewry during the Holocaust*, vol. 1 (New York, 1986), 499–504; ANR, Colecția Documentară Comunități Evreiești din România (CDCER) 21/1941, p. 9. The Jewish Center also participated in court contestations of Romanianization cases. ANR, Centrala Evreilor din România (CER) 14/1942, p. 13, CER 16/1942, pp. 2, 159; CDCER 1/1941, pp. 3–6, 9, 26.
33. Filderman, *Memoirs and Diaries*, 2:57.
34. Ibid., 2:77–78.
35. Ibid., 2:81.
36. Benjamin, *Strategii comunitare*, 197–98.
37. See Direcția Generală a Poliției report sent on 16 October 1942 to the Great Chief of Staff of the Romanian army. Ottmar Trașcă, ed., *"Chestiunea evreiască" în documente militare române, 1941–1944* (Iași, 2010), 699.
38. See the 13 February 1943 SSI informative note from a "serious source." United States Holocaust Memorial Museum Archives, Washington DC, Arhiva Serviciului Român de Informații, RG-25.004M, reel 96, file 2295, pp. 280–81.
39. See I. P. Prundeni, "Momentul Filderman," in Schafferman, *Dr. W. Filderman*, 159–60.
40. Lavi acknowledged, however, that Filderman's strategy was probably the only possible response in that particular political and military context. Schafferman, *Dr. W. Filderman*, 213.

41. For more examples of Antonescu's statements criticizing the illegal seizure of Jewish property by Legionaries, see Ancel, *History*, 116.
42. Filderman, *Memoirs and Diaries*, 2:29–43; Ancel noted that even though, initially, the Jewish leaders were happy to hear Antonescu's guarantees—such as those from September 1940—that the property and other rights of the Jews would be respected, they soon realized that the legionaries did not abide by them. Ancel, *History*, 170–71.
43. See Ancel, *Documents*, 2:285–317; Filderman, *Memoirs and Diaries*, 2:113–15.
44. See the 10 December 1940 petition of Filderman to Ion Antonescu, in Ancel, *Documents*, 2:78–80.
45. Filderman, *Memoirs and Diaries*, 2:113–15.
46. Ibid.
47. Ibid., 2:115.
48. See, for instance, Schwefelberg, *Amintirile*.
49. Ionescu, *Jewish Resistance*.
50. ANR, MEN-DS 48/1940, pp. 25–35.
51. Ciucă et al., *Stenogramele*, 3:219.
52. Ibid., 4:806–7.
53. Ibid., 5:238–39; for Filderman's version of this incident, see Filderman, *Memoirs and Diaries*, 2:253–54.
54. Filderman, *Memoirs and Diaries*, 2:243.
55. Other incidents show the irritation of Antonescu officials with Filderman's petitioning campaign. See, for instance, Mihai Antonescu's hostile and threatening response to one of Filderman's petitions from August 1941. Schafferman, *Dr. W. Filderman*, 196–97.
56. For more details on Filderman's efforts to stop the 1942 deportations, see Ancel, *History*, 494–503.
57. Traşcă and Deletant, *Al III-lea Reich*, 24.
58. On the Belzec plan, see Ancel, *History*, 457–509.
59. Traşcă and Deletant, *Al III-lea Reich*, 537.
60. Ibid., 538–39.
61. The memo sent by the representative of the Jewish Communities in Banat and Southern Transylvania was in fact drafted by Filderman. See Ancel, *Documents*, 4:244–49.
62. Traşcă and Deletant, *Al III-lea Reich*, 548.
63. The death threats and plots against Filderman started in 1918 and continued throughout the 1920s and 1930s. Schafferman, *Dr. W. Filderman*, 105–106, 157–59; Ancel, *History*, 83, 576n64.
64. Filderman, *Memoirs and Diaries*, 2:64.
65. For more details on the context of Filderman's deportation to Transnistria, see the testimony of one of his main collaborators, lawyer David Rosenkranz. Rosenkranz-Herscovici, *Dadu: Viaţa şi activitatea*, 53; Filderman, *Memoirs and Diaries*, 2:434–66.
66. See Eugen Cristescu's undated statement to SMERŞ in Radu Ioanid, ed., *Lotul Antonescu în ancheta SMERŞ, Moscova, 1944–1946: Documente din arhiva FSB* (Iaşi, 2006), 222.
67. Filderman, *Memoirs and Diaries*, 2:425–40; Friling, Ioanid, and Ionescu, *Final Report*, 201.
68. Ancel, *History*, 494–95.
69. Ancel, *History*, 464, 498; Jean Ancel, Introduction, 2:xvii.
70. See Siegfried Jagendorf's 30 April 1949 letter to Filderman, in Filderman, *Memoirs and Diaries*, 2:463.
71. See for instance, the testimony of Transnistria survivor Yosef Govrin. Yosef Gorvin, *Sub spectrul distrugerii* (Bucharest, 2015), 87.
72. Schafferman, *Dr. W Filderman*, 222.
73. Filderman, *Memoirs and Diaries*, 2:383–84.

Bibliography

Ancel, Jean. *The Economic Destruction of Romanian Jewry*. Jerusalem: Yad Vashem, 2007.
———. *The History of the Holocaust in Romania*. Lincoln and Jerusalem: University of Nebraska Press and Yad Vashem, 2011.
———. Introduction to *Memoirs and Diaries*, vol. 2, by Wilhelm Filderman, iii–xxiv. Tel Aviv: The Goldstein Goren Diaspora Research Center, Yad Vashem, 2004, 2015.
———, ed. *Documents Concerning the Fate of Romanian Jewry during the Holocaust*. 12 vols. New York: Beate Klarsfeld Foundation, 1986.
Benjamin, Lya, ed. *Evreii din România între anii 1940–1944: Legislația antievreiască*. Bucharest: Hasefer, 1993.
———. *Prigoană și rezistență în istoria evreilor din România: 1940–1944*. Bucharest: Hasefer, 2001.
———, ed. *Strategii comunitare de supraviețuire în contextul statului național legionar: Documente*. Bucharest: Hasefer, 2013.
Carp, Matatias, ed. *Cartea Neagră: Suferințele evreilor din România, 1940–1944*, 3 vols. Bucharest: Socec, 1946–1948.
Clark, Roland. "Fascists and Soldiers: Ambivalent Loyalties and Genocidal Violence in Wartime Romania." *Holocaust and Genocide Studies* 31, no. 3 (2017): 408–32.
Deletant, Dennis. *Hitler's Forgotten Ally: Ion Antonescu and His Regime, Romania 1940–44*. Basingstoke: Palgrave Macmillan, 2006.
Dumitru, Diana. *The State, Antisemitism, and Collaboration in the Holocaust: The Borderlands of Romania and the Soviet Union*. Cambridge: Cambridge University Press, 2016.
Dumitru-Ciucă, Marcel et al. eds. *Stenogramele ședințelor* Consiliului de Miniștri: *Guvernarea Ion Antonescu*, 11 vols. Bucharest: Arhivele Naționale ale României, 1997–2008.
Filderman, Wilhelm. *Memoirs and Diaries*. 2 vols., Tel Aviv: The Goldstein-Goren Diaspora Research Center, Yad Vashem, 2004, 2015.
Friling, Tuvia, Radu Ioanid, and Mihail Ionescu, eds. *Final Report*. Iași: International Commission on the Holocaust in Romania, Polirom, 2004.
Gorvin, Yosef. *Sub spectrul distrugerii*. Bucharest: Hasefer, 2015.
Heinen, Armin. *România, Holocaustul și logica violenței*. Iași: Editura Universității "Al. Ioan Cuza" din Iași, 2011.
Iancu, Carol. *Evreii din România: De la emancipare la marginalizare, 1919–1938*. Bucharest: Hasefer, 2000.
———, ed. *Lupta Internațională pentru Emanciparea Evreilor din România: Documente și mărturii, 1913–1919*, 2 vols. Bucharest: Hasefer, 2004.
Ioanid, Radu. *Evreii sub regimul Antonescu*. Bucharest: Hasefer, 1998.
———, ed. *Lotul Antonescu în ancheta SMERȘ, Moscova, 1944–1946: Documente din arhiva FSB*. Iași: Polirom, 2006.
Ionescu, Ștefan Cristian. *Jewish Resistance to "Romanianization," 1940–44*. Basingstoke: Palgrave Macmillan, 2015.

Iordachi, Constantin. *Liberalism, Constitutional Nationalism, and Minorities: The Making of Romanian Citizenship, 1750–1918*. Leiden: Brill, 2019.

Middleton-Kaplan, Richard. "The Myth of Jewish Passivity." In *Jewish Resistance against the Nazis*, edited by Patrick Henry, 3–26. Washington, DC: The Catholic University of America Press, 2014.

Popa, Ion. *The Romanian Orthodox Church and the Holocaust*. Bloomington: Indiana University Press, 2017.

Prundeni, I. P. "Momentul Filderman." In *Dr. W. Filderman: 50 de ani din istoria judaismului român*, by S. Schafferman, 159–60. Tel Aviv: Self-published, 1986.

Rosenkranz-Herscovici, Adina. *Dadu: Viața și activitatea avocatului David Rosenkranz*. Sydney: Rexlibris, 2018.

Schafferman, S[imon]. *Dr. W. Filderman: 50 de ani din istoria judaismului român*. Tel Aviv: Self-published, 1986.

Schwefelberg, Arnold. *Amintirile unui intelectual evreu din România*. Bucharest: Hasefer, 2000.

Solonari, Vladimir. *Purifying the Nation: Population Exchange and Ethnic Cleansing in Nazi-Allied Romania*. Baltimore, MD: John Hopkins University Press, 2010.

Stone, Dan. "Romania and the Jews in BBC Monitoring Service Reports." *East European Politics and Societies, and Cultures* 31, no. 3 (2017): 545–564.

Trașcă, Ottmar, ed. *"Chestiunea evreiască" în documente militare române, 1941–1944*. Iași: Institutul European, 2010.

Trașcă, Ottmar, and Dennis Deletant, eds. *Al III-lea Reich și România, 1940–44: Documente din arhivele germane*. Bucharest: Editura Institutului Național pentru Studierea Holocaustului din România Elie Wiesel, 2007.

Volovici, Leon. "The Response of Jewish Leaders and Intellectuals to Antisemitism." In *The History of the Jews in Romania*, vol. 3: *Between the Two World Wars*, edited by Liviu Rotman and Raphael Vago, 171–76. Tel Aviv: The Goldstein-Goren Diaspora Research Center, Tel Aviv University, 2005.

Chapter 5

ATTEMPTS TO TAKE ACTION IN A COERCED COMMUNITY
Petitions to the Jewish Council in the Łódź Ghetto during World War II

Svenja Bethke

Introduction

"Highly esteemed Praeses Rumkowski, we hereby address you with the following request"—salutations of this kind can be read in thousands of letters from the inmates of the Łódź ghetto to the Jewish Council head, Mordechai Chaim Rumkowski. These letters are found in comprehensive collections held in the Archiwum Państwowe in Łódź, comprising more than 35,000 letters sent internally in the ghetto.[1] Since the writers asked the Jewish Council head to take action in their favor, these letters can be classified as petitions. In them, ghetto inhabitants expressed concerns and queries relating to the harsh living conditions and the omnipresent danger to life in the ghettos created by the Germans during World War II.

The Łódź ghetto, which existed from April 1940 until July 1944, was the second largest and longest-running ghetto in German-occupied Eastern Europe. After the Germans attacked Poland on 1 September 1939, Reinhard Heydrich, Chief of the Reich Security Main Office, ordered the establishment of Jewish Councils and ghettos for the newly occupied territories initially as a provisional measure to prepare for the future resettlement of the Jewish population.[2] It was only in the second half of 1941 that the Nazi leadership decided to systematically murder the European Jews.[3]

In the city of Łódź, German city commissioner Albert Leister enforced the establishment of the Jewish Council with Mordechai Chaim Rumkowski as its head within weeks of the German army's arrival. By the time the

---

Notes for this chapter begin on page 130.

order was given on 13 October 1939, the Council head was fully responsible for fulfilling German decrees. Two months after Friedrich Uebelhoer, district president of the Warthegau, had formulated the plan to establish a ghetto on 10 December 1939, police president Johannes Schäfer ordered the Jewish population to move to the designated area in the old city of Łódź and the quarters of Bałuty and Marysin on 8 February 1940. The city administration sealed the ghetto on 30 April 1940. While the German ghetto administration, headed by Hans Biebow, had ultimate power over the ghetto, the Jewish Council was granted limited control over the Jewish population, and was able to collect taxes and form institutions.[4] Rumkowski established a comprehensive internal ghetto administration including a secretariat for petitions and complaints (Sekretariat für Bittschriften und Beschwerden) in October 1940, located at Dwórska Street 1. He employed four functionaries to answer the petitions, among them Renia Wółk as head, and four inspectors to investigate the material circumstances of the writers.[5] Jewish people started to write petitions almost immediately after Rumkowski's appointment and the volume increased after the establishment of the secretariat.

After the war, survivors and public representatives, especially in Israel, fiercely criticized Rumkowski, killed in Auschwitz in 1944, and called him a "tyrant"[6] who had betrayed his fellow Jews by carrying out the decrees of the German occupiers in a dictatorial manner.[7] In reaction to these criticisms, scholars have stressed the dilemma of the Jewish Councils, highlighting their desperate attempts to respond to the urgent needs of the ghetto inhabitants in the context of the brutal German occupation.[8] The petitions from the Łódź ghetto allow for a re-evaluation of these key debates.

After the Łódź ghetto was sealed, about 160,000 people were forced to live in a narrow space of 4.13 square kilometers. They belonged to a broad range of social strata, political groups, and religious traditions.[9] In autumn 1941, the population increased further when the German authorities deported twenty thousand Jews from Germany, Vienna, Prague, and Luxembourg and sent five thousand Sinti and Roma to the ghetto.[10] Between December 1941 and August 1942 another eighteen thousand Jews arrived from dissolved ghettos in the Warthegau.[11] Reflecting this broad range of origins, the authors wrote petitions in Polish, Yiddish, German, and Hebrew.

Although research on petition writing has shed light on the agency of allegedly passive individuals in various historical contexts, scholars have not yet systematically considered the practice of petitioning in a coerced community.[12] This chapter closes the gap by focusing on petitions from the Łódź ghetto as an expression of competing survival strategies. By doing so, it will ultimately rethink acts of individual and group resistance as more complex and ambivalent than scholars have previously acknowledged. Despite new research on life in the ghettos, the petitions have received little attention.[13]

The sheer number of ghetto inhabitants and Rumkowski's encouragement of petition writing has resulted in an exceptionally large number of letters in the Łódź ghetto.[14] Rumkowski preserved them in an internal ghetto archive set up in November 1940 with the aim of writing the history of the ghetto after the war.[15] For this chapter, the collections have been researched to identify changing patterns over time with regard to the background of the writers, the concerns they expressed and the language chosen. The chapter evaluates a sample of representative letters and petitions that allow us to address key topics against the background of changing German demands and resulting changes within the ghetto community.

This chapter analyzes the petitions in two ways that will significantly change our understanding of internal dynamics and patterns of behavior in the ghetto community. First, it looks at the letters as an expression of conflicting survival strategies within the ghetto community. Rumkowski pursued a collective survival strategy by trying to fulfill ever-changing German demands in the hope of saving at least part of the ghetto com-

FIGURE 5.1. A teenage boy hands a petition to Mordechai Chaim Rumkowski, Łódź ghetto, 17 August 1941. Photo Archives of the United States Holocaust Memorial Museum, Washington, DC, courtesy of Jehuda Widawski.

munity.[16] The establishment of the secretariat for petitionary letters and complaints and the practice of petition writing was key to this strategy.

Rumkowski aimed to keep the ghetto inhabitants calm by tempering their individual concerns and criticism. He did so to prevent internal conflicts and unrest that could potentially trigger brutal German intervention.

At the same time and often in contrast to Rumkowski's strategy, ordinary ghetto inhabitants sought to enforce their individual interests and survival strategies. Viewed in this light, the petitionary letters were a vehicle of communication between the Jewish Council and the ghetto inhabitants that offer new insights into a highly dynamic relationship. Second, by looking at the motivations of the writers and the content of the letters, this chapter reveals the multilayered survival strategies of individuals who were part of a heterogeneous community. It calls for the acknowledgement and assessment of the ambivalent patterns of behavior that complicate the overly dichotomous categories of resistance and complicity that still prevail in Holocaust research.

Due to a strong focus on the Germans' motivations, English and German-speaking scholars have long viewed ghettos as one step on the way to the "final solution," while the perspective of those defined as "Jewish" and forced to live in the ghetto was largely ignored.[17] Postwar debates on the alleged lack of Jewish resistance in scholarship, survivor communities, and public discourse have also contributed to a perceived dichotomy between "active" perpetrators and "passive" Jewish victims. In the 1960s, scholars such as Hannah Arendt and Raul Hilberg imposed clear categories of morally good and bad behavior on ghetto communities. This view limited Jewish resistance to armed resistance and classified any fulfilling of German demands, forced or not, as complicity or even collaboration.[18] The behavior of the Jewish Councils was defined as "the darkest chapter in the whole dark story," with Rumkowski as the archetype of the "evil" Jewish Council head.[19] Due to the forced submission of the ghetto inhabitants, scholars and survivors described the relationship between the inhabitants and the Councils as largely hostile.[20] In the late 1970s and 1980s, historians such as Isaiah Trunk and Jacob Robinson started to reevaluate the dilemma of the Jewish Councils to understand the motivations behind their actions.[21] They emphasized, in addition to forced cooperation, how the Councils tried to respond to the daily needs of the ghetto inhabitants by providing communal institutions, food, and health care by making use of their limited and changing scopes of action. A scholarly reexamination of Rumkowski's authoritative rule as part of his survival strategy is only a recent development.[22] However, changing dynamics within the ghetto community and the complicated relationship between the ghetto inhabitants and the Jewish Council remain understudied.

The opening of the archives after 1991 in the former Soviet Bloc and a new interest in history from below allowed new innovative research on everyday life in the ghettos.[23] As part of the reevaluation of Jewish survival strategies, Yehuda Bauer used the term *amidah* (standing up) to classify any group action against German intentions as resistance. Referring to this definition and making use of the new archival material, scholars since the 1990s have interpreted a broad range of activities in ghettos, such as smuggling, educating children, and fulfilling spiritual needs, as acts of cultural resistance.[24] In line with this research, petition writing in the ghetto can be classified as collective and individual acts of resistance. However, these acts should be understood as more complex by putting emphasis on the individual motivations and patterns of behavior within the historical context of the ghetto.[25] Ghetto inhabitants themselves did not explicitly classify their writing as an act of resistance, but revealed a broad range of other, often ambivalent and pragmatic, motivations that have so far largely been ignored.

In the last two decades, scholars have increasingly researched ambiguous patterns of behavior among the persecuted that cannot clearly be classified as "morally good or bad." Holocaust survivor Primo Levi has located these actions and decisions in the "gray zone" by emphasizing the often-blurred distinction between victim and perpetrator.[26] While recent research has focused on internal dynamics and hierarchies among inmates of concentration camps, much remains to be done with regard to ghetto communities.[27] Two reasons can explain the relatively limited state of research. First, scholars have to have the relevant language skills to work with the primary sources. Second, scholars often still hesitate to question the long prevailing assumption that the common experience of the ghetto inhabitants of being classified as "Jewish" led without exception to a sense of solidarity.[28] This chapter addresses these shortcomings by stressing ambivalent patterns of behavior in the ghetto inhabitants' struggle for survival and calls for the introduction of the term "community of coercion" when researching ghetto communities. In contrast to the phrase "Jewish community,"[29] previously used in research on ghettos, this new term emphasizes the fact that the Germans forcibly established these communities according to their racial criteria.[30] The ghetto inmates did not necessarily all identify themselves as Jewish and constituted a highly heterogeneous community, forced to live together in narrow spaces under unbearable conditions. Acknowledging this factor enables us to understand patterns of behavior and dynamics not as "Jewish," a classification that is often linked to certain expectations and moral judgments, but as human behaviors and survival strategies in the light of an existence subject to arbitrary decisions, misery, and fear of death under German occupation during World War II.

By looking at the victims of Nazi persecution, the chapter makes an important contribution to understanding how the most vulnerable individuals used petitions to take action despite the fact that the Germans had deprived the writers of legal rights, tried to dehumanize them, and tried to force them to remain passive.

Petition Writing and the Jewish Council: Tradition, Rupture, and Institutionalization

Prewar Jewish Communities in Eastern Europe (*kehillot*) had a limited degree of autonomy over internal matters, including organizing welfare, religious education, and settling smaller disputes.[31] While members of these Communities turned toward non-Jewish legal, financial, and political institutions in other matters, they were used to bringing internal issues to the Jewish authorities. The Jewish Councils forcibly established by the Germans after 1939 differed drastically from these Communities. Their main task was to fulfill the German decrees. Yet, at the same time, the Jewish Council was the only institution officially representing the Jewish community and its interests.[32] Furthermore, the German functionaries often chose previous representatives of the Jewish Community to take over key roles in the newly set-up Councils.[33] It is therefore not surprising that Jews continued to address the Council with petitions, especially when their need to express suffering and concerns was urgent as never before. And, rather than only harshly judging the Councils, writers also accepted their social authority.[34] In the initial occupation period, Jewish writers also wrote petitions to the German occupiers.[35] This practice can be understood as stemming from an impulse to address the overall official authorities as they had done prior to the war. Furthermore, it shows that the writers did not yet understand their individual experiences as embedded in the occupiers' more ideological and systemic policy. In the early phase, the writers still hoped to claim individual interests in the light of the brutality and arbitrariness they experienced.

In November 1940, the Germans forced the 63-year-old Rumkowski to take the role of the Jewish Council head. Prior to the war, Rumkowski had been working as an insurance agent and entrepreneur in Łódź's textile industry. As a member of the prewar Jewish Council and cofounder of a Jewish orphanage, he had been involved in Jewish public affairs.[36] From the beginning, Rumkowski pursued a strategy of complying with German orders and fulfilling German demands in the hope of securing the survival of the ghetto community. This strategy entailed keeping the community calm in light of the ever-changing German demands.[37] These changes had severe consequences for Rumkowski's survival strategy and the Łódź ghetto. In the early period of the establishment, the Germans forced the Jewish Council to hand over alleged valuables belonging to ghetto inmates and insisted that the Council members keep the ghetto calm.[38] When the Germans realized from early summer 1940 onward that the actual number of valuables in the ghetto was limited, Rumkowski offered to provide a Jewish labor force. For this purpose, he set up an internal work sphere in the ghetto with factories and departments to produce textiles for the German army.[39] Beginning in 1941, he also provided the German ghetto administration with ghetto inhabitants to work in camps outside the ghetto.[40] By doing this, Rumkowski tried to make the ghetto productive, hoping that this would ensure the survival of the inhabitants. This became known as the "rescue through work" strategy. Despite his efforts, Rumkowski was unable to convince the Germans that the ghetto inhabitants were an indispensable labor force.[41] From December 1941 onward, German ghetto administration head Biebow forced the Jewish Council to deliver ghetto inhabitants for deportation.[42] It was only from May 1942 onward that Rumkowski knew the deportees were being murdered in extermination camps.[43] Despite this knowledge, he continued fulfilling German demands in the hope of saving at least part of the community.[44] He first delivered those that he classified as endangering the survival of the ghetto community: the inhabitants who were unable to work and the "criminals."[45]

It is likely that Rumkowski set up the secretariat for petitions in October 1940 to deal with an increasing number of petitions written by ghetto inhabitants. In May 1941, the editor of the internal *Geto-Tsaytung* Szmul Rozenstajn commented on the function of the new institution in his newspaper: "It is, so to speak, the direct mediator between the ghetto population and the Praeses [the Jewish Council head], who is not able to get in touch directly with the crowd that wants to have a word with him."[46]

Rozenstajn does not explicitly mention the circumstances created by the Germans. Instead, the institution aimed at regulating the communication and the relationship between the Jewish Council head and the ordinary ghetto inhabitants. It allowed the Jewish Council head to appease inhabitants by offering a way to express concerns after the Germans had deprived them of opportunities to do so and of any legal rights.[47] It was thus an attempt to create a degree of normality and stability in a context defined by arbitrariness, brutality and constant uncertainty.

In the following months, the Jewish Council head publicized and anchored the institution and its function within the ghetto community. Rumkowski clarified the purpose of the secretariat in a number of proclamations and requested that the ghetto inhabitants make use of it. Rumkowski announced in March 1941 that letters would be answered within three weeks; otherwise the request could be regarded as declined.[48] On 2 May 1941, he proclaimed: "I explain categorically that from today on, I will not accept any more personal requests . . . Therefore I ask you to let me work in peace. Disturbances will not bring you any merits and will only bring harm for me."[49]

On 11 March 1944, a writer noted in the ghetto chronicle that Rumkowski had dissolved the main secretariat to make use of the personnel in the internal work sphere. The secretariat's personnel had been working until a few months before the Germans murdered almost all the ghetto inhabitants and dissolved the ghetto in August 1944. This suggests that up to the end, it fulfilled an important function within the ghetto community. While various languages were used in the ghetto, it is noticeable that the majority wrote petitions in Polish and German. This remained true even when German was not the writers' first language, resulting in spelling mistakes and words derived from Yiddish. In doing so, the petitioners tried to conform to the official languages used by the internal ghetto administration, probably hoping that this would positively influence the personnel's decisions.[50] The authors usually signed the letters and added their ghetto addresses to make sure that Rumkowski's replies would reach them.

On 2 May 1941, the *Geto-Tsaytung* reported that the secretariat had received 20,000 work offers and 6,700 petitions within the past six months.[51] In most cases, surviving sources do not explicitly reveal the outcome of petitions. Entries of the letters received were recorded, but not the decisions made.[52] On the letters, the personnel added a stamp with a note showing that it took them approximately two weeks to deal with the letters. Furthermore, the personnel classified the letters by adding content-related keywords. The comprehensive classification, filing, and answering of the petitionary letters can be understood as a practice that allowed the Jewish Council head to consolidate his power in the emerging ghetto administration.

Despite the missing information on the outcome of the queries, the preserved petitionary letters allow some conclusions to be drawn on the success of requests by identifying common topics, patterns, and phrases. It is likely that ghetto inhabitants discussed the content, phrasing, successes, and failures of their petitionary letters, since multiple letters used the same phrasing. For example, the brothers Abraham and Szyje Bankier, living at different addresses, used almost exactly the same letters in June 1940 to ask for work after they had lost their previous jobs as house guards.[53] The use of common phrases and expressions of concern in numerous petitions over a long time suggests that earlier letters had, to some extent, been successful. It is likely that ghetto inhabitants were motivated to submit requests, if they knew that Rumkowski had previously decided on similar issues in a positive way.

From Queries to Petitionary Letters and Complaints: Work, Financial Support, and Land

On 26 March 1940, shortly before the ghetto was finally sealed, Jakob Biegeleisen made the following request:

> To the highborn, the eldest of the Jews of the city of Łódź. With regards to the fact that a branch of the Łódź power station has been set up in the designated living area for the Jews of the city of Łódź, I have addressed the head of the branch, Mr. Weinbug, in person lately, in order to apply for a suitable position. However, Mr. Weinbug replied that he was not in charge and directed me to your Excellency as the Eldest of the Jews, who is the only one in charge of employing accountants.[54]

Biegeleisen's letter shows that he did not know to whom to address his query. The new Jewish Council's responsibilities had not yet been communicated. The need to find work in the new community of coercion was crucial in order to cover basic living costs. Similar letters were written by the thousand asking for the allocation of professions, while referencing previous work experience.[55] The forced relocation represented a drastic rupture with their previous lives. People had lost most of their belongings and found themselves in urgent need of new work to secure their livelihood. Their petitions expressed the extent to which German orders had created new needs and miseries. Furthermore, petitions in general show what the writers thought the authorities could decide in their favor.[56] In the context of the ghetto, the petitionary letters give insights into how the ghetto inhabitants addressed and perceived the Jewish Council's capabilities.

In 1940 and 1941, hundreds of letters also asked for certificates issued by the Jewish Council that would allow inhabitants to receive money from relatives outside the ghetto. On 4 December 1940, Ruda Brucha Brajbard wrote a letter to Rumkowski requesting that he issue a certificate of poverty, in order to receive support from her husband. He had stayed for a year in Białystok, while she had been resettled with her two-year-old child.[57]

Ruda Brajbard's experience was not unique. After September 1939, the Germans forced family members to move to different regions, while many Jewish people fled to other parts of the country.[58] What followed was a complex internal procedure that shows how Rumkowski expanded the ghetto administration and its regulations during the first year of the ghetto's existence. A Jewish Council inspector visited Ruda Brajbard twelve days after her letter to confirm her living conditions.[59] Following the inspection, she was issued a certificate, to be presented at the internal bank, which allowed her to have money transferred to the ghetto.[60] This is just one of hundreds of examples of this process during 1940 and 1941.[61]

Initially, the ghetto inhabitants addressed the Jewish Council as the intermediary instance, in the hope that Rumkowski could temper their needs, and in doing so indicated that they did not identify him as directly responsible for their miseries. However, the longer the ghetto existed and the more Rumkowski expanded its internal institutions and regulations, the more ghetto inhabitants identified Rumkowski, and not the Germans, as responsible for their problems. The letters increasingly took on the character of petitions or even supplications.

An early expression of this development dates from the summer of 1940, when numerous ghetto inhabitants wrote letters in response to Rumkowski's 18 June 1940 order to reduce the posts of the house guards.[62] Three months earlier, in preparation for the sealing of the ghetto, Rumkowski had established house guards who were responsible for organizing internal ghetto affairs at the level of the houses, such as cleaning, the allocation of food rations and soup kitchens.[63] In June 1940, seventy ghetto inhabitants signed and sent a petitionary letter in Polish to the Jewish Council head:

> After the summoning, we have fulfilled our duties during 14–15 hours under very difficult circumstances. During this time, there were approximately 300 men enlisted as house guards, a number that has now been reduced by orders of the esteemed Mr. Praeses. We are among those whose jobs have been made redundant. For this reason, we address the esteemed Mr. Praeses with the warm petition to show sympathy for the fate of a number of men, who are facing the consequences of the reduction of the house guards. Good work will not put us off, we just do not want to live at the expense of the community.[64]

Shortly after the dissolution, former house guards sent at least seventy-eight letters.[65] Similar phrases were employed repeatedly as the writers reminded Rumkowski of his responsibility for their situation and asked him to allocate new jobs.[66]

In the second half of 1940, the Jewish Council realized that despite their provisional status, ghettos were likely to exist for the time being. It is against this background and the need to regulate everyday life that Rumkowski expanded the ghetto's internal administration.[67] In response, more letters emerged complaining about specific internal problems. This shows that the ghetto community perceived the establishment of a specific institution dealing with petitions as a signal that their needs and concerns would potentially be heard. In addition, it suggests that the ghetto inhabitants believed at this point that the Jewish Council had room to maneuver in improving their living conditions under German occupation. They wrote both individually and collectively when facing similar problems. On 7 March 1941, Mr. Friedmann addressed the secretariat of the Jewish Council in a letter signed by six others, complaining that Rumkowski had confiscated their land and had promised compensation that had never been paid.[68]

In choosing specific phrases, the writers expressed the ambivalence they faced in writing to the Jewish Council head. On the one hand, they often voiced harsh criticism in making the Jewish Council head responsible for the severe conditions, misery, and even deaths in the ghetto. On the other hand, bereft of legal rights, Rumkowski was the only authority they could address with their desperate queries. This is evident in the use of formal language. In their salutations, writers praised Rumkowski as "highborn," "your Excellency," or "highly esteemed elder of the Jews."[69] The literary style expressed both the authors' dependency on being heard by the Council, and how they perceived Rumkowski and his authoritative role, in which he presented himself as the "savior" and, as some inhabitants put it, even "king" of the ghetto.[70]

To understand why ghetto inhabitants wrote petitions collectively, several reasons have to be taken into account. Not everyone was literate. Offering writing skills to people with similar concerns was an act of solidarity in some cases. Collective letters also highlight how ghetto inhabitants talked to one another about their concerns. They probably exchanged experiences with regard to writing petitionary letters and strategies to make them effective. Ultimately, writing as a group was a way to save paper. This factor became especially significant, as by the end of 1941, the ghetto chronicle was frequently noting the severe lack of paper in the ghetto.[71]

Writers Pleading for Justice: New and Old Definitions of Morality

Ghetto inhabitants wrote to express urgent concerns in light of the drastic changes and ruptures they faced. They formulated explicit and implicit notions of what they perceived as injustices in the new community of coercion. On 18 July 1941, Mordka Wajngot complained that he had been arrested by mistake and sentenced to imprisonment for two months. He claimed another ghetto inhabitant had accused him of stealing potatoes in order to avoid punishment for his own offense.[72] In this case, the Germans were not directly responsible for this incident. Wajngot had been arrested by the Jewish police and was imprisoned in the ghetto prison, set up by the Jewish Council.[73] Wajngot was criticizing Rumkowski's ghetto regulations and institutions.

After the ghetto was sealed, the Jewish Council head formulated new rules and definitions of criminal offenses that were enforced through internal legal institutions. Among them were offenses that resulted directly from German orders such as smuggling, but new offenses such as the illegal production of sweets and the spreading of rumors were also included. In line with Rumkowski's strategy, the latter were aimed at preventing individual behavior that posed a danger for the ghetto community.[74] For instance, Rumkowski feared that the illegal production of sweets under unhygienic conditions could lead to epidemics, triggering the liquidation of the ghetto by the Germans. In democratic societies, legal norms usually originate in the moral norms shared by the majority of their members; however, this was not the case in the ghetto. While the Jewish Council's definitions of "criminal" activities were part of a collective survival strategy, the same acts represented individual survival strategies for the ghetto inhabitants. They had their own perceptions of what was right and wrong, often anchored in the norms they were used to from the prewar period.[75] In their letters, the writers expressed their anger about the new regulations and the resulting persecution by the Jewish Council.

In many instances, women wrote petitions, especially in cases of injustice or interned family members. In May 1943, fourteen-year-old Fela Łomska asked for her sister to be released from the central ghetto prison that the Jewish Council administered. She claimed that her sister was the victim of a mix-up. When her sister had tried to collect food rations, a man attempted to steal potatoes. When the police arrived, he had escaped and the sister was arrested in his place.[76]

Many letters by female writers described a need for financial aid.[77] This shows that although women were integrated into the internal work sphere, they were nonetheless often dependent on male family members. Another reason for the high number of female petitioners is that based on the experience of other petition writers, concerns were supposedly heard, if the writers were female and pleading for their children. This strategy may have been a response to Rumkowski's self-presentation as the father and protector of children in his public speeches.[78]

Many petitions were formulated by mothers and wives trying to get their children or husbands released from prison.[79] These can be read as attempts to claim criteria of justice and notions of morality that differed from the Jewish Council's new norms. It is notable that in most of the cases the authors did not know why their family members had been arrested, as they were not used to these new, ever-changing norms.[80]

Scholars have noted that the percentage of male petition writers usually significantly exceeds the number of female writers.[81] This is only partly true for the ghetto. From the beginning, women addressed the Jewish Council head in significant numbers.[82] Two reasons have to be considered. In general, scholars have observed that petitions addressing welfare concerns were more likely to be written by women.[83] In ghetto petitions, such concerns were among the most often expressed. Furthermore, the German occupation enforced the redefinition of gender roles among the ghetto inhabitants, particularly as families were torn apart, for example, when the Germans forced the men to work in labor camps.[84] The pressure to work according to Rumkowski's strategy forced women to undertake tasks traditionally associated with male family members, and thus to assume responsibility in the struggle for survival of their families by writing petitionary letters.

Writers tried to enforce their individual interests by denouncing others and referring to the collective good as propagated by Rumkowski. Here, their individual interests and Rumkowski's interests in enforcing his survival strategy overlapped. The motivations behind denouncing other ghetto inhabitants were diverse. Some wanted the Jewish Council to punish "unjust" and "morally wrong" behavior or were hoping for compensation. Other cases were attempts to take revenge for personal conflicts and disputes.[85] In these cases, the ghetto inhabitants made pragmatic use of internal institutions to enforce their individual interests.

Despair and Pleading: Petitions in Times of Deportation

During 1942, the way in which some writers addressed Rumkowski and their concerns changed drastically. "Dear Mr. Praeses, have mercy on me! Until now you have not left me! . . . I ask you, if possible, to protect me from the expulsion and not to disrupt my remaining sad existence,"[86] wrote the 62-year-old G. Rawicz on 25 February 1942. On that day, Rawicz had received an order from the Jewish Council, informing her that she would be expelled from the ghetto. At this point, neither the ghetto inhabitants nor Rumkowski knew what "expulsion" meant.[87] The Sonderkommando Lange had been murdering deported ghetto inhabitants in the nearby extermination site of Kulmhof/Chełmno since December 1941. Yet, Biebow had told Rumkowski that twenty thousand ghetto inhabitants would have to leave the ghetto due to supply problems and would be provided with food in nearby villages. He asked Rumkowski to select the ghetto inhabitants for these relocations. Hoping to prevent the Germans from choosing arbitrarily, the Jewish Council head set up a commission on 5 January

1942, first selecting inhabitants that were "unfit for work."[88] Rawicz knew that it had become crucial to remain in the ghetto, but she was scared to be separated from her two children after her husband's death.[89] She wrote to the "only savior in this hour of need" that she was desperate to find work in handicraft, but due to her "age of 62 it seems as if no one wanted me."[90]

Following orders of expulsion in February and March 1942, other ghetto inhabitants wrote similar letters, employing a language of despair when pleading to Rumkowski to exempt them.[91] However, they knew that the Jewish Council had a limited scope of action. The 1942 German deportations meant a rupture in the relationship between the Jewish Council and the ghetto inhabitants. Prior to that, Rumkowski had propagated his "rescue through work" strategy. This strategy went hand in hand with attempts to suppress any stirring protest and underground resistance.[92] From July 1942 onward, the ghetto inhabitants knew that deportees would be murdered in the German extermination sites.[93] Correspondingly, their requests became increasingly urgent and desperate.

In September 1942, Lajzner Kuczyński typed a letter in Polish, explaining that his daughter Pesse-Sara was not born on 15 January 1933, but on 30 December 1932, because her parents had only been able to travel to Bydgoszcz to register the newborn two weeks after her birth.[94] At the end of August, the Reich Security Main Office (Reichssicherheitshauptamt) had ordered the deportation of twenty thousand ghetto inhabitants, including everyone under ten, over sixty-five, the sick, and those without work, to Kulmhof.[95] Thus, on 4 September 1942, Rumkowski asked the ghetto inhabitants to give away their children under the age of ten for the upcoming deportations.[96] The writer's desperate aim was to prove that his daughter was almost ten years old, pleading that she would not be "expelled."[97]

In 1942, the Gestapo deported more than seventy thousand ghetto inhabitants to Kulmhof. After the so-called *Sperre* of early September, only ninety thousand inhabitants remained in the ghetto.[98] Some petitions pleading for family members to be spared the deportations exist, but the number of these letters is comparatively small from 1942 onward. This is partly due to the reduced number of ghetto inhabitants and partly because the remainder stopped believing that the Jewish Council could respond to their individual needs.

However, thanks to Rumkowski's "rescue through work" strategy, labor continued to play a key role in petitions. In addition to the main secretariat, the Jewish Council head even set up petitionary institutions at every work department from August 1942 onward.[99] This was probably a response to an increasing number of work-related petitions, which in turn reflected the crucial role of work as a survival strategy. Those without work were the first to be deported. From 1943 on, petitions increasingly came from the supervisors of ghetto workshops, requesting medical care for specific employees. The supervisors informed the Jewish Council head about poor health conditions that could impact on the production process.[100]

The need to work had initially been a matter of individual and family survival. In 1942, work became crucial for the survival of the whole ghetto community. However, by 1943 Rumkowski had realized that the ghetto's productivity would not prevent the Germans from murdering the Jewish population. He now played for time in the hope that a victorious Red Army would arrive and end German occupation.

Conclusion

In examining the Łódź ghetto petitions, this chapter makes several contributions to scholarly debates. First, it shows that Jewish reactions to Nazi persecution and ghettoization were far from passive, but multilayered, flexible, and proactive. This was true for the Jewish Council head Rumkowski, who developed a collective, evolving strategy for survival, hoping that fulfilling German demands would prevent the occupiers from persecuting and, later, murdering the ghetto community. To this end, Rumkowski's establishment of the secretariat for petitions and complaints played a crucial role. Isaiah Trunk's influential 1981 essay asks the pressing question: "Why was there no armed resistance to the Nazis in the Lodz ghetto?"[101] He points to the strict sealing of the ghetto from the outside world and the ghetto's relative calm in 1943, when armed ghetto uprisings took place within other ghettos such as Warsaw. However, he does not link these observations to the survival strategy of the Jewish Council head.

This chapter has shown that Rumkowski's establishment of an institution that addressed needs and criticisms was in line with his overall strategy of appeasement. For Rumkowski, petitions allowed for an avenue of communication, in which anger and frustration could be safely expressed. Furthermore, his comprehensive administrative procedures allowed him to gather knowledge of the ghetto's atmosphere and to exert power over its inmates. These procedures can also be seen as part of an attempt to temper the miseries of the ghetto inhabitants. However, it eventually became tragically clear that Rumkowski had only limited room to maneuver in light of German coercion.

Second, analyzing the petitions leads to rethinking the allegedly hostile relationship between ghetto inhabitants and the Jewish Council by emphasizing a more dynamic approach. For pragmatic reasons, ghetto inhabitants made use of the Jewish Council's institutions, trying to enforce their individual concerns and interests where possible. They wrote petitions, trying to remedy the harsh living conditions by finding work and freeing family members. They created networks and exchanged knowledge on how to address the Jewish Council head. They helped other ghetto inhabitants in writing such letters and wrote collectively when sharing concerns. However, they also composed letters informing the Jewish Council about the "incorrect behavior" of others, highlighted what they perceived as "unjust," or wanted to take revenge for internal conflicts and disputes. The petitions contradict the long prevailing assumption that the common experiences of being classified as "Jewish" necessarily led to a sense of solidarity among the ghetto inhabitants.

The chapter therefore argues for an integration of ambivalent patterns of behavior into the history of the ghetto communities and, ultimately, Holocaust historiography. If we acknowledge these communities as communities of coercion, in which humans faced hunger, disease, fear of death, in cramped spaces, it is hardly surprising that their actions covered the whole range of human behavior: not only acts of solidarity, but revenge, envy, and egoism. The petitions were an expression of the inmates' limited ability to have their voices heard. The evidence mustered here leads to a broadening of our understanding of Jewish behavior and resistance in light of German persecution and murder.

Finally, the analysis contributes to an understanding of petition writing in a broader historical perspective. The ghetto inmates could be seen as emblematic of the passive individual. The research undertaken has shown that, despite their limited scope of action, the ghetto inhabitants made extensive and active use of petitions. Researching their petitions allows for the reintegration of their voices, their concerns, and fears into the historiography. However, those who were unable to write or had given up hope cannot be integrated. Petition writing was a practice that the ghetto inhabitants made use of during an emergency situation and struggle for survival. The decisions taken, the individual and collective strategies of survival and the patterns of behavior developed were diverse, dynamic, and ambivalent. Trying to understand these in their full complexity will allow for new insights into the ghetto communities as communities of coercion. This approach will facilitate comparison with other coerced communities such as those in concentration camps in order to explore patterns of human behavior at the edge of human existence.

Svenja Bethke is Associate Professor of Modern European History and Director of the Stanley Burton Centre for Holocaust and Genocide Studies at the University of Leicester. She is the author of *Dance of the Razor's Edge: Crime and Punishment in the Nazi Ghettos* (2021). For her current book project "Between Diaspora and the 'Land of Israel': Jewish Dress, Migration and Belonging, 1880s–1948," she was awarded a prestigious Marie Skłodowska-Curie Fellowship by The European Commission, hosted at the Avraham Harman Institute of Contemporary Jewry at the Hebrew University in Jerusalem from 2019–2021, and received an AHRC Research, Development and Engagement Fellowship (2023–2025).

Notes

For their comments and suggestions I am especially grateful to Roey Sweet, Richard Butler, Paul Moore, Sarah Goldsmith, Lauren Parsons, and the editors of this volume. I also thank Andrea Löw and Peter Klein for their kind advice.

1. Archiwum Państwowe w Łodzi (hereafter APŁ), Przełożony Starszeństwa Żydów w Getcie Łódzkim (PSŻ), 37/278/0, Sekretariat Próśb i Zażaleń (Secretariat for Petitions and Complaints). Unless otherwise specified, the translations of the letters from German, Polish, and Yiddish have been made by the author.
2. Dan Michman, *The Emergence of Ghettos during the Holocaust* (Cambridge, 2011); Dan Michman, "Why Did Heydrich Write the Schnellbrief? A Remark on the Reason and on Its Significance," *Yad Vashem Studies* 32 (2004): 433–47.
3. For a summary of this core debate, see Dan Stone, *Histories of the Holocaust* (Oxford, 2010), 64–112.
4. Peter Klein, *Die Gettoverwaltung Litzmannstadt 1940 bis 1944: Eine Dienststelle im Spannungsfeld von Kommunalbürokratie und staatlicher Verfolgungspolitik* (Hamburg, 2009), 25–26, 53–61; Michael Alberti, *Die Verfolgung und Vernichtung der Juden im Reichsgau Wartheland 1939–1945* (Wiesbaden, 2006), 148–92.
5. APŁ, PSŻ, 278/1076. *Geto Tsaytung*, No. 9, 2 May 1941, p. 3. For the procedures, see also Monika Polit, *"Moja żydowska dusza nie obawia się dnia sądu": Mordechaj Chaim Rumkowski. Prawda i zmyślenie* (Warsaw, 2012), 137–39.
6. Israeli President Zalman Shazar, quoted by Jacob Robinson, *Discontinuity or Continuity in Community Councils during the Nazi Era* [in Hebrew] (Jerusalem, 1967), 35. See also Salomon F. Bloom, "Dictator of the Lodz Ghetto: The Strange History of Mordechai Chaim Rumkowski," *Commentary* 7 (1949): 111–22; Philipp Friedman, "Pseudo-Saviors in the Polish Ghettos: Mordechai Chaim Rumkowski of Lodz," in *Roads to Extinction: Essays on the Holocaust*, ed. idem (New York, 1980), 333–52.
7. Michal Unger, *Reassessment of the Image of Mordechai Chaim Rumkowski* (Jerusalem, 2004), 7–9.
8. Crucial in this debate: Isaiah Trunk, *Judenrat: The Jewish Councils in Eastern Europe under Nazi Occupation* (New York, 1972), Isaiah Trunk, *Łódź Ghetto: A History*, ed. Robert M. Shapiro (Bloomington, 2006); Jacob Robinson, *And the Crooked Shall Be Made Straight: The Eichmann Trial, the Jewish Catastrophe, and Hannah Arendt's Narrative* (New York, 1965).
9. Andrea Löw, *Juden im Getto Litzmannstadt: Lebensbedingungen, Selbstwahrnehmung, Verhalten* (Göttingen, 2013), 55–56.
10. Ibid., 224; Julian Baranowski, *The Łódź Ghetto 1940–1944: Vademecum = Łódzkie getto 1940–1944*, (Łódź, 2003), 120.

11. Michal Unger, "Łódź," in *The Yad Vashem Encyclopedia of the Ghettos during the Holocaust*, ed. Guy Miron et al. (Jerusalem, 2009), 409.
12. On the research on petitions, see the introduction to this volume, pp. 4–7.
13. For an exception, see Polit, *Moja żydowska dusza*, 137–44; also Danuta Dąbrowska, "O projektach poprawy sitaucji ludności w getcie łódskim (Wnioski miesckańców getta z lat 1940–1942)," *Biuletyn Żydowskiego Instytutu Historycznego* 38 (1961): 118–27.
14. For petitions in much smaller numbers from the Warsaw and Vilna ghettos, see Svenja Bethke, *Tanz auf Messers Schneide: Kriminalität und Recht in den Ghetto Warschau, Litzmannstadt und Wilna* (Hamburg, 2015), 267–82.
15. Sascha Feuchert, "Die Getto-Chronik: Entstehung und Überlieferung. Eine Projektskizze," in *Die Chronik des Getto Lodz/Litzmannstadt, Supplemente und Anhang, vol. 5*, ed. Sascha Feuchert (Göttingen, 2007), 167–90.
16. Unger, *Reassessment*; Bethke, *Tanz*, 77–83.
17. E.g., Raul Hilberg, *The Destruction of the European Jews*, vol. 3 (New York, 1985); Christopher Browning and Jürgen Matthäus. *Origins of the Final Solution: The Evolution of Nazi Jewish Policy, September 1939–March 1942* (Lincoln, NE, 2004); on the state of research, see Dan Michman, "The Emergence of Ghettos under the Nazis and Their Allies: The Reasons behind Their Emergence," in Miron et al., *Yad Vashem Encyclopedia*, xiii–xxxix. An important exception from the 1950s includes Samuel Gringauz, "The Ghetto as an Experiment of Jewish Social Organization (Three Years of Kovno Ghetto)," *Jewish Social Studies* 11 (1949): 3–20.
18. Hannah Arendt, *Eichmann in Jerusalem: A Report on the Banality of Evil* (New York, 1978); Hilberg, *Destruction*, 1037; on the debates, see Michael R. Marrus, "Jewish Resistance to the Holocaust," *Journal of Contemporary History* 30, no. 1 (1995): 83–110.
19. Arendt, *Eichmann in Jerusalem*, 117.
20. Samuel Gringauz stressed that the ghetto inhabitants accepted the Jewish Councils to a certain extent as the social authority. Gringauz, "Experiment," 11. See also Aharon Weiss, "The Relations between the Judenrat and the Jewish Police," in *Patterns of Jewish Leadership in Nazi Europe 1933–1945: Proceedings of the Third Yad Vashem International Historical Conference, Jerusalem, 4–7 April 1977*, ed. Yisrael Gutman and Cynthia J. Haft (Jerusalem, 1979), 201–18.
21. Trunk, *Judenrat*; Robinson, *And the Crooked*; Aharon Weiss, "Jewish Leadership in Occupied Poland: Postures and Attitudes," *Yad Vashem Studies* 12 (1977): 335–66. More recently Dan Michman, "Reevaluating the Emergence, Function, and Form of the Jewish Councils Phenomenon," in *Ghettos 1939–1945: New Research and Perspectives on Definition, Daily Life, and Survival. Symposium Presentations*, ed. Center for Advanced Holocaust Studies (Washington, DC, 2005), 67–84.
22. Unger, *Reassessment*; Richard Rubinstein, "Gray into Black: The Case of Mordecai Chaim Rumkowski," in *Gray Zones: Ambiguity and Compromise in the Holocaust and Its Aftermath*, ed. Jonathan Petropoulos and John K. Roth (New York, 2005), 299–310; Polit, *Moja żydowska dusza*; Bethke, *Tanz*.
23. E.g., for the Łódź ghetto: Löw, *Juden*; for the Warsaw ghetto: Barbara Engelking and Jacek Leociak, *The Warsaw Ghetto: A Guide to the Perished City* (New Haven, CT, 2009).
24. See Yehuda Bauer, "Forms of Jewish Resistance during the Holocaust," in *The Jewish Emergence from Powerlessness* (Toronto, 1979), 26–40; Carol Battrick, "Smuggling as a Form of Resistance in the Warsaw Ghetto," *British Journal of Holocaust Education* 4, no. 2 (1995): 199–224; Joseph Rudavsky, *To Live with Hope, to Die with Dignity: Spiritual Resistance in the Ghettos and Camps* (Northvale, NJ, 1997); Samuel D. Kassow, *Who Will Write Our History? Emanuel Ringelblum, the Warsaw Ghetto, and the Oyneg Shabes Archive* (Bloomington, 2007) and this volume's introduction, pp. 7–10.

25. For a similar approach, see Amos Goldberg, "The History of the Jews in the Ghettos: A Cultural Perspective," in *The Holocaust and Historical Methodology*, ed. Dan Stone (New York, 2012), 79–100.
26. Primo Levi, *The Drowned and the Saved* (New York, 1988), 48. See Petropoulos and Roth, *Gray Zones*.
27. E.g., Nikolaus Wachsmann, *KL: A History of the Nazi Concentration Camps* (London, 2015), chap. 10; Falk Pingel, "Social Life in an Unsocial Environment: The Inmates' Struggle for Survival," in *Concentration Camps in Nazi Germany: The New Histories*, ed. Nikolaus Wachsmann and Jane Caplan (London, 2009), 70–93.
28. See, e.g., Gringauz, "Experiment," 6–7; Goldberg, "History," 85.
29. For alternative terms, such as "Jewish community" and "Jewish ghetto," see Gringauz, "Experiment," 5, 11; Trunk, *Judenrat*, 44; Yisrael Gutman, "Ghetto," in *Encyclopaedia of the Holocaust*, ed. Yisrael Gutman et al. (New York, 1990), 2:579.
30. Use of similar terms, e.g., Wachsmann, *KL*; Hans Günther Adler, *Theresienstadt, 1941–1945: The Face of a Coerced Community* (New York, 2017); Löw, *Juden*; Anna Hájková, "Prisoner Society in the Terezín Ghetto, 1941–1945" (Ph.D. diss., University of Toronto, 2013).
31. Michael Stanislawski, "Kahal (*kehilah*)," in *The YIVO Encyclopedia of Jews in Eastern Europe*, ed. Gershon David Hundert (New Haven, CT, 2008), 845–48.
32. Gustavo Corni, *Hitler's Ghettos: Voices from a Beleaguered Society, 1939–1944* (London, 2002), 61–62.
33. Aharon Weiss, "Judenrat," in Gutman et al., *Encyclopedia of the Holocaust*, 2:762–71, 762; Corni, *Hitler's Ghettos*, 61.
34. Gringauz, "Experiment," 11.
35. Polit, *Moja żydowskaja dusza*, 177–83.
36. Löw, *Juden*, 72.
37. Dan Diner, "Beyond the Conceivable: The Judenrat as Borderline Experience," in *Beyond the Conceivable: Studies on Germany, Nazism and the Holocaust*" (Berkeley, CA, 2000), 125.
38. Bethke, *Tanz*, 77–83.
39. Löw, *Juden*, 116–24.
40. Klein, *Gettoverwaltung*, 296–324.
41. General considerations on this dilemma: e.g., Diner, "Beyond the Conceivable," 123.
42. Unger, "Łódź," 409.
43. Löw, *Juden*, 283, Baranowski, *The Łódź Ghetto*, 33.
44. Diner, "Beyond the Conceivable," 123–24.
45. Löw, *Juden*, 266–67.
46. APŁ, 278/1076, *Geto Tsaytung*, no. 9, 2 May 1941, 1.
47. Bethke, *Tanz*, 41–50, 273.
48. APŁ, 278/1076. *Geto Tsaytung*, no. 1, 7 March 1941, 3.
49. APŁ, 278/1076. *Geto Tsaytung*, no. 11–12, 30 May 1941, Proclamation no. 175.
50. Petitioners frequently mentioned these skills. E.g., APŁ, PSŻ, L 18818, 27 Juli 1940, 8; 18821, Jetty Mandelbaum, June 1940, 4.
51. APŁ, 278/1076. *Geto Tsaytung*, No. 9, 2 May 1941, 3.
52. APŁ, PSŻ, L 18817.
53. APŁ, PSŻ, L 18818, 12–13.
54. APŁ, PSŻ, L 18819, 26 March 1940, 1.
55. APŁ, PSŻ, L 18819–18855.
56. Lex Heerma van Voss, *Petitions in Social History* (Cambridge, 2002), 6.
57. APŁ, PSŻ, L 18775, 4 December 1940, 1.

58. Löw, *Juden*, 81–84.
59. APŁ, PSŻ, L 18775, 16 December 1940, 2.
60. Ibid., 3.
61. E.g., APŁ, PSŻ, L 18775, Efraim Szlessera, 2 December 1940, 6–8; Szmuel Zaleberg, 20 December 1940, 15; Chaim Grajwer, December 1940, 97; Mindla Gertler, 6 February 1941, 106; Jakob Sałat, 2 March 1941, 112–13; Gitla Lipszyc, 21 January 1941, 116–17.
62. APŁ, PSŻ, L 18818.
63. Archives of the Jewish Historical Institute, Warsaw (hereafter ŻIH), RG 205/219, Rumkowski's proclamation no. 7 on the establishment, 26 March 1940, 20.
64. APŁ, PSŻ, L 18818, June 1940 (no exact date, but referring to 18 June), 4.
65. Number of letters preserved in PSŻ, L 18818.
66. E.g., APŁ, PSŻ, L 18818, 27 July 1940, 8; Jozef Majer, 27 June 1940, 9; Henryk Pfefer, 27 June 1940, 14; Szylem Pomerane, 27 June 1940, 30; Salomon Rogowski, 26 June 1940, 41; J. Migolałowiez, 27 June 1940, 73.
67. Löw, *Juden*, 97–223.
68. United States Holocaust Memorial Museum Archives, Washington, DC (hereafter USHMMA), RG 15.083M, 91/275, 5 March 1941, received 7 March 1941, 21.
69. E.g., APŁ, PSŻ, L 18818, Abram Bankier, 12; APŁ, PSŻ, L 18819, Jakob Biegeleisen, 1; APŁ, PSŻ, L 18820, Regina Friedman, 28 October 1940, 3–5.
70. Unger, *Reassessment*, 7–9; Polit, *Moja żydowska dusza*, chap. 1, 11–53.
71. Feuchert, *Chronik 1941*, 16 December 1941, 306; Feuchert, *Chronik 1942*, 11 June 1942, 291.
72. USHMMA, RG 15.083, 93/283, 5 February 1943, 18–19.
73. Ibid.
74. Bethke, *Tanz*, 293–294; Svenja Bethke, "Crime and Punishment in Emergency Situations: The Jewish Ghetto Courts in Warsaw, Lodz and Vilna in WW II — A Comparative Study," *Dapim: Studies on the Holocaust* 28, no. 3 (2014): 173–89.
75. Bethke, *Tanz*.
76. USHMMA, RG-15.083M, 91/283, 17 May 1943, 10.
77. E.g., USHMMA, RG 15.083, 38/118, Golda Frajndlich, 12 May 1941, 229–30.
78. See e.g., Rumkowski's speeches in Feuchert, *Chronik 1941*, 1 February 41, 55–56 and 30 August 1941, 214; Feuchert, *Chronik 1942*, 3 January 1942, 27, 39.
79. E.g., USHMMA, RG 15.083, 93/283, 14 August 1943, 4; RG 15.083, 93/283, 12 February 1941, 79; USHMMA, RG 15.083, 93/283, 7 February 1943, 22; USHMMA, RG 15.083, 93/283, 22 February 1941, 76–78.; USHMMA, RG 15.083, 93/283, 19 February 1941, 87; USHMMA, RG 15.083, 93/283, 7 February 1941, 93–94; ŻIH, RG 205/282, 15 August 1941, 76.
80. E.g., USHMMA, RG 15.083, 93/283, Chaja Faiflowiak, 23 February 1941, 90–92.
81. Voss, *Petitions*, 10.
82. The percentage of female writers ranged from approximately 25 up to 60 percent.
83. Voss, *Petitions*, 10.
84. E.g., Dalia Ofer and Lenore J. Weitzman, eds., *Women in the Holocaust* (New Haven, CT, 1998), 8–12.
85. USHMMA, RG 15.083, 93/283, Chaja Faiflowiak, 23 February 1941, 90–92; APŁ, PSŻ, L 18909, Chil Rosenzweig, 7 March 1941, 12.
86. APŁ, PSŻ, L18904, 25 February 1942, 38.
87. Feuchert, *Chronik 1942*, February 1942, 128; Löw, *Juden*, 269.
88. Löw, *Juden*, 264–66.
89. APŁ, PSŻ, L18904, 25 February 1942, 38.
90. Ibid.

91. APŁ, PSŻ, L18904, Mindla Krzepicka, 25 February 1942, 40; Ryfka Kowalska, 19 February 1942, 43; Rifka Kleinbaum, 20 February 1942, 50–51; Hersz Mendel Rozencweig, 25 February 1942, 52; U. Rawiez, 10 March 1942, 66; Fraja Marja Gepner, 14 March 1942, 67.
92. Löw, *Juden*, 328–49.
93. E.g., Oskar Rosenfeld, *Wozu noch Welt: Aufzeichnungen aus dem Getto Lodz*, ed. Hanno Loewy (Frankfurt am Main, 1994), 136; Dawid Sierakowiak, *Das Ghettotagebuch des Dawid Sierakowiak: Aufzeichnungen eines Siebzehnjährigen, 1941/42*, ed. Roswitha Matwin-Buschmann (Leipzig, 1993), 158 (17 August 1942); Löw, *Juden*, 284.
94. APŁ, PSŻ, L18904, [September] 1942, exact date illegible, 91. For the complete petition, see this volume's appendix, pp. 233–35.
95. Löw, *Juden*, 292.
96. Speech in Yitzhak Arad et al., eds., *Documents on the Holocaust: Selected Sources on the Destruction of the Jews of Germany and Austria, Poland, and the Soviet Union* (Amsterdam, 2014), 283–84; Löw, *Juden*, 296.
97. APŁ, PSŻ, L18904, [September] 1942, exact date illegible, 91.
98. Löw, *Juden*, 292.
99. ŻIH, RG 205/288, 20 August 1942, 1; Bethke, *Tanz*, 267.
100. APŁ, PSŻ, L 18816, n.d. (but in this collection mainly 1943), 4; supervisor of workshop no. 61, 3 April 1943, 5; 19 March 1943, 7; 12 June 1943, 11.
101. Isaiah Trunk, "Note: Why Was There No Armed Resistance against the Nazis in the Lodz Ghetto?" *Jewish Social Studies* 43, no. 3/4 (1981): 329–34.

Bibliography

Adler, Hans Günther. *Theresienstadt, 1941–1945: The Face of a Coerced Community*. New York: Cambridge University Press, 2017.
Alberti, Michael. *Die Verfolgung und Vernichtung der Juden im Reichsgau Wartheland 1939–1945*. Wiesbaden: Harrassowitz, 2006.
Arad, Yitzhak, Israel Gutman, and Avraham Margaliot, eds. *Documents on the Holocaust: Selected Sources on the Destruction of the Jews of Germany and Austria, Poland, and the Soviet Union*. Amsterdam: Elsevier Science, 2014.
Arendt, Hannah. *Eichmann in Jerusalem: A Report on the Banality of Evil*. New York: Penguin, 1978.
Baranowski, Julian. *The Łódź Ghetto 1940–1944: Vademecum = Łódzkie getto 1940–1944*. Lodz: Archiwum Państwowe, 2003.
Battrick, Carol. "Smuggling as a Form of Resistance in the Warsaw Ghetto." *British Journal of Holocaust Education* 4, no. 2 (1995): 199–224.
Bauer, Yehuda. "Forms of Jewish Resistance during the Holocaust." In *The Jewish Emergence from Powerlessness*, 26–40. Toronto: University of Toronto Press, 1979.
Bethke, Svenja. "Crime and Punishment in Emergency Situations: The Jewish Ghetto Courts in Warsaw, Lodz and Vilna in WW II—A Comparative Study." *Dapim: Studies on the Holocaust* 28, no. 3 (2014): 173–89.
_____. *Tanz auf Messers Schneide: Kriminalität und Recht in den Ghetto Warschau, Litzmannstadt und Wilna*. Hamburg: Hamburger Edition, 2015.

Bloom, Solomon F. "Dictator of the Lodz Ghetto: The Strange History of Mordechai Chaim Rumkowski." *Commentary* 7 (1949): 111–22.
Browning, Christopher, and Jürgen Matthäus. *Origins of the Final Solution: The Evolution of Nazi Jewish Policy, September 1939–March 1942*. Lincoln: University of Nebraska Press, 2004.
Corni, Gustavo. *Hitler's Ghettos: Voices from a Beleaguered Society, 1939–1944*. London: Arnold, 2002.
Dąbrowska, Danuta. "O projektach poprawy situaciji ludności w getcie łódskim (Wnioski miesckańców getta z lat 1940–1942)." *Biuletyn Żydowskiego Instytutu Historycznego* 38 (1961): 118–27.
Diner, Dan. "Beyond the Conceivable: The Judenrat as Borderline Experience." In *Beyond the Conceivable: Studies on Germany, Nazism and the Holocaust*, 117–29. Berkeley: University of California Press, 2000.
Engelking, Barbara, and Jacek Leociak. *The Warsaw Ghetto: A Guide to the Perished City*. New Haven, CT: Yale University Press, 2009.
Feuchert, Sascha, ed. *Die Chronik des Gettos Lodz/Litzmannstadt*. Vol. 1 (1941) and vol. 2 (1942). Göttingen: Wallstein, 2007.
―――. "Die Getto-Chronik: Entstehung und Überlieferung. Eine Projektskizze." In *Die Chronik des Getto Lodz/Litzmannstadt, Supplemente und Anhang*, vol. 5, edited by Sascha Feuchert, 167–90. Göttingen: Wallstein, 2007.
Friedman, Philip. "Pseudo-Saviors in the Polish Ghettos: Mordechai Chaim Rumkowski of Lodz." In *Roads to Extinction: Essays on the Holocaust*, edited by Philip Friedman, 333–352. New York: Jewish Publication Society, 1980.
Goldberg, Amos. "The History of the Jews in the Ghettos: A Cultural Perspective." In *The Holocaust and Historical Methodology*, edited by Dan Stone, 79–100. New York: Berghahn Books, 2012.
Gringauz, Samuel. "The Ghetto as an Experiment of Jewish Social Organization (Three Years of Kovno Ghetto)." *Jewish Social Studies* 11 (1949): 3–20.
Gutman, Yisrael. "Ghetto." In *Encyclopaedia of the Holocaust*, edited by Yisrael Gutman et al., 2:579–82. New York: Palgrave Macmillan, 1990.
Hájková, Anna. "Prisoner Society in the Terezín Ghetto, 1941–1945." Ph.D. diss., University of Toronto, 2013.
Hilberg, Raul. *The Destruction of the European Jews*, vol. 3. New York: Holmes and Meier, 1985.
Kassow, Samuel D. *Who Will Write Our History? Emanuel Ringelblum, the Warsaw Ghetto, and the Oyneg Shabes Archive*. Bloomington: Indiana University Press, 2007.
Klein, Peter. *Die Gettoverwaltung Litzmannstadt 1940 bis 1944: Eine Dienststelle im Spannungsfeld von Kommunalbürokratie und staatlicher Verfolgungspolitik*. Hamburg: Hamburger Edition, 2009.
Levi, Primo. *The Drowned and the Saved*. New York: Summit Books, 1988.
Löw, Andrea. *Juden im Getto Litzmannstadt: Lebensbedingungen, Selbstwahrnehmung, Verhalten*. Göttingen: Wallstein, 2013.
Marrus, Michael R. "Jewish Resistance to the Holocaust." *Journal of Contemporary History* 30, no. 1 (1995): 83–110.
Michman, Dan. *The Emergence of Ghettos during the Holocaust*. Cambridge: Cambridge University Press, 2011.

———. "The Emergence of Ghettos under the Nazis and Their Allies: The Reasons behind Their Emergence." In Miron et al., *The Yad Vashem Encyclopedia of the Ghettos during the Holocaust*, xiii–xxxix.

———. "Reevaluating the Emergence, Function, and Form of the Jewish Councils Phenomenon." In *Ghettos 1939–1945: New Research and Perspectives on Definition, Daily Life, and Survival. Symposium Presentations*, edited by Center for Advanced Holocaust Studies, 67–84. Washington, DC, 2005.

———. "Why Did Heydrich Write the Schnellbrief? A Remark on the Reason and on Its Significance," *Yad Vashem Studies* 32 (2004): 433–47.

Miron, Guy, et al., eds. *The Yad Vashem Encyclopedia of the Ghettos during the Holocaust*. Jerusalem: Yad Vashem, 2009.

Ofer, Dalia, and Lenore J. Weitzman, eds. *Women in the Holocaust*. New Haven, CT: Yale University Press, 1998.

Petropoulos, Jonathan, and John K. Roth, eds. *Gray Zones: Ambiguity and Compromise in the Holocaust and Its Aftermath*. New York: Berghahn Books, 2005.

Pingel, Falk. "Social Life in an Unsocial Environment: The Inmates' Struggle for Survival." In *Concentration Camps in Nazi Germany: The New Histories*, edited by Nikolaus Wachsmann and Jane Caplan, 70–93. London; New York: Routledge, 2009.

Polit, Monika. *"Moja żydowska dusza nie obawia się dnia sądu": Mordechaj Chaim Rumkowski. Prawda i zmyślenie*. Warsaw: Stowarzyszenie Centrum Badań nad Zagładą Żydów, 2012.

Robinson, Jacob. *And the Crooked Shall Be Made Straight. The Eichmann Trial, the Jewish Catastrophe, and Hannah Arendt's Narrative*. New York: Penguin Books, 1965.

———. *Discontinuity or Continuity in Community Councils during the Nazi Era* [in Hebrew]. Jerusalem: The Hebrew University of Jerusalem, 1967.

Rosenfeld, Oskar. *Wozu noch Welt: Aufzeichnungen aus dem Getto Lodz*, edited by Hanno Loewy. Frankfurt am Main: Neue Kritik, 1994.

Rubinstein, Richard. "Gray into Black: The Case of Mordechai Chaim Rumkowski." In *Gray Zones: Ambiguity and Compromise in the Holocaust and Its Aftermath*, edited by Jonathan Petropoulos and John K. Roth, 299–310. New York: Berghahn Books, 2005.

Rudavsky, Joseph. *To Live with Hope, to Die with Dignity: Spiritual Resistance in the Ghettos and Camps*. Northvale, NJ: Jason Aronson, 1997.

Sierakowiak, Dawid. *Das Ghettotagebuch des Dawid Sierakowiak: Aufzeichnungen eines Siebzehnjährigen, 1941/42*, edited by Roswitha Matwin-Buschmann. Leipzig: Reclam Verlag, 1993.

Stanislawski, Michael. "Kahal (*kehilah*)." In *The YIVO Encyclopedia of Jews in Eastern Europe*, edited by Gershon David Hundert, 845–48. New Haven, CT: Yale University Press, 2008.

Stone, Dan. *Histories of the Holocaust*. Oxford: Oxford University Press, 2010.

Trunk, Isaiah. *Judenrat: The Jewish Councils in Eastern Europe under Nazi Occupation*. New York: Macmillan, 1972.

———. *Łódź Ghetto: A History*, edited by Robert M. Shapiro. Bloomington: Indiana Univ. Press, 2006.

———. "Note: Why Was There No Armed Resistance against the Nazis in the Lodz Ghetto?" *Jewish Social Studies* 43, no. 3/4 (1981): 329–34.
Unger, Michal. "Łódź." In Miron et al., *Yad Vashem Encyclopedia of the Ghettos*, 403–12.
———. *Reassessment of the Image of Mordechai Chaim Rumkowski*. Jerusalem: Yad Vashem, 2004.
Voss, Lex Heerma van. *Petitions in Social History*. Cambridge: Cambridge University Press, 2002.
Wachsmann, Nikolaus. *KL: A History of the Nazi Concentration Camps*. London: Little, Brown, 2015.
Weiss, Aharon. "Jewish Leadership in Occupied Poland: Postures and Attitudes." *Yad Vashem Studies* 12 (1977): 335–66.
———. "Judenrat." In Gutman et al. *Encyclopedia of the Holocaust*, 2:762–71.
———. "The Relations between the Judenrat and the Jewish Police." In *Patterns of Jewish Leadership in Nazi Europe 1933–1945: Proceedings of the Third Yad Vashem International Historical Conference, Jerusalem, 4–7 April 1977*, edited by Yisrael Gutman and Cynthia J. Haft, 201–18. Jerusalem: Yad Vashem, 1979.

Chapter 6

PETITIONING MATTERS
Jews and Non-Jews Negotiating Ghettoization in Budapest, 1944

Tim Cole

Introduction

As the chapters in this volume show, petitions matter. This was brought home particularly forcefully when researching a socio-spatial history of the Holocaust in Hungary.[1] Working through documents from the regional archives, I came across a striking document. It was not a petition, but a memo penned in response to a petition. From this response, it was possible to work out what the original petitioner had requested. In May 1944, a Jewish father living in Budapest wrote to the local authorities in Vasvár asking them to remove his eleven-year-old son György András from the newly established Vasvár ghetto and return him to his family home in Budapest.[2] Reading between the lines, it appears that György András had been sent to the countryside in the early summer of 1944—perhaps fleeing the start of bombing in the capital, which saw the evacuation of the children to the safety of rural Hungary—to stay with the village tobacconist in Csehimindszent in western Hungary. However, in the middle of May 1944, György András was taken, along with other Jews from the village, to the ghetto established in the nearby city of Vasvár.[3] Finding out about this, his father petitioned the local authorities to remove his son from the ghetto and return him to Budapest, a city where the ghetto had not yet been created. On 23 May 1944, the chief constable (*főszolgabíró*) of Vasvár agreed to this request and a local lawyer was identified to accompany György András, as a minor, on his journey out of the Vasvár ghetto and back to the capital.[4]

This movement from one place to another—Vasvár to Budapest—in May 1944 ultimately saved the boy's life. A few weeks later the Jews in

---

Notes for this chapter begin on page 153.

the Vasvár ghetto were deported to Auschwitz-Birkenau. Here it is very unlikely that an eleven-year-old boy would have survived the initial selections, but would have been quickly dispatched to the gas chambers. However, the Jews in Budapest were not sent to Auschwitz after the deportations from Hungary were halted in early July 1944. Instead, Jews in Budapest continued living in a series of ghettos that were ultimately liberated—rather than liquidated—in January 1945. As a result of his father's petitioning, György András' name is missing from the Vasvár ghetto list that was in effect a de facto deportation list,[5] and instead appears on a list of Jewish survivors living in Budapest in the summer of 1945.[6] In this case, the petition literally saved György András' life.

This chapter examines the power of petitioning in Hungary in 1944, by moving from this single petition requesting that a Jewish boy be removed from the ghetto in Vasvár to hundreds of petitions that survive in the Budapest archives. There are a number of important differences aside from the issue of the sheer volume of these petitions. These petitions directed to the city's mayor and his officials were written not only by Jews, but also by their non-Jewish neighbors, who also saw themselves being impacted by measures enacted against Jews. They came in response to the publication of a list of houses the city's Jews were to move into, and non-Jews were to move out of, in June 1944. In most cases, petition writing brought Jews and non-Jews into conflict with each other as both sought to stay put, but in some cases petitions became vehicles for coalition building around shared concerns.

But these petitions from Budapest also differ from the letter penned by György András's father given that the relationship between petitioning and the results of petitioning was less direct. The flurry of petition writing in the middle of June 1944 was highly significant, but in more complex and indirect ways. In the aftermath of these days of letter writing, the local authorities changed not only the shape of the ghetto, but also the scale. In short, in Budapest in 1944, petitions mattered. This mass petitioning in Budapest—like the other examples that feature in this volume—raises important questions of agency, as well as the role for negotiation and room for maneuver during the Holocaust. But before turning to examine the nature and impact of the mass petitioning in Budapest in mid-1944, this essay starts by briefly sketching the background to this story.

Implementing Ghettoization in Budapest

On 19 March 1944, German forces occupied their increasingly reluctant ally Hungary. In the aftermath of the occupation, Hungarian Jews were swiftly subjected to a raft of anti-Jewish measures. Jews were marked with a yellow star, and then from April onward concentrated into ghettos. From mid-May onward, deportations to Auschwitz commenced from these short-lived ghettos. In the course of less than two months in the summer of 1944, more than 430,000 Jews were deported from across Hungary. The rapid implementation of ghettoization and deportation in spring and summer 1944 were not the first anti-Jewish measures implemented in Hungary. Long before the German occupation, the Hungarian authorities had implemented a series of anti-Jewish laws, primarily aimed at limiting economic participation, as well as specifically targeting young Jewish men who were drafted into unarmed labor battalion units that served alongside the Hungarian military and suffered massive loss of life.[7] Nonetheless, in the weeks and months after the German occupation, the scope, nature, and pace of anti-Jewish policy and practice changed. What has been seen by scholars as the "last chapter" of the Holocaust was marked not only by its late onset, but also its rapidity.[8]

While measures such as ghettoization were legislated nationally, they were implemented locally within a plan that broadly moved from the east to the west before finally shifting to the capital. As a result, the timescale for ghettoization in Budapest came a little later than elsewhere in the country (something that ultimately proved of critical importance for György András). National ghettoization orders and legislation from April 1944 were discussed by the mayor of Budapest and officials in the city housing department in May 1944 and implemented in the city in the middle of June 1944. But it was not simply the case that ghettoization came a little later in Budapest than elsewhere. It also took a rather different form. Rather than identifying a single ghetto, as was the case in Vasvár,[9] on 16 June 1944, the city authorities instructed Jews in Budapest to move within five days into 2,639 apartment buildings marked with a large yellow star dispersed throughout the city.[10]

The highly dispersed nature of the ghetto in Budapest was unusual but not unique, neither within Hungary nor outside of it. Jewish houses were set up in other cities in Central Europe—for example in Germany and Austria.[11] In Hungary, national ghettoization legislation issued in April 1944 presented local authorities with a choice of what form the ghetto within their town or city might take. Mayors in towns and cities with a population greater than ten thousand could determine which "parts, or rather specified streets, or perhaps designated houses" Jews had to move into. It was not only in Budapest that local authorities decided to designate the ghetto in a number of individual houses, rather than a single part of the town or city.[12] Nonetheless, there was nowhere else in the country where the nature and scale of dispersal of ghetto houses was as marked as it was in the capital.

It seems that a number of issues were particularly significant in the case of Budapest, where such a highly dispersed form of ghettoization was adopted. Both emerged in the pages of the press during the spring and early summer of 1944 as ghetto plans were discussed openly not only by the authorities but also by the public.[13] One plan came in the wake of the beginnings of Allied bombings of Budapest, which most likely led to György András being dispatched to what was seen as the safety of Csehimindszent. In the press, rumors began circulating that placing the Jews into a single, closed ghetto in Budapest would expose the rest of the city to Allied attacks. To prevent this, there were calls for Jews to be spread throughout the city to act as a human shield of sorts. Although this discourse was one that shifted across 1944, it does seem to have shaped emerging ghetto plans.[14] Certainly, the key Under Secretary in the Interior Ministry with responsibility for anti-Jewish measures, László Endre, responded to fears in a newspaper interview by reassuring readers that they did not plan to create a single, closed ghetto in Budapest but rather to "concentrate an appropriate number of Jews close to everywhere we expect to be attacked by terror bombers, for example, factories, railway stations."[15] This fitted with the early plans from May 1944 that identified seven ghetto areas in Budapest, many of which made sense given their location close to factories, railway stations , and government buildings.[16]

In the end, the ghetto list issued on 16 June stretched across not simply seven areas in Budapest but the whole city as a result of another set of concerns. These did not see ghettoization as a positive opportunity—the chance to create a human shield to protect the city from Allied bombing—but a negative necessity that would involve forcing large numbers of non-Jews (as well as Jews) to move.[17] It is clear that the authorities were well aware of the implications of ghettoization on non-Jewish residents, and so implemented a city-wide survey at the beginning of June that sought to establish whether the owner of each apartment building was Jewish or non-Jewish, the proportion of Jewish to non-Jewish tenants, and other information such as the age of the building and the cost of rents. From the surviving copies of these registration forms from one district of the city, it would seem that the proportion of Jewish and non-Jewish tenants was critical in deciding which houses would make up the ghetto. In the fourth district, officials added up the number of Jewish and non-Jewish tenants in the top left-hand corner of the form and then penciled in either "Zs" (*Zsidó*, Jew) or "K" (*Keresztény*, Christian) in the top right-hand corner of the form depending on which was in the majority. Those with a "Zs" penciled on them ended up on the ghetto list issued on 16 June, while those with a "K" were not on this list.[18] This was an attempt to "bring the ghetto to the Jew" and so, as much as possible, spare non-Jews from being forced to relocate.[19]

Designating a highly dispersed ghetto was intended to limit the numbers of non-Jews who would have to move from their homes. However, given that Jews and non-Jews lived in the same apartment buildings, even the most dispersed form of ghetto would necessitate some non-Jews having to move. According to press claims, as many as twelve thousand non-Jewish families would be forced to move as a result of ghettoization in the capital, alongside forty thousand Jewish families.[20] In the days that followed the issuing of the list of ghetto houses on 16 June 1944, hundreds of those non-Jews and Jews who would now have to leave their homes petitioned the mayor and his officials. These petitioners targeted those making the decisions about the shape of the ghetto.

Petitioning Ghettoization in Budapest

The flurry of petitioning in mid-June has been noted—although not fully explored—in the existing literature. In his early postwar work, Jenö Lévai wrote that "scores of complaints" were submitted after the list of ghetto houses was issued.[21] Randolph Braham described the city office in Budapest in the early summer of 1944 being "besieged by petitioners requesting changes from the original designations."[22] In total, I have located over six hundred petitions, although it may well be that more were written and submitted. Most were composed by owners or tenants themselves—both men and women, from across the city—although a few engaged the services of a lawyer to petition the authorities on their behalf. Braham is right to note that "the overwhelming majority of the pleaders were Christians requesting that their buildings not be designated as Yellow-Star houses; Jews usually had the opposite request."[23] Of the six hundred or so petitions I have read, the single largest group (just over two hundred) was requests from non-Jews for the cancellation of their apartment building or house from the ghetto list. The second largest group (just over a hundred and fifty) was requests from Jews for their apartment building or house to be included on the ghetto list. In short, the vast majority of petitions came from those—whether Jewish or non-Jewish owners or tenants—who simply wanted to stay put. That desire to stay put was particularly significant and poignant in the case of the third largest group of petitions (over a hundred) submitted by those living in mixed marriages who requested that both partners be permitted to remain together after the implementation of ghettoization.[24]

Given that the majority of petitions were requests to stay put, it is perhaps not surprising that some properties were contested through rival petitions submitted by Jewish and non-Jewish neighbors. In some cases, the fact that another petition had already been submitted, or was soon to be submitted, or was even rumored to have been submitted from the same address, was specifically referenced in the counter petition. Here is clear evidence of the way petitioning did not simply reflect attitudes, but also created attitudes. Petitioning could, and in some cases did, lead to counter-petitioning and so revealed and created fractures within the microworlds of apartment buildings, and even in one case, within families.[25]

The fault lines in the apartment building at Koháry u. 16 in the city's fifth district were clear and reflected the wider situation across much of the city as a whole. The building had not been included in the ghetto on the 16 June list, and in response, the Jewish owners wrote to the local authorities on behalf of the building's Jewish tenants requesting "Jewish house" status for their property. Their petition, which arrived in the mayor's office on 19 June, drew on the principle of majority occupation and pointed to the finding of the 1 June survey that twenty-six of the thirty-four tenants in the house were Jewish, or as they put it, were required to wear the yellow star, while only eight were Christian. They also pointed out that the house owners—and petition writers—were Jewish. Here their rhetoric mirrored that articulated in the local press and the logic captured in the questions of the 1 June survey. They did not dispute ghettoization and the logic of segregation of Jews and non-Jews. Rather they addressed the particular issue that faced them. In a few days time they would be forced to leave their homes, which in the case of three Jewish doctors would also mean leaving their surgeries. Their petition was directed at ensuring they could stay in their homes, so they worked with the principle of majority occupation being one of the key deciding factors and emphasized the number of Jews who lived in the building.[26] There are other cases from Hungary where Jews petitioned to challenge their designation as Jews or those required to wear the yellow star.[27] But this was not the case here. Rather, these petitioners saw the sheer number of Jews in their apartment building to be key as they asked the city authorities to include their home within the dispersed ghetto.

Still, they were not the only ones who wanted to stay put. In a direct and intentional act of counter-petitioning, all of the non-Jewish tenants wrote a couple of days later, asking that the building continue to be excluded from the ghetto list. Their petition came in response to a rumor that the house's Jewish inhabitants had submitted a request for inclusion in the ghetto. As they sought to counter this request, they drew in part on the question of how many tenants would have to move out. The statistics of majority occupation were not on their side, so they omitted any reference to how many Jewish tenants there were and instead noted simply that thirteen (a number higher than the figure of eight spelled out in the earlier petition) Christian tenants lived in the house and would have to move. Rather than arguing that these thirteen made up the majority of tenants, they pointed out that they included some illustrious individuals—lawyers, bank managers, business leaders—one of who had moved in with specific permission from the mayor just over a month earlier, and a number of bomb victims who could not afford to move elsewhere.[28] Ultimately these thirteen Christian tenants were not required to leave their apartments in Koháry u. 16 as it was not included in the revised ghetto list published on 22 June, which I return to below.

For the thirteen non-Jewish tenants living in Koháry u. 16, it is clear that relocation as a result of ghettoization would be more than simply an inconvenience. It was quite clear that they did not want to leave an apartment building that was both comfortable and affordable. These concerns with the quality of accommodation, and not simply the proportions of Jewish and non-Jewish inhabitants, meant that not all petitions simply followed the logic of non-Jewish requests to stay in a non-ghetto house and Jewish requests to stay in a ghetto house. A small but significant set of petitions came from non-Jewish tenants who called for their property to be included in the ghetto. In short, ghettoization afforded them an opportunity to leave their apartments and exchange them for better apartments, which some non-Jewish tenants and inhabitants were eager to seize.

A significant minority of petitions from non-Jewish tenants called for their property to be designated as part of the ghetto. One arrived in the mayor's office on 19 June from the non-Jewish tenants at Nagydiófa u. 11 in the city's seventh district who complained about how unhealthy and unsuitable the building was where they lived solely because they could not get an apartment anywhere else. Ghettoization was the opportunity they had been waiting for. The twenty-nine tenants wrote—ultimately unsuccessfully—requesting ghetto status with the hope of getting more decent apartments.[29] In this case as with others, there was an assumption that an unhealthy and unsuitable building would be considered fit for Jewish use, something echoed in some Jewish petitions in instrumental ways.[30]

A similar story, also ultimately ineffective as the second ghetto list makes clear, can be seen in the letter submitted by the non-Jewish inhabitants at Péterfy Sándor u. 3, also in the seventh district, who wrote to the mayor, calling for their house to be included in the ghetto as they wanted to move into other properties in the neighborhood. In particular, they had their eyes on a house a little further down the street—at Péterfy Sándor u. 17—which had been designated a ghetto house and was far more modern and much more desirable. However, their hopes for a direct swap failed to materialize. Péterfy Sándor u. 3 remained off the ghetto list and Péterfy

Sándor u. 17 remained on the ghetto list, no doubt influenced in part at least by the fact that non-Jews made up the majority of inhabitants in the former.[31]

Not all such requests from non-Jewish tenants for inclusion of their property in the ghetto so they could leave for better apartments were rejected. The non-Jewish inhabitants of Klauzál Square (*tér*) 5, also in the city's seventh district, were more successful in their request to move out. Their property was included on the list of Jewish houses published on 22 June 1944. Based on the penciled notes on the cover of this petition (more on this below), the acceptance of the petition appears to have more to do with the fact that Jews made up the majority of tenants than with the quality of the property.[32] A similar story can be seen in the successful petitioning by the non-Jewish inhabitants of the corner house at Károly király u. 7 and Rumbach Sebestyen u. 8 in the city's seventh district. Here the petitioners were quick to point out that Jews made up the vast majority of tenants and inhabitants (two hundred and twenty Jews living in thirty-three apartments compared with twenty-seven Christians living in seven apartments), but they also took pains to signal the terrible state of this dirty and smelly building.[33]

However, from reading through the petitions submitted by non-Jewish tenants requesting that their house be designated, it would seem that most were unsuccessful in a context where whoever made up the majority of tenants and inhabitants was the single most significant issue at play in the minds of officials. A telling example comes from the petition submitted by some of the non-Jewish tenants at Baross u. 116 in the city's eighth district, who wrote with a request for inclusion in the ghetto on the grounds that their apartments were small, poorly equipped, and in an old building. The local official, who checked this petition, scribbled on the cover in pencil "1 zsidó!" (1 Jew!).[34] The exclamation mark says it all. Desires for upward mobility on the part of the building's non-Jewish tenants were trumped by the pragmatics of whether Jews or non-Jews made up the majority of inhabitants.

Although it turned out to be largely unsuccessful, petitioning was taken up by a small number of non-Jews who saw ghettoization as an opportunity not a threat. For them, their plans could and did lead to a coming together of non-Jewish tenants' desire to leave and Jewish tenants' wish to stay put. In contrast, as the example of Koháry u. 16 shows, the desire on the part of the majority of both Jewish and non-Jewish tenants and inhabitants to stay meant that Jews and non-Jews tended to come into conflict with each other. In this conflict, both used petitioning as a way to express that conflict to the authorities as well as to call upon them to play a mediating role in their favor.

But it was not just opposing groups of tenants who used petitions to mediate conflict within apartment buildings. At times, ghetto designation brought building owners and their tenants into conflict with each other and fought these battles through petitioning. This can be seen in the case of two submitted petitions that related to the apartment building at Szent István Park 10. The building was not included in the 16 June ghetto list. On 17 June, a number of Jewish owner-occupiers wrote entreaties, requesting the inclusion of the building on the grounds of Jewish majority occupation. Their claim that fifteen of the eighteen apartments in the house were occupied by Jews no doubt explains why this building was included in the new ghetto list issued on 22 June.[35] However, its inclusion on that list was a cause of concern to non-Jewish owners who did not reside in the building, but owned investment properties within it. From their perspective, the overcrowding, which it is clear they understood ghettoization to entail, would lead to damage—they pointed in their petition in particular to "the beautifully painted white doors"—which someone would have to pay for.[36] It is clear that owners and tenants could, and did, have differing views on the inclusion in, or exclusion from, the dispersed ghetto in Budapest.

While on the whole the petitions point to the ways that ghettoization tended to bring Jews and non-Jewish inhabitants into conflict with each other and to mediate that conflict through petitioning, there is a striking subset of petitions that point to the ways petitioning was a means of coalition building. These petitions are particularly important because they proposed a novel solution to the key problem that ghettoization posed. As the majority of petitions show—and this was something that the local authorities were well aware of—ghettoization meant the physical separation of Jews and non-Jews and hence the forced relocation of both Jews and non-Jews. In this context, both Jews and non-Jews petitioned the local authorities with an eye to staying put and asked that their building be variously designated for Jewish or non-Jewish use. Nevertheless, what is significant is how a number of petitioners—and sometimes these were explicit coalitions of Jews and non-Jews within the same building—requested that they be permitted to remain in a new kind of category that was both within the ghetto and outside it. The idea of the *vegyes ház* (or "mixed" house) was coined in and through petitioning as both Jews and non-Jews sought to stay put *together*.

Calls for "mixed" status could and did come from Jewish or non-Jewish petitioners. For example, taking just one folder of fifty to sixty petitions from the archive, the non-Jewish inhabitants of Csengery u. 56 in the sixth district, and Nefelejts u. 15 and Hernád u. 11/a in the seventh district wrote with requests for Jewish or mixed status.[37] In this same folder, there are requests for Jewish or mixed status from Jewish owners and inhabitants at Dessewfy u. 21, Paulay Ede u. 33, and Szív u. 60 in the sixth district, Izabella u. 3/b in the seventh district, and Ráday u. 38 in the tenth district.[38] In these cases, there were often explicit references to the request being supported by others in the building, if not the inclusion of separate lists of Jewish and non-Jewish tenants. For instance, while the request for ghetto or mixed status for Dessewfy u. 21 in the city's sixth district came from the Jewish owner, the petition was explicitly presented as being written in the names of the Jewish and non-Jewish inhabitants of the building.[39]

This sense of coalition building was not total. At Hársfa u. 57 in the city's seventh district, a house that had not been included in the ghetto list published on 16 June (but was added to the 22 June list), the coalition of Jews and non-Jews petitioning for "mixed status" was, as one non-Jewish tenant wanted to make completely clear, not uniformly supported by everyone in the building.[40] Nonetheless, this opposition to calls for mixed status was the exception and not the rule. In far more cases, such requests saw joint petitioning by Jews and non-Jews who not only called upon the mayor to allow them all to remain living where they were, but to remain living together. Moreover, through their petitions, Jews and non-Jews directly challenged the national ghettoization legislation that stipulated that Jews and non-Jews would be placed in separate areas, streets, or houses.

Petitioning Matters: Changing the Shape of Ghettoization

It is one thing to find a stack of petitions carefully wrapped up in bundles in the archives, and another thing to identify if—and how—these petitions were taken seriously by the local authorities. However, in Budapest, it does seem that the large-scale petitioning in the middle of June 1944 led to rethinking on the part of the authorities. There was an immediate thoroughgoing reinvestigation of all properties included in the 16 June list, as well as the properties suggested for designation in individual petitions. Explicit reference to this reinvestigation is made in some of the petitions themselves. The Jewish owner of Lendváy u. 15 in the city's sixth district noted in his petition requesting the property continue to be designated for Jewish use that a representative of the district council had visited the building on the evening of 20 June to collect up-to-date data on the occupants in the building. It would seem that the district council official took with them the first petition related to this building that called for the cancellation of the building from the ghetto list. On the front of this petition, the official tallied up the numbers of Jewish and non-Jewish apartments and inhabitants in the building as well as recording whether the owner was Jewish or not.[41]

All this information had already been collected in the registration taken at the start of June upon which decisions about designations were made. However, it seemed that petitioning did enough to raise questions about the up-to-date accuracy of that earlier exercise. Certainly, in the sixth district of the city, there was a thorough investigation of properties in the middle of June that led to recommendations being made about which properties should be included in, or excluded from, a second definitive list of ghetto houses. Evidence of such a detailed reinvestigation also survived for the eleventh district, which—taken together with the evidence from the cover sheets of petitions with their annotation notes—suggests that there was meticulous reinvestigation of all designated or potentially designated properties in the days following this rush of petitioning, with a particular concern for identifying majority occupation, whether the owners were Jewish or non-Jewish, and further information about the type and nature of the property.[42]

After this rapid reinvestigation, the mayor issued a new—definitive—list of ghetto houses on 22 June 1944.[43] Less than one week after the ghetto was first outlined by the authorities, it changed shape with the addition of 149 new buildings that Jews could move into and the cancellation of 840 buildings. As a result, the dispersed ghetto in Budapest shrank from a total of 2,639 buildings on 16 June to 1,984 buildings six days later.[44] It is clear that there was not a direct line between each individual petition and these hundreds of additions and cancellations. The sheer number of cancellations far outweighs the number of surviving petitions submitted by non-Jewish tenants and owners for removal from the ghetto list. Moreover, not all of those surviving petitions calling for cancellation were successful. There was clearly more at play here in the reshaping of the dispersed ghetto, which saw the cutting of over a quarter of all those properties originally designated for Jewish use. Many of these cancelled buildings were smaller properties in the outlying districts of the city, and in particular villas or single-family homes, which were now to be explicitly excluded from the ghetto.[45] Although mass petitioning formed the general context to this redrawing of the ghetto, the number and nature of cancellations of particular property *types* (villas) and not just particular properties (where a majority of non-Jewish tenants lived) was not directly tied to specific petitions.

Nevertheless, the impact of petitioning should not be measured simply in terms of a direct correlation between a specific request for inclusion or cancellation and the resulting inclusion or cancellation of that property. There are cases where this kind of direct cause and effect can be seen, but petitioning had a more powerful effect at an aggregate level. It was the sheer number of petitions—which shows the importance of each individual petition—submitted that was more significant in drawing attention to the impact of ghettoization on the city's non-Jewish population in particular. As I have suggested, this resulted not in a simple case-by-case reinvestigation of particular properties that were specifically referenced in petitions, but a far more widespread, rapid reassessment of all properties within the ghetto. Even more significantly, the flurry of petitioning and the rethinking it generated led to changes not only in the shape of the ghetto, but also the scale at which ghettoization was enacted.

Petitioning Matters: Changing the Scale of Ghettoization

Three days after the second definitive list of 1,948 ghetto houses was announced, the city authorities issued a long list of regulations that marked the formal closing of this dispersed ghetto. The eighth point was particularly significant and represented a major compromise on the part of the authorities with important implications for both non-Jews and Jews. Forbidding non-Jews from allowing Jews to enter "for no matter how brief a period into either Christian houses or the Christian-tenanted portions of Jewish houses," this rule signaled that non-Jewish neighbors would be allowed to continue living in their apartments within the buildings that made up the ghetto.[46] This concept of "mixed" houses only operated in one direction. Non-Jews were permitted to continue living in ghetto houses, but Jews were not allowed to remain in non-ghetto houses. However, what this concession did point to was official recognition of the category of "mixed" houses that first emerged in petitions.

It seems that large numbers of non-Jewish tenants and inhabitants seized upon this concession and decided to stay put, which was, after all, the thing that most petitioners wanted to do. The journalist Jenö Lévai's postwar claim that twelve thousand non-Jews lived in ghetto houses is hard to substantiate, but it may well be not far off the mark. In the area of the city that later became the site of the closed Pest ghetto in the winter of 1944, non-Jews as well as Jews lived in 144 of the 162 ghetto houses throughout the summer and fall.[47] If we can extrapolate from these figures then it would seem that the vast majority of the 1,948 ghetto houses identified on 22 June were in reality "mixed" houses where Jews and non-Jews lived alongside each other, and the so-called "Aryan side" was as close as the other side of the apartment wall. In part, of course, the continued presence of non-Jewish tenants in ghetto houses meant that living conditions for Jews were even more overcrowded. Nevertheless, it also afforded opportunities for Jews to mobilize long-standing social-networks with non-Jewish neighbors.[48]

What this co-existence of Jews and non-Jews within individual ghetto houses meant in practice can be seen by looking at the experience of another eleven-year-old Jewish child from Budapest—Judit Brody. The Brody family was, in Judit's words, "lucky" given the city included their apartment building in the final list of 1,948 houses. This meant that the family remained living in their own apartment with their own furniture, but more critically stayed in a social space that meant continuing access to "connections" and "contacts". Outside the apartment building, it meant that Judit's mother could get hold of scarce foodstuffs through her network of good relationships with nearby shopkeepers. Inside the apartment building, it meant that Judit's family could draw on the help of their non-Jewish neighbors and the non-Jewish caretaker and his family in what was, like so many other ghetto buildings, in reality a "mixed" house. Given the increasingly difficult conditions during the summer of 1944, Judit's parents decided that it would be safer if she went into hiding outside of Budapest rather than staying with them. They therefore turned to their non-Jewish next-door neighbor who "helped find somebody who was willing, for payment of course, to take me away." Judit assumed a new persona, complete with forged papers, as Edit, the daughter of the caretakers evacuated to the countryside to avoid the bombing. While in hiding, the non-Jewish next-door neighbor served as the main point of contact between Judit and her parents. He was the recipient of letters sent from her to her "godfather" and also sent news from her parents back to her in a pre-agreed code. In short, he was a pivotal figure in facilitating hiding, as it seems was the building caretaker.[49] The caretaker and his wife continued to play an important role in the family's story of survival. After Judit returned to Budapest in the late summer and early fall, it was the caretaker's wife who warned the Brody family that members of the Arrow Cross (the native fascist *Nyilas* party that came to power in October 1944) had raided the building. While her husband kept these men talking at the gate, she found Judit's family a hiding place.[50]

The lived experience of the "mixed" house where Judit's family spent the summer and fall of 1944, forces a reimagining of the nature of segregation in the dispersed Budapest ghetto. Enacting ghettoization at the scale of the individual apartment as a result of mass petitioning, meant that the so-called "Aryan side" in Budapest was within many ghetto buildings, being found just along the corridor or up the stairs. Technically speaking, the wall between, and front door of, the Brody family apartment and their non-Jewish neighbor's apartment functioned as a ghetto boundary during the summer and into the fall of 1944. Nevertheless, tens of thousands of mini-boundaries like these were impossible to police.[51] With the caretaker on their side, Judit's family was able to take advantage of the presence of a sympathetic non-Jewish neighbor within this "mixed" ghetto house.[52]

Conclusions: Petitions and "Integrated" Histories

As shown here, petitioning the authorities in Hungary during 1944 were not simply acts in vain. Petitions could and did have significant effects. For two eleven-year-old children from Budapest, petitions were important in shaping their wartime experiences. In the case of György András, the link between petition and outcome is more direct and clear. His father petitioned the authorities and he was removed from the ghetto in Vasvár and returned to Budapest as a result of this intervention, where he ultimately survived the war. In the case of Judit Brody, the link was far looser. Her journey in the other direction—from Budapest to the countryside in the summer of 1944—was a less clear outcome of much more widespread petitioning. The fact that her non-Jewish next-door neighbor remained in the building can be seen as emerging from a compromise of sorts on the part of the authorities. While petitioning mattered for both György András and Judit Brody in 1944, it did so in different ways. For the former, the link was direct. For the latter, it was not an individual petition that was important, but rather the act of petitioning en masse that mattered.

The example of responding to ghettoization plans in Budapest in June 1944 forces a wider consideration of petitioning beyond simply the more binary example of a Jewish father petitioning the authorities as seen at the beginning of the chapter. There is a need to expand our thinking to include the (perhaps unexpected) impact of non-Jewish (as well as Jewish) petitioning on Jews (and non-Jews). This is part of a broader need to bring those, unhelpfully, dubbed "bystanders" more centrally into Holocaust historiography as active agents.[53] As Jan Gross has shown, those better described as neighbors play an important role in the story of the Holocaust.[54] In Budapest in June 1944, non-Jewish neighbors were active agents, just as Jewish neighbors were. In part, their agency was distinct and indeed opposed. As I have suggested, most non-Jews tended to call for their property to be excluded from the ghetto list, while Jews tended to call for the opposite. But there are also examples where their agency was entwined, either in opposition or solidarity. In some cases petitions beget petitions. In other cases, Jews and non-Jews came together in the same apartment building to argue a common cause. But more significant than each individual petition, it was the mass act of petitioning that led to important change. As I suggest, the impact of this complex web of petitioning in June 1944 was considerable for both non-Jews and Jews as the lived experience of ghettoization unfolded in "mixed" houses across Budapest in the summer and fall of 1944.

Here petitions offer one source for writing the kind of "integrated" histories of the Holocaust that Saul Friedländer called for. For Friedländer, bringing the voices of the victims together with those of the perpetrators was more than simply ethical necessity. It was also a way to better narrate the complex history of the Holocaust, given that

> Nazi attitudes and policies cannot be fully assessed without knowledge of the lives and indeed of the feelings of the Jewish men, women, and children themselves . . . their voices are essential if we are to attain an understanding of this past. For it is their voices that reveal what was known and what *could* be known . . . The constant presence of the victims in this book, while historically essential in itself, is also meant to put the Nazis' actions into full perspective.[55]

It should come as no surprise that petitions appear in Friedländer's study as one way of introducing victims' voices into his text.[56] Focusing attention on petitions brings victims' words directly into correspondence with those of perpetrators and forces us to reexamine the complex—and surprising—nature of power during the Holocaust. But as I have suggested, there is a need for "integrated" histories not to stop there, but also to bring the voices of non-Jewish neighbors into the mix. Petitions offer not simply a way of thinking about how Jews negotiated with the authorities, but also how non-Jews negotiated with the authorities over matters—such as ghettoization—that impacted both Jews and themselves.

Tim Cole is Professor of Social History at the University of the Bristol. He is the author of *Images of the Holocaust: The Myth of the Shoah Business* (1999), *Selling the Holocaust: From Auschwitz to Schindler* (1999), *Holocaust City: The Making of a Jewish Ghetto* (2003), *Traces of the Holocaust: Journeying in and out of the Ghettos* (2011), *Holocaust Landscapes* (2016), *About Britain: A Journey of Seventy Years and 1,345 Miles* (2021) and a co-editor of *Militarized Landscapes: From Gettysburg to Salisbury Plain* (2010) and *Geographies of the Holocaust* (2014).

Notes

1. Tim Cole, *Traces of the Holocaust: Journeying in and out of the Ghettos* (London, 2011).
2. For more reflections on this story, see Tim Cole, "The Return of György András M.: Writing Exceptional Stories of the Holocaust," *Journal of Jewish Identities* 1, no. 2 (2008): 29–48.
3. National Archives, Budapest (hereafter OL) I 101, 1330/1944, letter from Vasvár chief constable to deputy prefect (12 May 1944).
4. OL, I 101, 1500/1944, decision of Vasvár chief constable (23 May 1944).
5. OL, I 101, Vasvár ghetto name list (not dated).
6. *Counted Remnant: Register of the Jewish Survivors in Budapest* (Budapest, 1946), 755, 1131.
7. For a comprehensive discussion, see Randolph L. Braham, *The Politics of Genocide: The Holocaust in Hungary* (New York, 1994).
8. Christian Gerlach and Götz Aly, *Das letze Kapitel: Realpolitik, Ideologie und der Mord an den ungarischen Juden 1944/1945* (Stuttgart, 2002).
9. Randolph L. Braham ed., *A Magyarországi Holokauszt Földrajzi Enciklopédiája* (Budapest, 2007), 1288.
10. Tim Cole, *Holocaust City: The Making of a Jewish Ghetto* (New York, 2003), 101–15.
11. Marlies Buchholz, *Die hannoverschen Judenhäuser: Zur Situation der Juden in der Zeit der Ghettoisierung und Verfolgung 1941 bis 1945* (Hildesheim, 1987); Susanne Willems, *"Der entsiedelte Jude": Albert Speers Wohnungsmarktpolitik für den Berliner Hauptstadtbau* (Berlin, 2002); Hubert Schneider, *Die Entjudung des Wohnraums—Judenhäuser in Bochum: Die Geschichte der Gebäude und ihrer Bewohner* (Münster, 2010); Wolf Gruner, "Local Initiatives, Central Coordination: German Municipal Administration and the Holocaust," in *Networks of Nazi Persecution: Bureaucracy, Business, and the Organization of the Holocaust*, ed. Gerald D. Feldman and Wolfgang Seibel (New York, 2005), 269–94.
12. Cole, *Traces of the Holocaust*, 59.
13. Cole, *Holocaust City*, 81–125; on press debates in Szeged, see Cole, *Traces of the Holocaust*, 41–55.
14. Cole, *Holocaust City*, 115–25.
15. Article in *Magyarság* (16 April 1944), 4 cited in Cole, *Holocaust City*, 88.
16. Cole, *Holocaust City*, 84–88.
17. See wider sensitivities, in Tim Cole, "Contesting and Compromising Ghettoization, Hungary 1944," in *Lessons and Legacies IX. Memory, History, and Responsibility: Reassessments of the Holocaust, Implications for the Future*, ed. Jonathan Petropoulos, Lynn Rapaport, and John K. Roth (Evanston, IL, 2010), 152–66.
18. Cole, *Holocaust City*, 101–5.
19. Tim Cole and Alberto Giordano, "Bringing the Ghetto to the Jew: Spatialities of Ghettoization in Budapest," in *Geographies of the Holocaust*, ed. A. K. Knowles, T. Cole, and A. Giordano (Bloomington, IN, 2014), 120–57.
20. Cole, *Holocaust City*, 125.
21. Jenö Lévai, *Fekete Könyv a Magyar Zsidóság Szenvedéseiröl* (Budapest, 1946), 155.
22. Braham, *The Politics of Genocide*, 2:852.
23. Ibid.
24. Surviving petitions are housed in the Budapest Capital City Archive (hereafter BFL). Some are included in the so-called I collection of microfilms available at the National Archives, Budapest (OL).
25. Cole, *Holocaust City*, 147.

26. BFL 2783, 148001 (19 June 1944).
27. Cole, *Traces of the Holocaust*, 14–18.
28. BFL 2789, 148414 (21 June 1944).
29. BFL 2781, 147803 (19 June 1944).
30. Cole, *Holocaust City*, 139–40.
31. BFL 2781, 147851 (19 June 1944).
32. BFL 2783, 148031 (19 June 1944).
33. BFL 2786, 147766 (17 June 1944).
34. BFL 2786, 147741 (17 June 1944).
35. BFL 2785, 147686 (17 June 1944).
36. BFL 2791, 148794 (28 June 1944).
37. BFL 2781, 147822 (19 June 1944); 2781, 147821 (19 June 1944); 2781, 147833 (19 June 1944).
38. BFL 2781, 147802 (19 June 1944); 2781, 147864 (19 June 1944); 2781, 147857 (19 June 1944); 2781, 147811 (19 June 1944); 2781, 147846 (19 June 1944).
39. BFL 2781, 147802 (19 June 1944).
40. BFL 2784, 148115 (19 June 1944); 2784, 148191 (19 June 1944).
41. BFL 2789, 148419 (21 June 1944); 2784, 148128 (19 June 1944).
42. Cole, *Holocaust City*, 149–52.
43. Ibid., 149–59.
44. Ibid., 158; Cole and Giordano, "Bringing the Ghetto to the Jew," 124.
45. Cole, *Holocaust City*, 152.
46. Braham, *Politics of Genocide*, volume 2, 737–38.
47. Lévai, *Fekete Könyv*, 156; Braham, *Politics of Genocide*, 2:735; New Hungarian Central Archives (hereafter ÚMKL) XXXIII-5-c-1, XI.23 (23 November 1944).
48. Braham, *Politics of Genocide*, 2:853.
49. On the complex role played by caretakers, see Matyás Rigó, "Ordinary Women and Men: Superintendents and Jews in the Budapest Yellow-Star Houses in 1944–1945," *Urban History* 40, no. 1 (2013): 71–91; István Pál Ádám, *Budapest Building Managers and the Holocaust in Hungary* (Houndmills, 2016).
50. Interview with Judit Brody (Oxford, 26 November 2009); Judit Brody, unpublished memoir; Judit Brody (Edit), letter to her "Godfather" (11 July 1944, 14 July 1944).
51. My sense is that ghetto boundaries elsewhere were more porous than we often imagine. See my discussion of this in Tim Cole, "Building and Breaching the Ghetto Boundary: A Brief History of the Ghetto Fence in Körmend, Hungary, 1944," *Holocaust and Genocide Studies* 23, no. 1 (2009): 54–75.
52. For more on how the presence of non-Jews mattered to Jews, see Tim Cole and Alberto Giordano, "Rethinking Segregation in the Ghetto: Invisible Walls and Social Networks in the Dispersed Ghetto in Budapest, 1944," in *Lessons and Legacies XI. Expanding Perspectives on the Holocaust in a Changing World*, ed. Hilary Earl and Karl A. Schleunes (Evanston, IL, 2014), 277.
53. Tim Cole, "Writing 'Bystanders' into Holocaust History in More Active Ways: 'Non-Jewish' Engagement with Ghettoization, Hungary 1944," *Holocaust Studies: A Journal of Culture and History* 11, no. 1 (2005): 55–74; Robert M. Ehrenreich and Tim Cole, "The Perpetrator-Bystander-Victim Constellation: Rethinking Genocidal Relationships," *Human Organization* 64, no. 3 (2005): 213–24.
54. Jan T. Gross, *Neighbors: The Destruction of the Jewish Community in Jedwabne* (Princeton, NJ, 2001).
55. Saul Friedländer, *Nazi Germany and the Jews*, vol. 1:The Years of Persecution 1933–1939 (London, 1997), 2.
56. For further reflections on this, see Cole, "The Return of György András M."

Bibliography

Ádám, István Pál. *Budapest Building Managers and the Holocaust in Hungary*. Houndmills: Palgrave Macmillan, 2016.
Braham, Randolph L. *The Politics of Genocide: The Holocaust in Hungary*. New York: Columbia University Press, 1994.
———, ed. *A Magyarországi Holokauszt Földrajzi Enciklopédiája*. Budapest: Park Könyvkiadó, 2007.
Buchholz, Marlies. *Die hannoverschen Judenhäuser: Zur Situation der Juden in der Zeit der Ghettoisierung und Verfolgung 1941 bis 1945*. Hildesheim: A. Lax, 1987.
Cole, Tim. "Building and Breaching the Ghetto Boundary: A Brief History of the Ghetto Fence in Körmend, Hungary, 1944." *Holocaust and Genocide Studies* 23, no. 1 (2009): 54–75.
———. "Contesting and Compromising Ghettoization, Hungary 1944." In *Lessons and Legacies IX. Memory, History, and Responsibility: Reassessments of the Holocaust, Implications for the Future*, edited by Jonathan Petropoulos, Lynn Rapaport, and John K. Roth, 152–66. Evanston, IL: Northwestern University Press, 2010.
———. *Holocaust City: The Making of a Jewish Ghetto*. New York: Routledge, 2003.
———. "The Return of György András M.: Writing Exceptional Stories of the Holocaust." *Journal of Jewish Identities* 1, no. 2 (2008): 29–48.
———. *Traces of the Holocaust: Journeying into and out of the Ghettos*. London: Continuum, 2011.
———."Writing 'Bystanders' into Holocaust History in More Active Ways: 'Non-Jewish' Engagement with Ghettoization, Hungary 1944." *Holocaust Studies: A Journal of Culture and History* 11, no. 1 (2005): 55–74.
Cole, Tim, and Alberto Giordano. "Bringing the Ghetto to the Jew: Spatialities of Ghettoization in Budapest." In *Geographies of the Holocaust*, edited by A. K. Knowles, T. Cole, and A. Giordano, 120–57. Bloomington, IN: Indiana University Press, 2014.
———. "Rethinking Segregation in the Ghetto: Invisible Walls and Social Networks in the Dispersed Ghetto in Budapest, 1944." In *Lessons and Legacies XI. Expanding Perspectives on the Holocaust in a Changing World*, edited by Hilary Earl and Karl A. Schleunes, 265–91. Evanston, IL: Northwestern University Press, 2014.
Counted Remnant: Register of the Jewish Survivors in Budapest. Budapest: Hungarian Section of the World Jewish Congress, American Joint Distribution Committee & Jewish Agency for Palestine Statistical and Search Department, 1946.
Ehrenreich, Robert M., and Tim Cole, "The Perpetrator-Bystander-Victim Constellation: Rethinking Genocidal Relationships." *Human Organization* 64, no. 3 (2005): 213–24.
Friedländer, Saul. *Nazi Germany and the Jews*. Vol. 1: *The Years of Persecution 1933–1939*. London: Weidenfeld and Nicolson, 1997.
Gerlach, Christian, and Götz Aly. *Das letze Kapitel: Realpolitik, Ideologie und der Mord an den ungarischen Juden 1944/1945*. Stuttgart: Deutsche Verlags-Anstalt, 2002.

Gross, Jan T. *Neighbors: The Destruction of the Jewish Community in Jedwabne.* Princeton, NJ: Princeton University Press, 2001.
Gruner, Wolf. "Local Initiatives, Central Coordination: German Municipal Administration and the Holocaust." In *Networks of Nazi Persecution: Bureaucracy, Business, and the Organization of the Holocaust,* edited by Gerald D. Feldman and Wolfgang Seibel, 269–94. New York: Berghahn Books, 2005.
Lévai, Jenö. *Fekete Könyv a Magyar Zsidóság Szenvedéseiröl.* Budapest: Officina, 1946.
Rigó, Matyás. "Ordinary Women and Men: Superintendents and Jews in the Budapest Yellow-Star Houses in 1944–1945." *Urban History* 40, no. 1 (2013): 71–91.
Schneider, Hubert. *Die Entjudung des Wohnraums—Judenhäuser in Bochum: Die Geschichte der Gebäude und ihrer Bewohner.* Münster: Lit Verlag, 2010.
Willems, Susanne. *"Der entsiedelte Jude": Albert Speers Wohnungsmarktpolitik für den Berliner Hauptstadtbau.* Berlin: Edition Hentrich, 2002.

Chapter 7

GLOBAL JEWISH PETITIONING AND THE RECONSIDERATION OF SPATIAL ANALYSIS IN HOLOCAUST HISTORIOGRAPHY
The Case of Rescue in the Philippines

Thomas Pegelow Kaplan

Introduction

Throughout the 1930s and early 1940s, Jews in most countries across the European continent submitted a veritable "flood" of individual and collective petitions.[1] In their pleas, they addressed, as this volume's previous chapters demonstrate, a growing number of institutions and representatives of a distinct state, ruling party, camp administration, or civil society. Much of the still limited scholarly attention to Holocaust-era petitions has unfolded in the confines of national boundaries, even if altered by war and expansion.[2] Upon closer scrutiny, many Jewish petitioning practices, however, turn out to be influenced or even directly driven by transnational exchanges and networks. These dynamics are hardly unique to twentieth-century entreaties and built on older political-cultural practices. Transnational Jewish publics emerged by the middle of the nineteenth century propelled by, among other developments, the responses to the 1840 blood libel charges in Damascus. At this time, Jewish organizations and Communities in Europe, North America, and the Ottoman Empire frequently relied on petitions, for example to Viceroy Muhammed Ali, that drew on transnational networks and resources and quickly reached wider audiences by being reprinted in the mainstream press.[3]

A more nuanced analysis of Holocaust-era petitioning, therefore, draws our attention to the need for an ongoing rethinking of the spatial terms of analysis of European Jewish and Holocaust histories. The 2009 call

---

Notes for this chapter begin on page 175.

by Moshe Rosman—and more recently by Simone Lässig and Miriam Rürup— for European Jewish histories that take the challenges of the spatial term seriously and examine non-political, socio-economic, and cultural ties between Jewish communities in different European countries is equally valid for histories of Jewish responses during the Holocaust.[4] Indeed, the history of the Holocaust has to be regarded as a history of constant forced border crossings—most critically of refugees and deportees brought about by Hitler's Germany and its many allies.

Consequently, this chapter not only makes the case for petitioning practices as a key part of much-needed "integrated histories" of the Holocaust and means of individual and collective contestations,[5] but also engages in the emerging reconsideration of the spatial terms of Holocaust and Jewish historiographies. It does so by demonstrating and analyzing the widespread existence of trans-territorial networks, which connected Jewish communities and families in multiple countries and helped to create transnational spaces that shaped Holocaust-era Jewish petitions, while also drawing on entreaty-writing practices of previous centuries.

More specifically, the chapter turns to an examination of petitioning practices of Central European Jews who approached the Filipino administration of President Manuel L. Quezon and European and American-Jewish aid organizations along with German and eventually Japanese fascist authorities in their attempts to escape Nazi-controlled Europe and survive in the Southeast Asian island archipelago during the late 1930s and early 1940s. This chapter demonstrates the need to move beyond examinations restricted to specific nation-states and sole foci on victims or perpetrators to global spaces and interactive histories.

Writing Histories of the Rescue of European Jews in the Philippines

In recent years, American, Israeli, Austrian, and—to a much lesser extent—Filipino scholars have started to shed light on the complex ways in which more than a thousand European Jews managed to escape from Nazi-controlled Europe to the Philippines. This rescue can—and mostly has been—told as a story in the realm of conventional diplomatic relations and rescue operations.[6] In the late 1930s, the Philippines were a recently established Commonwealth that had received the promise of full independence from the United States, still the sovereign power. As scholars such as Sharon Delmendo have pointed out, the Philippine islands were largely exempt from the quota policy of US immigration legislation.[7] This gave Commonwealth leaders, especially President Quezon of the dominant Nacionalista Party, some flexibility in accepting immigrants to their territory as long as these men and women would not become "public charges." With the onset of the Sino-Japanese war in the summer of 1937, refugees arriving in Manila included Chinese nationals as well as thirty German-Jewish families who had escaped from Hitler's Germany to Shanghai.[8] The quickly assembled Jewish Refugee Committee of Manila headed by members of the Frieder family of Cincinnati, Ohio, took charge of these German-Jewish refugees and found them employment.

This 1937 rescue became the "precedent" for the subsequent immigration program for hundreds of Jews from Central Europe.[9] The New York City-based Refugee Economic Corporation (REC), an affiliate of the American Jewish Joint Distribution Committee (JOINT), helped to initiate the program in early 1938 and provided much-needed funds. Consulting with President Quezon, US High Commissioner to the Philippines Paul McNutt agreed to approve visas for the refugees and involved the State Department and its consulates in Central Europe in issuing the much struggled-for documents. The Jewish Refugee Committee of Manila assumed the role of distributing REC funds and also "select[ing] the type of people who were to come."[10] Historian Bonnie Harris, thus, has aptly dubbed this process a "rescue by selection."[11] In December 1941, the Japanese Imperial forces' invasion of the Philippines brought this rescue to a standstill and foiled even more ambitious plans to create a haven for tens of thousands of Jewish refugees.

At the same time, the Philippine rescue can and is beginning to be told as a story of belated and competing commemorations. In the postwar Philippines, the late 1930s arrival of Jewish refugees did not become part of the newly independent country's national memory cultures. Faced with up to one million Filipino victims of the Japanese occupation, Filipino memory activists had different priorities.[12] In the belated commemoration of the early twenty-first century, the remaining Jewish survivors, who had all left the Philippines, gave testimony and promoted the recognition of the Philippines as a place of rescue. Their efforts are part of a broader politics of memory that also encompasses the—so far unsuccessful—attempts of the Filipino diplomatic corps to lobby Yad Vashem, the World Holocaust Remembrance Center in Jerusalem, for the recognition of the Philippine Commonwealth's first President as a "Righteous Among the Nations."[13]

Yet, examinations of the successful escape of European Jews to the Philippines extend beyond foci on diplomatic relations, conventional immigration, and memory studies. The rescue involved a wide range of transnational networks, channels of communication, and actors par excellence that had a critical impact on European Jews' struggles for survival. Thus, it is also a story of the central, but still undervalued role of Jewish petitioning practices and their significance in (re-)shaping new languages of immigration in interaction with various international aid and fascist agencies that sheds new light on the Philippine rescue and our understanding of Holocaust histories as a whole.

Shaping Transnational Languages of Petitioning: Refugee Organizations, Jewish Communities, and Government Agencies

By late 1938, the number of Jews in the Reich, including the *Ostmark*, had shrunk to some 295,000. More than half of the Jewish population of early 1930s Germany and Austria had managed to emigrate.[14] The nationwide pogroms of November 1938 unleashed by the Nazi regime robbed the remaining Jewish population of the belief that there still might be a prospect for a future, albeit segregated, life in the country. Without allies, the overall mood changed to a struggle for immediate escape. For the more than thirty thousand German-Jewish men, whom the regime had interned in concentration camps during the pogroms, the situation was exceptionally desperate. In the assaulted Jewish communities, an affidavit and entry visa for another country emerged as the most highly desired objects that could provide ways out of even concentration camp imprisonment. Consequently, relatives and friends of the imprisoned engaged in remarkable activism to obtain visas. Between the pogroms and the start of the war in Europe, another 120,000 Jews managed to escape.[15]

In the long lines in front of the emigration departments of Jewish Communities and consular offices of countries such as the United States,[16] there was relatively little talk about the Philippines. Yet, in the desperate search for a refuge in late 1938, the remote Southeast Asian archipelago that not everyone could immediately find on a map became a location of hope.[17] Immigration to the Philippines or anywhere else required much more than completing questionnaires and lengthy bureaucratic maneuvers to secure a visa. Faced with most countries' highly restrictive immigration policies, Jewish men and women had to draw on an array of approaches to elicit support. Among the most prominent means were collective and individual petitioning practices.

These entreaties assumed many forms, were increasingly embedded in global networks, and depended on shaping and sharing in a transnational language of petitioning and immigration. For once, Jews from Vienna to Breslau and from Düsseldorf to Budapest, who had learned about the Philippines as a possible refuge, directly petitioned the Commonwealth's President Quezon. The Presidential papers held at the National Library of the Philippines contain entreaties by or on behalf of some fifty almost exclusively Jewish petitioners sent to Manila from Central Europe. All of these petitions were mailed after the November pogroms. Sigmund Tauber's second petition of June 1939 is representative of most pleas in this collection. Drawing the president's attention to the "sad situation of the German . . . Jews," Tauber "begg[ed]" Quezon "for a card of permission to enter the Philippines and to remain there with my family."[18]

Many of these petitions were indirectly part of the intricate process of "selective immigration" to the country, which the Refugee Economic Corporation, Jewish Refugee Committee of Manila, US High Commissioner, and Filipino president had established. The authors of these petitions aimed at being included in a process they did not always fully comprehend and that often followed applications to their Jewish Communities' emigration departments. In April 1939, for example, Franz Thurmann, a photographer, sent a petition to Quezon in the hope of reviving his June 1938 application to the Viennese Jewish Community's emigration department.[19] Yet, even the "regular" selective immigration process to the Philippines included various forms of petitioning along the way. Jewish organizations in the Reich soon received entreaties. Among these organizations was the Aid Society of the Jews in Germany (Hilfsverein der Juden in Deutschland) that adhered to the Refugee Economic Corporation' guidelines by collecting formal applications, CVs, photographs, and educational records of potential emigrants to be forwarded to the Refugee Committee in Manila for evaluation. Petitions also reached the JOINT in New York, the Bureau of Insular Affairs in Washington, DC, that supervised the Office of the US High Commissioner, and even the Manila-based Refugee Committee itself.[20]

Like Holocaust-era petitions in general, the authors of Philippines-related petitions sought to follow specific rules of communication and tried to adhere to fluid regulations that the addressed agencies or officials had developed and made accessible. Still, even the establishment of criteria for determining suitable candidates for immigration to the Philippines and successful entreaties took the form of drawn-out and somewhat fluid processes. From the onset, these processes were informed by transnational networks and actors.

Among these actors, the Jewish Refugee Committee of Manila was of particular importance. Enjoying support from High Commissioner McNutt and President Quezon, it temporarily gained the status of a legitimate place and site of an "authorized language" on immigration that temporarily oversaw much of the immigration flow to the islands.[21] The Committee consisted of a board of members of the wealthiest Jewish families of the largely Manila-based Jewish Community of some five hundred men and women. It included Isaac Beck, owner of Manila's first department store, and a representative of the Frieder family, whose tobacco enterprise had brought them from the United States mainland to the Southeast Asian islands.[22] Most of the Committee's continually increasing "volume of work" and processing of the "ever mounting mail" from Europe was carried out by a staff of initially three and soon six "refugee assistants."[23]

Headed by Morton I. Netzorg, who had come to the islands in 1911 to join the Philippine public schools' teacher corps, the Committee's staff included Dr. Kurt Marx, a more recent arrival from China, where he had directed the Committee for the Assistance of European Refugees in Shanghai.[24] In addition, the 39-year-old Margarete Stern, a former official of the Viennese Community, who arrived in Manila in March 1940, was involved in the Committee's work.[25] In the fitting words of Michael G. Müller and Cornelius Torp, these officials "live[d] within, and actively shape[d], various geographical orders" from Southeast Asia to the Americas and Europe, where they maintained close contacts with Jewish Community and refugee officials as well as members of the business communities and political elites. They also helped to create and remake the transnational networks that shaped the language of immigration and informed the crafting of entreaties of the growing refugee population.[26]

Drawing heavily on their own experiences as transnational actors, the Committee members fleshed out the criteria for the "system of selective immigration" in which, as Alex Frieder who led the family's enterprise in Manila from late 1938 to early 1940, dubbed it, "employment" was "the magic word which holds the solution to all our problems."[27] They crafted a new language that constituted a continuum of refugees from the ideal to the—quite literally—"abject." These constructs evolved around specific classifications of employment allegedly needed on the islands. "Medical specialists," "registered nurses," "chemical engineers," "farmers," "film and photograph experts," "women dressmakers-stylists," "accountants," and "auto mechanics" were classifications that made the list, as did "cigar and tobacco experts," a clear nod to the Frieder's economic interest.[28] Petitioners whom the Committee regarded as fitting these categories and approved were then deemed eligible for financial subsidies from funds provided by the American Jewish Joint Distribution Committee, REC, and prosperous members of the local Jewish Community. This language was hardly neutral and inconsequential, but material, productive, and, when informing rejection and exclusion, outright violent.

As Alex Frieder noted in a lengthy May 1940 report, the Committee had indeed turned away or—in his words—"successfully diverted" "literally thousands of applicants" whose arrival would "have created a very bitter social and economic problem."[29] In the broadening transnational networks, the language of immigration and petitioning continued to be (re-)shaped by the Committee along with the Office of the US High Commissioner and US Federal Government agencies. For once, High Commissioner McNutt and, after July 1939, his successors Weldon Jones and later Francis B. Sayre reiterated the notion that the accepted immigrants would not become "a financial burden on domestic society." Yet, they also sought to expand the language by inserting more of the lingo of US immigration laws. McNutt, for instance, endorsed a 22 November 1938 US Government memo that portrayed the acceptance of political refugees as an act based on "broad humanitarian grounds" and the "defence of essential human liberties." In its interactions with the Refugee Committee, the Office of the High Commissioner, which had to accept the Committee's refugee recommendations, eagerly conveyed this modifying language.[30]

The Filipino political leadership, especially the Office of the President, also influenced the language of immigration and petitioning. In a press conference after the November pogroms in Nazi Germany, which received significant attention in the Filipino press, President Quezon stressed the country's willingness to admit more German-Jewish refugees.

In the process, he explicitly participated in filling the "magic word" of "employment" with additional meaning by privileging the acceptance of "German-Jewish physicians" who were allegedly needed to establish new

FIGURE 7.1. President Manuel L. Quezon and US High Commissioner Paul McNutt, Manila, ca. 1938. National Library of the Philippines.

clinics. Within eighteen months, the lingo of the ideal immigrant, however, had changed. As Quezon emphasized in an April 1940 speech on the eventually unsuccessful plan to settle thousands of Jewish refugees on the island of Mindanao, Jewish immigrants now had to be "farmers." They could "not" be "only ... merchants," "monopoliz[ing] commerce in the Philippines." Reiterating contemporary Zionist discourses, the President praised the recent "experience in Palestine," where Jewish settlers had succeeded in making "even the most arid land ... produce plenty."[31]

In addition to the figure of the refugee, the changing language of immigration also featured the aid giver, which was especially pertinent for a country in the process of nation building. To admit "unfortunate human beings," Quezon indicated in a statement in January 1939, would reify the "just and hospitable character of our people," while reasserting the Philippines' place among the "general conduct of democratic nations." For Filipino government officials, refugee petitioners' appeals to these dynamics were part of speaking the right language.[32]

In late 1938, US State Department officials called on government agencies, including European consular offices, not to get out the word that the archipelago was becoming a refuge for Jews.[33] Nonetheless, the aid agencies largely ignored US government officials and relied on still widening transnational networks to transmit information, strategies, and suitable verbiage. Once informed by the Refugee Economic Corporation, the Berlin-based Aid Society of the Jews in Germany swiftly briefed its subsidiary offices and corresponded with Jewish Communities in the Reich. In early fall 1938, the Jewish Community in Vienna, by then restructured and under Gestapo supervision, learned about the Philippine refuge from the Far Eastern Jewish Central Information Bureau in Harbin, China. Viennese Community officials immediately approached the government of the Philippines and the Hilfsverein.[34]

Jewish Community members in search of ways to escape fascist Europe eagerly took advantage of these networks. By 1935, the Hilfsverein alone, which historian Tobias Brinkmann has fittingly dubbed a "transnational actor per se," had already advised some 110,000 visitors to its offices and assisted even more in the late 1930s.[35] At the same time, community members tapped into transnational webs of communication and global family networks that transmitted information also on the Philippines. The Löwensteins, an acculturated lower middle-class Jewish family in Berlin-Charlottenburg, for instance, approached a distant relative, who had long ago immigrated to the Philippine islands and provided the desired insight into procedures and strategies. Sometimes, these relatives even sent entreaties to persons of real or imagined authority. Rose Druyan, a US citizen based in Buffalo, New York, petitioned Quezon in February 1939 to admit her brother Richard Fischhof and his Viennese-born family to the Philippines.[36]

In light of the immense distances, soon war-related impediments, censorship in Europe, and even the communication of information and comprehension of language rules were no easy tasks. These dynamics only increased the importance of the press. As very few had access to the Manila newspapers, the *Jüdisches Nachrichtenblatt* (*JN*), which replaced the stunning variety of Jewish papers in November 1938, when the Nazi regime shut down the Jewish press, aided in the transmission.[37] In January 1939, the *JN*'s 35,000 copies-strong Berlin edition, for example, published Quezon's December 1938 press conference announcement to "speed up the immigration of Jewish persons in larger numbers." The front-page announcement also included his call for "Jewish physicians from Central Europe."[38]

Yet, publications like the *Nachrichtenblatt* or the Hilfsverein's *Jüdische Auswanderung* went beyond conveying information. In the face of increasing supervision by the Gestapo and Propaganda Ministry officials, these publications' editors, such as the *JN*'s Leo Kreindler, recalibrated their texts with the expectation that their audiences would grasp their contributions' multilayered meanings—also to prepare their petitions. Kreindler repeatedly called for a "break with the past," which included an end to claims to Germanness and veritable celebrations of past military contributions. Instead, there was an urgency to "adapt" (*umstellen*) to "modest employment relationships" as part of a new "migration."[39]

Other publications were more direct. The *JN*'s Viennese edition listed the privileged professions desired by Manila's Refugee Committee in late December 1939.[40] The *JN*'s Prague edition sought to instruct its readership by urging everyone to "learn from letters" that reached Central Europe. The *Jüdische Auswanderung* published anonymous letters solicited from Jewish transnational activists in the Philippines. Already in mid-1938, one of these letters mentioned a "small influential group of local Jews" in Manila that helped "individuals, whose aptitude and profession enabled them to work here." A May 1937 letter writer ruled out "tailors" as fitting immigrants, since Filipinos or Chinese migrants exclusively held these professions. Others presented narratives peopled with "healthy, young" immigrants with a "savoir-vivre" who also spoke Spanish. While these constructs overlapped with the lingo of Manila's Refugee Committee, others, strikingly, conflicted. One of the authors construed "lawyers," if fluent in English and passing the local bar exams, as potential immigrants. More strikingly, a March 1937 letter pointed to the harsh climate and strictly excluded "any physical labor" such as farming—an immigrant identity that would later gain considerable importance for President Quezon.[41]

Central European Jews in Berlin, Naples, Vienna, Copenhagen, Breslau, or Budapest, thus, had to navigate a complex terrain, grasp subtle meanings and avoid easy misreadings of less authorized languages, while facing increasingly brutal physical and linguistic violence by fascist agencies. To reimagine themselves as part of a "transnational community" partially created by the press and to speak the fluid language of immigration remained pivotal in their quest to escape Nazi-dominated Europe.[42]

Central European Jewish Petitioning Practices, Transnational Networks, and Language

Almost all of the Jewish men and women in Nazi-governed Central Europe eager to learn about the Philippines as a possible refuge were already immersed in interactions with various Jewish Community agencies, aid organizations, consulates of countries around the globe, and German officials at tax, police, and city offices. Admonished by aid organizations and their publications, many, like the parents of Breslau-born Margot Kestenbaum, née Cassel, started to study Spanish and English, languages of countries of possible immigration. However, they also consciously set out to comprehend new terminologies and adjust previous languages of petitioning. Walter Laqueur, who grew up in Breslau's Jewish community, home to a significant cohort of subsequent immigrants to the Philippines, remembered encountering a flurry of new terms from "retraining" (*Umschulung*) to "affidavit."[43]

The petitions submitted by those men and women who tried to take advantage of the news of a potential Philippine refuge reflect these complex tasks. While attempting to speak these new languages as part of multilayered strategies to cope with increasingly dire circumstances, some succeeded with their entreaties, whereas many more slipped back to an older lingo that was in danger of undermining the very prospect of securing support for their emigration plans.

The surviving petitions to President Quezon capture many of the discursive practices and strategies of the increasingly "harassed, worried and depressed" Central European Jews—as a family friend on board a ship with immigrants bound for Manila conveyed to Quezon—who authored entreaties that sought to secure permission to immigrate.[44] First, especially older male petitioners regularly stressed their past military service and sacrifice, particularly in World War I. Before giving any other details in his collective April 1939 petition to Quezon mailed from Vienna, Hungarian-born Sigmund Tauber underscored that "three of us were partaking of [*sic!*] the Great War." In his English-language entreaty from April 1939,

Franz Thurmann also did not fail to stress that he had been "decorated with a war order [sic!]." Since past military service had been the cornerstone of, literally, thousands of petitions for exemptions from the Nazi regime's anti-Jewish legislation of the early 1930s, this ongoing practice by male veterans is hardly surprising.[45] Historian Marion A. Kaplan has argued that acculturated German-Jewish men tended to be more involved in public life and displayed a greater "sense of patriotism," especially regarding their military service, which had led many to argue against emigration. Nevertheless, prominent references to wartime service were hardly limited to male Jews. In her aforementioned 1939 plea to the Filipino president to grant a visa to her brother, United States-based Rose Druyan underscored that he had "served in the World War."[46]

In the transnational languages and worlds of immigration, however, these references hardly held any sway. If anything, they conflicted with the new terminologies coined by transnational actors on refugee committees and often circulated in the Jewish press. Tauber's petitions and references to military service did not result in a favorable decision. The Viennese Gestapo deported him and his wife to the Terezín ghetto in September 1942. In October 1944, the couple was forced on a train to Auschwitz and murdered at the camp.[47] The rejection of Tauber's petition can hardly be reduced to a single factor—his age of fifty-four and profession of tailor also worked against him—but the reference to frontline service and patriotism did not help his case.

Second, the lingo of labor was even more prominent in virtually every petition. Any questionnaire from a Jewish Community's emigration department, often supported by entreaties, listed profession on the front page. When the 25-year-old Julius Klinger completed the questionnaire of the Viennese *Gemeinde* in May 1938, as one of more than twenty thousand Viennese Jews that month, he identified his "occupation (specialist subject)" as "mechanic" and emphasized work with tractors and cars along with his alleged English language skills. When submitted, along with pleas, to the Frieder-led Refugee Committee, its members decided in Klinger's favor, and with the support of Quezon and McNutt, a visa was issued in 1939. While it would be a gross oversimplification to tie this decision exclusively to his stated job skills, his language of labor constituted a key factor in securing a favorable decision.[48]

Others, by contrast, misread the stated criteria or sought assistance without drawing on strategies available via transnational networks. In his March 1939 petition to Quezon, Isac Grossmann pleaded to be granted an immigration permit by emphasizing his "occupation of bank official." Writing in German, the 45-year-old Grossmann also included his younger sister, whom he likewise identified as a "bank official." The author referenced a *Jüdisches Nachrichtenblatt* article that quoted Quezon's offer to admit Jews to his country.[49] There is no evidence that Grossmann, a resident of Berlin for twenty-five years, but Romanian by birth who had remained stateless, consulted the Hilfsverein or attempted to expand the "accountant" category of the Manila Committee by including banking. His efforts to obtain visas failed. Grossmann's highlighting of the banking profession blatantly clashed with the Frieder-led Committee's language of immigration. Moreover, it seemed to confirm the stereotypes in the lingo of antisemites not only in Nazi-controlled Europe, but also among Filipino opposition politicians and parts of the general populace. As the public discussions of the ever-more ambitious plans to settle thousands of Jewish refugees in the archipelago broadened in 1939, voices of religious anti-Judaism gained ground. In a newspaper interview, General Emilio Aguinaldo, the country's first President after its independence from Spain, argued that "the Jews are a dangerous people to have around in large number." "[B]y their training in business, they have succeeded in predominating [sic!] . . . the people of places they settled."[50] With his petition rejected and other attempts to emigrate unsuccessful, Grossmann was forced on a train to Birkenau in March 1943, where the SS killed him shortly after arrival. A day earlier, the Berlin Gestapo had already deported his sister.[51]

Yet, even those petitioners who had mastered the language of labor and immigration were not assured a positive outcome. After reading the *JN*'s January 1939 coverage of the Philippines, Oskar Hess petitioned Quezon for a visa for him and his family in Hagen, Westphalia. Hess underscored that he did "not shy away from any work" and was "experienced in agricultural labor," including cattle. Writing in German, he even assured the Filipino leader that he would "never become a burden to the state."[52] There is no evidence that Malacañan Palace officials ever forwarded the petition to the German-speaking staff of the Refugee Committee. While Quezon and his Executive Secretary Jorge Vargas had both visited Nazi Germany on separate occasions—Vargas was, among others, invited to a reception hosted at the Propaganda Ministry in Berlin in April 1938—they hardly read German. In March 1943, Hess, his spouse, and their teenage daughter were deported and murdered in Auschwitz.[53]

In his April 1939 petition from Berlin, Erich Friedlaender, by contrast, wrote in more than respectable Spanish and presented himself not only as an export specialist, but also as a professional translator. He eloquently made his case of employability in the trade of pharmaceutical and medical equipment. Several factors, nonetheless, worked against him, including his advanced age of almost sixty. The family never received the desired response from Manila. Aided by her parents' petitions and multiple interactions with fascist authorities, the nineteen-year-old Ilse Friedlaender, meanwhile, could prepare to go into hiding. According to the gentile woman who provided her with shelter in Berlin, Ilse succeeded for two years, but was caught by the Gestapo in late 1944 and died in Belsen a few months later.[54]

Third, petitioners, finally, relied on a language of humanitarian values and urgency in the face of imminent danger to the lives of those favored in the entreaties. Viennese-Jewish Community member Julius Klinger had not only used the "right" language of labor. In June 1938, he had also been arrested and deported to Dachau and later to Buchenwald concentration camp. Confronted with what a Viennese Community official readily accepted as a "decidedly huge emergency," Klinger's mother Elsa and the wife of his last employer, Katharina Wachmann, applied for a visa for the prisoner and petitioned the Viennese Community for financial support for his boat ticket. Both were granted. Due to the intervention by the two women and after the visa information had reached the Buchenwald administration, Klinger was released four weeks later and secured passage on a ship bound to Shanghai in July.[55]

The Nazi regime's increased targeting of male Jews, culminating in the mass arrests during the November 1938 pogroms, necessitated public interventions by middle-class Jewish women in largely unprecedented forms and numbers. In the process, they overcame and exploited pervasive and highly restrictive bourgeois gender norms of female passivity. After the pogroms of November 1938, the "most crucial task" for thousands of Jewish women was to get their husbands and other male relatives released from various concentration camps.[56] This task also translated into increased petitioning practices that were dominated by the utmost urgency and directed, as in Klinger's case, at both Jewish and Nazi officials. Fifteen percent of the entreaties written by European Jews to Quezon in the Presidential Papers had female authors. While still small, the figure is remarkable. Despite a robust tradition of petitioning by Central European Jewish women since the period of Emancipation, many of these past petitioners had been widows or sought support for underage children.[57]

As members of the Jewish Community in Graz, the thirty-year-old Margaret Welisch and her sister-in-law Doris survived the November pogroms. Yet, Austrian Nazi officials threatened them with arrest, if their husbands, who had narrowly escaped, would not turn themselves in. When the men emerged from hiding, the Gestapo deported them to Dachau. Trying to comprehend the flurry of new anti-Jewish regulations, the women quickly discerned the promise of release that came with the presentation of emigration papers. As Margaret Welisch later recalled, her sister-in-law went to Vienna. With the help of another family member, she obtained affidavits from a Catholic-Austrian Nazi opponent who had immigrated to the Philippines. Together, they also received a positive decision from the Refugee Committee. The two men were released after two weeks in Dachau and they all soon left for Manila.[58]

Speaking a language of humanitarian values and urgency, Margaret and Doris Welisch swayed a series of male officials. They emerged as veritable transnational actors, successfully mobilizing fluid family and organizational networks that reached all the way to Manila. They also contributed to the shifting language of immigration shaped by the Frieder-led Committee. Alex Frieder's prescript to withstand an "appeal made to our emotions" in favor of a "practical attitude" that favored suitable professions hardly presented a rigid rule.[59]

Jewish Refugees in the Philippines: New Struggles and Petitioning during the Japanese Occupation

By the fall of 1941, the Jewish refugee population in the Philippines had increased to about thirteen hundred.[60] Most of the adults had mastered and perfected languages of immigration and petitioning. Many joined Manila's Jewish Community based in Temple Emile. The Temple, completed in 1924, was the only synagogue on the archipelago. Navigating what was still largely a colonialist society with a metropolitan capital of more than 623,000 residents and largely rural communities in the rest of Luzon and the other islands presented a considerable challenge to many. Some regarded the Refugee Committee as involved in a policing of interactions between the mostly impoverished white European refugees and the native Filipino population.[61] For the refugees, petitioning practices—albeit once more adjusted—continued to play an important role, evolving mainly around questions of employment. Immigrant physicians in particular encountered obstacles as Filipino doctors and the medical board lobbied the Commonwealth Government to prevent the refugees from offering their services to the native population. All sides submitted entreaties to the Malacañan Palace, which, ultimately, sided with the Filipino physicians.[62]

The Japanese attack on the islands shortly after the bombing of Pearl Harbor profoundly changed the lives of the refugees, native Filipino population, and US officials. Weeks before the Imperial Army overran a basically abandoned capital city on 2 January 1942, Phillip Frieder had returned to the United States. High Commissioner Sayre and President Quezon followed suit in late December. The Japanese forces set up a military administration and a new collaborationist State Council Executive Commission chaired by former Executive Secretary Jorge Vargas as part of the Japan-dominated "Co-Prosperity Sphere in Greater East Asia."[63]

For most Central European Jewish refugees, the beginning of the occupation translated into a striking role reversal. Members of the Refugee Committee and Temple Emile congregation who held US passports, including Morton Netzorg and Samuel Schechter, Frieder's successor as the head of the now disbanded Refugee Committee, were arrested as enemy aliens. The Japanese brought them to Manila's Santo Tomas Internment Camp on the grounds of a Spanish-founded university by the same name. In 1944, it housed about 3,700 internees, mostly Americans along with some British, Australian, and a few citizens of other countries also at war with Japan, including 250 Jews.[64]

Jewish refugees with passports from countries allied with Imperial Japan, including Nazi Germany and fascist Hungary, by contrast, were not interned and fully assumed the leadership of the Temple. Rabbi Josef Schwarz, who had come from the German city of Hildesheim with the help of the Refugee Committee in October 1938, took on a leading role, especially as the congregation's official representative to the "Religious Section" of the Japanese Army and, as of July 1942, to the Japanese Military Administration's Department of Information.[65]

In recent testimonies, surviving refugees such as Ralph Preiss have often stressed that in the eyes of the Japanese who saw their Reich-issued passports, German-Jewish refugees in the Philippines had, ironically, become "good Germans again."[66] Yet, Japanese perceptions and European-Jewish-Japanese relations were far more complex. While some ordinary Imperial Army soldiers might indeed have drawn little distinctions between gentile and former Jewish Germans, the Army's "Jewish experts" and officials of the *Kempeitai*, the Japanese military police, hardly made any such conflations. *Kempeitai* officers were distinctly anti-Jewish, even suspecting the congregation to function as local representative of a worldwide Jewish conspiracy to rule the globe.[67] Still, at least initially, Jewish refugees from the Reich found themselves in a position of limited symbolic power they could use in interactions with Japanese occupation officials.

At both the community and family level, German Jewish refuges frequently resorted once again to petitioning practices as they addressed Japanese authorities over a range of issues. For that purpose, they distinctly modified these practices, combining lingo and strategies once obtained via ocean-crossing transnational networks with older responses to fascist authorities. Rabbi Schwarz and the refugee congregants specifically sought to come to the aid of precisely the same, now imprisoned Jewish Community members who had once helped them to find refuge in the Philippines. Securing the food supply for those held at the closed internment camp of Santo Tomas, especially for orthodox Jews committed to keep the prescribed dietary laws, spurred the congregants into action.

Furthermore, American-Jewish prisoners participating in High Holiday services officiated by Schwarz at the Temple became a concern. In his verbal entreaties to the Japanese Military Administration's Religious Section, Schwarz tapped into the proclaimed commitment of the Japanese "not to interfere with religious worship" but rather to engage in "conscious accommodation" to religious life on the islands.[68]

By drawing on discourses of religious practice, Schwarz relied on petitioning strategies once developed in exchanges with Nazi officials, whom Community leaders had temporarily convinced to accept a separate Jewish cultural and religious sphere in the Reich, and applied these strategies to their interactions with Japanese authorities. As the imprisoned Schechter later noted, the efforts initially prompted a steady supply of kosher food into the camp and the permission for some eighty Jewish prisoners—under armed guard—to attend Yom Kippur services at the Temple in the fall of 1942. The same strategy even helped to get Joseph Cysner, the Community's former cantor with a Polish passport, released from Santo Tomas. As historian Bonnie Harris has shown, Schwarz and Cysner also made a case for his release on humanitarian grounds, arguing that the cantor needed to take care of his sick mother outside the camp.[69]

Written and verbal petitioning played a critical role in a series of interactions between individual refugees and Japanese authorities. Shortly after the Japanese invasion, Salo Cassel, a former Tietz employee in Breslau who had escaped to Manila with his spouse, daughter, and his brother's family in October 1938, was dismissed from helping to run Ernest Berg's department store on Manila's Escolta Street. Berg, a German-born gentile who had arrived in the early 1920s, fired Cassel, his daughter later recalled, because her father "was Jewish." While Cassel and his spouse, a convert from Protestantism Berg continued to employ, debated possible ways to retaliate, they, ultimately, decided against it. They were, nonetheless, forced into action when the *Kempeitai* arrested Salo Cassel for changing prices at the store in an allegedly illegal manner at the onset of the Japanese occupation. Upon learning that her spouse was held at the *Kempeitai* headquarter, the site of systematic torture and execution of prisoners, Erna Cassel decided to rely on verbal entreaties articulated in person at Fort Santiago.[70] The 37-year old Westphalian emphasized her Germanness, and in an almost anachronistic step back to interwar petitioning practices, she also presented the Iron Cross her spouse had been awarded for wounds sustained on the Western Front. What had undermined petitions to Quezon and the Refugee Committee only months earlier now had some sway even with Lt. Col. Seichi Ohta's military police. Unlike the *Kempeitai* detachments outside Manila whose officers spoke little Tagalog or English and relied on interpreters, the Cassels could converse with the English-speaking staff at the Manila headquarters. In a universe of false accusations and arrests, the symbolism of the German war medal increased the legitimacy of their claims.[71]

Spouses of Jewish veterans imprisoned during the November pogroms had likewise produced war medals in their attempts to get their husbands released from concentration camps and it is not unlikely that Erna Cassel had learned about this practice. At a time prior to Imperial Japan's 1943 antisemitic turn, the practice succeeded and her husband was released. By contrast, Margarete Stern's efforts to end her imprisonment faced considerably more hurdles. For the *Kempeitai*, her work for the former "American" Refugee Committee continually undermined her pleas as a Reich passport holder and she had to endure several months of imprisonment and torture in Fort Santiago.[72]

Petitioning, meanwhile, became one of the primary ways in which the self-organized prisoner communities in camps like Santo Tomas interacted with Japanese prison administrations. In late February 1943, Morton Netzorg, for example, petitioned the Santo Tomas commandant for help with liquidating assets kept outside the camp to help his sick spouse. Her illness, Netzorg stressed, could not be "cure[d] under present war conditions." Netzorg's appeal on humanitarian grounds implicitly drew—like the entreaties by the inmates' Executive Committee—on international law on the treatment of prisoners during war, while also reiterating a discursive strategy of humanitarian appeals and sense of urgency that the former Refugee Committee staff member had encountered hundreds of times in petitions by European refugees.[73]

Conclusions

The escape of some thirteen hundred Central European Jews to the Philippines and their subsequent struggles on the archipelago during the Japanese occupation demonstrates the significance of petitioning practices as crucial tools for many of the persecuted to negotiate space and their survival. It also captures the significance of transnational spaces and networks that profoundly shaped these entreaties and their language of immigration. These petitions were not just words on paper. Their verbiage was productive and inherently linked to the reconstitution of their authors' identities often along with the "magic word" of employment. Albeit in a position of little to no power, the refugee petitioners negotiated with fascist authorities at home, Quezon administration officials, and the cross-national Refugee Committee in Manila and often managed to insert themselves in ruptures in the narrative of desired immigrants, while quickly turning into veritable transnational actors themselves.

Entreaties by and on behalf of Julius Klinger, as discussed in this chapter, partook in shifting languages of immigration, resonated with members of the Manila Refugee Committee and helped to get him released from Buchenwald. Entreaties by Dr. Hugo Alt succeeded in securing travel support from the Viennese Israelitische Kultusgemeinde (IKG) and a favorable recommendation by the Manila Committee. Speaking the language of immigration as a medical practitioner with claimed English skills and—in fulfillment of the gender norms of his community—of a caring father who had, as the IKG's emigration official noted, "spent most of his wealth" on the emigration of his daughter and other relatives, ultimately, helped to place him and his spouse on a ship to Manila.[74]

Yet, there were few, if any, assurances. As Berlin-based Erich Friedlaender's aforementioned Quezon petition proved, even speaking the language of immigration did not automatically result in the much-desired issuance of visas, especially if other factors such as age worked against it. The Friedlaenders were murdered in Riga in late 1942.[75] And still, petitioning and mastering the "right" verbiage was hardly superfluous or part of a deception on the part of fascist offices or overburdened aid agencies. Acknowledging this language's impact, Alex Frieder lamented a few months before the Japanese attack that "[p]erhaps we have been misled by the rather indiscriminate usage of the terms 'perfect,' 'expert' and 'specialist'" and "given visa recommendations" to those "prone to overstate their qualifications."[76]

Like the petitioning processes, this transnational language of immigration was fluid and constantly adjusted. As of early 1942, European-Jewish refugees in the Philippines, once again under an increasingly hostile regime, had to realize that almost exactly the same strategies and verbiage that had ended an entreaty to Quezon now could easily result in the desired outcome in interactions with new Japanese occupation authorities.

These transnational petitions enable us to grasp some of the complexity that integrated histories of the Holocaust require and remind researchers of the need to eschew oversimplified binaries of resistance versus collaboration in favor of more complex taxonomies and, in so doing, also rethink the spatial terms of analysis.

Thomas Pegelow Kaplan is the Louis P. Singer Endowed Chair in Jewish History, Professor of History, and Interim Director of the Program in Jewish Studies at the University of Colorado Boulder. He is the author of *The Language of Nazi Genocide* (2009) and *The German-Jewish Press and Journalism Beyond Borders, 1933-1943* (2023, in Hebrew) as well as the co-editor of

Beyond "Ordinary Men": Christopher R. Browning and Holocaust Historiography (2019) and Police and Holocaust (2023, in German). He is currently completing a manuscript entitled Naming Genocide: Protesters, Imageries of Mass Murder, and the Remaking of Memory in West Germany and the United States.

Notes

Research for this chapter was made possible by fellowships from Yad Vashem's International Institute for Holocaust Research, the Memorial Foundation for Jewish Culture, the Alexander von Humboldt Foundation, a Davidson College Faculty Study and Research Project Grant, and funds from the professional development budget of the Leon Levine Distinguished Professorship in Judaic, Holocaust, and Peace Studies, Appalachian State University.

I would also like to thank Racelle Weiman, Anatol Steck, Sharon Delmendo, and Leni Garcia for their invaluable research support as well as the National Library of the Philippines and Manuel L. Quezon III for granting me access to his grandfather's papers.

1. Raul Hilberg, "Petitionen von Juden zur Zeit ihrer Vernichtung," in *Mit Petitionen Politik verändern*, ed. Reinhard Bockhofer (Baden-Baden, 1999), 39–40.
2. For France, see, for example, Renée Poznanski, *Jews in France during World War II* (Waltham, MA, 2001); for the Reich, see John M. Steiner and Jobst Freiherr von Cornberg, "Willkür in der Willkür: Befreiungen von den antisemitischen Gesetzen," *Vierteljahrshefte für Zeitgeschichte* 46 (1998): 143–87.
3. Jonathan Frankel, *The Damascus Affair: "Ritual Murder," Politics, and the Jews in 1840* (Cambridge, 1997), 165; Tobias Brinkmann, *Migration und Transnationalität: Perspektiven deutsch-jüdischer Geschichte* (Paderborn, 2012), 37–39.
4. Moshe Rosman, "Jewish History across Borders," in *Rethinking European Jewish History*, ed. Jeremy Cohen et al. (Oxford, 2008), 15–29; Simone Lässig and Miriam Rürup, eds., *Space and Spatiality in Modern German-Jewish History* (New York, 2017), 4–5.
5. Saul Friedländer, "Eine integrierte Geschichte des Holocausts." *Aus Politik und Zeitgeschichte* 14–15 (2007): 9–10.
6. See, for example, Dean Kotlowski, "Breaching the Paper Walls: Paul V. McNutt and Jewish Refugees to the Philippines, 1938–1939," *Diplomatic History* 33 (2009): 865–96; Bonnie M. Harris, *Philippine Sanctuary: A Holocaust Odyssey* (Madison, WI, 2020); Christine Kanzler, "Zuflucht in den Tropen: Österreichische Emigranten auf den Philippinen," *Mitteilungen Dokumentationsarchiv des Österreichischen Widerstandes* 167 (2004): 5–7; Maya Guez and Robert Rockaway, "The Philippine Saving of Jews, 1938–1939," *Moreshet* 18 (2018): 13–37.
7. Sharon Delmendo and Noel M. Izon, *An Open Door: Jewish Rescue in the Philippines* (Washington, DC, 2012), 12.
8. Third Annual Report of the President of the Philippines to the President and Congress of the United States, 1938, p. 2, National Library of the Philippines (hereafter NLP), Presidential Papers of Manuel L. Quezon (PPMLQ), Series III, Box 26.
9. Frank Ephraim, *Escape to Manila: From Nazi Tyranny to Japanese Terror* (Urbana, IL, 2003), 23.
10. Memorandum of Conversation between Mr. Hyman and Morris Frieder of Cincinnati, Ohio, 28 November 1938, JDC Archives, New York (hereafter JDCA), AR 1933/44, File no. 784, frames 1343.
11. Harris, *Philippine Sanctuary*, 73.

12. Jose Maria Edito Kalaw Tirol, "Of Forgetting and Remembering: Social Memory, Commemorating and the Jewish Refugees in the Philippines during the Second World War" (Ph.D. diss., University of the Philippines, 2015), 297–98.
13. As Yad Vashem officials point out, Quezon's involvement did not come at the risk to his life and, thus, does not meet a key criterion. Irena Steinfeldt, past director of Righteous Among the Nations Department, conversation with author, Jerusalem, 12 December 2017; Neal Imperial, Philippines ambassador to Israel, conversation with author, Rishon LeZion, 13 November 2017; Max Weissler, interview by author, Hod Hasharon, 22 November 2017.
14. On emigration figures, see Wolfgang Benz, ed., *Die Juden in Deutschland 1933–1945: Leben unter nationalsozialistischer Herrschaft* (Munich, 1996), 733.
15. Alan E. Steinweis, *Kristallnacht 1938* (Cambridge, MA, 2009), 108, 112–15.
16. On the conditions in Breslau, see Katharina Friedla, *Juden in Breslau/Wroclaw 1933–1949: Überlebensstrategien, Selbstbehauptung und Verfolgungserfahrungen* (Cologne, 2015), 220–53.
17. See Weissler, interview by author.
18. S. Tauber to President Quezon, 19 June 1939, NLP, PPMLQ, Subject File, Box 171, Folder "Iwahig Penal Colony—Joint Preparatory Comm / 1939–1940—Jews." For a different reading of these sources, see Ber Kotlerman, "Philippine Visas-for-Jews from the Perspective of the Unanswered Letters of 1939 to President Quezon," *Darbai Ir Dienos* 67 (2017): 273–91.
19. F. Thurmann, Fragebogen, Israelitische Kultusgemeinde Wien, Auswanderungsabteilung, 22 June 1938, Central Archives for the History of the Jewish People (hereafter CAHJP), Jerusalem, Archiv der Israelitischen Kultusgemeinde Wien (AIKW), HMB/2410; F. Thurmann to President Quezon, 4 April 1939, NLP, PPMLQ, Subject File, Box 171. On the Viennese Community and emigration, see Ilana Fritz Offenberger, *The Jews of Nazi Vienna, 1938–1945: Rescue and Destruction* (Cham, 2017), 71–72, 130–33, 142–45.
20. See, for example, N. Dallant's plea to A. Fischer, Malacañan Palace, in response to a petition by K. Wachtl on behalf of Dr. A. Oczeret, 10 October 1938, National Archives II, College Park (hereafter NA), RG 350, Box 1338 and L. Fuhrman to JDC, 17 July 1939, JDCA, AR 1933/44, File no. 784, frame 1357–58.
21. Pierre Bourdieu, *Language and Symbolic Power* (Cambridge, MA, 1991), 107–13.
22. On the Jewish Community, see Jonathan Goldstein, *Jewish Identities in East and Southeast Asia* (Berlin, 2015), 45–81; John W. Griese, "The Jewish Community in Manila" (M.A. thesis, University of the Philippines, 1954), 23–24.
23. Alex Frieder to Jewish Refugee Committee, Manila, 7 May 1940, JDCA, AR 1933/44, File no. 784, frames 1274–75.
24. Ibid.; Morton J. Netzorg and Michael Onorato, *Jock Netzorg: Manila Memories* (Laguna Beach, CA, 1988), 1–2.
25. "Bericht von Frau Margarete Stern," March 1957, Yad Vashem Archives (hereafter YVA), O.3/7829.
26. Michael G. Müller and Cornelius Torp, "Conceptualizing Transnational Spaces in History," *European Review of History* 16 (2009): 609–17.
27. Frieder to Refugee Committee, 1940, JDCA, AR 1933/44, File no. 784, frame 1268.
28. Bruno Schachner to Hilfsverein der deutschen Juden, Berlin, 1 June 1938, JDCA, AR 1933/44, File no. 784.
29. Frieder to Refugee Committee, 1940, JDCA, AR 1933/44, File no. 784, frame 1262.
30. McNutt to State Department, 25 October 1938; State Department to US High Commissioner, Manila, Radiogram, 11 October 1938 and Department of State to Harry Woodring, Secretary of War, 2 December 1938, NA, RG 350, Box 1338, folder "28943-to: Jewish Race."

31. "Willing to Aid Refugees, Says Quezon," *The Tribune*, 6 December 1938; "Quezon explains Policy on Jews," *Philippines Herald*, 24 April 1940, 12; Bourdieu, *Language*, 113.
32. President Quezon, "The Refugee Problem," 5 January 1939, NLP, PPMLQ, Series III, Box 87.
33. Department of State to Secretary of War, 2 December 1938, NA, RG 350, Box 1338, folder "28943-to: Jewish Race.".
34. Bruno Schachner to Hilfsverein der deutschen Juden, Berlin, 1 June 1938, JDCA, AR 1933/44, File no. 784; "Bericht über den Stand der Philippinen-Angelegenheit," Vienna, 30 October 1938, YVA, O.85/217.
35. Hilfsverein der Juden in Deutschland, *Die Arbeit des Hilfsvereins der Juden in Deutschland 1934–1935* (Berlin, 1935), 14. On the Hilfsverein, see Salomon Adler-Rudel, *Jüdische Selbsthilfe unter dem Naziregime 1933–1939* (Tübingen, 1974), 86–94; Brinkmann, *Migration*, 79–85.
36. George L. Loewenstein, interview by author, Boca Raton, 2 November 2014; Rose Druyan to President Quezon, 22 February 1939, NLP, PPMLQ, Subject File, Box 171.
37. Reiner Burger, *Von Goebbels Gnaden: "Jüdisches Nachrichtenblatt," 1938–1943* (Münster, 2001), 46–48.
38. Ibid., 77; "Aussichten. . .," *JN (Berlin)*, 6 January 1939, 1; Siegfried Israel Mehler, "Die Hauptinseln der Philippinen," *JN (Berlin)*, 28 March 1939, 3.
39. See, for example, Leo Kreindler, "Aktive Bereitschaft," *JN (Berlin)*, 21 March 1941, 1.
40. "Die Jüdische Wanderung: Mitteilungen der Auswanderungsabteilung der Israelitischen Kultusgemeinde Wien," *JN (Vienna)*, 29 December 1939, 2.
41. "Aus Briefen lernen," *JN (Prague)*, 28 November 1941, 4; "Die Philippinen," *Jüdische Auswanderung*, July 1938, 93–95.
42. Yosef Gorni, *The Jewish Press and the Holocaust, 1939–1945* (New York, 2014), 4.
43. Margot Pins Kestenbaum, interview by author, Jerusalem, 21 November 2017; Walter Laqueur, *Thursday's Child Has Far to Go: A Memoir of the Journeying Years* (New York, 1992), 129–30.
44. N.N., aboard the *Scharnhorst*, to Quezon, 10 August 1939, NLP, PPMLQ, Series IV, Box 21, folder "Family correspondence, January–August 1939."
45. On exemptions, see Steiner and Cornberg, "Willkür," 146–49. Tauber to Quezon, Vienna, 11 April 1939, NLP, PPMLQ, Subject File, Box 171; Thurmann to Quezon, April 1939, NLP, PPMLQ, Subject File, Box 171.
46. Marion A. Kaplan, *Between Dignity and Despair: Jewish Life in Nazi Germany* (New York, 1998), 64–65; Druyan to Quezon, February 1939, NLP, PPMLQ, Subject File, Box 171.
47. Transport list to Auschwitz, 16 October 1944, 4959385; index card S. Tauber, 98541984, ITS Digital Archive (ITSDA), United States Holocaust Memorial Museum Archives, Washington, DC (hereafter USHMMA).
48. Julius Klinger, Fragebogen, Israelitische Kultusgemeinde Wien, Auswanderungsabteilung, 15 May 1938, CAHJP, AIKW, HMB/2321; McNutt to State Department, Washington, DC, Radiogram, 1 April 1939, NA, RG 350, Box 1338, Folder "28943 with 21. Jewish Refugees to Philippine Islands." On the number of applicants, see Offenberger, *Jews of Nazi Vienna*, 85.
49. I. Grossmann to President Quezon, 29 May 1939, NLP, PPMLQ, Subject File, Box 171. For a reproduction of his petition, see pp. 236–37, this volume.
50. "Jews Feared by Aguinaldo," *Manila Daily Bulletin*, 22 April 1939, 2–3.
51. Index card I. Grossmann, 11233575, ITSDA, YVA; Central Database of Shoah Victims' Names, Yad Vashem, retrieved 11 November 2017 from https://yvng.yadvashem.org/.
52. Oskar Hess to Quezon, 10 January 1939, NLP, PPMLQ, Subject File, Box 171.

53. The Central Database of Shoah Victims' Names, Yad Vashem, retrieved 11 November 2017 from https://yvng.yadvashem.org/. Invitation by Goebbels to Vargas, Berlin, April 1938, Office of the President of the Philippines, Scrapbook, Mar.–May 1938, Vargas Papers, Jorge B. Vargas Museum & Filipiniana Research Center, University of the Philippines Diliman; Quezon to Vargas, 12 April 1937, NLP, PPMLQ, Series I, Box 84, Folder "General Correspondence. April 1–15, 1937."
54. Friedlaender to Quezon, 17 April 1939, NLP, PPMLQ, Subject File, Box 171; index card Friedlaender, 84786039; Henning to IRC, 1 March 1949, 84945771, ITSDA, USHMMA.
55. J. Klinger, Prisoner file card Buchenwald, 6290520, ITSDA, YVA; Antrag Reisezuschuß J. Klinger, 6 April 1939; Ansuchen Elsa Klinger, 1 April 1939, Auswanderungsabteilung, Israelitische Kultusgemeinde Wien, 6 April 1939, CAHJP, AIKW, HMB/2321; McNutt to State Department, 1 April 1939; D. Wachmann, Fragebogen, Israelitische Kultusgemeinde Wien, Auswanderungsabteilung, 23 May 1938, CAHJP, AIKW, HMB/2414.
56. Kaplan, *Between Dignity and Despair*, 127.
57. André Holenstein, "Bitten um den Schutz: Staatliche Judenpolitik und Lebensführung von Juden im Lichte der Schutzsupplikationen aus der Markgrafschaft Baden(-Durlach) im 18. Jahrhundert," in *Landjudentum im deutschen Südwesten während der Frühen Neuzeit*, ed. Rolf Kießling et al. (Berlin, 1999), 97–153.
58. Margarete Welisch, interview 6090, Jamaica, New York, 1995, USC Shoah Foundation Visual History Archive Los Angeles (hereafter USC SF VHA), Segment 80–81; Welisch, "I Remember," in *Erinnerungen: Lebensgeschichten von Opfern des Nationalsozialismus*, vol. 4/1, ed. Renate Meissner (Vienna, 2015), 226–27.
59. Frieder to Refugee Committee, 1940, JDCA, AR 1933/44, File no. 784, frame 1268.
60. "Refugee Immigration to the Philippines" [c. October 1941], JDCA, AR 1933/44, File no. 784, frame 1175.
61. Ruth Jacoby et al., eds., *Mensch—Land—Gerechtigkeit: Die Erinnerungen Erich Hellmuth Jacobys, 1903–1979* (Berlin, 2013), 79–81; Griese, "Jewish Community," 26. See also Christine Kanzler, "Exilerfahrungen deutschsprachiger Emigranten auf den Philippinen," in *Alltag Im Exil*, ed. Daniel Azuélos (Würzburg, 2011), 95–108.
62. Georg Winternitz v. Veljenegg to Quezon, 15 June 1939, NLP, PPMLQ, Subject File, Box 171; Ralph Preiss, interview by author, Boone, 8 August 2017.
63. On the occupation and Filipino collaboration, see Ikehata Setsuho and Ricardo Trota Jose, eds., *The Philippines under Japan: Occupation Policy and Reaction* (Quezon City, 1999), 2–9; Sven Matthiessen, *Japanese Pan-Asianism and the Philippines from the Late Nineteenth Century to the End of World War II* (Leiden, 2016), 78–183. See also Ephraim, *Escape to Manila*, 82.
64. Ephraim, *Escape to Manila*, 91; Ephraim, Oral History Interview, 28 February 1997, USHMMA, RG-50.106.0068; Frederic Harper Stevens, *Santo Tomas Internment Camp* (New York, 1946), 519, 523; Santo Tomas Internment Camp: Census Reports, 1943–1944, STIC 3, American Historical Collection, Rizal Library, Ateneo de Manila University (hereafter AHC Rizal); Samuel N. Schechter, "Judaism in the Camp," in Stevens, *Santo Tomas*, 172.
65. Headed by Lt. Col. Narusawa Tomoji, the Section supervised religious life on the islands, including the Jewish Community. See Terada Takefumi, "The Religious Propaganda Program for Christian Churches," in Setsuho and Jose, *Philippines under Japan*, 217–22; Alfredo Parpan, Sr., "The Japanese and the Philippine Church, 1942–45," *Philippine Studies* 37 (1989): 451–66.
66. Preiss, interview by author.
67. Rabbi Josef Schwarz, "History of the Jewish Community Manila," Racelle Weiman private collection; Ephraim, *Escape to Manila*, 94. On the Imperial Army's "Jewish experts,"

see Bei Gao, *Shanghai Sanctuary: Chinese and Japanese Policy toward European Jewish Refugees during World War II* (Oxford, 2016).
68. Parpan, "Philippine Church," 463; Schechter, "Judaism in Camp," 172; Ephraim, *Escape to Manila*, 92.
69. Schechter, "Judaism in Camp," 172; Norbert Propper, interview 496, Bronx, New York, 1995, USC SF VHA, Segment 29; Harris, *Philippine Sanctuary*, 196–97.
70. Kestenbaum, interview by author. On the Japanese secret police, see Ma. Felisa A. Syjuco, *The Kempei Tai in the Philippines, 1941–1945* (Quezon City, 1988), 12.
71. Ibid., 48–49.
72. Kestenbaum, interview by author; Steinweis, *Kristallnacht*, 113; Gao, *Shanghai Sanctuary*; "Bericht Margarete Stern," YVA. On imprisonment at the Fort, see Syjuco, *Kempei Tai*, 64–73.
73. Netzorg to Commander, 27 February 1943; Executive Committee Santo Tomas to JMA, 2 February 1943, Santo Tomas Internment Camp: Requests, STIC 1, AHC Rizal.
74. Amtsrecherche, 8 November 1938; Hugo Alt, Fragebogen, Israelitische Kultusgemeinde Wien, Auswanderungsabteilung, 14 July 1938, CAHJP, AIKW, A/W 2590.4.4; State Department to War Department, 28 June 1939, NA, RG 350, Box 1338, Folder "28943 with 21. Jewish Refugees to Philippine Islands."
75. Index card Friedlaender, ITSDA, USHMMA.

Bibliography

Adler-Rudel, Salomon. *Jüdische Selbsthilfe unter dem Naziregime 1933–1939*. Tübingen: Mohr, 1974.
Benz, Wolfgang, ed. *Die Juden in Deutschland 1933–1945: Leben unter nationalsozialistischer Herrschaft*. 4th ed. Munich: Beck, 1996.
Bourdieu, Pierre. *Language and Symbolic Power*. Cambridge, MA: Harvard University Press, 1991.
Brinkmann, Tobias. *Migration und Transnationalität: Perspektiven deutsch-jüdischer Geschichte*. Paderborn: Ferdinand Schöningh, 2012.
Burger, Reiner. *Von Goebbels Gnaden: "Jüdisches Nachrichtenblatt," 1938–1943*. Münster: LIT, 2001.
Delmendo, Sharon, and Noel M. Izon. *An Open Door: Jewish Rescue in the Philippines*. Washington, DC: DC Asian Pacific American Film, 2012.
Ephraim, Frank. *Escape to Manila: From Nazi Tyranny to Japanese Terror*. Urbana: University of Illinois Press, 2003.
Frankel, Jonathan. *The Damascus Affair: "Ritual Murder," Politics, and the Jews in 1840*. Cambridge: Cambridge University Press, 1997.
Friedla, Katharina. *Juden in Breslau/Wroclaw 1933–1949: Überlebensstrategien, Selbstbehauptung und Verfolgungserfahrungen*. Cologne: Böhlau, 2015.
Friedländer, Saul. "Eine integrierte Geschichte des Holocausts." *Aus Politik und Zeitgeschichte* 14–15 (2007): 7–14.
Gao, Bei. *Shanghai Sanctuary: Chinese and Japanese Policy toward European Jewish Refugees during World War II*. Oxford: Oxford University Press, 2016.
Goldstein, Jonathan. *Jewish Identities in East and Southeast Asia*. Berlin: De Gruyter Oldenbourg, 2015.

Gorni, Yosef. *The Jewish Press and the Holocaust, 1939–1945*. New York: Cambridge University Press, 2014.
Griese, John W. "The Jewish Community in Manila." M.A. thesis, University of the Philippines, 1954.
Guez, Maya, and Robert Rockaway. "The Philippine Saving of Jews, 1938–1939." *Moreshet* 18 (2018): 13–37.
Harris, Bonnie M. *Philippine Sanctuary: A Holocaust Odyssey*. Madison, WI: University of Wisconsin Press, 2020.
Hilberg, Raul. "Petitionen von Juden zur Zeit ihrer Vernichtung." In *Mit Petitionen Politik verändern*, edited by Reinhard Bockhofer, 39–41. Baden-Baden: Nomos, 1999.
Hilfsverein der Juden in Deutschland. *Die Arbeit des Hilfsvereins der Juden in Deutschland 1934–1935*. Berlin: n.p., 1935.
Holenstein, André. "Bitten um den Schutz: Staatliche Judenpolitik und Lebensführung von Juden im Lichte der Schutzsupplikationen aus der Markgrafschaft Baden(-Durlach) im 18. Jahrhundert." In *Landjudentum im deutschen Südwesten während der Frühen Neuzeit*, edited by Rolf Kießling et al., 97–153. Berlin: Akademie Verlag, 1999.
Jacoby, Ruth, et al., eds. *Mensch—Land—Gerechtigkeit: Die Erinnerungen Erich Hellmuth Jacobys, 1903–1979*. Berlin: Hentrich & Hentrich, 2013.
Kanzler, Christine. "Exilerfahrungen deutschsprachiger Emigranten auf den Philippinen." In *Alltag Im Exil*, edited by Daniel Azuélos, 95–108. Würzburg: Königshausen & Neumann, 2011.
———. "Zuflucht in den Tropen: Österreichische Emigranten auf den Philippinen." *Mitteilungen Dokumentationsarchiv des Österreichischen Widerstandes* 167 (2004): 5–7.
Kaplan, Marion A. *Between Dignity and Despair: Jewish Life in Nazi Germany*. New York: Oxford University Press, 1998.
Kotlerman, Bert. "Philippine Visas-for-Jews from the Perspective of the Unanswered Letters of 1939 to President Quezon." *Darbai Ir Dienos* 67 (2017): 273–91.
Kotlowski, Dean. "Breaching the Paper Walls: Paul V. McNutt and Jewish Refugees to the Philippines, 1938–1939." *Diplomatic History* 33 (2009): 865–96.
Lässig, Simone, and Miriam Rürup, eds., *Space and Spatiality in Modern German-Jewish History*. New York: Berghahn Books, 2017.
Laqueur, Walter. *Thursday's Child Has Far to Go: A Memoir of the Journeying Years*. New York: Scribner, 1992.
Matthiessen, Sven. *Japanese Pan-Asianism and the Philippines from the Late Nineteenth Century to the End of World War II*. Leiden: Brill, 2016.
Müller, Michael G., and Cornelius Torp. "Conceptualizing Transnational Spaces in History." *European Review of History* 16 (2009): 609–17.
Netzorg, Morton J., and Michael Onorato. *Jock Netzorg: Manila Memories*. Laguna Beach, CA: Pacific Rim Books, 1988.
Offenberger, Ilana Fritz. *The Jews of Nazi Vienna, 1938–1945: Rescue and Destruction*. Cham: Palgrave Macmillan, 2017.

Parpan, Alfredo, Sr. "The Japanese and the Philippine Church, 1942–45." *Philippine Studies* 37 (1989): 451–66.
Poznanski, Renée. *Jews in France during World War II*. Waltham, MA: Brandeis University Press, 2001.
Rosman, Moshe. "Jewish History across Borders." In *Rethinking European Jewish History*, edited by Jeremy Cohen et al., 15–29. Oxford: Littman Library of Jewish Civilization, 2008.
Schechter, Samuel N. "Judaism in the Camp," in Stevens, *Santo Tomas*, 172–73.
Setsuho, Ikehata, and Ricardo Trota Jose, eds. *The Philippines under Japan: Occupation Policy and Reaction*. Quezon City: Ateneo de Manila University Press, 1999.
Steiner, John M., and Jobst Freiherr von Cornberg. "Willkür in der Willkür: Befreiungen von den antisemitischen Gesetzen." *Vierteljahrshefte für Zeitgeschichte* 46 (1998): 143–87.
Steinweis, Alan E., *Kristallnacht 1938*. Cambridge, MA: Belknap Press of Harvard University Press, 2009.
Stevens, Frederic Harper. *Santo Tomas Internment Camp*. New York: Stratford House, 1946.
Syjuco, Ma. Felisa A. *The Kempei Tai in the Philippines, 1941–1945*. Quezon City: New Day, 1988.
Takefumi, Terada. "The Religious Propaganda Program for Christian Churches." In Setsuho and Jose, *Philippines under Japan*, 215–46.
Tirol, Jose Maria Edito Kalaw. "Of Forgetting and Remembering: Social Memory, Commemorating and the Jewish Refugees in the Philippines during the Second World War." Ph.D. diss., University of the Philippines, 2015.
Welisch, Margarete, "I Remember." In *Erinnerungen: Lebensgeschichten von Opfern des Nationalsozialismus*. vol. 4/1, edited by Renate Meissner, 218–41. Vienna: Nationalfonds der Republik Österreich für Opfer des Nationalsozialismus, 2015.

Chapter 8

PETITIONING FOR "EQUAL TREATMENT"
The Struggles of Intermarried Holocaust Survivors in Postwar Germany

Maximilian Strnad

Introduction

Jews who were married to gentile partners had a far greater chance of surviving the Holocaust than all other persons who were classified as Jews in Nazi Germany after the Nuremberg Laws. This is why German, Allied, and Jewish authorities often treated them differently than other Holocaust survivors after liberation. In the worst case, these institutions denied that they experienced outright persecution.[1] The historical background is rather complicated, which is one reason why until now their destiny has played only a minor role in the historiography.[2] This is all the more striking, because these men and women constituted a large proportion—more than 60 percent—of German-Jewish Holocaust survivors who stayed behind and did not manage to emigrate.[3] Their fate, in particular after the war, is widely unknown.[4]

In Nazi Germany, the persecution of intermarried Jews varied significantly according to the status they had been assigned by Nazi officials. From December 1938 onward, Jewish women with non-Jewish spouses were in a slightly better position than Jewish men with non-Jewish wives because they were categorized as in a "privileged mixed marriage." In Nazi ideology, Jewish men were perceived as a threat to the impurity of the "German race." Thus the impact of persecution on intermarried Jews was highly gendered, although Jewish men and their non-Jewish spouses could also obtain privileged status if the children of those families were raised non-Jewish.[5]

Notes for this chapter begin on page 197.

Because of their "half-Aryan" children and their "Aryan" family members, intermarried Jews with a privileged status received better food rations during the war and were not required to wear the yellow star after it was introduced in September 1941.[6] Moreover, they were not ghettoized and spared from several persecution measures that all other Jews had to endure. The Gestapo exempted all intermarried Jews, as long as the marriage was intact, from deportation until February 1945.[7] However, Nazi party officials were aware that the term "privilege" was misleading. They used it intentionally in order to drive a wedge between the various groups of persecuted Jews. They did this with some success until 1945, but the consequences of this policy extended to German postwar society and affected the living conditions of this group for decades. Again, gender played a major role. It is important to clarify that, despite the exceptions mentioned above, Jews living in all kinds of mixed marriages, as well as their spouses and children, had to endure many of the same severe persecution measures as all other Jews. They lost their jobs, were deprived of their property, and forced to do hard physical labor. They were humiliated, arrested, mistreated, and sometimes killed for being Jewish, even if they had converted to Christianity decades earlier, or for being related to a Jew. Being married to a non-Jew was by no means a guarantee for survival.[8]

Nevertheless, intermarried Jews possessed family ties to the so-called "people's community" (*Volksgemeinschaft*) that granted them more room for maneuver and influenced their situation during the Nazi period. In some families, these ties were disrupted due to the efforts the regime made to isolate the partners in mixed marriages from their surroundings. But often the relationships of the intermarried partners to non-Jewish family members, (former) colleagues, friends, and fellow Christians remained strong enough to form a basis for interventions by the latter in dangerous situations. Time and again, non-Jewish relatives and friends, usually directly prompted by the intermarried couples, submitted petitions on their behalf. Monica Kingreen, for example, has pointed out that the efforts of Nazi Party officials and the Gestapo in Hesse-Nassau in late 1942 and 1943 to systematically deport intermarried Jews to Auschwitz was aborted not entirely, but at least partially, due to numerous petitions by non-Jews, some of them highly decorated Nazis, including industrial or political leaders.[9] In other cases, it is well documented that petitions in favor of intermarried Jews had an effect on their recruitment or employment as forced laborers or could even delay and prevent their deportation to a labor camp or to the Theresienstadt ghetto in 1944 and 1945.[10] One has to be cautious not to overestimate the significance of those interventions, but it cannot be denied that these petitions from non-Jewish family members, relatives, and friends could increase the chances for survival for intermarried Jews.

In the summer of 1945, approximately thirteen thousand intermarried Jews were by far the largest group among German-Jewish Holocaust survivors. Most of them remained in cities like Berlin, Breslau, Frankfurt, Hamburg, or Munich.[11] 50 percent of those intermarried survivors were women whose marriages generally had a "privileged" status. Thus, the survival rate of Jewish women in "mixed marriages" was far higher than of Jews who survived the camps.[12] They also had a far better survival rate than intermarried Jewish men, who had constituted the majority in mixed marriages in 1933.[13] Due to the intensified persecution of Jewish men in general and the inferior food supply of not "privileged" marriages, the chances for survival of intermarried Jewish men proved to be lower than of intermarried Jewish women.

After liberation, Jewish survivors submitted compensation claims in manifold ways and to various German and Allied organizations and institutions from local governments to the High Commissioners of the occupied zones. As they faced rejection from official quarters, they started to petition for their interests. They strongly believed in their right to reclaim what had been taken from them and to receive reparations for the mistreatment they had suffered under Nazi rule. A belief in a better future had been crucial for their will to survive, as many victims recalled after the end of war. Max Kruse from Breslau, who resettled in Berlin, expressed his and his Jewish wife's feelings with the following words: "In the dark years of persecution, we did not become desperate, because we were certain that one day Hitler's reign would come to an end and that we would then finally be free and get compensation for all the suffering." But their expectations were not met in postwar German society. Non-Jewish citizens wallowed in self-pity and were not interested in being reminded of their own involvement in crimes or their failure to help the persecuted. While this was certainly a major reason for all political and racial victims of the Nazi regime to publicly complain about their situation, it was especially true for Jewish survivors in general and for intermarried Jews and their family members in particular. Kruse and his family became more and more desperate as their hopes for a better future seemed to "break into smithereens," as he described it one year after liberation.[14]

To understand their concerns, we have to briefly examine the overall situation in postwar Germany. Surviving Jews in occupied Germany basically consisted of three different groups: non-German Jews who had survived the Holocaust in Eastern European concentration camps or in the

Soviet diaspora and who arrived in Germany after the war as so-called Displaced Persons (DPs); German Jews who survived the camps and ghettos in the east or who had gone underground; and German Jews who had survived in the territory of the German Reich as partners in mixed marriages. The displaced Jews found shelter mainly in large DP camps often located at the site of former labor or concentration camps such as Buchenwald. In general, they had no deep connection to German society and were not interested in establishing such connections because they were primarily interested in emigration. The DPs appreciated the special protection of the United Nations and received assistance from the Relief and Rehabilitation Administration (UNRRA), which was reorganized as International Refugee Organization (IRO) in January 1947.[15]

The German-Jewish ghetto and camp survivors mostly returned to their former places of residence, where they reestablished Jewish Communities, often together with remaining survivors of mixed marriages. Like the DPs, the main goal for most of them was to leave the country of the perpetrators as soon as possible. But as German nationals, they had no access to UNRRA/IRO relief and relied instead on German authorities for supplies.[16] On 17 May 1946, Wilhelm Meyer, a member of the Jewish Community in Berlin, expressed the frustration of many German Jews in the gazette *Der Weg* (The path): "Except for some small but negligible forms of relief, all Jews carry the same burden as the rest of the German population. While the Germans ruined themselves and the rest of the world, all innocent victims of the Nazis have to share the same fate."[17]

This was also the case for the German Jews from mixed marriages who had not been deported or were deported only in February 1945 for a short time to the Theresienstadt ghetto. But in contrast to other Jews, most members of mixed marriages were also excluded from foreign relief shipments and, therefore, had no access to supplementary food rations, supplies of clothes, or medicine. As a result, partners from mixed marriages approached different organizations in order to try to improve their personal situation in postwar Germany. They addressed, often in the form of petitions, military headquarters in their zones of occupation, state and municipal authorities, international refugee and aid organizations as well as religious authorities, national aid agencies and other NGOs. Among their main goals was to secure better provisions for themselves.

Over time, they joined forces with the large group of the so-called *Mischlinge* (half-breeds) in local associations of persons who had been persecuted for racial reasons during the Nazi period. These individual groups ultimately formed a nationwide network. Since they constituted a significant percentage of surviving German persecutes and had close ties to German society, one might think that these organizations and their networks had a major effect on the distribution of relief and on the pending legislation relating to reparation and compensation claims. But, in fact, it seems that their influence was rather limited. So far, little is known about this advocacy, and additional research will be necessary to analyze the impact of these networks and their constituent organizations on the distribution of international relief and on German politics.[18]

This chapter will examine how intermarried persons intervened by appealing to refugee and relief organizations for treatment similar to that received by other victims of the Nazi regime. The analysis will focus on their petitions to public, Jewish, and Christian authorities. Since they did not have a strong lobby in public or in religious contexts, individual petitions were the only option most partners in mixed marriages had at their disposal to improve their position in the immediate postwar period. In doing so, this chapter will take a close look at the arguments they used in their petitions and at the official reactions in order to assess what position intermarried families had among the victims of National Socialism and how the competition for resources affected their lives in Germany immediately after the war. I therefore use a broad conceptualization of the term *petition*. In their correspondence of diverse nature and to different institutions, many protagonists used similar arguments and developed comparable patterns in their approach for being recognized and treated as victims of the Nazi regime. These entreaties often exhibited an official or semiofficial character and tone. Many complaints to an array of German and non-German agencies also can be defined as petitions. They relied on similar arguments and pleaded for help or for reconsidering rejections based on their suffering as persecutes in mixed marriages under Nazi rule.[19]

Claiming Recognition as Victims of Fascism

After liberation, the general supply situation of the German population was precarious. Especially in bigger cities, where most of the formerly persecuted lived, food, coal, and living space were scarce, and the struggle for provisions of rare goods determined the daily lives of most individuals. Most of the surviving German Jews were elderly—marriages between Jews and "Aryans" had already been forbidden by the Nuremberg Laws in 1935—and, therefore, they often were not capable of undertaking physical labor.[20] They only received a minimal amount of food stamps. Due to the economic crisis and the scarce food production in postwar Germany compounded by the lack of imported goods, it was often impossible to obtain even these small rations. In any case, the supplies were insufficient for the rehabilitation and survival of people who had faced hunger for years and thus possessed little physical stamina.

From the beginning of the war in 1939, Jews had received less food and coal rations than other Germans. They were also excluded from many other rationed goods such as new clothing and shoes.[21] Moreover, Jews who went into hiding had no access to food rations at all, depended on help from others to survive, not to mention those who survived the atrocities in the concentration camps and ghettos.[22]

After liberation, German authorities granted additional supplies, living accommodations, medicine, and loans to people who were officially recognized as victims of the Nazi regime so that they might launch a business or buy furniture. Of course, this supplementary assistance was not sufficient to fully recover and reintegrate themselves into the economic and social fabric of German society. But after all the years of privation, the supplementary calories and additional health care was a first step toward improving physical strength, and it was an important signal that their claims for compensation had been officially recognized.

Many of the local committees charged with determining who would be officially accepted as a victim of the Nazi regime were dominated by former political prisoners. In their understanding, only those persons who had suffered imprisonment for resisting the Nazis deserved the right to obtain this badly needed status.[23] Due to their supposedly lesser degree of persecution, and especially because they had not been compelled to wear the yellow star and had not been imprisoned for a long time, former persecutes from privileged mixed marriages, and therefore about 75 percent of all survivors of mixed marriages, were not officially recognized as victims of the Nazi regime.[24] The modus operandi differed from region to region, and over time assistance was extended to a small degree also to members of privileged mixed marriages.[25] But generally speaking, their access to public benefits and later also to compensation was greatly inferior to that enjoyed by members of other victim categories.

In the German capital of Berlin, where most German Jews had lived before the war and where a large number of survivors were stranded in mid-1945, the main committee of the Victims of Fascism (Hauptausschuss Opfer des Faschismus) only started to accept Jews who had been imprisoned for less than one year after the Allied headquarters of the Western zone pressured the Berlin magistrate to do so. But the status Victim of Fascism (Opfer des Faschismus, OdF) was generally not granted to Jews who had lived in privileged mixed marriages and who had not been forced to wear the yellow star. Officials also refused to include non-Jewish spouses of Jews and *Mischlinge* because they "had not suffered any considerable persecution during the Nazi past," as one member of the committee emphasized.[26]

After twelve years of persecution, it was a real shock for these intermarried Jews and their family members to be excluded from assistance programs and to be treated like other non-Jewish Germans. Their experience was casually dismissed, and they were perceived as equal with those who had humiliated, maltreated, and killed Jews. In April 1946, Fritz Behrend, for example, complained in his petition to the OdF committee in Berlin that this decision is "utter mockery" and a "glaring injustice."[27] In the absence of a strong lobby, sending individual petitions to the OdF committee often was the only way for ordinary men and women to at least somehow influence the decisions about compensation and to be finally recognized as Victims of Fascism. In particular, Jewish men like Behrend, whose marriage had been classified as "privileged," aired their grievances and emphasized that they also had to suffer under most of the same persecution measures that intermarried bearers of the yellow star had been forced to endure, listing numerous examples in their petitions. These included loss of their professional career and property, imprisonment and maltreatment during Kristallnacht, forced labor, social ostracism, the ban on social and cultural participation, and the fact that they had been forced to adopt the discriminatory middle names Sara and Israel. They also underscored the emotional stress that they had suffered by being forced into helplessness against the defamation of their children and the deportation of relatives, always fearing to be the next on the Gestapo's lists.[28]

Similarly non-Jewish members of mixed marriages like Max Kruse, who had lost his position as a civil servant in the mid-1930s for being married to a Jewish woman and whose family suffered severe economic losses, complained in several letters to the Berlin magistrate and to other authorities. Kruse stressed that as a consequence of the fact that neither his nor his wife's petition was accepted, "we lack any legitimation as victims of fascism." He desperately asked: "We surely were lucky to survive, but aren't we, thus, in need of special assistance?"[29]

All of these numerous complaints shared similar features: intermarried Jews and their family members requested equal, or at least some, help in restarting their lives and demanded recognition as persecutes of the Nazi regime. Consequently, they expected the right to receive compensation for the injustice they experienced over more than a decade. The process of petitioning was not simply to get more supplies or compensation. Being fully accepted as victims of the Nazi regime was essential for their self-understanding. Their struggles for recognition were a crucial part of the self-determination process many members of mixed marriages were subjected to in these first years after the war as Thomas Pegelow Kaplan has pointed out.[30]

As a small concession to those demands, the OdF committee introduced the new category of "Victims of the Nuremberg Laws" in August 1946. This special identification card, which demonstrated that its owner had also suffered from "restrictions" under the Nazi regime, had a different color, but did not entitle its owner to any assistance, as the committee clarified.[31]

The decision to discriminate against one of the major groups of persecutes in the immediate postwar era and to exclude them either fully or partially from special assistance programs for victims of the Nazi regime was applied generally in postwar Germany with some regional differences in the four occupation zones.[32] Intermarried Jews had to apply for help at other authorities, also often with little success, as we will see below.

Persecuted "Jews" Petitioning for Equal Treatment

Another very important opportunity for former persecutees to fill the resource gap was international aid. Immediately after liberation, the Allies prevented relief organizations other than UNRRA from operating on German soil. Germans were to accept their responsibility for Nazi crimes and not feel like victims entitled to generous assistance. This is why international relief organizations started their work only in the late spring of 1946, after public pressure increased in some of the donor countries due to the dire supply situation of the German population.[33]

From the beginning, however one important exception existed for German Jews. The Allied headquarters for Germany allowed direct aid to Jewish survivors by the American Jewish Joint Distribution Committee (JOINT). The JOINT had already started to support surviving Jews in Germany in the summer of 1945. Most of its assistance was directed to the DPs, but the newly re-established Jewish Communities in Germany also frequently received assistance. In Berlin, all members of the Jewish Community received one parcel per month. The packages contained precious items of high nutritional value such as butter, cheese, eggs, and powdered milk. These products were almost impossible to acquire with food stamps and very expensive on the black market.[34] Consequently, assistance from the JOINT became crucial for the surviving German Jews.

But the JOINT provided this help only to people of the Jewish faith. With their marriage to non-Jewish partners, or in a futile effort to avoid persecution, many intermarried Jews had left the Jewish community before 1945 and were therefore now barred from this vital assistance. Those who were affected could not understand why. Heinz Gerber was Catholic, but had been persecuted as an intermarried Jew under the Nazi regime.

In his petition addressed to a Catholic aid organization in Berlin, he complained, "The mixed marriages, where the Jewish partner is also Jewish by faith, have lived under the same conditions as we did."[35] Jewish men whose marriages were classified as non-privileged felt especially belittled, as they had been subjected to the same restrictions as other Jews.

This decision of the JOINT affected several thousand people. More and more of them publicly raised their voices against it, and eventually the press took note of their situation. In April 1946, the *Chicago Sun* published the article "Many in Berlin, Jews to Hitler, Get No Relief." "If the angels took Adolf Hitler straight to Valhalla, as some Germans piously believe," the *Sun* polemicized,

> you can imagine him interrupting his favorite sport of carpet chewing for a few moments each day to indulge in a spasm of wild laughter at the mess that his race theories have left in Germany. Hitler would be diverted particularly by the plight of certain Berliners who were considered Jews and wore the Yellow Star of David during the Nazi regime, but today are denied privileges that religious Jews enjoy.

The JOINT, the *Sun* continued, "does not accept Hitler's racial definition."[36]

In fact, numerous articles like the one above surfaced in 1946 and 1947.[37] More and more letters and petitions from individuals and organizations reached the JOINT from all over Germany. Some of them pointed out that the distribution policy of the JOINT would abet injustice, because it was not the degree of persecution but only the faith that was relevant to who might qualify for assistance.[38] But the JOINT did not change its policy. First of all, it was a question of capacity. From the beginning of 1946, the number of Jewish DPs in Germany rose from about 50,000 to more than 150,000, and it was one of JOINT's main tasks to help UNRRA/IRO in providing food and other kind of help for these Jews.[39]

On the other hand, the JOINT collected its contributions specifically for the relief of religious Jews who identified themselves as such. Its focus was on saving the last Jewish remnants and helping them to establish a new life, not on helping other victims of fascism, even if they had been persecuted as Jews on the basis of Nazi racial definitions. As the JOINT pointed out, "Trade unionists, Communists, gypsies and priests suffered at the hands of the Nazis too. But since the committee does not have sufficient supplies to aid all victims of fascism—and indeed collected its contributions specifically for the relief of religious Jews—it is bound to be restricted to the job of helping those who were members of the Jewish religious community."[40]

Like many other foreign Jewish organizations, the JOINT did not believe that Jewish life could be re-established in the country of the perpetrators. But many intermarried Jews did not want to leave their country. This is why the director of the JOINT in Berlin claimed the following in his quarterly report in June 1946: "Because of their high degree of assimilationism in the past and their lesser degree of persecution suffered at the hands of the Nazis, [they] feel Germanic tendencies even today." JOINT officials were not willing to invest more than necessary in a community of "marginal Jewish character." Resources should be reserved for those who suffered most and who would probably receive no help from other sources, which basically meant the DPs and those who remained loyal to the Jewish community during the Nazi period. JOINT officials were persuaded that "generally speaking, the converted are not subject to the same degree of persecution as were those who were members of the Jewish Community, and this is another reason why the communities are unable to extend relief to them."[41]

For the JOINT and Jewish leaders in Germany, it was necessary to redefine the Jewish Community as a union of Jews defined by religion and not as an organization of people who had been racially persecuted, as Hans-Erich Fabian, one of the leaders of the Jewish Community in Berlin, proclaimed.[42] JOINT officials pointed to the responsibility of public and Christian aid organizations to help all non-Jewish victims, and even gave a positive spin to the report of the *Chicago Sun*: "This item may serve to awaken Catholic and Protestant circles to the need of doing something for their religious brethren. I do not think that, because the Jews recognize their responsibility and try to help Jews, they are to be called upon to assist non-Jews as well. This responsibility lodges elsewhere."[43] Thus, the survivors of Nazi racial persecution were not only divided between former bearers of the yellow star and those who had been "privileged" due to their specific kind of intermarriage but by religion as well.

Intra-Jewish Discourse on Relief for Mixed Marriages

Let us take a closer look at how the distribution of relief was organized inside the Jewish Communities, and how this affected intermarried survivors. The JOINT's decision to provide only assistance to Jews who were members of the Jewish Community was a pragmatic one regarding "the size of the problem and our limited resources," as an internal comment of one of its officials shows. "Since we ourselves could not determine who was Jewish and who was not Jewish, we had to follow some criterion," went the argument. "This was the best rule of thumb we could find, by reasoning that, if people were Jewish and were willing to apply for membership to the Jewish community . . . the greatest number of Jews could be reached for our aid."[44]

The JOINT was aware that "since they knew that admission carried with it supplementary assistance," becoming a member of the Jewish Community was very attractive. As a consequence, the Communities received many petitions from Jews who had previously left the Jewish community and now wanted to rejoin. Non-Jewish family members of intermarried Jews in particular applied for membership, often not for religious reasons, but rather to be part of a collective of those who shared the experience of persecution. Of course, gaining access to the much sought-after care packages provided one important reason. In fact, Jewish leaders were not always happy about this development. The newly founded Jewish Communities wanted to preserve a genuine Jewish character, and it was not in their interest to share the scarce resources. These proselytes often were derisively called "package Jews" (*Paketjuden*) and many Communities restricted their admission.[45] In Berlin, the rabbinate rejected more than two-thirds of the membership applications.[46] The unsuccessful applicants countered with petitions, in which they highlighted "the irony of being denied their Jewish identity now that being Jewish could mean life rather than death."[47]

On the other hand, due to their high survival rate, intermarried Jews were the largest group among the surviving German Jews in the postwar Jewish Communities of Germany.[48] Many Jewish Communities had been re-established by intermarried Jews immediately after the end of war, often even before the liberated Jews returned from the concentration camps.[49] In April 1946, for example, 60 percent of the 7,822 members of Berlin's Jewish Community had survived the Holocaust because they were married to a non-Jewish spouse, divided evenly between "privileged" and "not-privileged" Jews.[50] Now they pleaded for support for their non-Jewish family members, often without success, as the following example shows. Again, the JOINT played a major role here. According to the JOINT's guidelines, the Jewish Communities were only allowed to grant assistance to Jews. Again especially Jewish men who had been forced to wear the yellow star regarded it as a question of fairness that their non-Jewish wives receive assistance as well. During the Nazi period, these women had suffered severely under persecution. They had to move into ghetto houses together with their husbands and to share their food rations with them. Moreover, they protected their Jewish husbands from deportation by resisting social pressure and personal threats as well as by staying married.[51]

In Düsseldorf, where the majority of the Community members were intermarried, twenty-three Jewish men submitted petitions to the board of the Jewish Community in November 1946. They pointed out that, during the Nazi period, "our non-Jewish wives have experienced unimaginable suffering and heroically endured our fate. They have been discriminated [against] because of our Jewishness, today they are disadvantaged because of their non-Jewishness."[52] However, the JOINT did not deviate from its policy. The non-Jewish spouses and children remained excluded from its relief programs. Its answer to this petition shows again that the JOINT was generally not willing to provide help for intermarried families:

> We must say after reading this, that it is still not clear to us why American Jewry must assist as a reward the non-Jewish spouse of a mixed marriage in Germany because the non-Jewish husband or wife stuck to his or her partner during the difficult days. Do these people really think that American Jewry owes something to the non-Jewish spouse or is the Jewish spouse trying to be a good fellow to the non-Jewish member at the expense of American Jewry?[53]

In cases involving mixed marriages, the JOINT always restricted its support solely to the family members who were Jewish by faith.

Christian Answers to the Petitions of Intermarried Families

During the Nazi period, Jewish Communities had to care for all persons who the regime racially defined as Jews, not just those identifying as Jews and religious Jews. Meanwhile, church-supported relief organizations and the Quakers gave assistance to non-Jewish family members in mixed marriages. These organizations also contributed spiritual support. After 1945, this shifted to a division of labor based entirely on religious affiliation. While the Jewish Communities took responsibility only for people of the Jewish faith, the churches provided for racial persecutes who were Protestant or Catholic, while the Quakers focused on non-religious ones.

In Berlin, help for racially persecuted Protestants after 1945 was again organized by the well-known office of Provost Heinrich Grüber, whereas Catholics could appeal to the relief organization of the episcopal chair, the so-called Hilfswerk am bischöflichen Ordinariat Berlin, led by Margarete Sommer until 1952. While the activities of these organizations during the Third Reich are well documented, their history after 1945 remains largely unknown.[54]

There are three main reasons why Christians persecuted as Jews faced disadvantages in comparison to their Jewish fellow sufferers. As shown above, international relief for all Germans started only in mid-1946, after which it took some time before help could be provided to the broader public. Second, Christian aid organizations distributed their share of international relief according to the principle of need. According to this logic, racial persecutes fared better, or at least no worse, than the mass of fugitives who had escaped the Red Army in the eastern territories of the German Reich, arriving in the western part of Germany with no possessions. This opinion was held mainly by the Protestant Relief Organization, the Hilfswerk der Evangelischen Kirche in Deutschland, which was one of the most influential German welfare institutions. Its leader, the future President of the German Federal Parliament, Eugen Gerstenmaier, had been arrested by the Nazis for his membership in the Kreisauer Kreis and then sentenced to seven years imprisonment after the assassination attempt on Hitler on 20 July 1944. Gerstenmaier strongly rejected assistance targeted specifically at racial persecutees among Christians. In his opinion, it was an article of faith that relief be dispensed "without regard to race, religious or political opinion and nationality" and solely according "to priority and need."[55]

Gerstenmaier also feared a negative effect on the Christian community. His argument points to the third reason why the churches did not respond satisfactorily to the needs of their fellow Christians. The Churches were traditionally suspicious of the "Jewish Christians." "Due to the wish from abroad to especially help this group, their fusion into the Christian community is impeded and this only leads to the fact that resentments against them will rise again," Gerstenmaier observed.[56]

Heinrich Grüber, who had established a nationwide network to support racially persecuted Christians and whose Berlin office had to deal with requests from several thousand victims, strongly opposed this argument, which, in effect, held the former victims responsible for antisemitic prejudices in German society. The World Council of Churches (WCC) in Geneva, which was one of the institutions "from abroad" that strongly intervened on behalf of racially persecuted Christians, also forcefully argued "that all efforts to establish the church as a real home to the brethren of Jewish descent and to help them to circumvent their mistrust of the former and perhaps also today's failures is of ecumenical relevance" and would, in the end, help to coalesce the Christian community.[57]

Nevertheless, the Hilfswerk of the Protestant Church in Germany did not change its position. Grüber only received permission from his superiors to distribute the supplies that were expressly donated to his clientele. Thanks to his celebrity and the help of Pastor Alfred Freudenberg at the WCC in Switzerland, who had already organized help in the 1930s and early 1940s, more and more assistance to racially persecuted Christians reached Germany from 1947 onward. Grüber dispensed this aid across the country, where in several cities, such as Frankfurt, Munich, and Stuttgart, local relief organizations specifically for Christians persecuted as Jews had been founded. He distributed the supplies not only to Protestant institutions, but also shared them with Catholic organizations and the Quakers. Despite this relatively late success of Grüber's numerous petitions to religious organizations and circles all over the world in favor of the Christians persecuted as Jews, this help only was a drop in the bucket considering the large number of persons who required assistance. In October 1945, the Grüber Office alone had 5,146 clients. The Catholic Hilfswerk and the Quakers in Berlin were in charge of another 1,500 persons. In February 1947, when the larger deliveries reached the former racially persecuted Christians, the number of those who were supported by the Grüber Office had risen to 14,017. Ten percent of these had been persecuted as Jews during the Nazi period, most of them as members of mixed marriages. A quarter had been non-Jewish spouses in mixed marriages. The rest had mainly been persecuted as *Mischlinge*.[58]

In view of these numbers, it is no wonder that there were insufficient supplies to satisfy all needs or to provide regular assistance to those who needed it the most. Individual care packages were split up in order to reach more people. Nevertheless, most of the former persecutes received assistance only once or twice in those first three years after the war, when special assistance was so important for regeneration. Otto Hawelleck, a non-Jewish husband who was unable to take care of his family because he had suffered injuries during his time as a forced laborer for the Organisation Todt,[59] complained in early 1946 that "all of these registrations have not yet put any food on the table, and I would like to see at least once some practical help and not simply read in the newspapers about how so much has been done for the Victims of the Nuremberg Laws."[60] At the same time Georg Jaretzki, an intermarried Jew who had been forced to wear the yellow badge, aired his grievances in his petition to the Hilfswerk for supplementary relief: "In contrast to the Jews by faith, I did not receive any help until now, although I am in desperate need of the most necessary things. I possess no clothes, no shoes; I was barely able to save my life. My food situation is very bad, too."[61] Still lacking any help from the Catholic Hilfswerk in Berlin, he wrote again in November 1946: "I believe that it should be possible for our worldwide operating [Catholic] organizations to achieve the same help as Jewish organizations get for their people."[62]

The situation was identical for the former racial persecutees who had unionized in special organizations outside the religious networks, like those in Hamburg did. Here some of the affected had founded the so-called Notgemeinschaft der durch die Nürnberger Gesetze Betroffenen.[63] Like the Grüber Office and the Hilfswerk, this association of persons who had experienced severe disadvantage resulting from the Nuremberg Laws provided access to relief in the form of emigration assistance or legal aid regarding compensation and reparations. When in 1947 the association distributed the first care packages, the reactions of members show how desperately they ached for recognition, and how important this acknowledgement of their victimhood was both for their social standing as well as for their positions within their families. Emmy Bothmann, née Cohn, had been persecuted as a Jew living in a "privileged mixed marriage." She had not been a member of the Jewish Community and therefore had no claim to relief. She was wracked with guilt for being responsible for all the negative experiences and suffering her family had to undergo during the Nazi period, and as a consequence, also for its bad situation after the war. Now for the first time, she was able to contribute to providing for her family. This was important for her self-esteem, as the last sentence of her thank-you letter to the donors demonstrates: "It is of particular satisfaction to me that I am now able to provide some delight to them [her family] with this lovely package."[64]

Conclusion

After surviving Nazi persecution, partners in mixed marriages strongly believed that society owed them the status of victims of the Nazi regime and compensation for their suffering. Recognition as a part of the community of victims was a central issue to them and can be identified as a pattern of self-determination in most of their petitions. While this recognition was denied to many of them, and while people with the same experience of persecution were treated differently depending on their religious faith, they started to regain agency in petitioning for what they believed to be their right. Jewish men, especially those whose "mixed-marriage" had been categorized as "non-privileged" and who were not members of the Jewish community, resisted the inequality in the distribution of relief and compensation that many of them experienced as injustice. But also non-Jewish spouses, especially men of "privileged mixed marriages" tried to be fully recognized as victims of the Nazi regime and to obtain compensation for their loss of employment and social standing.

During the Nazi period, petitions on behalf of intermarried Jews were often submitted by non-Jewish relatives and friends. Frequently they were composed by lawyers or acquaintances somehow related to the family. After liberation the intermarried Jews themselves were usually proactive, especially by penning petitions to a range of agencies. They used their moral integrity as victims not solely for their own good, but also for their non-Jewish family members and friends who had supported them.

Intermarried Jews, their spouses, and their children constituted a large group of several tens of thousands of persons in postwar Germany. However, their status among the victim groups was rather low. They were confronted with the prejudice of having belonged to a "privileged" group from 1933 to 1945. Not only the authorities but also other groups of victims, such as political prisoners and Jewish survivors of camps and ghettos, regarded them as not having suffered real persecution, and therefore denied to them the full status of victims of the Nazi regime. Moreover, they had no strong lobby in the Jewish and Christian communities. Thus, in the early years after liberation, when they needed help the most in order to recover from the consequences of deprivation and mistreatment, their individual complaints to public authorities, international help organizations such as the JOINT, churches, and the Jewish Communities went widely unheeded.

The organizations specializing in assisting these categories of victims—who commonly were called Victims of the Nuremberg Laws—attempted to influence the distribution of relief as well as the legislation governing reparation, which was still in its formative stage in the late 1940s. Far too little is known about the extent to which their lobbying was successful over the long term. But with regard to the immediate postwar period, it can be asserted that the help they were able to provide starting in 1947 was of limited consequence for the intermarried Jews and their family members who had survived twelve years of Nazi persecution. Under these circumstances, a new start in postwar Germany was often difficult for intermarried couples, who were generally older persons, and who frequently depended on welfare. The lack of adequate assistance all too often delayed or even prevented their physical recovery and their reintegration into society.

Maximilian Strnad received his PhD in Contemporary History from the Ludwig- Maximilians University in Munich, Germany. He is a historian at the Cultural Department of the City of Munich. In addition to a series of articles and book chapters, he is the author of *Zwischenstation "Judensiedlung." Verfolgung und Deportation der jüdischen Münchner, 1941-1945* (2011), *Flachs für das Reich. Das jüdische Zwangsarbeitslager "Flachsröste" bei München* (2013) and *Privileg Mischehe? Handlungsräume "jüdisch versippter" Familien 1933-1949* (2021). He also co-edited (with Michael Brenner) *Der Holocaust in der deutschsprachigen Geschichtswissenschaft* (2012).

Notes

1. Parts of this essay draw from the last chapter of my unpublished dissertation. See Maximilian Strnad, "Privileg Mischehe? Handlungsräume sogenannter 'jüdisch versippter' Familien 1933–1949" (Ph.D. diss., University of Munich, 2016). Very special thanks to Alan Steinweis for helping to edit the English translation of this chapter.

2. For some exceptions, see Ursula Büttner, *Die Not der Juden teilen: Christlich-jüdische Familien im Dritten Reich* (Hamburg, 1988); Beate Meyer, *"Jüdische Mischlinge": Rassenpolitik und Verfolgungserfahrung 1933–1945* (Hamburg, 1999); Adrienne Edgar and Benjamin Frommer, eds., *Intermarriage from Central Europe to Central Asia: Mixed Families in the Age of Extremes* (Lincoln, 2020).
3. Maximilian Strnad, "The Fortune of Survival—Intermarried German Jews in the Dying Breath of the 'Thousand-Year Reich,'" *Dapim* 29, no. 3 (2015): 190.
4. For a few exceptions, see Siegfried Hermle, *Evangelische Kirche und Judentum: Stationen nach 1945* (Göttingen, 1990); Thomas Pegelow Kaplan, *The Language of Nazi Genocide: Linguistic Violence and the Struggle of Germans of Jewish Ancestry* (Cambridge, 2009), 219–71; Thomas Pegelow Kaplan, "Jüdische Holocaustüberlebende und sprachliche Gewalt im besetzten Deutschland der frühen Nachkriegsjahre," in *Zwischen Erinnerung und Neubeginn: Zur deutsch-jüdischen Geschichte nach 1945*, ed. Susanne Schönborn (Munich, 2006), 250–67.
5. Telex of Hermann Göring, 28 December 1938, reprint in Paul Sauer, ed. *Dokumente über die Verfolgung der jüdischen Bürger in Baden-Württemberg durch das nationalsozialistische Regime 1933–1945*, vol. 2 (Stuttgart, 1966), 83–84. See also Büttner, *Not der Juden*, 44.
6. Polizeiverordnung über die Kennzeichnung von Juden, 1 September 1941, in *Reichsgesetzblatt* (RGBl.) 1941 I, 547.
7. Secret decree of Gestapo Düsseldorf, 11 October 1942, cited in Alfred Gottwaldt and Diana Schulle, *Judendeportationen aus dem Deutschen Reich 1941–1945* (Wiesbaden, 2005), 56. See also Strnad, *Fortune of Survival*, 185–93.
8. Beate Meyer, "The Mixed Marriage," in *Probing the Depths of German Antisemitism: German Society and the Persecution of the Jews, 1933–1941*, ed. David Bankier (New York, 2000), 54–77. See also Wolf Gruner, *Widerstand in der Rosenstraße: Die Fabrik-Aktion und die Verfolgung der "Mischehen" 1943* (Frankfurt am Main, 2005).
9. Monica Kingreen, "'Die Aktion zur kalten Erledigung der Mischehen': Die reichsweit singuläre systematische Verschleppung und Ermordung jüdischer Mischehepartner im NSDAP-Gau Hessen-Nassau 1942/1943," in *NS-Gewaltherrschaft: Beiträge zur historischen Forschung und juristischen Aufarbeitung*, ed. Alfred Gottwaldt et al. (Berlin, 2005), 187–201.
10. Maximilian Strnad, "Die Deportationen aus München," *Münchner Beiträge zur Jüdischen Geschichte und Kultur* 8, no. 2 (2014): 88. See also several cases in *Gegen Vergessen—Für Demokratie e.V./Regionalgruppe Mittelrhein: Projekt-Abschlussbericht zu erkundeten Rettungen von Juden und als Juden Verfolgten 1933–1945 mit Bezug zur Region Mittelrhein* (April 2015).
11. Statistics of the Reichsvereinigung der Juden in Deutschland from 1 Nov. 1944, Bundesarchiv Berlin, R 8150, 32; For more details, see "Statistik und Deportation der jüdischen Bevölkerung aus dem Dritten Reich," retrieved 2 January 2019 from www.statistik-des-holocaust.de/stat_ger_pop.html; Strnad, *Fortune of Survival*, 190.
12. Jael Geis, *Übrig sein—"Leben danach": Juden deutscher Herkunft in der britischen und amerikanischen Zone Deutschlands 1945–1949* (Berlin, 2000), 45.
13. Kerstin Meiring, *Die christlich-jüdische Mischehe in Deutschland 1840–1933* (Hamburg, 1998), 84, 91–92; Meyer, *"Jüdische Mischlinge,"* 28–29.
14. All citations in this paragraph, Max Krause to Hilfswerk, 5 Sept. 1946, Landesarchiv Berlin (hereafter LA Berlin), C-118–01 Nr. 35274.
15. For the DPs, see Angelika Königseder and Juliane Wetzel, *Lebensmut im Wartesaal: Die jüdischen DPs (Displaced Persons) im Nachkriegsdeutschland* (Frankfurt am Main, 1994); Margarete Myers Feinstein, *Holocaust Survivors in Postwar Germany, 1945–1957* (Cambridge, 2010); Avinoam J. Patt and Michael Berkowitz, eds., *"We Are Here": New Approaches to Jewish Displaced Persons in Postwar Germany* (Detroit, MI, 2010).

16. Constantin Goschler, *Wiedergutmachung: Westdeutschland und die Verfolgten des Nationalsozialismus 1945–1954* (Munich, 1992), 73–75.
17. Wilhelm Meyer, "Unsere Sorgen," *Der Weg*, vol. 1, no. 12, 17 May 1946, 1–2.
18. The only one who addresses this topic is Hermle, *Evangelische Kirche und Judentum*.
19. For more details on the definition of petitions, see pp. 5–7, this volume.
20. For the impact of the Nuremberg Laws on mixed marriages see Cornelia Essner, *Die "Nürnberger Gesetze" oder Die Verwaltung des Rassenwahns 1933–1945* (Paderborn, 2002); Alexandra Przyrembel, *Rassenschande: Reinheitsmythos und Vernichtungslegitimation im Nationalsozialismus* (Göttingen, 2003).
21. Konrad Kwiet, "Nach dem Pogrom: Stufen der Ausgrenzung," in *Die Juden in Deutschland 1933–1945: Leben unter nationalsozialistischer Herrschaft*, ed. Wolfgang Benz and Volker Dahm (Munich, 1993), 605–6.
22. Generally on hiding, see Wolfgang Benz, ed. *Überleben im Dritten Reich: Juden im Untergrund und ihre Helfer* (Munich, 2003). For a regional focus on Munich, see Susanna Schrafstetter, *Flucht und Versteck: Untergetauchte Juden in München: Verfolgungserfahrung und Nachkriegsalltag* (Göttingen, 2015).
23. Goschler, *Wiedergutmachung*, 70.
24. Strnad, *Fortune of Survival*, 189, 195.
25. In Bavaria, for example, Jewish members of "privileged mixed marriages" received smaller rations than so-called star bearers. See letter of the Bayerisches Hilfswerk to the Notgemeinschaft, 19 August 1946, Forschungsstelle für Zeitgeschichte Hamburg (hereafter FZH), 18–1 Nr. 6.1, vol. 1.
26. Cited from Christoph Hölscher, *NS-Verfolgte im "antifaschistischen Staat": Vereinnahmung und Ausgrenzung in der ostdeutschen Wiedergutmachung (1945–1989)* (Berlin, 2002), 54.
27. Letter from Fritz Behrend to the main committee OdF, 13 April 1946, Diözesanarchiv Berlin (hereafter DAB), I/1–71.
28. See, e.g., letter from Georg Jaretzki to the Hilfswerk, 8 September 1946, DAB, I/1–77.
29. Letter from Max Krause to the Hilfswerk, 5 September 1946, LA Berlin, C Rep. 118–01 Nr. 35274.
30. Pegelow Kaplan, *Language*, 255–71.
31. Circular of the Magistrate of Gross-Berlin, 12 December 1946, LA Berlin, C Rep. 118-01 Nr. 39019. The identification cards for intermarried Jews, their non-Jewish spouses, and their children had different colors in other regions of Germany and qualified the owner for varying kinds of assistance, Letter from Eduard Meyer to Bayerisches Hilfswerk, 28 June 1946, in Bayerisches Hauptstaatsarchiv, LEA 24258.
32. The situation was more severe in northern and eastern Germany than in the US occupied zone. For Bavaria, see, e.g., Tobias Winstel, *Verhandelte Gerechtigkeit: Rückerstattung und Entschädigung für jüdische NS-Opfer in Bayern und Westdeutschland* (Munich, 2006), 28–33.
33. Karl-Ludwig Sommer, *Humanitäre Auslandshilfe als Brücke zu atlantischer Partnerschaft: CARE, CRALOG und die Entwicklung der deutsch-amerikanischen Beziehungen nach Ende des Zweiten Weltkriegs* (Bremen, 1999), 80–108; Volker Ilgen, *Care-Paket & Co. Von der Liebesgabe zum Westpaket* (Darmstadt, 2008), 70–74; Peter Hammerschmidt, *Wohlfahrtsverbände in der Nachkriegszeit: Reorganisation und Finanzierung der Spitzenverbände der freien Wohlfahrtspflege 1945 bis 1961* (Weinheim, 2005), 82–88.
34. There has only been limited scholarly attention to the work of the JOINT in Germany after 1945. See Atina Grossmann, *Jews, Germans and Allies: Close Encounters in Occupied Germany: Close Encounters in Occupied Germany* (Princeton, NJ, 2007), esp. 233–41, 251–60. For general information on the JOINT after 1945, but no details on its work in Germany, see Oscar Handlin, *A Continuing Task: The American Jewish Joint Distribution*

Committee 1914–1964 (New York, 1964). For its work until 1945, see Yehuda Bauer, *My Brother's Keeper: A History of the American Jewish Joint Distribution Committee, 1929–1939* (Philadelphia, 1974); Yehuda Bauer, *American Jewry and the Holocaust: The American Jewish Joint Distribution Committee, 1939–1945* (Jerusalem, 1981).

35. Letter from Heinz Gerber to Hilfswerk, 7 December 1945, DAB, I/1–74.
36. Edd Johnson, "Many in Berlin, Jews to Hitler, Get No Relief," in *Chicago Sun Foreign Service*, 8 April 1946, DAB, I/1–79.
37. Letter with press clippings from God's Word is pre-eminent Scripture supply service, 17 January 1947, to the American Jewish Joint Distribution Committee (AJDC), JDC Archives, New York, (hereafter JDCA, NY), AR194554 / 4 / 17 / 119.
38. Letter from Curt Radlauer Bureau Grüber, Berlin to AJDC, 24 March 1946, JDCA, NY AR194554 / 4 / 32 / 304.
39. For details see Königseder and Wetzel, *Lebensmut im Wartesaal*; Feinstein, *Holocaust Survivors*; Patt and Berkowitz, *We Are Here*.
40. Johnson, "Many in Berlin."
41. For all citations in this paragraph, see Quarterly report from AJDC Berlin, 1 June 1946, 10–11, JDCA, NY, AJDC Jerusalem, 44–52 / 2 / 3 / JER.298.
42. Hans-Erich Fabian, "Rasse und Religion," in *Der Weg*, vol. 1, Nr. 20 12 July 1946, 1–2.
43. Letter from Herbert Katzki AJDC Arolsen to AJDC Paris, 24 May 1946, JDCA, NY, 45–54 / 4 / 32 / 304.
44. Ibid.
45. See Grossmann, *Jews*, 96–100; Pegelow Kaplan, *Language*, 256.
46. Statistik der Wiedereintrittsgesuche zwecks Aufnahme in die jüdische Gemeinde zu Berlin, Stand Juli 1946, Centrum Judaicum Archiv (hereafter CJA), 5A1 Nr. 46, p. 15.
47. Grossmann, *Jews*, 98. In other Communities, rabbis often decided more pragmatically and accepted non-Jewish relatives of mixed marriages as members. See Lida Barner, "Von Irmgard zu Irith: Konversionen zum Judentum im Deutschland der 1950er und 1960er Jahre" (MA thesis, University of Munich, 2008), 99.
48. Six to eight thousand of the surviving German Jews joined the postwar Communities according to Harry Maor, "Über den Wiederaufbau der jüdischen Gemeinden in Deutschland seit 1945" (Ph.D. diss, Mainz, 1961), 15.
49. Atina Grossmann and Tamar Lewinsky, "Zwischenstation," in *Geschichte der Juden in Deutschland von 1945 bis zur Gegenwart: Politik, Kultur und Gesellschaft*, ed. Michael Brenner (Munich, 2012), 122–39.
50. Report "Die Lage der jüdischen Gemeinde zu Berlin und ihrer Mitglieder, Bericht der jüdischen Gemeinde Berlin," April 1946, CJA, 5A1 Nr. 3, 31. In most other cities, the rate of intermarriage in the Communities was even higher than in Berlin, where many more Jews survived in hiding than elsewhere.
51. One of the best documented cases is the marriage of Victor and Eva Klemperer. See Victor Klemperer, *Ich will Zeugnis ablegen bis zum letzten: Tagebücher* (Berlin, 1998).
52. Letter to the Jewish Community of Düsseldorf, 4 November 1946, Zentralarchiv zur Erforschung der Geschichte der Juden in Deutschland, Heidelberg, B 1.5, Nr. 86. See Donate Strathmann, *Auswandern oder Hierbleiben? Jüdisches Leben in Düsseldorf und Nordrhein 1945–1960* (Essen, 2003), 206–7.
53. Letter from Herbert Katzki AJDC Paris to Joseph Fink AJDC Berlin, 9 February 1948, JDCA, New York, AJDC Geneva, 45–54 / 4 / 8 / 48 / GER.790.
54. For Berlin, e.g., Jana Leichsenring, *Die Katholische Kirche und "ihre Juden": Das "Hilfswerk beim Bischöflichen Ordinariat Berlin", 1938–1945* (Berlin, 2007); Hartmut Ludwig, *An der Seite der Entrechteten und Schwachen: Zur Geschichte des "Büro Pfarrer Grüber" (1938 bis 1940) und der Ev. Hilfsstelle für Ehemals Rasseverfolgte nach 1945* (Berlin, 2009).

55. Letter from Hilfswerk to Walter Hennighausen, 4 July 1946, in Archiv des Evangelischen Werkes für Diakonie und Entwicklung Berlin (hereafter ADW), ZB 842.
56. Minutes of a meeting at the central bureau of the Hilfswerk, 23 June 1947, ADW, ZB 842.
57. Letter of the WCC to the Hilfswerk, 12 August 1946, ADW, ZB 842.
58. Hermle, *Evangelische Kirche*, 67.
59. On forced labor of non-Jewish spouses of mixed marriages and *Mischlinge* in camps of the Organisation Todt, see Wolf Gruner, *Jewish Forced Labor under the Nazis: Economic Needs and Racial Aims 1938–1944* (Cambridge, 2006), 89–102; for the forced labor of intermarried Jews at the Organisation Todt, see Strnad, *Fortune of Survival*, 176–85.
60. Letter from Otto Hawelleck to Hilfswerk, 9 January 1946, DAB, I/1-80.
61. Letter from Georg Jaretzki to Hilfswerk, 17 February 1946, DAB I/1-80.
62. Letter from Georg Jaretzki to Hilfswerk, 8 September 1946, DAB I/1-80.
63. Harald Schmid, "'Wiedergutmachung' und Erinnerung: Die Notgemeinschaft der durch die Nürnberger Gesetze Betroffenen," in *Opfer als Akteure: Interventionen ehemaliger NS-Verfolgter in der Nachkriegszeit*, ed. Katharina Stengel (Frankfurt am Main, 2008), 27–47.
64. Letter Emmy Bothmann, 23 February 1947, FZH, 18–1 Nr. 7.7 Bd.1.

Bibliography

Barner, Lida. "Von Irmgard zu Irith, Konversionen zum Judentum im Deutschland der 1950er und 1960er Jahre." MA thesis, University of Munich, 2008.

Bauer, Yehuda. *American Jewry and the Holocaust: The American Jewish Joint Distribution Committee, 1939–1945*. Jerusalem: The Institute of Contemporary Jewry, Hebrew University, 1981.

———. *My Brother's Keeper: A History of the American Jewish Joint Distribution Committee, 1929–1939*. Philadelphia, PA: Jewish Publication Society of America, 1974.

Benz, Wolfgang, ed. *Überleben im Dritten Reich: Juden im Untergrund und ihre Helfer*. Munich: C.H. Beck, 2003.

Büttner, Ursula. *Die Not der Juden teilen: Christlich-jüdische Familien im Dritten Reich. Beispiel und Zeugnis des Schriftstellers Robert Brendel*. Hamburg: Christians, 1988.

Edgar, Adrienne, and Benjamin Frommer, eds. *Intermarriage from Central Europe to Central Asia: Mixed Families in the Age of Extremes*. Lincoln: University of Nebraska Press, 2020.

Essner, Cornelia. *Die "Nürnberger Gesetze" oder Die Verwaltung des Rassenwahns 1933–1945*. Paderborn: Schöningh, 2002.

Feinstein, Margarete Myers. *Holocaust Survivors in Postwar Germany, 1945–1957*. Cambridge: Cambridge University Press, 2010.

Geis, Jael. *Übrig sein—"Leben danach": Juden deutscher Herkunft in der britischen und amerikanischen Zone Deutschlands 1945–1949*. Berlin: Philo, 2000.

Goschler, Constantin. *Wiedergutmachung: Westdeutschland und die Verfolgten des Nationalsozialismus (1945–1954)*. Munich: Oldenbourg, 1992.

Gottwaldt, Alfred, and Diana Schulle, *Judendeportationen aus dem Deutschen Reich 1941–1945*. Wiesbaden: Marix Verlag, 2005.

Grossmann, Atina. *Jews, Germans, and Allies: Close Encounters in Occupied Germany*. Princeton, NJ: Princeton University Press, 2007.
Grossmann, Atina, and Tamar Lewinsky. "Zwischenstation." In *Geschichte der Juden in Deutschland von 1945 bis zur Gegenwart: Politik, Kultur und Gesellschaft*, edited by Michael Brenner, 67–152. Munich: Beck, 2012.
Gruner, Wolf. *Jewish Forced Labor under the Nazis: Economic Needs and Racial Aims 1938–1944*. Cambridge: Cambridge University Press, 2006.
———. *Widerstand in der Rosenstraße: Die Fabrik-Aktion und die Verfolgung der "Mischehen" 1943*. Frankfurt am Main: Fischer-Taschenbuch-Verlag, 2005.
Hammerschmidt, Peter. *Wohlfahrtsverbände in der Nachkriegszeit: Reorganisation und Finanzierung der Spitzenverbände der freien Wohlfahrtspflege 1945 bis 1961*. Weinheim: Juventa, 2005.
Handlin, Oscar. *A Continuing Task: The American Jewish Joint Distribution Committee 1914–1964*. New York: Random House, 1964.
Hermle, Siegfried. *Evangelische Kirche und Judentum: Stationen nach 1945*. Göttingen: Vandenhoeck & Ruprecht, 1990.
Hölscher, Christoph. *NS-Verfolgte im "antifaschistischen Staat": Vereinnahmung und Ausgrenzung in der ostdeutschen Wiedergutmachung (1945–1989)*. Berlin: Metropol, 2002.
Ilgen, Volker. *Care-Paket & Co. Von der Liebesgabe zum Westpaket*. Darmstadt: Primus-Verlag, 2008.
Kingreen, Monica. "'Die Aktion zur kalten Erledigung der Mischehen': Die reichsweit singuläre systematische Verschleppung und Ermordung jüdischer Mischehepartner im NSDAP-Gau Hessen-Nassau 1942/1943." In *NS-Gewaltherrschaft: Beiträge zur historischen Forschung und juristischen Aufarbeitung*, edited by Alfred Gottwaldt et al., 187–201. Berlin: Edition Hentrich, 2005.
Klemperer, Victor. *Ich will Zeugnis ablegen bis zum letzten: Tagebücher*. Berlin: Aufbau-Verlag, 1998.
Königseder, Angelika, and Juliane Wetzel. *Lebensmut im Wartesaal: Die jüdischen DPs (Displaced Persons) im Nachkriegsdeutschland*. Frankfurt am Main: Fischer Taschenbuch, 1994.
Kwiet, Konrad. "Nach dem Pogrom: Stufen der Ausgrenzung." In *Die Juden in Deutschland 1933–1945: Leben unter nationalsozialistischer Herrschaft*, edited by Wolfgang Benz and Volker Dahm, 545–659. Munich: Beck, 1993.
Leichsenring, Jana. *Die Katholische Kirche und "ihre Juden": Das "Hilfswerk beim Bischöflichen Ordinariat Berlin," 1938–1945*. Berlin: Metropol Verlag, 2007.
Ludwig, Hartmut. *An der Seite der Entrechteten und Schwachen: Zur Geschichte des "Büro Pfarrer Grüber" (1938 bis 1940) und der Ev. Hilfsstelle für Ehemals Rasseverfolgte nach 1945*. Berlin: Logos Verlag, 2009.
Maor, Harry. "Über den Wiederaufbau der jüdischen Gemeinden in Deutschland seit 1945." Ph.D. diss., Mainz, 1961.
Meiring, Kerstin. *Die christlich-jüdische Mischehe in Deutschland 1840–1933*. Hamburg: Dölling und Galitz, 1998.
Meyer, Beate. *"Jüdische Mischlinge": Rassenpolitik und Verfolgungserfahrung 1933–1945*. Hamburg: Dölling und Galitz, 1999.

———. "The Mixed Marriage—A Guarantee of Survival or a Reflection of German Society during the Nazi Regime?" In *Probing the Depths of German Antisemitism: German Society and the Persecution of the Jews, 1933–1941*, edited by David Bankier, 54–77. New York: Berghahn Books, 2000.

Patt, Avinoam J., and Michael Berkowitz, eds. *"We Are Here": New Approaches to Jewish Displaced Persons in Postwar Germany*. Detroit, MI: Wayne State University Press, 2010.

Pegelow Kaplan, Thomas. *The Language of Nazi Genocide: Linguistic Violence and the Struggle of Germans of Jewish Ancestry*. Cambridge: Cambridge University Press, 2009.

———. "Jüdische Holocaustüberlebende und sprachliche Gewalt im besetzten Deutschland der frühen Nachkriegsjahre." In *Zwischen Erinnerung und Neubeginn: Zur deutsch-jüdischen Geschichte nach 1945*, edited by Susanne Schönborn, 250–67. Munich: Martin Meidenbauer, 2006.

Przyrembel, Alexandra. *Rassenschande: Reinheitsmythos und Vernichtungslegitimation im Nationalsozialismus*. Göttingen: Vandenhoeck & Ruprecht, 2003.

Schmid, Harald. "'Wiedergutmachung' und Erinnerung: Die Notgemeinschaft der durch die Nürnberger Gesetze Betroffenen." In *Opfer als Akteure: Interventionen ehemaliger NS-Verfolgter in der Nachkriegszeit*, edited by Katharina Stengel, 27–47. Frankfurt am Main: Campus, 2008.

Schrafstetter, Susanna. *Flucht und Versteck: Untergetauchte Juden in München. Verfolgungserfahrung und Nachkriegsalltag*. Göttingen: Wallstein, 2015.

Sommer, Karl-Ludwig. *Humanitäre Auslandshilfe als Brücke zu atlantischer Partnerschaft: CARE, CRALOG und die Entwicklung der deutsch-amerikanischen Beziehungen nach Ende des Zweiten Weltkriegs*. Bremen: Staatsarchiv Bremen, 1999.

Strathmann, Donate. *Auswandern oder Hierbleiben? Jüdisches Leben in Düsseldorf und Nordrhein 1945–1960*. Essen: Klartext-Verlag, 2003.

Strnad, Maximilian. "Die Deportationen aus München." *Münchner Beiträge zur Jüdischen Geschichte und Kultur* 8, no. 2 (2014): 76–96.

———. "The Fortune of Survival—Intermarried German Jews in the Dying Breath of the 'Thousand-Year Reich.'" *Dapim* 29, no. 3 (2015): 173–96.

———. "Privileg Mischehe? Handlungsräume sogenannter 'jüdisch versippter' Familien 1933–1949." Ph.D diss., University of Munich, 2016.

Winstel, Tobias. *Verhandelte Gerechtigkeit: Rückerstattung und Entschädigung für jüdische NS-Opfer in Bayern und Westdeutschland*. Munich: Oldenbourg, 2006.

Conclusion

Thomas Pegelow Kaplan and Wolf Gruner

Petitions mattered. This volume aims at shifting scholarly perceptions of the role and impact of Jewish petitions from the early 1930s until the late 1940s. Its authors draw on conceptualizations of petitioning practices that take issue with attempts to present them as evidence of a fundamental failure to grasp the deadly threat of the Nazis and their collaborators. Instead, the volume demonstrates in various case studies that range from Jewish pleas to authorities in Nazi Germany to entreaties by Jews to local Hungarian officials in the Budapest ghetto that Jewish Holocaust-era petitions have to be taken seriously and substantially reevaluated.

Written by the thousands, these petitions constitute inherently hybrid sources that bring together the competing voices of the Jewish petitioners and the petitioned, often officials involved in the persecution and eventually outright genocidal policies. The authors in this volume analyze Holocaust-era entreaties as more complex, multi-voiced sources, in contrast to recent attempts to classify petitions as ego-documents. In other words, these petitions comprise active practices of victims and perpetrators that provide fresh insights into the difficult renegotiations of persecuted populations that the kind of integrated histories of the Holocaust with multiple combined perspectives call for.[1]

The collection's chapters reveal the various ways European Jews with their entreaties sought to counter the Nazi or another authoritarian regime's discriminatory actions and its imposition of racialized public subjectivities on the petitioners. To understand these petitions as manifestations of protest and self-determination gives agency back to the victims of oppression. The persecuted often used these entreaties as a political means despite their exclusion from political participation and representation. Without altering the asymmetrical power relations, many entreaties, as the authors of this volume have shown, reshaped the practices, languages, and often realities of petitioners and petitioned alike. The analysis of Jewish petitioning increases our understanding of the agency of perse-

---

Notes for this chapter begin on page 217.

cuted groups and their struggle for survival during periods of systematic persecution and mass violence.

Who then were the authors of petitions composed immediately before, during, and after World War II in Europe? Petitioners, as the essays in this volume demonstrate, came from across the European Jewish communities, as well as from Jewish converts to Christianity and their children, whom Nazi or other fascist laws labeled "Jews." Petitioners were not limited to the leaders of communities and organizations like Wilhelm Filderman in Romania or Leo Baeck, the head of the Reich Representation of German Jews (Reichsvertretung der deutschen Juden), even if they played a prominent role in petitioning activities. Indeed, many ordinary Jewish men and women composed and submitted entreaties. A severely disabled war veteran and former tobacco kiosk owner in Vienna, who petitioned Hitler's deputy Rudolf Hess for access to public parks in Vienna and to not live as a "pariah," was among them as well as a desperate father, dwelling in one of the "Jewish" houses in Budapest, who begged local authorities to return his son from the Vasvár ghetto to the Hungarian capital and a French-Jewish woman who attempted to persuade Vichy officials to release her husband from one of the country's transit camps.[2] The breadth is astounding and documents the ingenuity, agency, and room to maneuver—however limited—of these men and women under often devastating circumstances.

While many authors were of an urban middle or upper middle-class background with substantial education and access to lawyers or legal aid, there were also many Jewish petitioners from rural areas of Europe or of a lower-class background. Some in the coerced communities of ghettos, as Svenja Bethke's chapter revealed, also lacked the basic skills to compose an entreaty, but were able to join a collective petition penned by others. As several contributions, for instance by Stacy Veeder and Thomas Pegelow Kaplan demonstrated, a growing number of Jewish women engaged in entreaty writing. On occasion, as in the case of late 1938 and early 1939 entreaties that requested the release of their husbands, sons, brothers, and fathers imprisoned in the course of the November pogroms, women even constituted the vast majority of the authors.

Like the petitioners, the reasons for crafting entreaties were manifold. Many petitions in Nazi Germany and elsewhere, as Wolf Gruner has shown in his analysis of entreaties authored by Jewish organizations such as the Reich Representation of German Jews and the Zionist Federation for Germany (Zionistische Vereinigung für Deutschland), directly protested the rapidly increasing persecution of the Jewish population and demanded a stop of physical and verbal violence, be it in 1933 or 1938.

With the rising promulgation of antisemitic legislation and decrees, more and more individual petitioners requested either the abolishment of laws or exemptions from an ever-widening range of measures, be it the dismissal from employment and school or the prohibition to marry a non-Jew, denial of access to public parks, payments of arbitrary fees and "atonement levies" (*Sühneleistungen*) and the wearing of the notorious yellow star.

Throughout the 1930s, the *petitum* often evolved around opposition to anti-Jewish policies and practices as well as support for emigration in the form of securing an affidavit and visa from countries the petitioners sought to immigrate to. By the late 1930s and early 1940s, entreaties protested anti-Jewish segregation and aimed at exemption from forced labor and deportation as well as the release from camps of various types and ghettos. After the war, the few remaining Jews in post-genocidal societies such as occupied Germany petitioned for aid to increase the chances of their physical recovery and survival.

Some requests and their effects were rather unexpected, but all the more insightful for an understanding of anti-Jewish persecutions. As Tim Cole discussed, Budapest-based Jews petitioned to have their building or apartment designated as part of the evolving ghetto to avoid moving to an unknown location where they would lose their social infrastructure of close neighbors, friends, and families with their respective resources. As Ben Frommer's analysis of petitions for honorary Aryan status in the Protectorate of Bohemia and Moravia demonstrated, pleas from people, who had converted to Christianity, could also include the denial of the petitioner's legal parent.

Like the authors and their reasons for petitioning, there was also a myriad of petitioned individuals, organizations, state officials, and even party agencies across and beyond the European continent. The targets of entreaties ranged from fascist leaders to local mayors, from government administrators and camp managers to business executives and any person who held power. Some agencies and officials were directly identified by antisemitic laws and regulations as the addressees of petitions. Other individuals enjoyed influence in a specific regime and appeared, therefore, as promising recipients.

The identity and position of the petitioned, generally speaking, profoundly shaped the language and form of an entreaty. Romanian Jewish leader Wilhelm Filderman's plea to Antonescu's personal physician Dr. Nicolae Gh. Lupu was much less formal and structured than petitions prompted by exemption clauses in racial laws in Germany, Vichy France, or Romania. In many cases, the latter were accompanied by supplementary decrees and commentaries that often provided very specific lingo and criteria.

Many Jewish petitioners did not have a full grasp of the petitioning processes and the broader politics shaping them. Especially in the case of entreaties to local, regional, or national government agencies, they often used petitions as political tools and consciously or unconsciously drew on the language and regulation of the petitioned bodies to increase their chances of being heard and to obtain a desired outcome. Time and again, European Jews spoke or wrote the language of the petitioned agency and officials because they had to. These dynamics clearly reveal petitions as hybrid sources that encompass the lingo and goals of the petitioners and petitioned alike as well as key documents of integrated histories of the Holocaust.

All of these dynamics still do not fully explain why so many European Jews resorted to petitioning. No monocausal reading suffices. There was a range of reasons that again could differ quite substantially among individuals and communities. Among the most obvious factors were the explicit provisions in anti-Jewish laws and decrees that allowed for and explicitly required petitioning, especially for exemptions. In this sense, the *Statuts des Juifs* in Vichy France resembled anti-Jewish legislation in the Reich and other European countries with authoritarian or fascist governments such as Romania.[3]

The mere promulgation of a law with exemptions does not automatically prompt tens of thousands of men and women to petition. Further encouragement was needed. For once, the Jewish Community leadership in various parts of German-controlled Europe, coerced or non-coerced, often directly urged its members to write entreaties to address grievances or ask for support.

Furthermore, petitioning remained an option for communication for communities and individuals suffering from increasing persecution and a striking lack of political representation or material recourse. In authoritarian regimes, gaining access to a leading figure with power, influence, and resources, appeared to be the only way to potentially have any impact. Since the number and variety of anti-Jewish measures and laws were huge, Jewish petitioners had the opportunity to address a myriad of national, regional and local institutions that had issued these measures or somebody with the power to overrule them.

Even at the height of the Holocaust, there were, albeit on a rather minuscule scale, rulings in favor of individual entreaty writers' requests by fascist administrators. For many Jewish petitioners, the promise of a reprieve from harassment and a looming deportation, be it in Hungary or France, Germany or Romania, proved to be a powerful incentive. Moreover, petitioning was often easily carried out. It did not, by necessity, require many resources. Most members of the Jewish population segregated in Berlin or Budapest could find pen and paper to compose a petition or present it verbally. In many cases, the local Jewish Community, as shown by Wolf Gruner for Prague, also addressed the needs of the individuals and intervened on behalf of Community members or even drafted petitions for them. In some cases, however, especially involving intricate legal discussions and commentary or cases over racial classification that required genealogical research, petitioning practices could be very costly for individuals and include lawyers, researchers, fees for documents, and many related expenses.

The widespread use of entreaties and even their form and composition in the 1930s and 1940s, finally, cannot be fully explained without taking the long history of Jewish and non-Jewish petitioning practices into account that extended back for centuries. Both past practices internal to Jewish Communities on the continent and the long interactions of Jewish Communities and individuals with gentile city, territorial, and Reich administrations were significant. Support of members in need had long been part of the work of Jewish Communities run by acculturated Jewish post-Haskalah leaders in Western and Central Europe and were a key feature of Jewish religious practices. The *kehillot* in prewar Poland, as Svenja Bethke's contribution pointed out, with their semi-autonomy over internal and social affairs established strong traditions of seeking support echoes through the entreaties of Jews confined to ghettos run by Nazi-imposed Jewish Councils.

Petitions by Jewish women, even to non-Jewish authorities, especially in questions of divorce, inheritance, and the rights of children, too, had a *longue durée*. While female petitioning activities differed in scope and frequency in the early 1940s, it could and did draw on these traditions. The same was the case with the employment of gentile lawyers and scribes, which in some parts of the continent, especially those once controlled by the Ottoman Empire, also included an almost exclusive reliance on professional petition writers.

Raul Hilberg has noted that centuries of petition writing and finding accommodations with gentile rulers even during and after expulsions misled Jewish Communities into believing that they could achieve similar agreements with Nazi authorities.[4] Yet, the research results of this volume often contradict Hilberg's claims that these expectations and perceptions of Jewish petitioners were wrong. The volume's chapters demonstrate the extent to which Jewish leaders and ordinary community members were often able to adjust their entreaties and turn them to tools of survival and considerable agency under impossible circumstances.

Furthermore, European Jews directed their entreaties not only to representatives of oppressive and eventually genocidal regimes but also Jewish Community organizations, offices, and leaders and, during the war years, Jewish Councils and other bodies of Jewish dignitaries created by the Nazis or their allies. International aid organizations such as the American Jewish Joint Distribution Committee and the Aid Society of the Jews in Germany (Hilfsverein der Juden in Deutschland) were increasingly among the recipients as well as heads of state, foreign governments, and their embassies in Europe. The latter often required different approaches and languages, but key features of Holocaust-era petitions remained, including a prevalent sense of urgency.

Despite the multitude of voices emanating from the tens of thousands of entreaties, Jewish petitioning practices throughout Europe during and after the Holocaust reveal distinct patterns. For once, the timing and time European Jews crafted and submitted petitions was significant.[5] Jewish organizations and Communities frequently petitioned new authoritarian regimes and rulers such as Hitler in 1933 or General Ion Antonescu in 1940, often responding to early sets of antisemitic laws and violence. Soon, individual Jewish men and women joined in and petitioned authorities at the local, regional, or national levels against discrimination, robbery, and sometimes racial reclassification.

Similarly, location mattered and shaped petitioning patterns. Specific acts of segregation produced distinct waves of Jewish reactions. Entreaties penned against facets of the anti-Jewish laws excluding Jews from the German army in 1935 differed from those written against the internment of Jews in camps in France in 1940 and 1941. Petitions prompted by the June 1944 publication by the Budapest mayor's office of a list of houses to which the remaining Jewish population was required to move were different from pleas to the Łódź ghetto leadership after its issuance of names of inhabitants to be "relocated." The end of a regime and genocidal campaign prompted the survivors to return to entreaty writing one more time as part of their ongoing struggles for survival, even if the addressee, by necessity, changed. Reflecting the increasing desperation of the petitioners, even announcements that petitions would no longer be accepted did not completely stop petitioning practices, but partially prompted a redirecting to different agencies and officials.

The content and discursive strategies of Jewish petitioners also followed some distinctive patterns. First, in the early stages, Jewish organization and Community leaders—often lawyers by training—evoked Jewish civil and minority rights as enshrined in the post-World War I order or older legal prescripts to make their case. Wilhelm Filderman, as Ștefan C. Ionesco demonstrated, worked closely with a group of lawyers who meticulously studied the Romanian regime's antisemitic legislation. Union Générale des Israélites de France officials and individual French and non-

French Jews in camps in Vichy France, as Stacy Veeder has shown, initially engaged in similar practices as did the German-Jewish members of the Reichsvertretung and organizations such as the Central Association of German Citizens of Jewish Faith (Centralverein deutscher Staatsbürger jüdischen Glaubens), as Wolf Gruner correctly stressed.

Second, the reference to past military service and sacrifice along with patriotism and devotion to the fatherland were important hallmarks of individual Jewish petitioning practices throughout large parts of Europe during the early years of fascist rule and even at the onset of the Holocaust. References to individual or collective Jewish contributions to a nation or a city, ranging from military service and political participation to tax payments and cultural accomplishments, can be found in many petitionary letters to strengthen the applicant's case, fight anti-Jewish stereotypes, and reclaim their identity as true citizens of the fatherland.

In Austria and Germany, even during World War II, many Jews emphasized their service during the previous world war. This could save lives, since war decorations repeatedly exempted Jewish veterans from being deported to extermination sites in Nazi-occupied Poland. Instead, the Gestapo relocated them to the Theresienstadt ghetto. In Vichy France, as Stacy Veeder convincingly argued, evoking French patriotism and past sacrifices remained common. Faced with the threat of deportation, it constituted a convenient means for French-Jewish petitioners to set themselves apart from non-French Jewish refugees in the country. There were of course exceptions. Zionist officials drew much less on or even shunned these discursive patterns. In the Nazi-established ghettos, as Svenja Bethke demonstrated, in which the population mainly petitioned the Jewish leadership, such lingo also rarely surfaced.

Third, most petitioners spoke the language of the petitioned regime and its legislation, even an antisemitic one. They did so out of necessity, since an outright rejection or ridiculing of racial classifications or other measures would have quickly ended an entreaty. Paradoxically, many survivors, as Maximilian Strnad has shown, confronted the same exclusionary language and racial classification imposed on them by the Nazi state even after the regime's demise. In their petitions, they also had to use this lingo themselves to stake their claims for aid.

As several of this volume's chapters convincingly argue, Jewish and other petitioners of partial Jewish ancestry did not simply subject themselves to this often violent language. Instead, they sought to forge their own constructs that sometimes entered the lexicon of the petitioning process, found a level of acceptance by the petitioned agency, and yielded outcomes desired by the authors. Jewish petitioners, for instance, managed to introduce terms like "mixed" houses with Jewish and gentile tenants in the debates over the changing Budapest ghetto in ways that gave them more room to maneuver. Others appealed to wishes and interests of the recipients of the petition, exploited languages of nationalism, even of racism and exclusion, to their own advantage, or inserted themselves in languages of labor and immigration as part of their efforts to escape the continent.

Fourth, Jewish petitioners rarely remained restricted to just one entreaty to a single agency or person. Not only did Jewish men and women often compose a series of petitions to various agencies of real or imagined power. They also frequently tried to set one agency of an oppressive state or political party against another in ways that supported their request. In prewar Germany, as Wolf Gruner's chapter demonstrated, Jewish organizations repeatedly did so to their advantage in simultaneous petitions to the Interior Ministry, local Gestapo, and Nazi party activists. But even during wartime, the remaining Jewish institutions tried to manipulate various perpetrator institutions or their differing interests in emigration, property, or preserving economic improvement, or pit them against each other as one could see in Prague and Vienna.

Fifth, Jewish Holocaust-era practices of entreaty writing increasingly took on transnational dimensions. These phenomena are not limited to the reliance of border-crossing networks and communication flows that were a necessity for any effort to escape the Nazi-controlled parts of the European continent. Inhabitants in ghettos like Łódź, violently deported from various parts of Central Europe, had often crossed multiple borders, spoke various languages, and negotiated new ones in the ghettos' many transnational spaces. These experiences eventually entered their petitions. Furthermore, petitioning strategies of men and women in the Czech lands, as discussed by Ben Frommer, which amounted to a questioning of their Jewish "race" by claiming that their seventeenth-century Protestant Czech Brethren ancestors had converted to Judaism, did not remain limited to the Protectorate. By means of transnational scholarly and other networks, these strategies were shared with other petitioners elsewhere in Europe and started to inform their writing.

Finally, petitioners also often played up gender stereotypes and hierarchies in the hope of appealing to a petitioned official's sensibilities. Indeed, like Jewish history and Holocaust studies in general, histories of Jewish petitioning practices cannot be written without considering gender. As the chapters of this volume demonstrate, the writing, content, and contexts of Holocaust and post-Holocaust Jewish entreaties were profoundly shaped by gender hierarchies and the construction of gender relationships, which constitute primary ways, drawing on Joan Scott's classic conceptualization, in which power was articulated.[6] Wilhelm Filderman, the head of the Jewish Community in Romania acted as the patriarchal leader who emphasized hyper-masculine practices such as the past frontline fighting of Romanian-Jewish men and, as Ștefan C. Ionesco revealed, even evoked a sense of male camaraderie with the Romanian dictator General Antonescu.[7] Others tried to evoke solidarity directly with their former fellow soldiers in the trenches. Fathers, husbands, and brothers, often of bourgeois background and sensitivity, petitioned on behalf of their families and female relatives to meet gender expectations and norms. However, as we have seen in cases like Isac Grossmann's petition for permission to enter the Philippines discussed in Thomas Pegelow Kaplan's chapter, this evoking of gender norms did not always have the desired outcome as petitioners failed to overcome racial hierarchies and stereotypes.

Yet, even the undermining of prevalent gender hierarchies as a result of the racist policies by way of a middle-class husband's loss of income, status, and freedom, profoundly influenced the gendered production of petitions. Faced with persecution and violence, many Jewish women swiftly adjusted their responses to what they perceived as necessary to secure their families' and their own survival. As the chapters of this volume reveal, they made use of petitions with an unprecedented frequency, especially in the late 1930s and early 1940s. From Austria and Bohemia to Vichy France and in exile as far away as the Philippines, middle-class Jewish women in particular turned to entreaties to secure the release of a family member, battle discriminatory restrictions, avoid deportation or, in the case of converts, obtain a racial reclassification. Even while speaking the language of the petitioned, they asserted a sense of agency that often transgressed gender norms. Scholars have stressed gender differences in perceiving danger or developing strategies to survive.[8] In many cases, however, such as attempts to escape Vichy camps, as Stacy Veeder revealed, these women relied on similar strategies as men in emphasizing their patriotism or highlighting military service. As German historian Gisela Bock astutely noted, there is a need for a greater sensitivity to similarities—and not only differences—when turning to gender analysis.[9]

Male and female petitioners alike hoped—often desperately—for an outcome that helped them in their struggles for a reprieve from persecution and outright survival. In many cases, even against seemingly impossible odds, Jewish Holocaust-era petitioners obtained a desired decision on their plea. The Reichsvertretung in Germany, for instance, successfully petitioned the Gestapo to release Jewish teachers who had been arrested during the 1938 November pogrom. The Jewish Community in Prague convinced Eichmann's office to intervene against local ghettoization in a few cases, as Wolf Gruner has shown in this volume. Individual petitions helped, as Tim Cole convincingly demonstrated, to shape the size and even form of the Budapest ghetto. French and non-French Jews interned in camps controlled by the Vichy regime managed to secure aid and, albeit rarely, their release. After the Gestapo's first deportations comprised elderly, forced laborers, and Jews in mixed marriages, interventions led to more specific deportation decrees that excluded certain categories from transports.[10] Hence, quite a few petitions generated the desired outcome: they stopped certain anti-Jewish measures, provided access to resources, and secured exemptions from racial laws and support for emigration.

Almost all chapters in this volume, meanwhile, also document entreaties that were ignored, dismissed, or rejected by the addressed authorities. Intermarried Jews, not just in the postwar German lands, experienced painful rejections when international aid organizations such as the American Jewish Joint Distribution Committee pointed out their allegedly privileged status during the Nazi years and consistently turned down their requests for support. During the war, Jewish converts to Christianity in "mixed marriages" in the Nazi-established Protectorate of Bohemia and Moravia, as Ben Frommer demonstrated with powerful examples, did not fare much better and had their petitions for a racial reclassification consistently rejected by the Reich Protector's Office. Vichy official Xavier Vallat habitually alluded to the prerogative of German occupation agencies when rejecting petitions. Vallat, nonetheless, succeeded, as Stacy Veeder argued, in creating the illusion that the leaders of Jewish organizations such as Union Générale des Israélites de France had some influence they could evoke by means of petitions. Indeed, Veeder's and Frommer's explorations of specific cases border on arguments that much of the conventional scholarship on Jewish petitioning has used to dismiss the practice in general.[11]

Yet, as the studies in this volume indicate, it is the very question of what constitutes "success" that needs to be revisited and carefully probed. Even an evaluated and then rejected petition could offer the author a much-needed partial reprieve from persecution or stay of deportation. The processing of petitions often provided invaluable time to prepare to go underground, which often was a strikingly laborious process that required substantial resources.[12] While the petitions by Ilse Friedlaender's parents were not approved, as Thomas Pegelow Kaplan's chapter revealed, and they did not manage to emigrate, the young woman could prepare and managed to go into hiding in the Berlin area.

Again, the timing was significant. Authors of entreaties submitted and rejected in 1933–34, for example, could most often craft new petitions to different agencies or even the courts. By 1943–44, these opportunities were much harder to come by and, in the Reich, the Gestapo and radicalized parts of the Nazi party often turned the very use of petitions into a distinguishing feature of a petitioner's Jewishness to be unequivocally rejected.[13]

Overall, however, the question of "success" cannot be convincingly tied to a mere rejection or acceptance of a plea. Instead, it needs to be regarded as a relative and complex process, as the contributions to this volume underline. All along, the involvement of many different local, regional, and national government and party agencies and officials on the perpetrator side from Berlin to Vichy and Prague to Bucharest as well as the allocation of considerable resources, including time, information, legal advice, and manpower, points to the fact that such written complaints were taken seriously—even if sometimes for dubious and antisemitic reasons like the perceived power of "the Jew."

More importantly, entreaty writers who responded to racial policies by the Nazi state and its allies used these practices in many cases to assert a sense of agency that proved critical in challenging and withstanding these regimes' increasingly radical policies. Hence, the question is, to what extent might we be justified to understand petitioning practices as individual or group acts of contestation or even resistance?

Applying a broad understanding of resistance that includes all acts that challenged plans and actions of the Nazis, other dictatorial or authoritarian governments and their helpers, leaves no doubt that many of the entreaties can be seen as acts of resistance. Jewish men and women put their opposition on paper and signed it with their names, hence being vulnerable to personal repercussions such as incarceration and violence. They challenged anti-Jewish laws and measures or protested violence and humiliation. Such petitionary letters, authored alone by an individual, by groups of individuals, or even representatives of communities constituted the only political tools available for the oppressed Jewish population deprived of their political representation and civil rights.[14] To write directly to the responsible figures, be it authoritarian leaders or city officials, could potentially crosscut the vastly asymmetrical relationships of power by addressing interests, goals, fears, and convictions of the recipients. In any event, it opened a channel of communication, especially under increasing circumstances of segregation; saved time; and provided potential access to resources.

In addition to challenging anti-Jewish measures, many of the petitioners did not shy away from negating the racial classifications imposed on them by the regimes. Most often, they questioned the validity of these impositions on their own public identities by drafting elaborate exemption requests. On a few occasions, petitioners also denied the categories' correctness. Many Jews employed sophisticated ways to resist racial categorization and discrimination when they frequently reclaimed their sense of self and identity by not putting forward their forced names or ID numbers, by listing their earned titles and national awards, or by directly claiming their rights as citizens or patriots referring to their contributions to their homelands.

However, not every petition amounted to an act of contestation or resistance. There were some, as Ben Frommer's chapter highlighted, whose authors readily reified Nazi antisemitic constructions. Others were part of a denunciation of Jewish Community members, as Svenja Bethke's chapter has documented, and a few even led to collaboration with the petitioned regime.[15] The study of Holocaust-era petitions indeed demonstrates the need to avoid easy binaries of resistance versus complicity. Many unfolded on a more complex continuum or "gray zone."[16]

Further avenues of research would need to study this gray zone and relate petitioning practices more extensively to the broad range of Jewish acts of contestation. Studies should also look more comparatively into petitioning practices as well as into entreaty writing in other countries not represented here. Studies of petitions by Jews in other Nazi occupied countries such as the Netherlands and Greece or allied nations like Italy, whose leadership introduced their own racial legislation, would further increase our understanding of these practices across the continent. More specifically, future research could determine if and to what extent different types of Nazi occupation and control influenced petition practices. Were there, for example, discernible differences between the use of entreaties in states with semi-autonomous governments such as the Protectorate of Bohemia-Moravia and those under military government such as northern France, Belgium or, later, Italy? Did these differences have an impact on the number, scope, content, and direction of entreaties?

This collection of investigations cannot be a substitute for in-depth studies that explore the many facets of petitions in their distinct regional and local contexts. Rather, this volume points to a need for monographic studies of these phenomena. Petitioning in the Nazi-established ghettos, for example, already took on specific forms and fulfilled different objectives. Petitions in the ghetto of Budapest differed from those in the ghetto of Łódź/Litzmannstadt, where Jewish Council head Mordechai Chaim Rumkowski, as Svenja Bethke's chapter demonstrated, skillfully integrated petitioning in his authoritative rule and leadership. The practices of writing entreaties took on even different manifestations in other ghettos such as Kovno, Radom, or Odessa, whose leadership did not create an administrative office to process them.

Furthermore, Andreas Würgler's dictum for the study of early modern petitioning that these entreaties are open to an array of approaches from "close reading in the hermeneutic tradition" and serial analysis to micro-historical reconstructions and linguistic analysis is equally valid for Holocaust-era entreaties.[17] Although this volume has started to examine petitions from different methodological perspectives, it could hardly exhaust the full range of distinct disciplinary and interdisciplinary approaches available to analyze this genre. While some of the volume's authors are working on larger studies on petitioning, we hope the results of the volume's inquiries will serve to entice other scholars to integrate studies of these insightful sources and significant practices prominently into their works on the Holocaust.

Future research on Jewish petitioning also needs to focus even more on the interactions between Jews and non-Jews and take entreaties by both populations into consideration that were often in direct competition with one another. Time and again, pleas by persecuted Jews responded to antisemitic petitions by gentiles that had demanded anti-Jewish measures from the authorities.[18] In the Nazi state, for instance, the Reich Propaganda Ministry and the Chancellery of the Führer of the Nazi Party received thousands of gentile petitions of this type, which continued a long history of anti-Jewish entreaties throughout Europe.[19] At the same time, there were telling cases, in which, as Tim Cole's chapter revealed, Jewish and non-Jewish tenants wrote joint petitions to city officials to advance a shared agenda.

In addition, the extensive transnational spaces and forms of communication that critically informed Jewish petitioning practices even in remote areas of Eastern Europe require more scholarly analysis. Finally, Jewish Holocaust-era petitioning practices seen as forms of contestation or even resistance should lead us to rethink entreaty strategies of non-Jews against the Nazi regime and its European allies. Broadening the focus further, this rethinking also demands a review of petitions as tools of non-violent resistance in dictatorships and genocidal societies, be it in Latin America and elsewhere in world history.

Petitions, as the authors of this volume have shown, mattered. They were used by persecuted Jewish Communities, organizations, and individuals across the European continent and beyond during the 1930s and 1940s. Entreaties constituted one practice of many, used by increasingly embattled minorities in their struggle against persecution and, ultimately, for survival, and self-determination. In most cases, these Jewish petitions opposed a broad array of increasingly radical and eventually deadly policies by the Nazi regime and its many European allies. They ranged from general protest against persecution to demands for the abolishment of specific anti-Jewish restrictions, from requests to release relatives from internment and deportation to inquiries about exemptions from racial classification.

Even when Jews in their entreaties only claimed the right of self-determination, whether in Nazi Germany, Austria, France, or Romania, it was this practice in particular that challenged or took away power from the oppressors, namely the power of definition. Manifestations of self-determination gave agency back to the victims and proved critical as a political means despite their exclusion from political participation and representation. This book, thus, makes an important contribution to our understanding of petitions as overlooked tools of Jewish survival, contestation, and resistance. Petitions authored by male and female Jews during the Holocaust were anything but written for a bureaucrat's wastepaper basket and deserve a new appreciation and rereading as part of new integrated and integrative Holocaust histories that fully restore Jewish agency even against impossible odds.

Thomas Pegelow Kaplan is the Louis P. Singer Endowed Chair in Jewish History, Professor of History, and Interim Director of the Program in Jewish Studies at the University of Colorado Boulder. He is the author of *The Language of Nazi Genocide* (2009) and *The German-Jewish Press and Journalism Beyond Borders, 1933-1943* (2023, in Hebrew) as well as the co-editor of *Beyond "Ordinary Men": Christopher R. Browning and Holocaust Historiography* (2019) and *Police and Holocaust* (2023, in German). He is currently completing a manuscript entitled *Naming Genocide: Protesters, Imageries of Mass Murder, and the Remaking of Memory in West Germany and the United States*.

Wolf Gruner is the Shapell-Guerin Chair in Jewish Studies, Professor of History and Founding Director of the USC Dornsife Center for Advanced Genocide Research at the University of Southern California, Los Angeles. He is the author of eleven books, ten of them on the Holocaust, including *Jewish Forced Labor under the Nazis* (2006), *The Holocaust in Bohemia and Moravia* (2019) and *Resisters: How Ordinary Jews fought Persecution in Hitler's Germany* (2023).

Notes

1. Saul Friedländer, *Den Holocaust beschreiben: Auf dem Weg zu einer integrierten Geschichte* (Göttingen, 2007), 7–27.
2. See pp. 222–37, this volume, for reproductions and translations of some of these petitions.
3. On Romania, see Ştefan Cristian Ionescu, *Jewish Resistance to "Romanianization," 1940–44* (Basingstoke, 2015) and Ioanid Radu, *The Holocaust in Romania: The Destruction of Jews and Gypsies under the Antonescu Regime, 1940–1944* (Chicago, 2000). On France, see Renée

Poznanski, *Jews in France during World War II* (Waltham, MA, 2001) and Michel Laffitte, *Juif dans la France allemande: Institutions, dirigeants et communautés au temps de la Shoah* (Paris, 2006). On the Reich, see Saul Friedländer, *Nazi Germany and the Jews*, vol. 1: *The Years of Persecution 1933–1939* (New York, 1997).
4. Raul Hilberg, *The Destruction of the European Jews* (Chicago, 1961), 666.
5. On the importance of time, see Guy Miron, "'The Politics of Catastrophe Races On. I Wait.': Waiting Time in the World of German Jews under Nazi Rule," *Yad Vashem Studies* 43 (2015): 45–76.
6. Joan W. Scott, *Gender and the Politics of History* (New York, 1988), 43.
7. On Jewish masculinity during this period more broadly, see Maddy Carey, *Jewish Masculinity in the Holocaust: Between Destruction and Construction* (London, 2017) and Benjamin Maria Baader, Sharon Gillerman, and Paul Lerner, eds., *Jewish Masculinities: German Jews, Gender, and History* (Bloomington, IN, 2012).
8. Marion A. Kaplan, *Between Dignity and Despair: Jewish Life in Nazi Germany* (New York, 1998); Zoë Waxman, *Women in the Holocaust: A Feminist History* (New York, 2017); Chae-Ran Y. Freeze, Paula Hyman, and Antony Polonsky, *Jewish Women in Eastern Europe* (Oxford, 2007).
9. Gisela Bock, "Ordinary Women in Nazi Germany: Perpetrators, Victims, Followers, and Bystanders," in *Women in the Holocaust*, ed. Dalia Ofer and Leonore J. Weitzman (New Haven, CT, 1998), 96.
10. See pp. 28–50, this volume. For a more in-depth discussion, see Wolf Gruner, *Der geschlossene Arbeitseinsatz deutscher Juden: Zur Zwangsarbeit als Element der Verfolgung 1938–1943* (Berlin, 1997); Wolf Gruner, *Widerstand in der Rosenstrasse: Die Fabrik-Aktion und die Verfolgung der "Mischehen" 1943* (Frankfurt am Main, 2005).
11. See, for example, Beate Meyer, *"Jüdische Mischlinge": Rassenpolitik und Verfolgungserfahrung 1933–1945* (Hamburg, 1999), 158.
12. Susanna Schrafstetter, *Flucht und Versteck: Untergetauchte Juden in München: Verfolgungserfahrung und Nachkriegsalltag* (Göttingen, 2015); Wolfgang Benz, *Überleben im Dritten Reich: Juden im Untergrund und ihre Helfer* (Munich, 2003); Richard N. Lutjens, *Submerged on the Surface: The Not-so-Hidden Jews of Nazi Berlin, 1941–1945* (New York, 2019); Jacques Sémelin, *The Survival of the Jews in France, 1940–44* (Oxford, 2018).
13. For a longer discussion, see Thomas Pegelow Kaplan, "Determining 'People of German Blood,' 'Jews,' and '*Mischlinge*': The Reich Kinship Office and the Competing Discourses and Powers of Nazism, 1941–1943," *Contemporary European History* 15 (2006): 43–65. For the Protectorate, see Ben Frommer's analysis on pp. 72–91, this volume.
14. On the necessity to rethink narrower resistance concepts, see also Peter Steinbach, "Widerstand von Juden," in *Menora: Jahrbuch für Deutsch-jüdische Geschichte 1998*, eds. Julius H. Schoeps et al. (Bodenheim, 1998), 31–69.
15. See, for example, the case of Erich Goldmann, a Stuttgart-based dentist and World War I veteran, who, free of coercion, worked for the SD, the Secret Service of the SS, and the Gestapo during the war. See Erwin Goldmann Collection, Center for Research on Antisemitism Archive, Technical University of Berlin; Traut Graeber, interview by Thomas Pegelow Kaplan, tape recording, Bernau am Chiemsee, 11 August 2001; Wolfgang Benz, *Patriot und Paria: Das Leben des Erwin Goldmann zwischen Judentum und Nationalsozialismus: Eine Dokumentation* (Berlin, 1997).
16. Jonathan Petropoulos and John K. Roth, eds., *Gray Zones: Ambiguity and Compromise in the Holocaust and Its Aftermath* (New York, 2005). For a more recent study that includes a new model of "the coercion-resistance spectrum" that is more dynamic and adequate to understand individual behavior than the "gray zone" metaphor, see the relevant chapter in Sari Siegel, "Between Coercion and Resistance: Jewish Prisoner-Physicians in

Nazi Camps, 1940–1945" (Ph.D. diss., University of Southern California, Los Angeles, 2018).
17. Andreas Würgler, "Voices from among the 'Silent Masses': Humble Petitions and Social Conflict in Early Modern Central Europe," *International Review of Social History* 46, Supplement 9 (2001): 34.
18. See the compilation in Simon Dubnow's classic *History of the Jews in Russia & Poland*, vol. 1 (Philadelphia, PA, 1916), 316, 369–71.
19. See complaints and inquiries from the German population to Joseph Goebbels, National Archives II, College Park, RG 242, T-580, reel 654–655.

Bibliography

Baader, Benjamin Maria, Sharon Gillerman, and Paul Lerner, eds. *Jewish Masculinities: German Jews, Gender, and History*. Bloomington: Indiana University Press, 2012.

Benz, Wolfgang. *Patriot und Paria: Das Leben des Erwin Goldmann zwischen Judentum und Nationalsozialismus: Eine Dokumentation*. Berlin: Metropol, 1997.

———, ed. *Überleben im Dritten Reich: Juden im Untergrund und ihre Helfer*. Munich: C.H. Beck, 2003.

Bock, Gisela. "Ordinary Women in Nazi Germany: Perpetrators, Victims, Followers, and Bystanders." In *Women in the Holocaust*, edited by Dalia Ofer and Leonore J. Weitzman, 85–100. New Haven, CT: Yale University Press, 1998.

Carey, Maddy. *Jewish Masculinity in the Holocaust: Between Destruction and Construction*. London: Bloomsbury, 2017.

Dubnow, Simon. *History of the Jews in Russia & Poland*. Vol. 1. Philadelphia, PA: Jewish Publication Society of America, 1916.

Freeze, ChaeRan Y., Paula Hyman, and Antony Polonsky. *Jewish Women in Eastern Europe*. Oxford: Littman Library of Jewish Civilization, 2007.

Friedländer, Saul. *Den Holocaust beschreiben: Auf dem Weg zu einer integrierten Geschichte*. Göttingen: Wallstein, 2007.

———. *Nazi Germany and the Jews, 1933–1939*. Vol. 1: *The Years of Persecution*. New York: HarperCollins, 1997.

Gruner, Wolf. *Der geschlossene Arbeitseinsatz deutscher Juden: Zur Zwangsarbeit als Element der Verfolgung 1938–1943*. Berlin: Metropol, 1997.

———. *Widerstand in der Rosenstrasse: Die Fabrik-Aktion und die Verfolgung der "Mischehen" 1943*. Frankfurt am Main: Fischer Taschenbuch Verlag, 2005.

Hilberg, Raul. *The Destruction of the European Jews*. Chicago: Quadrangle Books, 1961.

Ionescu, Ştefan Cristian. *Jewish Resistance to "Romanianization," 1940–44*. Basingstoke: Palgrave, 2015.

Kaplan, Marion A. *Between Dignity and Despair: Jewish Life in Nazi Germany*. New York: Oxford University Press, 1998.

Laffitte, Michel. *Juif dans la France allemande: Institutions, dirigeants et communautés au temps de la Shoah*. Paris: Tallandier, 2006.

Lutjens, Richard N. *Submerged on the Surface : The Not-so-Hidden Jews of Nazi Berlin, 1941–1945*. New York: Berghahn Books, 2019.

Meyer, Beate. *"Jüdische Mischlinge": Rassenpolitik und Verfolgungserfahrung 1933–1945*. Hamburg: Doelling und Galitz, 1999.
Miron, Guy. "'The Politics of Catastrophe Races On. I Wait.': Waiting Time in the World of German Jews under Nazi Rule." *Yad Vashem Studies* 43 (2015): 45–76.
Pegelow Kaplan, Thomas. "Determining 'People of German Blood,' 'Jews,' and '*Mischlinge*': The Reich Kinship Office and the Competing Discourses and Powers of Nazism, 1941–1943." *Contemporary European History* 15 (2006): 43–65.
Petropoulos, Jonathan, and John K. Roth, eds. *Gray Zones: Ambiguity and Compromise in the Holocaust and Its Aftermath*. New York: Berghahn Books, 2005.
Poznanski, Renée, *Jews in France during World War II*. Waltham, MA: Brandeis University Press, 2001.
Radu, Ioanid. *The Holocaust in Romania: The Destruction of Jews and Gypsies under the Antonescu Regime, 1940–1944*. Chicago: Ivan R. Dee, 2000.
Schrafstetter, Susanna. *Flucht und Versteck: Untergetauchte Juden in München: Verfolgungserfahrung und Nachkriegsalltag*. Göttingen: Wallstein Verlag, 2015.
Scott, Joan W. *Gender and the Politics of History*. New York: Columbia University Press, 1988.
Sémelin, Jacques. *The Survival of the Jews in France, 1940–44*. Oxford: Oxford University Press, 2018.
Siegel, Sari. "Between Coercion and Resistance: Jewish Prisoner-Physicians in Nazi Camps, 1940–1945." Ph.D. diss., University of Southern California, Los Angeles, 2018.
Steinbach, Peter. "Widerstand von Juden." In *Menora: Jahrbuch für deutsch-jüdische Geschichte 1998*, edited by Julius H. Schoeps et al., 31–69. Bodenheim: Philo, 1998.
Waxman, Zoë. *Women in the Holocaust: A Feminist History*. New York: Oxford University Press, 2017.
Würgler, Andreas. "Voices from among the 'Silent Masses': Humble Petitions and Social Conflict in Early Modern Central Europe." *International Review of Social History* 46, Supplement 9 (2001): 11–34.

APPENDIX
European-Jewish Petitions during the Holocaust

DOCUMENT 1. Petition of Hans Kauders, Vienna, to Reich Minister and Deputy of the Führer Rudolf Hess, Munich, 1940 (Wiener Stadt- und Landesarchiv, Rassenpolitisches Amt der Stadt Wien, Gauleitung, Diverses, A-Z Nr. 1, 1938–45)

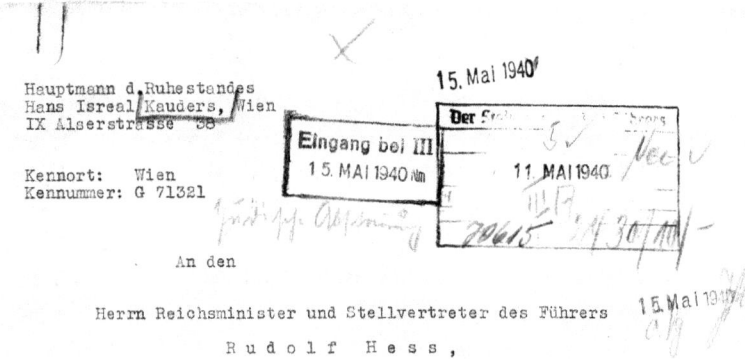

Hauptmann d. Ruhestandes
Hans Isreal Kauders, Wien
IX Alserstrasse 58

Kennort: Wien
Kennummer: G 71321

15. Mai 1940

Eingang bei III
15. MAI 1940 Nm

11. MAI 1940

An den

Herrn Reichsminister und Stellvertreter des Führers

R u d o l f   H e s s ,

München.

Sehr geehrter Herr Reichsminister !

Als nichtarischer, schwerstkriegsbeschädigter, ehemaliger Frontoffizier des Weltkrieges gestatte ich mir hiemit nachfolgende Ausführungen an Sie, Herr Reichsminister, mit der ergebenen Bitte zu richten, diese einer wohlwollenden Kenntnisnahme zu würdigen.

Ich bin gebürtiger Wiener, verheiratet, kinderlos, Hauptmann des Ruhestandes, stehe im 60. Lebensjahre und wohne seit meiner Geburt ununterbrochen in Wien.

Die Minderung meiner Erwerbsfähigkeit (Amputation des linken Oberschenkels infolge Schussverletzung und konsekutive Belastungs-Arthritis im rechten Kniegelenk) beträgt lt. Rentenbescheid des Versorgungsamtes Wien II, G.L. Nr 420.355, 90 vom Hundert.

Infolge der Eingliederung der Ostmark in das Deutsche Reich musste ich schon im März 1938 die mir im Jahre 1917 verliehene Tabak-Trafik in Wien I Kärntnerstrasse 43, die mir bis zu obigem Zeitpunkte eine bürgerliche Existenz gewährte, zurücklegen, da ich als Jude nicht länger Vertragspartner des Reiches bleiben durfte.

Seither gänzlich verdienst- und arbeitslos bin ich mit meiner Gattin auf die monatlichen Versorgungsgebühren von RM 164.95 angewiesen

14. MAI 1940

und von allen Kultureinrichtungen ausgeschlossen. Sogar das **Betreten** eines öffentlichen Gartens, um ein wenig frische Luft zu schöpfen, ist mir verboten, und dies alles nur aus dem Grunde, weil ich 4 jüdische Grosselternteile habe.

Bezüglich meiner Kriegsdienstleistung melde ich ergebenst Folgendes :
Am 2.September 1914 wurde ich als Leutnant i.d. Reserve des k.u.k. Infanterie-Regiments Nr 40 an der Spitze meines Zuges in Feyslavice vor Lublin 2 mal schwer verwundet, geriet dadurch trotz tapferster Gegenwehr in russische Kriegsgefangenschaft, wurde im Oktober 1914 in Homel(Russisch-Polen) im letzten Drittel des linken Oberschenkels in einem russischen Spital amputiert und nach 3 monatigem Krankenlager als einbeiniger Kriegskrüppel bei grimmigster Kälte nach Kansk-Jenniseisk in Zentralsibirien verschleppt. Hier blieb ich während des sibirischen Winters und wurde im August 1915 als Austausch- Invalide in die Heimat zurücktransportiert.

Nach meiner Heimkehr rückwirkend mit 1. März 1915 zum Oberleutnant befördert, wurde ich am 1.Juli 1916 als" invalid auch zu jedem **Landsturm**dienste ungeeignet " superarbitriert und in den Ruhestand versetzt.

Am 1.Dezember 1916 meldete ich mich freiwillig wieder zur Dienstleistung, wurde mit 10. Dezember 1916 reaktiviert und als Bezirks-Instruktions-Offizier der " Propaganda für Feindesabwehr " zugeteilt. Mit 1.April 1919 erfolgte meine Uebersetzung in das frühere Ruhestandsverhältnis. Am 23.Juli 1919 wurde ich ganz ausnahmsweise für " sehr erspriessliche Dienstleistung " durch Verleihung des Titel und Charakter als Hauptmann d.Ruhestandes ausgezeichnet.

Für " tapferes Verhalten vor dem Feinde " verlieh mir weiland Kaiser Franz Joseph I. schon am 11.Dezember 1915 das Militärverdienst-Kreuz 3.Klasse m.d. Kriegsdekoration u.d. Schwertern, überdies wurden mir folgende Kriegsauszeichnungen zuerkannt:

    Die Verwundeten-Medaille für 2 malige Verwundung,
    das Karl-Truppen-Kreuz,
    die oesterr. Kriegsmedaille m.d. Schwertern,
    die ungarische Kriegsmedaille mit Helm und Schwertern,
    die bulgarische Kriegsmedaille am Roten Bande.

Trotz meiner schweren Körperbehinderung, die den Dienst mit der Waffe unmöglich machte, stellte ich mich dem Vaterlande neuerlich zur Verfügung, indem ich mit Förderung des oesterr. Kriegsfürsorgeamtes mehr als 100 öffentliche Lichtbildervorträge über meine Erlebnisse in 12 monatiger russischer Kriegsgefangenschaft veranstaltete, die auf die Zivilbevölkerung beruhigend und aufklärend einwirkten, und deren Reinerträgnis zur Gänze dem Vaterländischen Frauenverein vom deutschen Roten Kreuz, dem oesterr. Roten Kreuz und dem türkischen Roten Halbmond zufloss.

Für diese ehrenamtliche und völlig uneigennützige Betätigung im Interesse der Kriegsfürsorge wurde ich mit nachstehend genannten Dekorationen ausgezeichnet:

    Preussische Rote-Kreuz-Medaille 3. Klasse,
    Ehrenzeichen 2. Klasse m.d. Kriegsdekoration vom oest. Roten-Kreuz
    Silberne Medaille vom türkischen Roten Halbmond,
    Fürstl. Liechtenstein'sche Regierungs-Jubiläums-Medaille.

Die Briefe des vaterländischen Frauenvereines in Berlin lege ich in Photokopien bei und werde die Dekrete über meine Ernennungen und Auszeichnungen auf Befehl sofort einsenden.

Anlässlich der Mobilmachung im September 1938 habe ich mich lt. Beilage 2 beim Wehrbezirkskommando Wien II freiwillig zur Dienstleistung gemeldet.

Meine Bemühungen, mir in einem neutralen Lande eine neue Existenz zu gründen, scheiterten überall an meiner schweren Kriegsbeschädigung und an meinem Alter. Ich hänge an meinem Vaterlande mit allen Fasern meines Herzens und möchte ihm in irgendeiner Weise noch weiter dienen.

Im alten Oesterreich bekleidete ich durch 7 Jahre das öffentliche Ehrenamt eines Beisitzers beim Berufungssenate des Gewerbegerichtes in Wien, wurde vom Handelsgericht Wien zum beeideten Sachverständigen und Schätzmeister bestellt und war ausserdem behördlich ernanntes Mitglied der Einkommensteuer-Schätzungs-Kommission f.d. 9. Wiener Gemeindebezirk.

I-9 Bl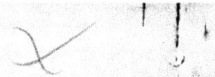

      Ich bin polizeilich und gerichtlich vollkommen unbescholten und habe mich niemals politisch betätigt.

      Der Führer und Reichskanzler hat anlässlich der Machtergreifung in der Ostmark das schöne und edle Wort geprägt : " Die Kriegsinvaliden sind die ersten Bürger des Staates" und im Vertrauen auf diesen Ausspruch stelle ich hiemit die ergebene Bitte, mein unverdientes, trauriges Los günstiger zu gestalten.

      Herr Reichsminister wollen überzeugt sein, dass Ihre Menschenfreundlichkeit keinem Unwürdigen zuteil werden würde, sondern einem Manne, der einst Schulter an Schulter mit den arischen Kameraden tapfer für das gemeinsame Vaterland gekämpft und ein schweres Blutopfer für Heimat und Volk dargebracht hat, und der es als Offizier und aufrechter, ehrliebender Mann unsagbar schmerzlich empfindet, nunmehr ohne irgendein Verschulden als Paria dahinleben zu müssen.

      Genehmigen Herr Reichsminister den Ausdruck meines gehorsamsten Respekts, womit ich verharre

Wien, am 9. Mai 1940.   ergebenst

   5 Beilagen
   einschreiben !

Captain (Retired)
Hans Israel Kauders, Vienna
[District] IX Alser Street 38
ID location: Vienna
ID number: G 71321

[Various stamps and signatures
"Received by III: 15 May 1940,"
"The Deputy of the Führer, 11 May 1940"
Handwritten in red: "Jewish ancestry"]

To Reich Minister and Deputy of the Führer Rudolf Hess, Munich

Dear Reich Minister!

As a non-Aryan, severely war-disabled, veteran frontline officer of the world war, I take the freedom to direct the following elaborations to you, Reich Minister, with the humble request to honor them with a favorable perusal.

I am Viennese-born, married, without children, a captain (retired), sixty years old, and have lived in Vienna all my life.

The impairment of my earning capacity (amputation of the left thigh resulting from a gunshot wound and consecutive stress arthritis in the right knee joint) amounts to 90 percent according to the pension award of the Pension Office Vienna II, G. L. No. 420.355.

As a result of the incorporation of the Ostmark into the German Reich, already in March 1938, I had to give back the tobacco kiosk license (*Tabak Trafik*) in Vienna 1, Kärnterstrasse 43, awarded to me back in 1917, which had provided me a middle-class livelihood up to this point, since as a Jew, I was no longer permitted to stay on as a contractor of the Reich.

Since then entirely without income and work, my wife and I depend on the monthly pension payments of 164.95 R[eich] M[ark] /

[Stamp: 14 May 1940] and are excluded from all cultural establishments. For me, even entering a public garden to get a breath of fresh air is prohibited; and everything only for the reason that I have four Jewish grandparents.

Regarding my service during the war, I respectfully report the following: On 2 September 1914, leading my platoon as Lieutenant of the reserve of the K.u.K. Infantry Regiment No. 40 in Feyslavice outside of Lublin, I was gravely injured twice, was therefore, despite the most courageous resistance, taken prisoner of war by the Russians; my left thigh was amputated at the upper third in a Russian hospital in Homel (Russian Poland) in October 1914 and after three months of sickbed, I was deported, as a one-legged war cripple, in the grimmest cold to Kansk-Jenniseisk in Central Siberia. Here I stayed during the Siberian winter and, in August 1915, I was transported back to the homeland as part of a disabled swap.

After my return, promoted retroactively to first lieutenant effective 1 March 1915, I was declared unfit for duty as "disabled and unsuitable even for service as a militia man (*Landsturmdienst*)" on 1 July 1916 and placed on the retired list.

On 1 December 1916, I voluntarily reported back for duty, was reactivated on 10 December 1916 and assigned as district instruction officer to the "propaganda for enemy defense" (*Propaganda für Feindesabwehr*). On 1 April 1919, I was retired again to my former pension status. On 23 July 1919, as a total exception, I was awarded the title and status of a captain (retired) for "very fruitful service."

For "brave conduct facing the enemy," the former Emperor Franz Joseph I already awarded me the Military Merit Cross 3rd Class with War Decoration and Swords on 11 December 1915; in addition, I was honored with the following war decorations:

The Wound medal for 2 wounds,
The Karl Troop Cross,
The Austrian war medal with swords,
The Hungarian war medal with helm and swords,
The Bulgarian war medal with red ribbon./

Despite my severe physical disabilities, which made service under arms impossible, I offered my services to the fatherland again, mounting, with the support of the Austr[ian] War Welfare Department, more than 100 public slide presentations about my experiences during 12 months of Russian captivity, which had a calming and illuminating effect on the civilian population; and all net proceeds went in their entirety to the Fatherland Women's Association of the German Red Cross, the Austr[ian] Red Cross, and the Turkish Red Crescent.

For this voluntary and entirely selfless activity in the interest of the war welfare, I was honored with the following decorations

Prussian Red Cross medal 3rd class,
Mark of distinction 2nd class w[ith] t[he] war decoration by the Austrian Red Cross,
Silver medal by the Turkish Red Crescent,
Royal Liechtenstein Government Jubilee medal

I attach the letters from the Fatherland Women's Association in Berlin in photocopy and will, when ordered, immediately submit the decrees about my appointments and accolades.

On the occasion of the mobilization in September 1938, I voluntarily reported for duty at the recruiting district headquarters Vienna II, as can be seen in attachment B.

All my efforts to establish a livelihood in a neutral country failed everywhere, because of my severe war disability and age. Yet, I am tied with all the fibers of my heart to my fatherland and would love to serve it further in any capacity.

In the old Austria, I held the honorary public office of an assessor at the appeals senate of the industrial court in Vienna for 7 years, was appointed as a sworn expert and appraiser by the commercial court Vienna, and, in addition, was chosen as a member of the income tax appraisement commission f[or] t[he] 9th District of Vienna by the authorities./

[II- 9 fol.]

I have neither a criminal nor a court record and have never been politically active.

On the occasion of the seizure of power in the Ostmark, the Führer and Reich Chancellor coined the elegant and noble phrase: "The war disabled are the first citizens of the state." And trusting his words, I make the humble request to improve my undeserved, sad fate.

Reich Minister, you shall be convinced that your philanthropy (*Menschenfreundlichkeit*) would not be bestowed on somebody undeserving, but on a man, who once fought courageously shoulder to shoulder with the Aryan comrades for their mutual fatherland and who offered a heavy blood sacrifice to his homeland and his people, and who, as an officer and an honest and sincere man, feels deeply hurt now that he is forced to live as a pariah without any fault.

Reich Minister, allow the expression of my utmost obedient respect, in which I adhere.

Vienna, 9 May 1940
5 Attachments   Respectfully,
Certified Mail!   [Handwritten signature: Hans Israel Kauders]

DOCUMENT 2. Petition by the Paris-based spouse of the interned Jewish refugee to the *Commissariat Général Aux Questions Juives*, March 1942 (Archives Nationales, Paris, AJ 38/67: 22043)

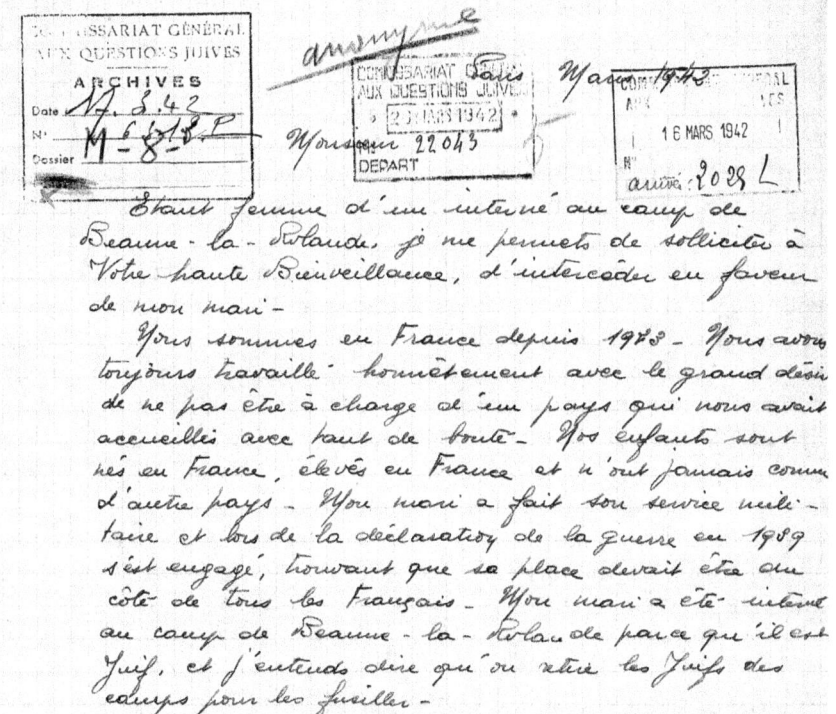

[Handwritten letter]

[Handwritten in blue: "Anonymous"
Various stamps
"General Commissariat for Jewish Affairs Archives, Date: 17 March 1942, No.: 6313 P, Dossier: M-8"
"General Commissariat for Jewish Affairs, 23 March 1942, Sent, 22043"
"General Commissariat for Jewish Affairs, 16 March 1942, Arrived, 2029 L"]

Paris, March 1942

Sir,

As the wife of an internee at the camp of Beaune-la-Rolande, I am taking the liberty of soliciting your great kindness, to intercede in my husband's case.

We have been in France since 1913. We have always worked honestly with the great desire not to be separated from the country that has welcomed us with such kindness. Our children were born in France, raised in France, and have never known any other country. My husband did his military service and at the outbreak of war in 1939, he enlisted, believing that his place should be on the side of the French forces. My husband was interned in the Beaune-la-Rolande camp because he is a Jew, and I hear that Jews in the camps were being shot to death.

Understand my anguish and worry. I live in constant terror of receiving a letter telling me that my children no longer have a father. I beg you to intervene on their behalf and I hope to owe you all of my gratitude.

Please, Sir, accept the expression of my most distinguished sentiments.

The wife of an internee at Beaune-la-Rolande*

---

* Many of the relatives and friends who appealed to French authorities on behalf of Jewish internees in the Occupied-Zone camps were of Eastern or Central European origin or descent, and likely learned French as a second language. Letters sometimes contain minor grammatical errors or awkward phrasing, but largely maintained a competent understanding of written French.

Document 3. Wilhelm Filderman to the Romanian Minister of the National Economy, 1941 (Arhivele Nationale Ale României, Bucharest, Ministerul Economiei Naționale-Direcția Secretariat 64/1941)

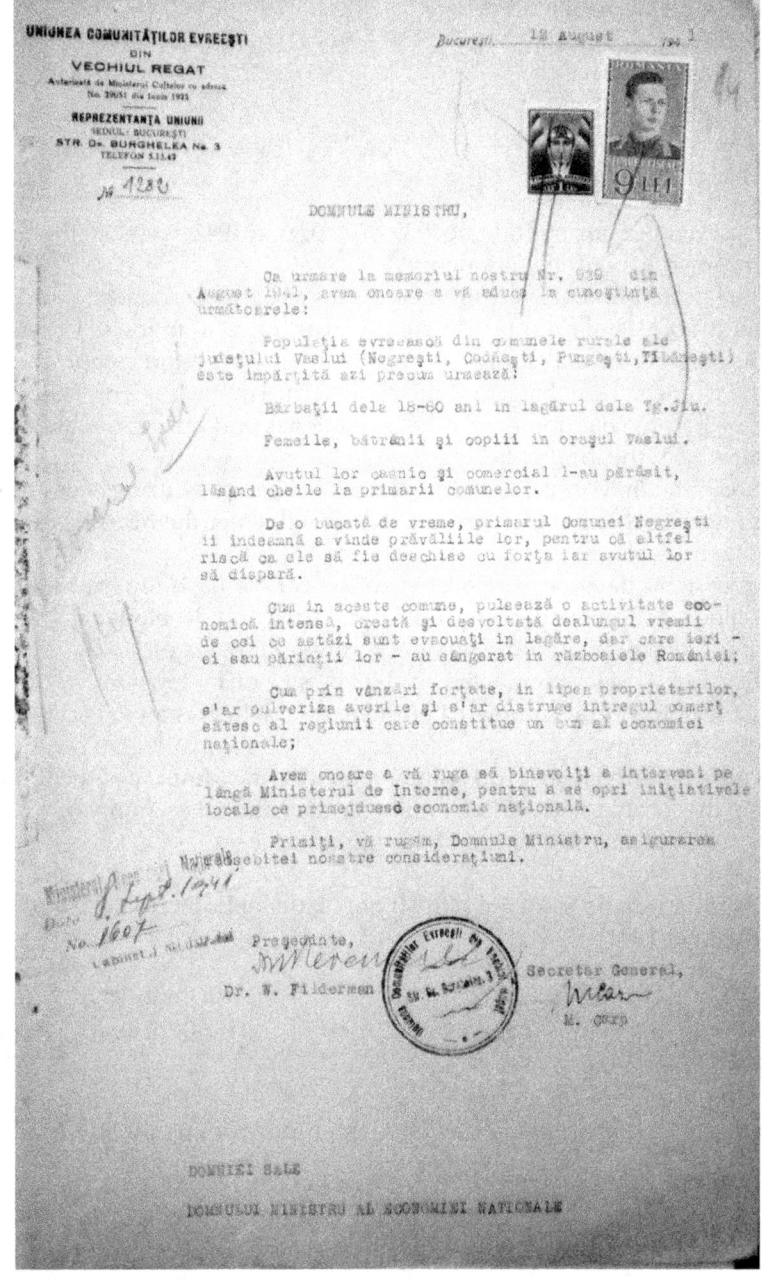

The Union of the Jewish Communities   Bucharest, 12 August 1941
from the Old Kingdom
Authorized by the Minister of Religious Affairs
through order no. 19051 from 1922
The Union's Representative
Bucharest headquarters
3 Dr. Burghelea Street
Phone 5.13.42
No. 1282

Minister,

As a result of our petition no. 939 of 7 August 1941, we have the honor to inform you about the following:

The Jewish population from the villages (Negrești, Codăești, Pungești, Țibănești) of Vaslui County is currently distributed as follows:

The men between 18 and 60 years old are in T(argu) Jiu camp.

The women, the elderly, and the children are in the town of Vaslui.

They had to abandon their household assets and businesses and leave the keys with the local policemen.

Lately, the mayor of Negrești village has been pressuring them to sell their businesses; otherwise the authorities will enter their businesses and seize their assets.

Those who have been relocated to the camps have fought and shed their blood in Romania's wars and have started and developed an intense commercial activity in those villages throughout the ages.

Such forced sales conducted in the absence of the owners would destroy the entire rural commerce of the region, which is a vital part of the national economy.

We are honored to ask you to intervene with the Ministry of the Interior to stop the local initiatives that endanger the national economy.

Minister, please be assured of our highest esteem.

[Registration stamp from the Ministry of National Economy no. 1607 from 8 September 1941]

President	Secretary General
[Handwritten signature]	[Handwritten signature]
Dr. W. Filderman	M. Carp

[Round stamp of the Union of Jewish Communities from the Old Kingdom]

To His Honor
the Minister of the National Economy

Document 4. Petition by Lajzer Kuczynski to Mordechai Chaim Rumkowski, Łódź ghetto, 1942 (Archiwum Państwowe, Łódź, PSŻ, L18904)

To:
The Head of the Jewish Council of Elders in Litzmannstadt-Ghetto

From:
Lajzer Kuczynski
Franciszkanska Street 75/10

STAMP OF RECEIPT: Received on 23 [September]* 1942

PETITION:

Pertaining to the ongoing evacuation of children, and considering that:

I have a daughter, Pesse-Sara, born in Bydgoszcz, in fact on 30 December 1932.

Because of a whole series of problems after [her] birth, I was able to visit the civil registry office Bydgoszcz (Urzad Stanu Cywilnego) two weeks after the child's birth, namely on 15 January 1933, reporting the date of childbirth as 11 January 1933, to be within the seven-day period required by law for reporting childbirths.

That way, of course not being able to foresee back then today's dire results of my action, I personally caused her to be placed on the current evacuation list due to the only eleven-day difference between the actual and reported age difference.

My wife, mother of this child, Chana-Szajndla, has died here not long ago, on 8 June of the current year, so now I am both the father and the mother for the child.

The child is in every way very slick, both mentally and physically, and fully realizes the tragedy she suffered because of the loss of her mother and now the tragedy awaiting her because of the expulsion.

I cannot imagine how I will be able to continue living and working without such a slick and beloved child, who is everything to me in my life, without whom life has no value to me, or sense, and at the same time it

---

*In the original: mistakenly March. The order to "evacuate" children under ten years of age was issued in September.

will be the same for the child without parents with whom she had such a close, tight bond.

For these unique reasons, in my sorrow, I am forced to appeal to your sense of kindness and beg you, Mr. Chairman, to decide that my delay in reporting the act of childbirth should not be the cause of a tragedy for an innocent child and, moreover, to decide that the actual date of birth of the child is in fact 1932 and give an order to remove my daughter Pessa-Sara Kuczynska from the evacuation list.

For that I thank you in advance from the depths of my fatherly heart.

With high regards,
[Handwritten signature]
L. Kuczynski

DOCUMENT 5. Petition by a stateless Jew in Berlin to the President of the Filipino Commonwealth Manuel L. Quezon, 1939 (National Library of the Philippines, Presidential Papers of Manuel L. Quezon, Subject File, Box 171)

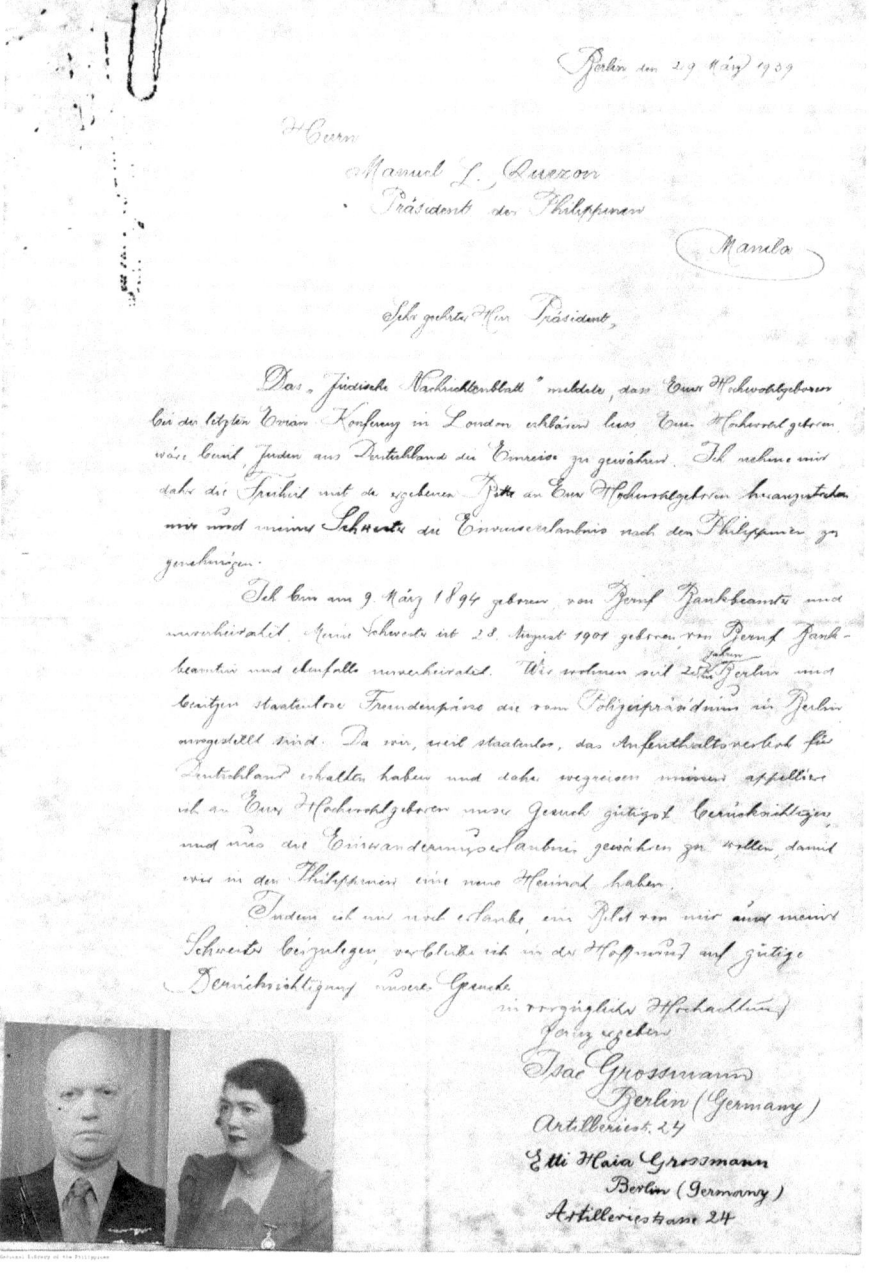

[Handwritten letter]
Berlin, 29 March 1939
To
Manuel L. Quezon
President of the Philippines
Manila

Dear Mr. President,
    The *Jüdische Nachrichtenblatt** reported that your Honor had a statement read at the last Evian conference in London, declaring that your Honor would be willing to grant entry to Jews from Germany. I, therefore, take the liberty to approach your Honor with the humble request to grant me and my sister entry permits to the Philippines.
    I was born on 9 March 1894, my occupation is bank official, and I am not married. My sister was born [on] 28 August 1901, her occupation is bank official, and she is also not married. We have been residing in Berlin for twenty-five years and are in the possession of stateless alien's passports issued by the Police President of Berlin. Since we have, because we are stateless, received a residency prohibition for Germany and have to leave, I appeal to your Honor to consider our entreaty benevolently and grant us entry permits, so that we can have a new homeland in the Philippines.
    Taking the liberty to include a picture of myself and my sister, I remain with the hope of benevolent consideration of our entreaty.

With the deepest admiration completely devoted

Isac Grossmann
Berlin (Germany)
Artilleriestr. 24

[Two passport photographs attached]

Ettie Haia Grossmann
Berlin (Germany)
Artilleriestrasse 24

*In 1939, the *Jüdische Nachrichtenblatt* was the only remaining "Jewish" news bulletin in Nazi Germany, edited by German-Jewish officials, but supervised by the Nazi Propaganda Ministry and the Gestapo.

INDEX

accountants, 122, 162, 168
agency, 19, 139, 151
    of Jewish petitioners, 1–2, 8–9, 13,
        18–19, 28, 30, 44, 58, 108, 115, 196,
        204–5, 208, 212, 214, 217
Aguinaldo, Emilio, 168
aid, 17, 56–57, 64–65, 125, 164, 189–91,
    194–95, 205–6, 210, 213
aid organizations, 17, 51, 57, 61, 65, 158,
    160, 164, 166, 174, 185, 191, 193, 209, 213
    Aid Society of the Jews in Germany
        (Hilfsverein der Juden in
        Deutschland), 161, 164, 168, 209
    American Friends Service
        Committee, 57
    American Jewish Joint Distribution
        Committee (JOINT), 57, 95, 159,
        161, 189–93, 197, 209, 213
    Children's Aid Society (Oeuvre de
        Secours aux Enfants, OSE), 53,
        57, 62
    Grüber Office, 195
    HICEM (HIAS-JCA-Emigdirect), 57
    Inter-movement Committee to
        Aid Evacuees (Comité inter-
        mouvements auprès des évacués,
        CIMADE), 57
    International Committee of the Red
        Cross, 57
    International Refugee Organization
        (IRO), 185
    Organization for Rehabilitation
        and Training (Organisation
        Reconstruction Travail, ORT), 57
    Red Cross, 42, 57–58, 64
    Refugee Economic Corporation
        (REC), 159, 161–62, 164
    Relief Organization for Those
        Affected by the Nuremberg
        Laws (Notgemeinschaft der
        durch die Nürnberger Gesetze
        Betroffenen), 195
    Relief Organization of the
        Episcopal Chair of Berlin
        (Hilfswerk am bischöflichen
        Ordinariat Berlin), 193, 195
    Relief Organization of the
        Evangelical Church in Germany
        (Hilfswerk der Evangelischen
        Kirche in Deutschland), 194
    Rue Amelot Committee, 53, 56–57, 62
    United Nations Relief and
        Rehabilitation Administration
        (UNRRA), 185, 189–90
Alexander II (Tsar), 14
Alliance Israélite Universelle, 95
Allies, 95–96, 108, 141, 182, 184, 187, 189
Alt, Hugo, 174
American Jewish Joint Distribution
    Committee (JOINT). *See under* aid
    organizations
Amidah (liturgy), 11
amidah (standing up), 8, 30, 93, 107, 118
Ancel, Jean, 94
András, György, 138–41, 151
antiquity, 5, 11
antisemitism/antisemites, 15–16, 85, 87,
    94–95, 100, 107, 168

Antonescu, Ion, 2, 4, 92–94, 96–108, 206, 209, 212
    and Jewish petitioning, 2, 4, 92–94, 97–98, 101–3, 106–7, 209, 212
    persecution of Jews, 92, 96, 103–4, 106–7
apartment buildings, 140–44, 146, 150, 152
apartments, 35, 39–40, 144–47, 149–51, 206
appeals, 1, 3, 11, 28–29, 43, 52–53, 56, 64–65, 76, 78, 164, 170, 173. *See also* petitions
Arendt, Hannah, 7, 117
Armenians, 98
arrests, 34, 38–39, 43, 53–57, 59–62, 64, 85, 94, 97, 169, 173
Arrow Cross (Nyilas party), 150
Aryanization, 36, 65, 77, 103, 107
Aryanness, Aryan, 40, 42, 72–73, 78, 80, 82, 84, 86–87, 186
    honorary Aryan status, 7, 73, 75, 81, 86–87, 206
assassination, 107, 194
assimilation, 52–53, 58, 81
asylum-seekers, 58, 60
asymmetrical power relations, 2, 204, 214
Auschwitz-Birkenau. *See under* extermination camps/sites
Austria/Austrians, 18, 31, 39, 41–43, 80, 100, 140, 160, 169, 210, 212, 216
Austrian Jews, 28, 30, 39, 44
Austrian veteran welfare department, 42
authoritarian governments/regimes, 1, 7, 9, 15, 17–18, 204, 207, 209, 214
autobiographies, 72
Axis, 92, 96, 106, 108

Baeck, Leo, 32, 205
Balkans, 1
Banat, 104–5, 115
bank employees, 144, 167
Bankier, Abraham, 121
Bankier, Szyje, 121
Bauer, Yehuda, 7, 118
Baur, André, 62
Beer, Fritz, 38
Behrend, Fritz, 188
Belcredi, Count Karel, 84

Belgium, 215
belonging, 9, 52, 58, 60
Benjamin, Lya, 94
Beran, Rudolf, 84
Bergen-Belsen. *See under* concentration camps
Berlin, 31–35, 38, 57, 105–7, 164–66, 168–69, 174, 184–85, 187–95, 207, 213–14
Bessarabia, 17, 98
Bettelheim, Bruno, 7
Białystok, 122
Biebow, Hans, 115, 120, 126
Biegeleisen, Jakob, 122
birth certificates, 59
bishops, 12, 15, 32, 65, 79
Bock, Gisela, 212
Böhme, Horst, 80
borders, 14, 80, 158, 211
Boskowitz, Anna, 40
Bothmann, Emmy, 196
boycotts, 8, 38, 43, 95
    April 1933 boycott, 31–32, 43
Braham, Randolph, 142
Brajbard, Ruda Brucha, 122–23
Brătianu, Constantin, 105
Breslau, 160, 166, 172, 184
Brinkmann, Tobias, 184
Brno, 80
Brody, Judit, 150–1
Bronstein, Jacques, 55
Brunner, Alois, 54
Bucharest, 92–93, 97–98, 101–7, 214
Buchenwald. *See under* concentration camps
Budapest, 3, 9, 17, 81, 138–41, 147, 150–52, 160, 166, 205–6, 208–9
Bulletin de l'Union Général des Israélites de France, 57
Bürckel, Josef, 2, 39, 43
Burgenland, 39
Bydgoszcz, 127

Carol I (king), 102
Carol II (king), 95–6
Carp, Matatias, 100
Cassel, Erna, 172–3
Cassel, Salo, 172
Catholic Church/Catholics, 81, 83, 169, 189, 191, 193

censorship, 53, 165
  police prefecture Censorship
    Bureau (Préfecture de Police-
    Bureau de Censure), 53
Central Association of German Citizens
  of Jewish Faith (Centralverein
  deutscher Staatsbürger jüdischen
  Glaubens), 16, 33, 210
Central Europe, 140, 159, 161, 165–66,
  208, 211
Central Office for the Emigration of the
  Jews (Prague), 36–37
Certificate of Non-Belonging to the
  Jewish Race (Vichy), 62, 64
České Budějovice (Budweis), 90
Chicago Sun, 190–1
children, 15, 36, 41, 55, 57, 59, 62, 64–65,
  75–76, 78–80, 82–83, 89n21, 89n40, 93,
  102, 118, 122, 125, 127, 138, 150–52,
  169, 182–83, 188, 193, 196, 205, 208
Children's Aid Society (Oeuvre de
  Secours aux Enfants, OSE). *See under*
  aid organizations
China/Chinese, 159, 162, 164–5
Chmelařová, Olga, 81
Christendom, 12
Christianity/Christians, 59, 72, 78–81,
  86–87, 98, 183, 142–45, 183, 186, 193–
  95, 197, 205–6, 213
  Jewish Christians, 194
Cincinnati, 159
citizenship, 33, 37–38, 52–53, 58–59, 61,
  66, 73–74, 94–95
civil service/civil servants, 38, 188
class
  lower class, 205
  middle-class, 93, 164, 169, 205, 212
coerced communities, 115, 129, 205
communication, 2–3, 6, 18, 64, 117, 120,
  128, 159, 161, 164–5, 207, 211, 214, 216
Communist regimes/Communists, 4, 15,
  53, 58, 94, 106, 190
concentration camps, 34–35, 39, 54, 118,
  129, 160, 169, 173, 184–85, 187
  Bergen-Belsen, 169
  Buchenwald, 139, 169, 174, 185
  Dachau, 81, 169–170
collaboration/collaborator, 8, 17, 30, 52,
  84, 117, 174, 204, 215

conformity, 7
constitution, 11, 97
  Weimar Constitution (Germany), 16
consular offices, 160, 164
converts, 8, 72, 80–81, 83, 86–87, 172, 183,
  191, 205–6, 211–13
Copenhagen, 166
Costiner, Elias, 100
courts, 6, 13, 41, 83, 96, 100, 102, 107, 213
  Supreme Court (Romania), 105
Cristescu, Eugen, 106
Csehimindszent, 138, 141
culture, 13, 58, 87
  German culture, 29, 80
curfew, 85
Cysner, Joseph, 172
Czech Brethren, 81, 211
Czech Jews, 28, 30, 44
Czechoslovak Republic, 35, 73

Dachau. *See under* concentration camps
Dachy, Nana, 58
Damascus, 14, 157
Dannecker, Theodor, 54–55
Darquier de Pellepoix, Louis, 51, 55,
  60–61
David, Lisa, 58
Deletant, Dennis, 94
Delmendo, Sharon, 158
denunciation, 6, 84–85, 215
Department of State (US), 159, 164
department stores, 162, 172
deportations, 1–2, 7, 15, 17, 37, 43, 53, 55,
  57, 59–60, 76, 87, 93, 96–97, 101, 104–8,
  120, 127, 139–40, 183, 188, 192, 206–7,
  210, 212–13, 216
  exemptions from, 1, 183, 206
designated Jews (*Geltungsjuden*), 78, 82,
  89n21, 89n40
diaries, 8, 10, 93, 95
diaspora, 11, 13, 185
dictatorships/dictatorial regimes, 3, 4,
  6, 9, 11, 15–16, 28, 43–44, 95, 107, 214,
  216
dietary laws, 171
diplomats, 93, 96, 100, 105–7
disabilities/disabled, 39–42, 98, 205
discursive contestation, 8
disease, 51, 55, 57, 129

Displaced Persons (DPs), 185, 189–91
divorce, 82–83, 208
doctors, 34, 73–74, 77, 86, 143, 170. *See also* physicians
Dorohoi, 1
Drancy. *See under* transit camps
Dworzecki, Meir, 8
Düsseldorf, 160, 192

Eastern Europe, 6, 17, 57, 114, 119, 216
Eastern Front, 42, 94
education, 15, 33–34, 72, 75–76, 119, 205
ego-documents, 7, 10, 204
Eichmann, Adolf, 36–37, 212
Eliáš, Alois, 73
Emancipation, 3, 12, 95, 107, 169
embassies, 209
emigration, 17, 33, 35–36, 74, 81, 100, 160–61, 166–67, 169, 174, 185, 195, 206, 211, 213
employers, 28–29, 38, 43, 64, 76, 169
Endre, László, 141
engineers, 83, 162
entreaties, 1–7, 9–19, 28–29, 32–33, 35, 37, 39–41, 43–44, 52, 54–55, 58, 60–61, 65, 97, 100, 146, 157–58, 160–2, 164, 166–67, 169–70, 172–74, 186, 204–16. *See also* petitions
Eschwege, Helmut, 8, 30, 38
ethnic Germans (*Volksdeutsche*), 36
Europe, 1, 4–6, 8–11, 14–15, 16–18, 197, 157–58, 160, 162, 164–66, 168, 205, 207–11, 216
evictions, 35, 37, 39–40, 97
executions, 56, 97
extermination camps/sites, 17, 120, 126–27, 210
    Auschwitz-Birkenau, 54–55, 58–59, 87, 115, 139–40, 167–68, 183
    Kulmhof/Chełmno, 126–27

Fabian, Hans-Erich, 191
families, 7, 9, 36–39, 51, 55–60, 62, 64–66, 72, 75–76, 79–84, 87, 93, 99, 122, 125–29, 138, 142–43, 150–51, 158–59, 161–62, 164–66, 168–72, 182–84, 186, 188, 192–93, 195–97, 206, 212
farmers, 162, 164
Faroqhi, Suraiya, 13

fascism/fascists, 6, 11, 95–98, 101, 158, 160, 166, 168, 171, 173–74, 190, 206–7
fathers, 39, 64–66, 78–79, 83, 93, 125, 138–39, 150–51, 172, 174, 205, 212
fear, 53, 64, 81, 93, 108, 118, 129, 141, 214
Federation of Jewish Communities (Romania), 92, 94, 100, 103
Filderman, Wilhelm, 92–108, 205, 209, 211
    and petition writing, 92–93, 97–98, 100–102, 104, 106–8, 205, 209
Fischl, Artur, 79, 85
Fitzpatrick, Sheila, 7, 84
Fleischmann, Adolf, 39
food, 17, 35, 56–57, 117, 123, 125–26, 150, 171–72, 184, 186, 190, 195
    food rations, 183, 185, 187, 192
    food stamps, 189
    kosher food, 172
forced labor/forced laborers, 35, 41, 55, 188, 195, 206
forged papers, 53, 150
Fort Mont-Valérien, 56
France, 1–2, 9, 15, 18, 51–54, 56, 58–61, 64–66, 94–96, 207, 209, 215–216
    Vichy France, 1, 11, 51–55, 58–64, 205–207, 210, 212–14
    Occupied Zone, 54–57
Frankel, Jonathan, 14
Frankfurt, 13, 184, 194
Frederick II (King of Prussia), 12
French Jews, 60, 65, 205, 210
Freudenberg, Alfred, 194
Frick, Wilhelm, 32
Frieder, Alex, 162, 174
Frieder, Phillip, 170
Friedlaender, Erich, 168, 174
Friedlaender, Ilse, 168, 213
Friedländer, Saul, 3, 8, 38, 42, 142
friends, 52–53, 56–57, 62, 64–65, 72, 76, 79, 84, 160, 183–84, 196, 206
Fromm, Julius, 38
Fuchs, Alfred, 81

gas chambers, 139
gender, 19, 82, 182–83, 211–12
    gender hierarchies, 19, 211–12
    gender norms, 169, 174, 212
    gender roles, 126

General Commissariat for Jewish Affairs
    (Commissariat général aux questions
    juives, CGQJ), 51–52, 55–56, 59–63
General Union of Israelites in France
    (Union Général des Israélites de
    France, UGIF), 56–58, 61–64, 69n62,
    209, 213
Geneva, 194
genocide/genocidal, 1, 5, 8–10, 18–19,
    204, 206, 208–209, 216
Gerber, Heinz, 189
German Foreign Office, 32–33
German Jews, 16–17, 28, 30, 32–33, 38,
    44, 159–60, 163, 167, 171, 182, 184–87,
    189, 192, 210
German Military Commander in France
    (Militärbefehlshaber in Frankreich),
    53
Germany, 16, 32, 40, 43–44, 61
    East Germany (German Democratic
        Republic), 17
    Nazi Germany, 2, 6, 11, 17–18, 30,
        32–33, 35, 43–44, 80, 95, 100, 105,
        115, 140, 158–60, 163, 168, 171,
        182, 204–7, 210–11, 216
    occupied Germany (early postwar),
        17, 182, 184–86, 189–94, 196–97, 206
    Weimar Germany, 9, 16, 31
Gerold, Hubert, 86
Gerstenmaier, Eugen, 194
Gestapo (Secret State Police), 34–36,
    38–39, 54, 81, 85, 127, 164–65, 167–69,
    183, 188, 210–13
Geto-Tsaytung, 120–21
ghettoization, 9, 17, 36, 40, 97, 128, 140–
    47, 149–52, 212
ghettos, 6, 17, 72, 107, 114, 116–18, 123,
    128, 139–40, 185, 187, 197, 205–6, 208,
    210–11, 215
    Budapest, 139–152, 204, 211, 213,
        215
    Kovno, 215
    Łódź, 6, 76, 86, 114–129, 215
    Mogilev, 107
    Odessa, 215
    Pest, 149
    Radom, 215
    Terezín (Theresienstadt), 87, 167,
        183, 185, 210

Vasvár, 138–40, 151, 205
Warsaw, 128
Glattauer, Moritz, 41
Glücklich, Viktor, 82
Goga, Octavian, 95
Goldner, Arnold, 39–40
Goldschmidt, James, 38
Göring, Hermann, 34
Graf, Philipp, 11
gray zone, 118, 215, 218n16
Graz, 169
Great Depression, 83
Greece, 215
Gross, Jan, 151
Grossmann, Isac, 167–68, 212
Grüber, Heinrich, 193–95

Hácha, Emil, 72, 74, 78
Hagen, 168
Hamburg, 2, 41, 51, 184, 195
Harbin (China), 164
Harris, Bonnie, 159, 172
Harz Mountains, 40
Haskalah movement, 12, 14, 208
Hawelleck, Otto, 195
Hayek, Karl Robert, 86
Hebrew. *See under* language
Heidelberg, 9
Hejdová, Luisa, 79
Helbronner, Jacques, 62
Hess, Oskar, 168
Hess, Rudolf, 2, 41–43, 205
Hesse-Nassau, 183
Heydrich, Reinhard, 72, 75, 86, 114
HICEM (HIAS-JCA-Emigdirect). *See
    under* aid organizations
Hilberg, Raul, 1–2, 7, 117, 208
Hildesheim, 171
Himmler, Heinrich, 34
Hindenburg, Paul von, 28, 38, 44
Hirsch, Otto, 32–33
Hitler, Adolf, 2, 28–29, 31–33, 38, 40,
    42–44, 96, 190, 194, 209
    Führerkult, 16
    and petitions, 2, 28–29, 32–33, 40,
        43–44, 209
Hitler Youth, 34
Hoare, Reginald, 100
Holocaust studies, 10, 18, 211

integrated history of the Holocaust, 3, 10, 42, 151–52, 158, 174, 204, 207, 217
Holy Roman Empire of the German Nation, 12
Honorius III (Pope), 12
houses, 123, 139–42, 147, 149–50, 209
    ghetto houses, 140, 142, 148–51, 192
    Jewish houses, 140, 143, 145, 149, 205
    "mixed" house (*vegyes ház*), 146, 149–52, 210
Hungarian Interior Ministry, 141
Hungarian Jews, 105, 139
Hungary/Hungarians, 1, 15, 18, 98, 138–40, 143, 151, 166, 171, 204, 207
husbands, 39–40, 52, 55, 59–62, 66, 79, 82, 84, 122, 125, 127, 150, 169, 173, 192, 195, 205, 212

identification/identity cards, 41, 59, 62, 86, 189
identity, 31, 52–53, 59, 65, 165, 173, 192, 206, 210, 214
immigration/immigrants, 13, 57–60, 66, 100, 105, 158–68, 163–66, 170, 173–74, 211
internees, 51–61, 63–66, 171. *See also* prisoners
internment camps, 54, 58, 209
    Argelès-sur-Mer, 54
    Beaune-la-Rolande, 54–55, 59
    Compiègne, 52, 54–56
    Gurs, 54
    Pithiviers, 52, 54–56
    Poitiers, 54–55
    Rivesaltes, 54
    Saint Cyprien, 54
    Santo Tomas, 171–73
    Vernet, 54
Israel, 7, 17, 115
Istanbul, 13
Italy, 215

Japan, 8, 170–71, 173
Japanese Imperial Army, 170
Japanese Military Administration (Philippines), 171–72
Jaretzki, Georg, 195
Jellinek, Walter, 9

Jerusalem, 159
The Jew and France exhibitions, 60
Jewish Army (Armée juive, AJ), 53
Jewish cemeteries, 97–8
Jewish Combat Organization (L'organisation juive de combat, OJC), 53
Jewish (Religious) Communities, 1, 4–5, 11–15, 17, 29, 30–31, 33, 35–37, 43, 53, 73, 76–78, 81–83, 85, 87, 92–95, 98, 100, 102–3, 106, 108, 119, 157–58, 160–62, 164, 166, 185, 189, 190–93, 196–97, 205, 207–8, 212, 216
    in Berlin, 31, 33–34, 185, 189, 191–92
    in Breslau, 166
    in Bucharest, 97
    in Damascus, 14
    in Düsseldorf, 192
    in Essen, 34
    in Graz, 169
    in Jitschin, 36
    in Jungbunzlau, 36
    kehillot (Eastern European Jewish Community structure), 119, 208
    in Manila, 161–62, 170–71
    in Merzig, 34
    in Minsk, 15
    in Munich, 33
    in Prague, 36–37, 212
    in Semil, 36
    in Turnau, 36
    in Vienna, 34, 164, 169
    in Vilna, 12
Jewish Councils, 6, 114–15, 117, 119–29, 208–9, 215
Jewish passivity (alleged), 8, 30, 93, 108, 115, 117, 119, 128–29, 169
Jewish police, 125
Jewish press. *See under* press
Jewish Refugee Committee (Manila), 159, 161
"Jewish Question," 72, 80, 94, 96, 105
Jewish Scouts (Éclaireurs israélites de France, EIF), 53
Jewish Statutes, 52, 95
    Statut des Juifs (Vichy), 1, 52, 60
Jewish youth, 33
Jones, Weldon, 163
Judeo-Bolshevism, 105

Jüdische Auswanderung, 165
Jüdisches Nachrichtenblatt, 165, 168

Kalusová, Jana, 82
Kantorowitz, Hans, 38
Kaplan, Jacob (rabbi), 1
Kaplan, Marion A., 167
Kárný, Miroslav, 73
Katzenstein, Adolf, 41
Kauders, Hans, 41–42, 222–28
Kaufmann, Karl, 41
Kempeitai, 171–173
Kestenbaum, Margot, 166
Kindler, Heinrich, 40
Kingdom of Castile, 12
Kingreen, Monica, 183
Klinger, Adele, 39
Klinger, Elsa, 169
Klinger, Isidor, 39
Klinger, Julius, 167, 169, 174
Kolben, Emil, 83, 87
Koppenheim, Albert, 40
Korsakov, Rudolf, 79–80
Koziol, Geoffrey, 5
Kraus, František, 78–79
Kreindler, Leo, 165
Krejčí, Tomáš, 84
Kristallnacht. *See under* pogroms
Krotoszynski, Ronald J., 14
Kruse, Max, 184, 188
Kuczyński, Lajzner, 127
Kwiet, Konrad, 8, 30, 38

Lambert, Raymond-Raoul, 62–63
landsmanshaftn, 57
language, 3, 5, 7–8, 11–12, 15, 17–18, 34, 53, 58, 78, 84–85, 116, 118, 121, 124, 127, 160, 162–67, 174, 204, 206–7, 209–12
    Czech, 78–79
    English, 117, 165–67, 173–74
    German, 5, 80, 84, 107, 115, 117, 121, 167–68
    Hebrew, 60, 115
    of humanitarian values, 169–70, 173
    of immigration, 160–64, 166, 168, 170, 173–74, 211
    of labor, 167–69, 211
    Polish, 115, 121, 123, 127
    of rights, 15. *See also* rights
    Spanish, 165–66, 168
    speaking Nazi, 84
    Yiddish, 15, 60, 115, 121
Lantz, Fanny, 62
Laqueur, Walter, 166
Lässig, Simone, 158
Latin America, 216
Laval, Pierre, 52, 60
Lavi, Theodor, 94, 101
laws, 6, 8, 10, 30–31, 35, 43, 61, 79, 86, 92, 97, 103, 163, 171, 205–7, 213
    anti-Jewish/antisemitic laws, 4, 28–29, 38, 43, 100–101, 140, 206–7, 209, 214
    Decree Law (no. 169) for the Revision of Citizenship (Romania), 95
    exemptions from, 1–2, 6, 9, 17–19, 39–40, 43, 63, 72–76, 78, 80, 82–87, 167, 206–7, 213–14, 216
    Nuremberg (Racial) Laws, 2, 9, 72–74, 82, 182, 186, 195
    Reich Law for the Restoration of a Professional Civil Service, 16
lawyers, 5, 10, 36, 38, 73–74, 76–77, 83, 86, 92–93, 100, 104, 138, 142, 144, 165, 196, 205, 208–9
League of Jewish Women (Jüdischer Frauenbund), 33
League of Nations, 11, 95
Legion of the Archangel Michael/ legionaries, 93, 95–97, 102, 106
Legionary Rebellion (Romania), 93, 96, 98, 101
Leipzig, 40–41
Leister, Albert, 114
letters, 3–4, 6–7, 15, 29–30, 33, 35, 37, 42–43, 52–56, 58–59, 61–62, 64, 76, 81, 83–4, 86, 103, 114, 116–17, 120–25, 127, 129, 150, 165, 188, 190. *See also* petitions: petitionary letters
    protest letters, 32, 34, 38
Leucutia, Aurel, 105
Lévai, Jenö, 142, 149
Levi, Primo, 118
Levit, Jan, 86–87
liberals, 13
liberation, 54, 64, 101, 182, 184, 187–89, 196–97

Lippert, Julius, 32–33
Lissa, 36
Łódź (city), 114–15
Łomska, Fela, 125
Lupu, Dimitrie G., 105
Lupu, Nicolae Gh., 105, 206
Lupu, Nicolae L., 105
Luxembourg, 115

Magna Carta, 14
Mandelík, Ervín, 83
Manila, 159, 161–162, 165–166, 168, 170–174
Maniu, Iuliu, 105
Marburg, 40
marriages, 12, 17, 53, 62, 78–79, 82, 87, 183–86, 188–90
    intermarriages, 72, 78, 82, 89–90n40, 191
    mixed marriages, 89n21, 142, 183–88, 190, 193, 195–96, 213
    non-privileged mixed marriages, 184, 196
    privileged mixed marriages, 182, 184, 187, 196
Manoilescu, Mihail, 105
Marx, Kurt, 162
massacres, 96, 103
mayors, 6, 29, 34–35, 39, 139–40, 142–44, 147–48, 206, 209
McNutt, Paul, 159, 161, 163, 167
mechanics, 162, 167
medicine, 56, 72–73, 84, 185, 187
memo(randa), 6, 29–30, 33, 35, 43, 63, 102, 105, 108, 138, 163. *See also* petitions: petitionary memoranda
memoirs, 10, 93, 95–96, 101
memory, 159
    memory cultures (Philippines), 159
Mendelssohn, Moses, 12
merchants, 38, 164
Meyer, Beate, 2
Meyer, Wilhelm, 185
Michman, Dan, 3
Middle Ages, 11
migration/migrants, 57, 59, 165
Mihalache, Ion, 105
military service, 53, 60–61, 98–99, 166–67, 210, 212

Mindanao, 164
Minsk, 15
Mischlinge, 2, 8, 78, 80, 86, 187, 195
Moldenhauer, Rüdiger, 13
morality, 59, 125
mothers, 38, 51–52, 60, 64, 56, 78–80, 83, 93, 125, 150, 169, 172
Müller, Ludwig (Reich Bishop), 32
Müller, Michael G., 162
Munich, 33, 184, 194
Munich Pact, 73, 80

Naples, 166
National Assemblies, 13. *See also* parliaments
National Christian Party (Romania), 95
National Library of the Philippines, 160
National Partnership, 73–74
National Revolution (Vichy), 53, 60
National Socialism, 80, 186
nationalism, 78, 211
naturalization, 52–53, 58–59, 66
Nazi Party (NSDAP), 32, 35, 39–40, 43, 80, 183, 211, 213
    Chancellery of the Führer of the Nazi Party, 16, 216
    Gauleiters, 39, 41
    as recipient of petitions, 39–40, 43, 80, 211
neighbors, 3, 62, 65, 72, 96, 139, 142, 149–52, 206
Netherlands, 215
networks, 18, 30, 52–53, 56–57, 60, 64–65, 129, 150, 160, 164, 170, 185–86, 194–95. *See also* under transnationalism
Netzorg, Morton, 162, 171, 173
Neubacher, Hermann, 39
Neumeyer, Alfred, 32
Neurath, Konstantin von, 72, 74
New York (City), 14, 79, 159, 161
North Bukovina, 17, 96–97
Nová, Alice, 82, 85
Nový, Oldřich, 82
Nowak-Reismann, Karel, 76–77
Nuremberg Racial Laws. *See under* laws
nurses, 162

occupation (military), 80
    Allied occupation, 184–85, 189

German occupation, 52–53, 63, 74, 83, 87, 115, 118–19, 124, 126, 128, 139–40, 213, 215
Japanese occupation, 159, 170–74
Romanian occupation, 96
Odessa, 80
Office of the Reich Protector (Bohemia and Moravia), 74–75, 79–80, 82
Ohta, Seichi, 172
Old Kingdom (Romania), 105
opportunism, 52
orders, 36, 119, 122–23, 125, 127, 140
Organisation Todt, 195
orphans, 1, 102
Ostmark, 160. *See also* Austria
Ottoman Empire, 13–14, 157, 208

Pacelli, Eugenio (Cardinal), 81
package Jews (*Paketjuden*), 192
Pale of Settlement, 14–15
Palestine, 13, 100, 105, 164
Paris, 13, 51, 54–56, 58–59, 62, 65, 81, 94, 97
Paris Peace Treaty, 97
parks, 40–41, 80, 205–6
parliaments, 6, 13, 14, 16, 194. *See also* National Assemblies
passport, 171–73
patriotism, 98, 167, 210, 212
Pekař, Josef, 84
pensions, 37, 41, 102
people's community (*Volksgemeinschaft*), 38, 183
perpetrators, 2–4, 9–10, 18, 28–29, 31, 42–43, 59, 117–18, 152, 158, 185, 204, 207, 211, 214
persecutions, 8, 30–31, 35, 37, 96, 104, 119, 182–84, 187–88, 190–92, 196–97, 204–06
    Jewish responses to, 1, 10, 28, 31, 36, 39, 42–43, 73, 92–93, 100, 125, 128–29, 189, 205, 212
    and petitioning, 1–3, 7, 9, 29, 31, 41, 43–44, 81, 87, 207, 212–13, 216
Pétain, Philippe, 51, 59, 61, 64–65
petitions, 1–19, 28–44, 51–53, 55, 58–59, 61, 63, 75–81, 83–87, 92–94, 97–98, 100–108, 114–29, 138–39, 142–49, 151–52, 157, 161, 165–68, 172–74, 183–86, 188, 190, 192–93, 195–96, 204–13, 215–17
    antisemitic petitions, 216
    collective petitions, 5–6, 12, 43, 157, 205
    conceptualization of, 4–10, 186
    counter petitions, 143
    history of, 11–17
    and Muslim petition writers (*arzuhalsi*), 13
    petitionary letters, 2, 29–31, 33, 35, 66, 117, 121–24, 126, 210, 214
    petitionary memoranda, 6, 29, 32–33
    and petitum, 6–7, 15, 206
    as resistance, 1–2, 7–9, 18–19, 31, 42–44, 53, 87, 93, 214–17
    secretariat for petitions and complaints, Łódź ghetto (Sekretariat für Bittschriften und Beschwerden), 115, 120, 128
    success of, 2, 4, 8–9, 12–13, 15, 17, 29–30, 34–36, 82, 93–94, 97, 108, 121, 145, 159, 161–62, 170, 183, 189, 195, 197, 212–14
    and supplications, 3, 5, 11, 15–16, 123
    and writers' guides, 13, 23n72
Philippines, 6, 18, 158–61, 163–65, 166, 168, 170–1, 173–74, 212
photographs, 9, 161
physicians, 32, 36, 86, 105, 163, 165, 170, 206. *See also* doctors
Pick, Emil, 83
pleas, 6, 10–11, 15, 72, 76, 80, 85–87, 157, 161, 167, 173, 204, 206, 209, 216. *See also* petitions
pogroms, 15, 28, 96, 102
    Bucharest Pogrom (1941), 102
    Kristallnacht (1938 November Pogrom), 34–35, 38–39, 43, 160–161, 163, 169, 173, 188, 205, 212
Poland, 1, 12, 14–15, 18, 100, 104–5, 114, 208, 210
police, 33, 38, 43, 51, 53–55, 58–59, 62, 67, 76, 81, 85–86, 97, 101, 106, 115, 125, 151, 166. *See also* Gestapo; Jewish police; Kempeitai
Pomerania, 38
Popescu, Dumitru, 103

post (mail), 53, 55, 62, 78
Poznan, 81
Prague, 36–37, 85–86, 115, 165, 208, 211–12, 214
Preiss, Ralph, 171
press, 3, 62, 76, 103, 107, 141–43, 157, 163, 165–67, 190
    Jewish press, 58, 165, 167
priests, 15, 62, 65, 190
prisoners, 34, 54–55, 98, 172, 187, 197
    prisoners of war (POWs), 42, 54, 60, 173
prisons
    Fort Santiago, 172–73
    Łódź central ghetto prison, 125
    Theresienstadt Small Fortress, 85
propaganda, 33–34, 60
property, 15, 18, 36, 44, 65, 74–75, 97–98, 101–2, 104, 108, 143–45, 147–48, 151, 183, 188, 211
protected Jews (*Schutzjuden*), 12
Protectorate of Bohemia and Moravia, 31, 35–36, 43, 72–75, 82, 87, 206, 211, 213, 215
Protectorate Government (Czech), 35–36, 72, 74–77, 80–82, 86
Protectorate Ministry of Education, 37
Protectorate Ministry of Finance, 37
Protectorate Ministry of the Interior, 79
Protectorate Ministry of Justice, 36
Protestant Church/Protestants, 191, 193–94
Prundeni, I. P., 101
Prussian Ministry for Education, 38
Prussian Ministry of the Interior, 34
public opinion, 51, 64–65, 95, 101

Quakers, 193, 195
Quezon, Manuel L., 158–61, 163–70, 172–73

race, 60, 79, 84, 190, 194
    German race, 182
    Jewish race, 60, 62, 84, 211
    mixed race, 82
racism, 78, 211
Ramet, Gabriel, 58–59
Rapoport, David, 62
Red Army, 94, 128, 194

refugees, 54–55, 57, 59–60, 66, 100, 158–59, 162–64, 167–68, 170–74, 210
Reich Association of Jewish Frontline Soldiers (Reichsbund jüdischer Frontsoldaten), 33
Reich Chancellery, 32–33
Reich Ministry of Defense, 32
Reich Ministry of Foreign Affairs. *See* German Foreign Office
Reich Ministry of the Economy, 38
Reich Ministry of the Interior, 9, 16, 34, 211
    Expert in Racial Research at, 16
Reich Ministry of Labor, 32
Reich Ministry of Popular Enlightenment and Propaganda, 165, 216
Reich Ministry of War, 38
Reich Representation of German Jews (Reichsvertretung der deutschen Juden), 31–33, 35, 43, 205, 210, 212
Reich Security Main Office (Reichssicherheitshauptamt), 114, 127
Reich Union of Orthodox Synagogue Communities (Reichsbund gesetzestreuer Synagogengemeinden), 33
religion, 11, 33, 39, 60, 65, 76, 191
    definition of Jewishness by, 191
reparations, 93, 101–2, 184, 195
republicanism, 52
rescue, 94, 159–60
    through work, 120, 127
resistance, 1–2, 7–8, 18–19, 31, 42, 44, 52–53, 57, 62, 65, 96, 118, 127, 174, 214–17
    amidah, 8, 30, 93, 107, 118,
    armed resistance, 3–4, 7, 42, 53, 93, 107, 117, 128
    collective/group, 7–8, 19, 30, 42, 52, 116, 118, 214
    conceptualization of, 7–8, 18, 117–18
    individual, 7–8, 19, 30, 87, 116, 214
    Jewish resistance, 2, 4, 7–8, 30, 107, 117, 129
    legal resistance, 93, 96, 99–101, 107
    oversimplified binaries, 2–3, 117, 174, 215

polemic resistance, 53
spiritual/cultural resistance, 8, 118
unarmed/non-violent resistance, 7, 19, 30–31, 52–53, 93, 216
Resler, Kamill, 83
restitution, 34, 93, 98, 100–102
Richter, Gustav, 107
Riga, 174
Righteous Among the Nations, 159
rights, 6, 9, 11, 16, 19, 28, 44, 52, 58, 65–66, 92, 94, 96–7, 100–102, 104, 119–20, 124, 208–9, 215
civil rights, 6, 44, 209, 214
Rings, Werner, 53
Rioşanu, Alexandru, 97
Ritter von Epp, Franz, 32
Robinson, Jacob, 117
Romania/Romanians, 2, 15, 18, 92–98, 100–101, 103–8, 205–7, 212, 216
Romanian Jews, 92–95, 100–101, 105–6, 108, 212
Romanian Ministry of Interior Affairs, 97, 103, 105
Romanianization, 96–97, 102–3, 105, 107
National Romanianization Center, 103
Rosenkranz, David, 100
Rozenstajn, Szmul, 120
Rosman, Moshe, 12, 158
Rue Amelot Committee. *See under* aid organizations
Rumkowski, Mordechai Chaim, 114–17, 119–24, 126–28
rumors, 75, 87, 101, 103, 105, 125, 141, 143
Rürup, Miriam, 158
Russia, 1, 8, 14–15

SA (Sturmabteilung), 34
Saar, 34
Salzburg, 81
Sayre, Francis B., 163, 170
Schacht, Hjalmar, 32
Schäfer, Johannes, 115
Schechter, Samuel, 171–72
Schlafman, Joseph, 60
Schlafman, Sarah, 55
schools, 14, 33, 35–36, 75, 79, 82, 93–94, 162, 206

Schwarz, Isaïe (chief rabbi), 62
Schwarz, Josef (rabbi), 171–72
Schwefelberg, Arnold, 100
Scott, James, 3, 8
Scott, Joan, 211
Second Balkan War, 98
Security Service of the SS (Sicherheitsdienst, SD). *See under* SS
segregation, 43, 143, 150, 206, 209, 214
self-determination, 8–9, 18–19, 58, 65, 188, 196, 204, 216–17
Sephardic Jews, 13
Shanghai, 86, 159, 162, 169
Siberia, 42
Sino-Japanese war, 159
Sinti and Roma ("gypsies"), 115, 190
Slavonice, 80
smuggling, 118, 125
solidarity, 32, 98, 108, 118, 124, 129, 152, 212
Sommer, Margarete, 193
soup kitchens, 57, 123
Southern Dobrogea, 96
Soviet Union, 96
Spain, 15, 168
spatial terms of analysis, 18, 157–58, 174
SS (*Schutzstaffel*), 34, 54, 80, 107, 168
Security Service of the SS (Sicherheitsdienst, SD), 53–54, 80
SS vocational labor camp Linden, 86
Stahl, Heinrich, 33
starvation, 33
Stein, Rudolf, 86
Šteindler, Stanislav, 81
Stern, Adolphe, 93
Stern, Margarete, 162, 173
Sternberg, Count Leopold, 84
Stockfisz, Paulette, 59
Stoicescu, Constantin, 104
Stow, Kenneth R., 12
Streicher, Julius, 32
Stülpnagel, Otto von, 53
Stürmer, Der, 32
Stuttgart, 194
Sudeten crisis, 42
Sudeten German Party, 80
Suhard, Emmanuel Célestin (Archbishop of Paris), 65
supplications. *See under* petitions

survival/survivors, 8–9, 17–18, 94, 102, 107–8, 115, 117–20, 126, 128–29, 139, 150, 159, 173, 182–85, 187, 189, 191–92, 197, 205–6, 208–10, 212, 216–17
   collective survival, 116, 125
   survival strategies, 56, 66, 116–18, 120, 126–28
Switzerland, 194
synagogues, 15, 36, 57, 170
   Coral Temple (Romania), 102
   Merzig synagogue, 34
   Temple Emile (Manila), 170–72

Tábor, 81
Tauber, Sigmund, 161, 166–67
taxes, 12, 37, 41, 44, 65, 115
teachers, 34–36, 74, 162, 212
teenagers, 34–35, 168
Terezín (Theresienstadt). *See under* ghettos
testimonies, 100
   survivor testimony, 8, 159, 171
Third Reich, 28, 160–61, 164, 171–72, 193. *See also* Germany: Nazi Germany
Thurmann, Franz, 161, 167
Tobias, Paula, 38
Torp, Cornelius, 162
trade unionists, 190
transit camps, 9, 54, 205
   Drancy, 51, 54–60, 62, 64
transnationalism/transnational, 211
   actors, 161–62, 164–65, 167, 170, 174
   communities, 166
   languages, 160, 166–67, 174
   networks, 4, 14, 18–19, 157, 159, 161–64, 166–67, 171, 173, 211
   spaces, 4, 158, 173, 211, 216
Transnistria, 94, 96, 100–101, 104, 106–8
Trunk, Isaiah, 117, 128

Uebelhoer, Friedrich, 115
Ukraine, 97
Union of Native Jews (Uniunea Evreilor Romani, UER), 92, 94
United Kingdom, 14
United Nations Relief and Rehabilitation Administration (UNRRA). *See under* aid organizations
United States of America, 95, 103, 158, 160, 162, 167, 170

United States Holocaust Memorial Museum, 10
universities, 15, 38, 171
   Bucharest Medical University, 105
   Heidelberg University, 9
   Sorbonne University, 94
   University of Bucharest, 94

Vallat, Xavier, 11, 51–52, 61–64, 213
Van Buren, Martin, 14
Vargas, Jorge, 168, 170
Vatican, 106
Verdun, 61
veteran welfare department (Austria), 42
veterans, 1, 39, 41–42, 52, 60–62, 66, 98, 167, 173, 205, 210
victims, 2–3, 7, 10, 17–18, 39, 42, 44, 55, 59, 61, 98, 102, 117–19, 125, 144, 152, 158, 159, 184–91, 194, 196–97, 204, 217
   Victims of Fascism (Opfer des Faschismus, OdF), 186–88, 190
   Victims of Fascism committees, 17, 187
   Victims of the Nuremberg Laws, 189, 195, 197
Vienna, 39–42, 115, 160, 166, 169, 205, 211
villages, 79, 126, 138
violence, 4, 6–10, 15, 28–29, 31, 34–35, 44, 93, 96–97, 101–2, 166, 205, 209, 212, 214
   linguistic violence, 8, 166, 205
visas, 160, 167–69, 174, 206
Vlădescu, Ovidiu, 104

Wachmann, Katharina, 169
Wajngot, Mordka, 124–25
war medals/ribbons, 39–40, 42, 61, 173
   EK (Iron Cross), 40, 79, 172
Warsaw, 81
Warsaw Ghetto. *See under* ghettos
Warthegau, 115
Washington, DC, 161
Weg, Der, 185
Wehrmacht (German army), 32, 38, 56, 72, 80, 120, 209
Weimar Republic. *See* Germany: Weimar Germany

welfare, 33–35, 119, 126, 194, 197
Welisch, Margaret, 169–70
Western Front, 172
widows, 1, 84, 102, 169
Wischau, 36
wives, 38, 51, 56, 59, 80, 82, 125, 182, 192
Wółk, Renia, 115
Wolzig, 34
women, 1, 4, 8, 10, 14, 37–38, 75, 82, 125–26, 142, 159, 162, 166, 169, 184, 188, 192, 205, 207, 209, 211–12
    Jewish women, 3, 10, 13, 29, 42–43, 60, 82, 152, 160, 162, 166, 169, 182, 184, 205, 208, 211–12, 214
    as petitioners, 3–4, 10, 13, 37–38, 43, 125–26, 166, 205, 207–9, 211
World Council of Churches (WCC), 194
World Jewish Congress, 95
World War I, 32, 39–41, 79, 93, 95, 97–98, 166–67, 210
World War II, 92, 95, 106, 108, 114, 118, 205, 210

Yad Vashem, 159
yellow star, 64, 97, 140, 142–43, 183, 187–88, 190–92, 206

Zimmer, Viktor, 80
Zimmermann, Moshe, 8
Zionism/Zionists, 164, 210
Zionist Federation for Germany (Zionistische Vereinigung für Deutschland), 32–33, 205
Zionist Youth Movement (Mouvement de la Jeunesse Sioniste, MJS), 53
Zwiedeneck, Eugen, 103–4

www.ingramcontent.com/pod-product-compliance
Lightning Source LLC
Chambersburg PA
CBHW070121110526
44587CB00017BA/2868